1995

Time's Children

Phyllis M. Yaburke
1976

Time's Children
Impressions of Youth

by Thomas J. Cottle

foreword by David Riesman

Little, Brown and Company — Boston – Toronto

LIBRARY OF CONGRESS CATALOG CARD NO. 74-149168

SECOND PRINTING

The author gratefully acknowledges permission to quote from the following sources:
"Student, Mischievous — Fire at the Architectural Institute" from *Selected Poems* by Andrey Voznesensky, translated by Herbert Marshall. Copyright © 1966 by Herbert Marshall. Reprinted with permission of Hill and Wang, Inc.

An excerpt from *Mallarmé: Selected Prose Poems, Essays and Letters,* translated by Bradford Cook. Copyright © 1956 by The Johns Hopkins Press. Reprinted with permission of The Johns Hopkins Press.

An excerpt from *The Words* by Jean-Paul Sartre, translated by Bernard Frechtman, pages 230–231. Copyright © 1964 by George Braziller, Inc. Reprinted with permission of George Braziller, Inc.

"Letter to George Izambard" from *Illuminations* by Arthur Rimbaud, translated by Louise Varèse. Copyright 1946 © 1957 by New Directions Publishing Corporation. Reprinted with permission of New Directions Publishing Corporation.

A quotation from page 11 of *Such, Such Were the Joys* by George Orwell. Copyright 1945, 1952, 1953 by Sonia Browell Orwell. Reprinted with permission of Harcourt Brace Jovanovich, Inc.

"Praise of Learning" from *Selected Poems* by Bertolt Brecht, translated by H. R. Hays. Copyright 1947 by Bertolt Brecht and H. R. Hays. Reprinted by permission of Harcourt Brace Jovanovich, Inc.

"The Way" from *Ten Rungs: Hasidic Sayings,* collected and edited by Martin Buber. Copyright 1947 by Schocken Books, Inc. Reprinted with permission of Schocken Books, Inc.

A letter from *The World as I See It* by Albert Einstein, pages 21–22. Copyright 1949 by the Philosophical Library. Reprinted with permission of the Estate of Albert Einstein.

A letter to Scottie from *The Letters of F. Scott Fitzgerald,* edited by Andrew Turnbull, pages 32–34. Copyright © 1963 by Frances Scott Fitzgerald Lanahan. Reprinted with permission of Charles Scribner's Sons.

An excerpt from *Let Us Now Praise Famous Men* by James Agee and Walker Evans, pages 289–291. Copyright © 1969 by Mia Fritsch Agee. Reprinted with permission of Houghton Mifflin Company.

Sections of this book originally appeared in *Saturday Review, Sociological Quarterly, Sociological Inquiry,* and *Change Magazine.*

Chapter 5, "The Mosaic of Creativity," is from *Confrontation: Psychology and the Problems of Today,* edited by Michael Wertheimer. Copyright © 1970 by Scott, Foresman and Company. Reprinted by permission of the publisher.

Chapter 7, "Simple Words, Simple Deeds," is adapted from an article of the same title which originally appeared in *Urban Education,* Vol. V, no. 3 (October 1970). It is reprinted by permission of the publisher, Sage Publications, Inc.

Published simultaneously in Canada
by Little, Brown & Company (Canada) Limited

PRINTED IN THE UNITED STATES OF AMERICA

To my family and to students

And the birds will go on and the snappy words will go on
And the tea sky and the sloped marine sky
And the hustle of beans will go on and the unserious canoe
It will all be going on in connection with you, peace, and my poem, like
   a Cadillac of wampum
Unredeemed and flying madly, will go exploding through
New cities sweet inflamed, planispheres, ingenious hair, a camera smashing
Badinage, cerebral stands of atmospheres, unequaled, dreamed of
Empeacements, candled piers, fumisteries, emphatic moods, terrestialism's
Crackle, love's flat, sun's sweets, oh peace, to you.
Kenneth Koch, The Pleasures of Peace

Contents

Contents

Part One: Youth

Part Two: Education

Part Three: ...

Part Four: Conclusion

Acknowledgments

There are many ways in which one's friends help one in the writing of a book. There are intellectual guidance and critical insight; there are encouragement, kindness and, even more, tolerance. So many people have graciously responded to my work that I fear I may be omitting some important names in the lists below. Heaven only knows where one gets ideas or the strength and temerity to write about them. I suspect, however, that many of the ideas contained in this volume and much of the strength that it does require to keep at one's work have come through my friendships with many, many people. As the various chapters required working in different cities with different groups, the list perhaps is rather long, but that is as it should be.

For so many reasons I wish to thank Erik H. Erikson, David and Evey Riesman, Mary C. McClelland, Christina Platt, George W. Goethals, Chad Gordon, James Cass, Ernest and Rebecca Lockridge, Robert and Gail Melson, Homer O. and Betty Brown, Geoffrey and Marjorie Gault, Craig and Betsy Eisendrath, James S. and Adele Dalsimer, John and Virginia Demos, Judith Jordan, Stuart Pizer, Daniel and Nancy Ogilvie, Robert F. Bales, Diane Divoky, Philip E. and Dori Slater, Leonard Saphier, Joseph Pleck, Lane Conn, James McGoldrick, Knute Larsen, Hans Toch, Jacob W. Getzels, Fred L. Strodtbeck, John and Marcia Cooper, Donald Kaplan, John Kitsuse, Bernard Beck, David Pines, Betty Yankwich, Wallace Roberts, Edward and Elizabeth Pattullo, Benson Snyder and Merton Kahne.

In addition, there were my teachers at the Francis W. Parker School, then considerably later on, my colleagues in the Department of Social Relations at Harvard University, at the Center for Advanced Study at the University of Illinois, where much of the book was written during a marvelous fellowship year, and in the Education Research Center and Medical Department at the Massachusetts Institute of Technology. Grants from these latter three institutions made this book possible. Several people have typed portions of the manuscript, and while their work is no longer visible it is in fact what at this time I continue to envision as my book and I wish to thank them: Linda Janus, Cynthia Sparrow, Constance Bunker, Julye Rogers, Jane Lee and Rose Sullivan.

Several people have worked very hard in my behalf to bring the manuscript to readable form, each having read all or portions of it. Jerome Kagan, David C. McClelland, Alfred Browne, Marian Weil, Leonard Stevens and Mary Purcell have been extraordinarily helpful and generous in this task, and Robert Coles, Gerald M. Platt, William Phillips and Peter Schrag have given me something profoundly rare, days of confidence and pride. There is an aesthetics as well as a business to writing, I have learned, and anyone who writes needs those special friends who gently guide one's hand on the page, soothe or lift a constantly lagging spirit and then, as a truly lovely reward, bring the manuscript to publishers and ultimately readers. I shall always be indebted to Bill Phillips and Peter Schrag.

And how do I thank my wife, Kay, who has read this manuscript over and over again and heard it read aloud, who has suffered through the setbacks and given perspective to the moments of satisfaction? It is she who, through her teaching and being, knows youth and the compassion this knowing must take as a partner. It is she who brings students and writers steps closer to mature triumphs and makes their reality genuine and glorious.

Foreword

Thomas Cottle's last year at Harvard College, 1958–1959, was my first as a faculty member. He made on me as on others a vivid impression: tall, spirited, ferociously energetic, expansive, alternately self-mistrustful and euphoric. After a year's try at medical school (his father's profession), he entered the Sociology Department at the University of Chicago and, his work completed there, returned to teach at Harvard in the Department of Social Relations. He became a Teaching Fellow in the undergraduate General Education course I have been giving since I came here. This was only one of his many engagements as teacher and scholar. As some of these essays indicate, he led what are termed self-analytic groups (less intrusive precursors of current encounter groups, though in my own critical view, subject to some of the same risks and extravagances). The range of his interests and talents made him at home in the different compartments of an interdisciplinary Department of Social Relations, with its clinical, social-psychological, ethnographic, and more strictly sociological wings. Some of the essays reflect these intellectual involvements and clinical opportunities, but Mr. Cottle ranged far outside even these permeable boundaries, into the philosophy of time, with a personal bent for metaphysics. (All this is in the past tense because he is no longer at Harvard, and the department, although still united in undergraduate teaching, has separated at the graduate level.)

To those of us who worked with him in the General Education course I direct, Mr. Cottle brought his special virtuosity and impetuosity. He says a great deal in these essays about youth and its energies, and how these are refracted upon adults who look backward in sorrow, envy, anger or with pride. For some senior faculty at Harvard, Mr. Cottle represented heedless impatience and profligate energy, dramatizing as a slightly older spokesman the complaints and affections of activist or alienated students, as for example those pictured in "Voices in the Yard." This impression was not just, and I believe that a reading of these essays will clearly demonstrate the ambivalent stance Thomas Cottle takes concerning cross-generational confusions. He seeks to be someone who describes or interprets youth, but he is not its prisoner or unambiguous defender; he knows that not all youth qualify as "Youth."

In recent years, there have been a good many faculty members of all chronological ages who project onto the activist young their own hostilities, their own aspirations. Such student-watchers, as Mr. Cottle notes in his introduction, frequently embarrass those they observe, because the latter know better than to believe the fulsome praise they hear; students are generally, in my observation, more tortured and troubled by their own actions than are many older persons who applaud them from the sidelines or even lead the charge. Mr. Cottle is so vulnerably open to the moodiness and shadow-boxing of adolescence, as in "The Children of Nine Lives," that he can listen to all that is being said in young people's fluctuations of spirit and self-dramatization — listen responsively, yet with compassionate humor or needful deflation.

But like many who work therapeutically with children, he occasionally cannot help himself from getting angry with those parents and with those institutions which he believes have warped children, cabined their creativity, or in some of the terrible cases he describes in "Of Youth and the Time of Generations," intruded on them too soon with their parental loneliness, sexual and otherwise. There are times, as in "The Mosaic of Creativity," when his writing would almost seem to propose a society consisting principally of poets, controlling the imagery of William Blake and the sensibility of Wordsworth. More exactly, this essay asks for a world that honors the humanity and imagination of all people, young and old. When touched by the young, Mr. Cottle is not afraid, as the Japanese put it, to be wet rather than dry, as is the case with "The Children of Nine Lives" and "Leo's Child in the Age of

Aquarius." In the former essay, he reveals his concern for a group of young people for whom the events of childhood have been bitter and terrifying. In the latter essay, his interest shifts to what some would call the simple or normal life of a fourteen-year-old girl, her friends, brother, and parents, as well as her rich imagination.

Sometimes these sorts of identifications lead him to flippancy or sharpness vis-à-vis powerful or simply unresilient adults. The lyrical account of children in "Prospect Street Moon" takes a sideswipe at a city mayor, which at first glance seems almost ritualistic but which later is recognized to be a call for help from those people who share the author's compassion. Nonetheless, I found uncompelling the perspectives on Wellesley Senior High School in "Simple Words, Simple Deeds," which is a perspective returned to in "Dressing Down the Naked Ape." I have argued against putting vulnerable public school teachers in the position of having to be brave through involving them in social studies and social questions — a view that many teachers and students now regard as at once too protective and too quixotic. I recognize that my own view asks much less of teachers, parents, and students than does Mr. Cottle's, and that it is more resigned and skeptical: that it places less hope in mutual understanding and thrashing things out.

There are times in some essays when I feel that Mr. Cottle is straining at the cosmic, the resonant. Thus, in contrast, I welcome the documentary detail and vivid bursts of dialogue in "Prospect Street Moon," with its lovely discussion of the fantasy life of two eleven-year-old chums, their awareness of the wizardry of technology in the first moon landing, and their prompt return to baseball. So, too, with the reportorial account "College and Career Night in Bristol Township," with its vivid human geography.

For me, one of the most fascinating essays is "Tutoring for Democracy," which reports on two different groups of student tutors of inner city black youth, and of the ways in which the tutors dealt with each other and with their tutees. One group of tutors, called the Uplifters, sought to help mostly grade-school children to fare less badly in school, leaving it to the tutees to decide what to do about society when they had more options in hand.

This group of tutors organized itself soberly, bureaucratically, efficiently, for the short-run task. The other group of tutors, whom the essay calls Reformers (but who actually seem more like revolutionaries) , sought out teen-age boys for what they termed "picket training." They wanted to channel the admired energies of the uneducated young into organized alienation and group antagonism. And in their relations to each other, these tutors practiced what would now be called the SDS style of participatory democracy, rejecting any organized or hierarchical procedures as death itself. My experiences with efforts at participatory democracy are more limited than Mr. Cottle's. Many such efforts seem to create a physiological democracy, giving weight to those who are tireless, usually male, often abrasive, and generally taking what appears as the uncompromising line. Having a less exalted view of the uses of democracy and no doubt a more Hobbesian sense of its abuses, and being intensely skeptical of children's crusades, I found "picket training" a rather immoral exploitation of other people's energies. While Mr. Cottle's account is compassionate toward the more politicized groups of tutors, nevertheless he includes the negative evidence; he does not hide the dangers, nor the personal problems and projections among some of the tutors. Indeed, in this essay, he suggests some sympathy for the institutions in which the tutees live, even as he recognizes the rage these institutions evoke or channel among the tutors. (In some experiences with Peace Corps Volunteers in training, I have found it not too difficult to engender sensitivity to the lot of the deprived in a host culture, but far more difficult to engender any understanding or sympathy for the qualities and dilemmas of host culture bureaucrats or elites.)

In other essays also, Mr. Cottle exhibits the range of his moral sensibility: for example, in "Thank God for the Simple People" he tells about election night 1968 and about how seemingly sophisticated students who expected to gloat over Humphrey's defeat found themselves almost in tears at the prospect of Nixon's victory. They had thought they could have their purity of view without paying a price for it. As Mr. Cottle is vibrantly aware, he is always at some emotional and temporal distance from students, never simply a pal, never simply leading the troops in the way some of his colleagues once thought he was. (If the colleagues had asked the troops, they would have seen how often they were furious at Mr. Cottle for not sharing their hatreds or parroting their simplicities.)

I remember, in this context, a visit to the University of Illinois in June 1970, where Mr. Cottle was a Fellow at the University's Center for Advanced Study. We had lunch at the Student Union with a group of student leaders — one of whom, an assertive young woman, started to talk sympathetically about the post-Cambodian violence that had erupted on campus. Mr. Cottle, from the base-line of his own principled nonviolence, was angrily critical of her. He was not seeking to remain "credible" to her and the other young around the table through oversympathy, but rather to use the leverage of his closeness of concern to ask her to recognize that she was rationalizing, sliding along out of fear not to seem pure or wholly committed.

It is an ability for resourceful response that makes Mr. Cottle an extraordinary teacher. Some of his flavor comes through in these essays, despite what I feel to be an occasional unevenness and over-flow. The post-Cambodian conversations — "The Spring of Death" — capture the mood of expanded antiwar politics and confrontation in a mosaic of bulletins, snatches of dialogue, glimpses of mood and event. As the essay on the two tutoring projects illustrates, Mr. Cottle brings to work of this sort a journalist's flair but also a social scientist's frame of reference. The term often used for this kind of enterprise is "participant-observation." Mr. Cottle is very observant, and at the same time, extremely participant. He knows that this is a difficult dialectic, but he also conveys the sense throughout the essays that all human encounters, all human understanding, are perilous and precarious. So he is always turning back on himself, watching himself watching others, yet also surprisingly gaily expressive, as now, in print.

DAVID RIESMAN
Cambridge, Massachusetts
January 1971

Introduction

There is an intriguing distinction many of us in the social sciences tend to make. Oversimplified, the distinction has to do with the value of feelings and impressions versus the systematic collection of facts through disinterested observation. Subjective versus objective investigations, perhaps, is what it all boils down to, or soft science versus hard science. Maybe better labels are phenomenological knowledge versus rational or empirical knowledge. Truthfully, I hold too feeble a grasp on the philosophies of science and mind to be able to elaborate these distinctions. But, more importantly, among all those momentous words like hard, soft, systematic, phenomenological, the word that troubles me most is versus, especially when versus is meant to refer to people and our understanding of people. And especially, too, when versus implies a distinction between the others and myself.

This book most definitely belongs in the category of soft science, phenomenology, or humanistic psychology, as we have also called it. More exactly, it is a book containing impressions of people, in the main young people: the schools they attend; the social and political activities they contrive, work at; about what it means to be young or old, and what it means, perhaps, to live with the feeling that while some groups of people clearly join with you in your sense of time, others seem to have discovered a time uniquely their own.

By impressions I mean the union of my own feelings and perceptions with the feelings and perceptions of those with whom I have visited, those whom I have studied, one might say. While to some extent I can separate myself from those other ones whose names throughout the text I have changed, there is an area where our senses, perceptions and social and psychological contacts tend to blur our differentiations, and where something intensely human happens. Often, for example, in exploring our impressions, I found myself asking questions of young people I might not dare to answer myself. But surprisingly, those whose eyes met my own rarely retreated from my words or from the facts of my age or my status or job. Indeed, they frequently made their stand right where I should have been, where they wanted me to be and where they believed my research efforts should be directed. And often, too, they pointed to that convergence of our impressions: the feelings, the themes of childhood and adulthood as we experienced them and as we displayed them simultaneously to ourselves and to one another. Then would occur the sometimes staggering collision of their ideas and musings about race, sex, authority, and aging and their looking forward, backward, and, presumably, at times nowhere at all, with my own responses to these very same things and to different things which also mattered greatly to me. And finally, all of this would be conjoined with our sentiments and impressions about being young or at least younger, or being old, older, too old or too young.

One is never certain in this brand of work, as one travels to schools with "the kids," attends their parties, talks to them about parents, about careers, girls and boys, that any general concepts can ever be formulated, or that from out of the impressions, singular and vivid as they are, sociological concepts or psychological propositions might emerge. In fact, the data, as we call them, of another person's life come at us in these interviews and friendships so forcefully and in such quantity that we almost never know where we are at, unless, of course, we disregard everything the other person says until he speaks directly to what we want to know. But then, one of the best ways to learn whether or not what we want to know matters at all to this other one is by trying to get a feel of his emotions, or of his own sense of intensity and commitment to the data. So there we are, having been returned to that fuzzy area of impressions.

The chapters which follow were written at different times over a period of several years, always interposed with other work, other obligations, so much so that I actually needed someone else to tell me that despite varying intentions and moods the same themes remained constant, both in the lives of the young people with whom I worked, and in my own life. The themes of a person's relation with authority, with people of another age group, with people of another race or of the other sex, the deciphering of boundaries between the single person and those he calls his family, his friends or his crowd, his feelings of intimacy and hatred, and feelings about everyone else in school, teachers, classmates, the best friend, are among the most dominant themes comprising this book and, hence, forming the lives of those of us about whom it is written.

The single most striking issue recurring in these pages is the concept of ambivalence. On the one hand, the concept suggests the simultaneous existence in a single heart of ostensibly opposing sentiments or ideologies (like objective versus subjective without the versus) , while, on the other hand, it symbolizes the complexity and richness of not only every human being but every human interaction. I think, for example, of the way so many of my young captives, I almost said subjects, spoke of their parents, even those few who had never met their parents. There was in their language and in their responses to the questions they themselves constructed when they were compelled to disregard some of my own queries, such hatred and love that I simply could not distinguish the direction in which they were headed. Nor could they themselves on some occasions.

The ambivalence, particularly about such things as dependence and independence, caring and hurting, fighting on and giving up, destroying and preserving, was always present. So little about the lives of these people seemed unequivocal, or sufficiently discrete and "right" that I could actually put it in my notebook for safe-keeping; the best that I could do was check it out in my own imagination. But even that was unsatisfactory because, after locating my own ambivalent yearnings and sensibilities, I then had to ask just who had initiated this ambivalent imagery in the first place: was it they or I? Or was it all of us, and was this ambivalence, therefore, the presence of our mutual convergence of impressions?

Throughout the work, I have tried to hold to the notions that I could never fully know these young people I would "study"; that I could never speak for them, and that I could never totally articulate the impressions born from our contacts together. And yet, just as we learn that no one can speak wholly for us, so do we also realize that others' impressions, theories and words do speak for substantial parts of us. And because they help us to sort out that convergence of feelings and events that comprise our involvements, intellectual and social, they assist us in taking a step or overcoming error.

But, if this is too abstract, I learned that I didn't care for some of these young people as much as I did others and, at times, that I didn't care for any of them as much as I was fascinated by, or at least rather pleased with, the stuff that came out of my own head after long encounters on school playfields, in restaurants, hangouts, homes and all those places where one travels to seek out that thing we call "youth culture." Studying youth, after all, is a bit like surfing, in that we can watch the ways in which our source of fascination moves from the gush of the water, to the smooth and slippery planes of the board, to, finally, the erotic patterns that are the muscles holding us aloft amid the spray and chopping motion of natural currents that play about the sleds we manufacture to ride these currents. And yet, everything seems to pass by so quickly and with such devastating finality that in the long run some of the best time is the time we make stand still by recalling our impressions of the ride. For in the recollections and the impressions they guard, we have a chance not only to replay past experiences, but to shape them any way we want with a fluidity and boundaryless majesty that the ocean itself might envy.

But does this mean that our impressions of youth or of the past are untrue or true only in their special way? Does it mean that the essence of any experience, the stress point, in fact rests just slightly beyond the beat of the experience so that to capture the genuine impulse of youth, the flow of younger people through life, is just about an impossibility? Do we perhaps make young people bigger than life by writing about them and laying on them the wit and elegance as well as the blandness and foolishness of our own perceptions of them? And how does one manage best the business of maintaining what at our old high school dances the faculty determined to be "proper distance"?

[2]

From all sorts of varying distances and intensities, I have tried to locate an appropriate closeness with the young people in this book whose worlds I was deeply touched by, attracted by, and at times angered or threatened by. The writing is divided into three parts of four chapters each and a concluding chapter. Part One is devoted to describing some of the young people I have come to know. There are first in "Prospect Street Moon" several young boys who revealed to me their fascination with Americans walking on the moon, while at the same time speaking, in their quiet ways, of the poverty and especially the hunger they have known since their time began. "Prospect Street Moon" is also about a life tempo, a tempo quite different from what we in the middle and upper classes know to be suitable or congenial. Then there is in "Leo's Child in the Age of Aquarius" a fourteen-year-old girl, a friend, and what really amounts to her simple life and simple efforts. Some would call this chapter a case study of a normal adolescent female. There are clinical features about the chapter, I suppose, but more importantly there is the story of a young woman's fantasies and hard-earned adaptations to the life that she treasures and that too many of us find lacking. "Leo's Child" is also about a style of approaching young people and about the ethics this approach assumes. The final two chapters of the first part are about parents and children and the "generation gap" business about which so many of us have wondered. More conceptually, "The Children of Nine Lives" and "Of Youth and the Time of Generations" deal with the relationship of social structure and personal development, identity, if you will, and the emergence of self-consciousness, personal understanding, trust and hope.

Part Two is devoted to education, to schools, those who attend them, those who are employed by them, and those who control them. The part begins or tries to begin inside the minds of students — "The Mosaic of Creativity" — and concludes with a rather orthodox sociological examination of suburban high schools — "Dressing Down the Naked Ape." Whereas Part One includes portraits of the poor, Part Two includes impressions of the rich and very rich. For some reason, the studies of suburban high schools are often ignored or glossed over. Suburban schools experience problems other than drugs and long hair. They have scandals erupting over events like nasty language and the introduction of black literature. So, after emerging from the creative minds of young students, Part Two turns to the problems of the working class knocking on the door of colleges — "College and Career Night in Bristol Township" — and then to the people in suburban high schools — "Simple Words, Simple Deeds" — feeling the surging rush of a culture which touches them every once in a while even though it perhaps is not supposed to, at least according to the social and institutional insurance policies they have taken out.

Finally, Part Three is addressed to the political activities in which some students find a new kind of breathing room. By now many people know quite a lot about this campus political stuff. By the time this volume is published more will be known, hence I fear that some will have decided just what they are going to do about these students and maybe about this country, too. Nevertheless, there is a history to campus unrest, that marvelous euphemism, a tiny portion of which is traced in Part Three. Commencing with the tutorial movements in 1963 — "Tutoring for Democracy" — this part reveals young people falling in and out of love with American democracy and what we call "the system," hoping that their efforts might have some effect somewhere, and maybe even such an enormous effect that they might be able to make a life of these actions or retreat from them for good. From the university tutorial programs, to observing students begin to recognize the ambivalence toward their own politics that crept in during the 1968 American elections — "Thank God for the Simple People" — and then to the events of Harvard's special

Spring of 1969 — "Voices in the Harvard Yard" — and America's tragic spring semester and national campus strike of 1970 — "The Spring of Death" — this third part focuses over and over again on the main theme I so often find to be lacking on all sides of all political issues: the people involved. As time went on, I found myself moving away from the uncomfortable objectivity I had seen come over me on my trips to suburban high schools. I was becoming involved in the politics and with the people. No, it wasn't exactly that. It was the very thought of human life that I found missing in much of the political materials, in the braggadocio, in the blasphemy as well as in the serious programs that thoughtful people were outlining. My temptation to reminisce or wish that I could call a "time out" and run away to the most pastoral, silent and elitist solitude were clues, perhaps, to my fright and insecurity as well as indicators that people's feelings were being mistreated or that people, young and old, were being used or ignored or forgotten altogether. Others, of course, had these same feelings and published words like "Cops are people too." Such an incredible cliché, but how important it was that some would remember to utter such an admonition.

Someone pointed out to me that the rhetoric of *Time's Children* is excessive. It *is* excessive, just as the emotions of the young seem excessive, and as their actions and demands, their trials and their boredom seem excessive. Exaggeration is the happy disease of many young people, though certainly not all, and while I am unaware of many of youth's excesses, I guess they become ensnared or even ingrained in some of my writing. Partly, of course, the excess is my imagination, or their imagination, but in the main it may just be the natural end product of that convergence, of that presence we have called an impression. It is for this reason, perhaps, that impressions appear to lack a scientific validity, a certainty and ultimately a graceful clarity. Perhaps, too, excess is the reason for children and young people often to be treated not as whole human beings by so many institutions but as either half human or doubly human. It seems, in other words, that those of us who spend time with the young tend to crunch them under the feet of our rules and rituals and thereby render them half human, or overromanticize their talents and activities to such an extent that the young themselves begin to doubt the worth of their very worth-while beings. It is as though we may be flunking too many students and giving A+'s to too many others.

The young themselves know as well as we do that their position in society, their status, really, is meant to be standing upright and proud alongside any pedestal anyone might wish to erect. Upright and proud alongside any pedestal; not crushed under its weight, not hidden by its girth, and not elevated by its height.

[3]

A typical conclusion to a book summarizes its major points and urges the reader to linger one last time on thoughts which seem especially significant. I held these guiding notions in mind when writing the last chapter, but instead something else forced its way in. The chapter concerns the effort of "studying" youth, becoming older, looking back at oneself and then over there at them and, generally, just musing about how one's past and present fit together, and how our present and youth's present might possibly fit together. What lies behind much of the writing in the concluding chapter is the way in which young people confront the inequalities and asymmetries in their lives and in their society. While some would call these inequalities inequities, it is not always the case that what we might see as a pernicious strain in a community is seen in the same way by that community's children. Indeed, what made many episodes with the young people in this book so poign-ant for me was their frequent disinterest in situations I felt to be so serious and crippling.

Most striking, perhaps, was that ambivalence of theirs toward parents and teachers, and the lack of clear-cut and unequivocal attitudes in this group of people whom we foolishly believe to be dogmatic, unyielding and exaggeratedly settled in their approach to contemporary life-styles. Where all young people, it seems, find a common source of complicated anger and attachment is with their parents, their schools and finally, as they mature, with the so-called established order that represents to them the symbolic reenactment of the prior social order they have known, or a new social order some now have come to oppose, or even a social order just too discrepant from their expectations, languishing wishes and recently conceived demands.

In a sense, the concluding chapter is devoted to aging, recollection, anticipation, or what in a word appears as maturation. To be sure, maturational processes shift as though the elements themselves were in revolution: the past is made strong again, the present recontextualized, and the future envisioned in totally new settings. But through it all, certain figures, certain symbols and existential properties remain frightfully constant. And it turns out, often to the surprise of some young persons, that the foundations and inevitabilities of time and its properties, such as our pasts, presents and futures, are still there. It turns out, too, that a society's properties, like poverty, hunger, stratification, power, illness and oppression, and a single person's properties, like sadness, loneliness or despair, contentment and courage, are also still there. And these discoveries require adjustments as well.

Each of us is capable of making those calculations which prove the existence of inequalities and asymmetries both in ourselves and in the institutions we structure and bequeath to our children. Each of us, moreover, works to comprehend the variables, the figures and integers which must go into these computations of maturity. We wonder, for example, about our individuality and our need for group coherence; our interior privacy and external displays; and our loyalty to authority demonstrated through our compliance and our desires to topple it, often through rather creative or ingenious enterprises. We wonder about success and failure, fame and anonymity, youth and old age, life and death, mothers and fathers, parents and children, and we, all of us, avoid the temptation to insert the word "versus" between these "options" and "properties" because we know without professional training, without therapeutic intervention, without it being taught to us by anyone directly, that we maintain all of these urges and the images of all these people simultaneously. Not only that, but we cannot accurately predict which urge or image might take psychological or social precedence over another, or whether one stimulus might send all the urges and images scurrying in one or a million directions at once.

All of us possess a limited understanding of youth culture, or whatever one chooses to call it. I shudder, however, from the certainty with which some investigators speak about the young or the old, or just about people. Tentativeness often seems to be a stigmatized word, whereas certainty, in personal action or carriage and scientific inquiry, has become the ideal. But as yet there is no certainty in our comprehension of human behavior as much as we might wish for it. How much of a young person's actions, I wonder, are made in response to his fear (or wish?) that people like myself might try to understand too much, and that his privacy, his secret interior, his impressions of himself and of his life, those feelings he cherishes the most might be taken away from him.

Most young people are resilient, and because they are they replenish what might have been taken away from them. Others are less so, and we must do more than wonder about them. Still others find their resiliency irrelevant when faced with an implacable reality that simply will not budge one inch to accommodate them, their styles or their patterns of growth. But more than anything, it seems, "studies of youth" make us question whether now is the time to be hopeful or despairing. For during these days of such extreme confusion, unsettled plans and purposes, and outright danger there just seems to be no middle ground of denial and safety, and no easy passage through time or through childhood to freedom and peace.

part 1: Youth

part 1: Youth

chapter 1

Prospect Street Moon

The young beings groped around indecisively for what suited
them best, and out of the awareness of sameness grew the desire
for differentiation, and in some cases awakened for the first time
the growing germ of a personality out of its childhood slumber.
Indescribable little scenes of affection and jealousy took place,
grew into pacts of friendship or into declared and stubborn
animosities and ended, as the case might be, in a tender
relationship with long walks or in wrestling and boxing matches.
Hermann Hesse, *Beneath the Wheel*

In the bedroom of his mother's apartment, Gino
Calibrieti is actually no more than four feet from the bathroom
where Israel Raymond showers every day, or at least where he tells
his mother he showers every day. They live so close together that
when they were seven and eight, some two or three years ago, they
used to meet on the street and make plans to knock on the walls
of their respective rooms at a special time, the four-foot separation
between these walls apparently not making such a significant scientific impact on them. Somehow they just figured out that their
friendship was sufficiently close to make possible the conduction of
sound waves through one brick fire wall, one wood frame wall,
and a four-foot area of outer space.

A year ago, they laughed together as they recounted their plan
to run pipes through the building of such a width that with one
fan blowing the air through one end and another fan sucking it
out at the other they might be able to "zap" their secretly serious
messages from room to room in the dead of night, or, even better,
just when they got into bed before falling asleep. "Are you sleeping?" a message might read.

"No, are you?"

"No. Who do you like better, Reggie Smith or Rico Petrocelli?"

"I don't know. Wanna play basketball tomorrow?"

"I can't. We're going shopping."

"Ugh."

Then the Boston winter came. For a time it seemed as though there would be few calls for their small snow shoveling business, but when February and March finally arrived, their business "turned the corner," as Israel would always say when things "got good." Walking to school each day together, Gino and Israel whispered, dreamed and plotted. After school they shoveled snow in the streets and driveways of their neighborhood. Gino's mother gave birth to a son early in the spring. Israel's sister got married on almost the same date. Both events confirmed the fact that time was moving. Worn-out dates suddenly had become brand-new dates, even special dates to remember. Yet those days of celebration also meant no baseball and, instead, long trips by subway and bus to a hospital and a church.

Although I had been seeing the boys during the previous year, I had lost touch with them for many months. I had my work to do, they had theirs; but one summer event surely would bring us together and give us much to talk over. Weeks before the space shot of Apollo 11, I received a phone call. Could I inspect the most recent drawings of the boys' rocket and maybe help them to purchase some small batteries for another mysterious project? We agreed to meet at my office. As always, they were early, their pockets bulging with bottle caps collected by carefully dipping bent hangers into the slots of vending machines. They had spent a bit of time riding the elevators to the top of our office building where, indefatigably, they constructed their plans for the bombing of Harvard, a task undertaken about ten times a week during the summer from the top of the fifteen-story structure.

Within minutes of their arrival they had spread their maps and charts all over the floor. We all laughed in deciding to take our shoes off for fear of damaging the "blueprints" and illustrations. "You watch, man," Israel cackled, "your boss is gonna catch you in here with your big, fat ugly feet staring up at him and you're gonna end up . . ." He couldn't finish. Laughter exploded out of him and, tottering around, he ripped one of the drawings. Gino's exhilaration stopped, cut off short. He went to swing at his friend, shoving him against the desk. When tempers subsided, we settled matters with Scotch tape, and soon the three of us, side by side, our bodies barely touching, were kneeling on the floor, our knees tucked under our chests, our elbows planted on the "blueprints" supporting our chins. Then, as the noises of corridors and elevators slipped away in time and silence, all that could be heard was the heavy breathing of three men, three boys, hard at work, concentrating on a plan that would send them thousands of miles, no, not this special and supreme time — hundreds of thousands of miles into space.

And in those moments, broken for me only by a vivid image of our hands pointing to the lines and diagrams, labels and erasings, we three were on our way. Together, we were on our way to the moon. I remember looking hard at Israel Raymond's hands and thinking to myself that when a black man turns his palms upward, as if to show his mother he has washed them, they are the color of a white man's hands. Actually, Israel's palms were more the color of Gino's than mine, there being a noticeable difference between Gino's dark, smooth skin and my own.

These were more pleasant times now than the rainy September afternoons after school when these two young men and their friends would come around to others' offices for psychological testing or physical therapy. It was more comfortable now and of course more exciting, because Captain Calibrieti, Commander Raymond and Doctor Tom were headed for the moon. So the deep breathing continued and we all became very brave men, the first to set foot on the crusty edges of the moon's most awesome craters, and I became more than the sum of the smaller boys who rode my flanks, my two bodyguards. I became eight and eleven, fourteen and six all over again. All the while, these two young men, these two pilots, these two young adolescents, unbeknownst to but a few, were engineering a two-week flight with a payoff the size of outer space itself. No longer that "kid's stuff," Gino would remark several days later in referring to the now obsolete message-pipe-sucking apparatus. "This is adult work."

Truly it was to be the work of three adults. The proposal called for a three-man cockpit. Gino and Israel would face forward in the direction of a giant window. Built into the window were radio signals that would direct the spacecraft to the moon. I would face the rear of the cabin. Sitting in a distinctly less luxurious chair, their design called for me to have a smaller slit of a window housing less powerful radio beams that would stay in direct contact with the earth on the "trip out," as they called it. It was almost as if my job was to keep us in touch with real or earthly realities.

This was what the whole venture was about. Filled with television screens and tubing, batteries and boxes of circuits, tunnels to other spacecraft and conspicuously unlike the professional model, an enormous galley, this most marvelous invention, a hybrid of the U.S. Enterprise, the Apollo 11 and, most importantly, the creation of the minds of two young men eleven and twelve years old from homes no more than four feet apart, was about to enjoin the fantasies and realities of generations of people. It was going to settle so lightly, so deftly, so silently on the moon that not even the spirit of history would notice the ripple that would be made then felt, as if with a smile it settled backward and forward in time. We were going to the moon, I kept thinking, an Italian American, a black American, a Jewish American. And while it all seemed as corny as anything, it also seemed, in a way one hates to admit, just about right, and kind of nice after all.

"It all seems just about perfect," I said finally, my words waking us from daydreams. Had we already been there? Were we already back from the darkest side of the moon, or even from beyond? Gino and Israel were proud. Having received my approval, they beamed a dazzling pride. For there in the plans and dreams where reality and fantasy also disappear behind the moon, and where in a vast darkness each of us loses contact with earthly realities and all attempts at communication with ourselves and those we love the most and hardest, lay the end of one logical and tightly closed destiny and the beginning of a new and open one. There on the paper lay the most poignant and sublime sense of possibility.

The two young men were talking hard science now, plain, unadulterated science. They jabbered about circuit breakers, override systems, yaw, generators of alternating voltages, electrical currents, burn capacities and reentry configurations. Their collaboration was immaculate. When one faltered, the other provided the language. When one ran out of ideas, the other always had one or two more, usually additions to the plan which meant, naturally, an entire redrawing of the rocket with the most recent innovation drawn in last. Never forgotten were those two special chair-couches etched with their initials, nor the elaborate storage spaces and psychedelic instrument panel. Never forgotten either, was the oversized and overstuffed galley, its cabinets filled with all sorts of marvelous foods packed in specially designed outer space preservatives. Food storage cupboards were sketched in everywhere. Even sections of the galley floor could be mechanically rolled aside, laying bare racks of canned goods, freezing units for beef, vegetables, fruits and ice cream, and uniquely tailored baking trays for breads, cookies, cakes and pies. "You know you don't get that hungry in weightlessness," Gino reported. "But just in case the ship has difficulty in its return mission we're gonna be well stocked."

At twilight, we were still on the office floor making arrangements to meet a second time. The boys planned to enter the building, using my key, to climb again to its broad rooftop lookout, this time to plot the course of the moonship against a backdrop of all the stars that they could count together. The plans to bomb Harvard were "junked," as they said. "Bigger things on deck to do." But, importantly, their gaze, their very attention was moving upward and outward, away from the ground and the earth, away from the mud-caked postage stamp of dead land the city had given to them and their comrades as a local play area for the summer. Away, too, from the virulent and destructive noises of a city and the malnutrition which brought these boys to the nearby city hospital where I first heard about them. Away from all this, for the galleys on the veritably hundreds of rockets they had conceived carried more food than existed on all of Prospect Street and the surrounding streets. More food, for that matter, than in all the kitchens of Harvard and M.I.T. and probably Cambridge and Boston themselves. Even if trouble were to occur on the way to or back from the moon, there would be enough food to feed large families, neighborhoods and nations of families. Of this we could all rest assured.

For weeks before the adventure Gino Calibrieti and Israel Raymond, with the help of Lemoine Tanner, Bobby Clamper, Skippy Green, the twins Roddie and Roger Gaut, Roberto Visoni, whom everybody called "Toto," and the others, spoke nothing but the street, baseball and moon shots. By the time July finally came, they had just about traded every ballplayer on the Red Sox and Orioles, returned Ted Williams to Boston and redesigned their spacecrafts from top to bottom. The only features remaining constant were the initialed chairs and the galley. All new machinery was projected one week, then scrapped. Then out of the clear blue sky special German equipment was being flown in for undisclosed purposes. Then this too was canceled, and transistorized computer consoles, made by a company in Japan, were installed. Toto reassured me that American interests possessed full purchasing and controlling rights of this company so that it "wasn't as bad as it might have been. You know like in South America. Don't we make Cadillacs or something like that in Mexico?" he asked.

It was a coming together of polished business transactions and scientific achievement. It was all so perfectly thought out. While less than three blocks away, local organizations continued their week-long trucking strike, good and eager friends had turned benchtops, tables and a small shack in which garbage cans stay hidden from the street into nothing less than an awe-inspiring military-industrial complex. Its aim: to get Gino Calibrieti and Israel Raymond to the moon.

Two days before the mission, everything was set. As more and more I became a member of their Mark Twain raft of characters, they readied systems, and although they hadn't quite memorized the names of these most recent astronauts, the frequent television reminders had driven them to fever pitch excitement. Not so much, however, that the day before the mission, which would be seen on Gino's "television," they couldn't find time for swimming in the shallow pools adorning our "home base" office building. Ignoring the No Swimming signs, they splashed about the cement

ledges in their Levi's and T-shirts which now clung to them in
the oppressive July heat. They even pushed Toto's dog into the
pool with them at one point. We all laughed, and kept an eye out
for the police, who would assuredly make us leave the premises.

Thought of the moon shot had aroused a sleeping childhood in
each of us, even those in the group who, chronologically anyway,
still are categorized as children. Sending people away from the
earth meant to all of us around the pool not merely a colossal scientific achievement. In fact, after the familiar "wow" shaking of
the head and that expression having to do with mind boggling,
we all seemed to have feelings and thoughts transcending even
the science of it all. It was just fantastic, the impossible come true.
It was the stuff of the mind and imagination, the food of fantasy
just plopped down right in front of you. "This is what makes it
extraordinary for me," I said, trying to explain it to Israel one
afternoon over ice cream. "It's like what was once imagined and
made into fantasy is now coming true. But everyone says that,
don't they? Well, does that make it less or more true, I wonder?"
But the thing that made it all great, although a bit frightening,
was that the barriers to these fantasies, the very things which make
fantasies safe because fantasies with barriers forever remain impossible, had been dissipated.

Without the impossible, fantasies aren't fantasies anymore,
they're intentions. It's the barrier that guarantees that fantasies
stay fantasies. Like the command module, our fantasies too and
maybe even the entire temporality of childhood which encases
fantasies and renders them pure if not wholly comprehensible
were about to break out of the past's atmosphere and explode
into the atmosphere of adulthood and adult truth. Even more,
but how could I communicate this to Israel who had stopped outside a shop window and now stood swooning over sports equipment, was there not something analogous between the psychological boundaries of fantasies and the atmospheric boundaries of the
earth? Is there not some primitive or symbolic similarity in the
substance of the invisible nature of air and fantasy? "Can you see
gravity?" Israel once asked. And Bobby, too, wondered at one
point, "If there is no air between the earth and the moon, why

can they see anything at all? I'd think you couldn't even see the moon." We all pondered that a good long while.

What Israel and Gino did indicate in response to all my own foolish wonderings was essentially that television had prepared them for all of this and evidently much more. The clichés were true. To a great extent, the wonderment and awe were mine, not theirs. My generation not theirs had a queasy feeling, because comic books and science fiction never could usurp or rob the truth of private fantasy as television does. In a way, to hear them talk was to realize that the space shot would do more than make congruent the images of television with the images of men and science. It was as though the rational images of reality and television would finally now be superimposed, placed in focus. It would be like peering through the viewfinder of an expensive camera and moving the focus button so that all of reality's wondrous edges would come together and all the unwanted ghosts would disappear behind the images soon to be made permanent.

At least this was the way they spoke of the event. It was not the melding of fantasy and reality or however one chooses to describe the event. It was the collision of two external sources, two inputs, that would meet and, like the rocket's own fuel components, explode into a unique storm of wonderment, a storm quite different from my own, comprehensible to be sure, but not genuinely mine. "You gotta learn to think like all those scientists do," Gino always said. "You gotta learn to think like those big guys."

I'll never know if our reactions were so different because of their lack of adult years, my own private history, or just the personal preparations each of us quietly preserves, displaying to others in the day and to himself at night. "But that's it," I wanted to exclaim to Israel, who stood peering through the glass at plastic batting helmets and tennis rackets. This trip of theirs, I mean of ours, in that giant rocket, was a bizarre and marvelous dream. There simply wasn't a thread of truth to it. The string of the kite, the tether of the balloon, would be severed and up and up we'd float, higher and higher, higher and higher. It was power and achievement and life itself that would be ignited on Cape Kennedy. It was Icarian. But not for the boys. For them, it was the

logical end of perception, cognition, attention and work. It was a
graduation ceremony of a sort. It was a rite, a natural and fitting
conclusion to something.

"Man, I'd like to get me a baseball hat like that. It's off the wall,
Reggie's got it. There's the throw to second. It's gonna be close.
He's . . . out . . . It's not real, you know."

"What's not real?"

"That hat. The hat's not real. They make 'em for kids."

The four feet of space between Gino's and Israel's apartment
houses have long been filled with crushed rock and rubbish. Over
three years ago, an apartment building in the rear burned down
and the city has never finished cleaning away the rubble and the
large concrete pieces that once served as a foundation for eight
families. "D'you know that a baby died in that fire?" Gino recalled
for us on several occasions. Most of the stones have just been
ground more deeply into the earth so that the dust adheres to the
pants and shoes of the boys who play in this area every day when
the late afternoon light slips between the houses and throws the
shadows of the people walking by onto the tan wooden fence in
the rear.

It's dirty here. The air always so heavy makes one feel as though
nearby buildings had just been razed causing the dust to rise from
the crashing walls and roofs. Almost all of the mothers in the community have been on or contemplate going on welfare. They speak
about the problems of their lives to strangers and wonder aloud
about their presents and futures as well as the futures of the
children who run under the rotting porches or sit upstairs in bare
rooms, listening to radios and keeping the flies away from a baby
brother or sister asleep in a carton or on a pillow whose stuffings
have been flattened by time. "My uncle saves the biggest orange
crates from Florida for Mrs. Bisconti," Gino once remarked, his
uncle being the owner of a small grocery store several blocks
away. "He says she has so many children he's got to get her a
new box every three months."

"That's a lot of children, Gino. You sure he said every three
months?"

"Yeah, I know. There's too many damn children on this street.

There's too many on this earth. That's why so many of them are hungry. That's why they don't do nothing."

"That's the thing, man," added Israel. "Everyone's always just sitting around here, thinking of this and that. You can't get 'em to do things."

"You mean the other guys?" I asked.

"No, not really, you know. You know who I mean!"

"You mean the men?"

"Yeah, kind of."

"Your father?"

"Man, I'm not even so sure I know my father. My mother always talks about some guy. He sounds like a bad guy, but I've never seen him. I think she probably still likes him."

"He's bad, bad, bad." Israel was laughing. "He's bad like you're bad like we're all bad. You ever bad, Tom?"

"Yes. I'm sure I am."

"You bad like Gino's old man?"

"I don't know Gino's old man."

"Gino don't know Gino's old man." Both boys had blurted out practically the identical words. It ended the topic.

Walking back from the store, we spoke about the space shot and money.

"I'll bet it cost a lot of money to send those guys to the moon," Israel said. "Jillions, I'll bet."

"Jillions? Those guys are going to be millionaires," Gino responded. "They're gonna be rolling in money. They'll make more than you make, I'll bet." And they laughed again. "I'll bet they do."

"Think of all that money they're going to get. Hey, do they get it before they go or after? I'll bet before just in case something bad happens. Then at least they can say they had it."

"Naw, you nuts, man!" Israel charged. "You think old Nixon's gonna give them all that stash knowing he may lose it?" Suddenly Israel had become his country's President: "You did a good job Neil, now here's your reward. Give 'em the bread." He held his small hand out, palm up, and Gino laughed and spanked him a handshake. Then they both laughed.

The theme of personal fortune stayed with the boys just as it did with their friends. Little else about money seemed to matter to them. The astronauts would get rich, become heroes, and "probably never do anything that dangerous again." Nothing was said about priorities, how else money might be spent. Nothing at all. To broach the subject, to push it on them as they rode the elevators or pulled the bottle tops out of the machine at Chauncey's, the neighborhood ice cream parlor, was to enter a dead end street. It wasn't to be. The older kids had spoken to them of finding money for the "poor programs," as several called them, and all that, but the shifting of priorities, like the dizzying dreams, was something for my head.

Israel and a new friend of his from Rhode Island spoke about the Black Panthers and their battles with the police. At age eleven they knew the front and back sides of the facts as only those "on the street" know them. But the time perhaps wasn't quite right for an appreciation of what I soon stopped pursuing.

It was not ignorance, however, that limited them and forced them and me to catch on to new interests. Nor was it that they lacked a sense of sociology. In their way, they probably know all the sociology that will ever matter to them. Indeed, for those anxious to help, they have graduated from informant to expert. What inhibited them came out in their fantasies of the moon shot itself. For while we all shared fears of imminent crises, failure or destruction, for these two Prospect Street neighbors there emerged two prophecies, repetitions perhaps of their own lives, of such extreme and panicked certainty that within days after lift-off they had for both Gino and Israel extinguished the glow of the entire enterprise and blocked the flood of hope and exhilaration the boys had invested in and then derived from those magical "blueprints."

Armstrong and Aldrin would not return from the moon. Upon landing on its surface they would themselves discover that essential elements, indispensable tools, or fuel or something had been forgotten. They would remain hopelessly and, more importantly, permanently stranded. Rescue attempts would be made by others who for years would struggle to the moon almost begrudgingly on their way from Mars and the sun. New astronauts with more modern gear and uniforms would trudge about craters, bored and exhausted, looking for the remains of boots, space suits, equipment and human bones. Armstrong and Aldrin would receive messages of sorrow and sadness and be bathed in the apologies and guilts of millions of Americans, young and old, "and Europeans, Russians and Chinese. But they're not gonna come home."

"They'll never be forgotten," Gino said, embellishing his and Israel's mutual sense of loss as but a few weeks before they had reinforced their divine scientific collaboration with mounds of ideas and inventions. "All the best heroes die," Israel muttered to us. Then he thought a moment about his words. "I mean, you know. Like President Kennedy and Martin Luther King. I have a picture of Martin Luther King in my room. I saw him once when he came to Boston. He looked right at me. . . ."

The good would go away, and while someone or everyone — it didn't make a difference, really — would know precisely where they were, and maybe even be able to telephone them or see their face in a photograph or on a television screen or reflected in the velvet of wrinkled and outworn memories, they could neither be returned nor reunited.

The boys told as well of imagined explosions just at reentry or lift-off, the failure of the command module to make connections with the LEM as one hunted furiously in darkness for the other, and equipment failures of all varieties. Clarence Carver came up with the notion that the astronauts would return to earth with what he described as "a strange and heavenly disease" and would die. "Ain't too many cats gonna go back up there and see what happened to their buddies. Those guys dead on the earth and all those brainy scientists sitting in their big offices scratching their heads asking, what do you suppose happened to *those* guys?" But the theme of omission, inadequate planning and death persisted. That no one was around to be blamed!

"It's not like war where the generals do the easy work and those other guys get it," Israel said. The punishment was their own, inflicted by themselves on themselves.

This was for them and their age and most essentially their time the nub of priorities. Undoubtedly they are all too old to believe in the "What would you do if you had a million dollars?" game. Thank God the few of us who once did ask that of America's poor children have stopped. Not to know their wishes and aspirations at this point in our history, much less theirs, without using such "unobtrusive" measures as "I wish" games borders on the unforgivable. What Gino and Israel, Bobby and Clarence and the girls, too, have learned in their homes and schools, in the shabby playgrounds three blocks away, at Chauncey's, at church and most particularly in that four feet of space between their houses, is precisely what a neighbor woman uttered a few years ago: "Ain't nothing coming to no one unless they got something already. The most important thing I got to teach my children is that if they sit around waiting, they're gonna get armfuls of air. You make a move, the world's gonna make a move right back at you. You take this moon business. You know about that? You think it's bad and I think . . . I don't know. But it's gonna teach them a lesson. No one from the moon's coming here. We want to know about the moon, we go to the moon. We up and get up and go."

There will be no one coming to the people on Prospect Street. Not from the moon, not from City Hall. As filled as their streets are with noises and smells, children, animals, garbage, and cars that no one seems to own, they are as empty really, as these streets are of people who matter. The children who spend their summers procuring wrenches to switch on the spray of water from the hydrants, then back into it squealing with a chilled ecstasy that echoes deep into the blackened stairwells of their homes and probably into their private histories as well, have learned about wishing. None of the young men and women who romp around the streets on those brilliantly hot days or duck under porches or into stores during the intense summer flashes of rain is quite able to articulate notions of reapportionment of federal funds from war and space programs to cities and communities and ultimately, possibly, to themselves. But they know what they have learned, and their urban explorations, such as they are, have been thorough and comprehensive.

"Gino, what do you think you might do when you get older?"

We all sat together on a bench, several of its slats missing, allowing the boys to jiggle their bottoms over the cracks and spaces. Copies of the Boston *Globe* were spread out on the ground. Clarence and his cousin Arthur from Dorchester crouched over them examining the fresh headlines, crinkled pictures and accounts of triumphant astronauts.

"I'm going to be a welder. There's this factory here in Cambridge. My brother works there and he says when I get older he can get me a job there, too."

"Maybe someday you'll be making space capsules."

"Naw. Big companies do that. This place is only a small outfit."

"Some deal that moon shot, eh?"

The shot to the moon, even the successful ascent from it and docking procedure were not having the "proper" effect on any of the boys. Only brief mention was made of the moon walk.

"You see them jump around?"

"Yeah."

"I liked it when they jumped around."

"Yeah, but they should have been more excited. They shoulda said, 'Hey you on earth, it's green cheese all right, and there are tiny little moon people here too. They're all so serious.' "

"Aw, I got tired. They kept doing the same thing over and over again."

"Yeah."

The exuberance of their planning days had diminished. The impact of the mission seemed to be wearing out. Grains of tedium had risen on the surface of their conversation and recollections. Each, naturally, wanted to preserve a moment of the event, a newspaper photograph or button or banner, but their talk no longer thumped with the hardware, science, manliness and daring of lunar landings. The next few days would drag by until the capsule returned. As it headed home, nine boys passed a summer morning speaking of the Red Sox and a Mr. "V." who had thrown Arthur out of a Dorchester cleaning shop while accusing him of stealing a pair of pants.

"Let's go back and get him," Clarence urged, without even lifting his face from the newspaper. "He'd probably drop dead if we all walked in."

"You sure you wanna go all the way over there? That's some trip!"

"Hey, d'you see this thing about Senator Kennedy and his girl?" Arthur began reading aloud.

"He died, didn't he?"

"No, you ninny. They had this big accident. Was it on the Cape, Tom?"

"I think on an island near the Cape."

"What happened?"

"I'm not sure. He was driving a woman home and they had an accident."

"Was it his wife?"

"No."

"Did they die?"

"No, well, the woman did and Senator Kennedy got hurt."

"Gee." We felt the morning's first still silence. Even the bench wigglers stopped. They looked to Clarence, Arthur and me for information and to tell them the end of the story.

"Pretty bad, pretty bad, pretty bad," Clarence said.

"What's going to happen?" Israel asked, just as he might have of a story his mother had read to him. "I mean, is he still Senator?"

"Of course he is. You gotta be unelected before you're no longer Senator," Bobby counseled.

"There ain't no such thing as unelected," Gino said, and they laughed. "Is there, Tom?"

"Well, there are ways that people who elect officers and senators can try to get them out of office."

"Hey, they did that in the Reptiles. You remember? Isn't that right, Clarence? They had a guy they didn't like so they pulled a fast one and before the next meeting this guy was out of a job." They jabbered together of a Cambridge gang they all knew, admired and feared.

"I remember. I was supposed to go to that meeting."

"Yeah?"

"Yeah!"

"Senator Kennedy gonna lose his job?"

"I hope not."

"Me too."

"You like him, Tom?"

"Yes, I do."

"Me too." And that was that. Soon they were off to buy something to eat.

Several days later I met Gino, Israel and a few boys I previously had seen but did not know. Gino and Israel were introducing the boys to the office building, which meant several elevator rides and excursions to the roof deck. I went up with them and recalled our first trip aloft when I had discovered how almost totally disoriented the boys were from fifteen stories above the city. Buildings they knew from street level had become unrecognizable, and as for their homes, they barely had known in which direction to point. As I had guided them through Cambridge and Somerville from our hallowed perch, they gradually had begun to catch on. Upper space had renewed meanings.

"Hey, there's St. Peter's."

"Is that it? Yeah, you're right. There's St. Peter's."

"Can you see my house from here? I'll bet I can."

"Not a chance."

"Over there. Over there. See where I'm pointing? Not there, there!"

"It's hard to get located from up here, isn't it? I wonder sometimes how pilots and astronauts find their way home."

"They're back, you know."

"Yes," I said. "I was just reading about it."

"Yeah, we saw them come down."

"Were you at home?"

"No, we were at Chauncey's. He's got a color television, but you couldn't see that much, so we left."

"Hey. Is that Prospect Street? Hey. That's Prospect Street. See it?"

"Where?"

"There. Over there!"

But I wanted them to speak more of the space shot and of the astronauts. After all, I had research interests. Would they discover new heroes? Would the trip stay with them? It *had* mattered, hadn't it? Would my own conflict between scientific achievement and political priorities reach them, or maybe teach them? Was it fair exposing my politics or even boyish ecstasy? For that matter, was it fair to send men to the moon? Did they know of the trucker's strike still going on in their community? And what actually is a community or neighborhood, especially if you can't even recognize it from fifteen stories up? Why shouldn't all children know about elevators and really high rooftops? Why didn't they know of the hills around Boston before their climbs, or their proximity to the ocean and what waits for them and only them on the other side? And why does an elevator ride to a public yet still secret lookout and a chance to peer into the offices not of famous men but of strange men or just plain men always end in a stop for food? And why, come to think of it, was I the only adult I ever saw them with? Where was everybody else? Where were Washington and Cambridge? Where were Mayor White and Mr. Calibrieti?

Then, as we rode down to the ground floor and walked past the wading pools, I came to see my special ones, Gino and Israel, not only apart from their novitiates, but separated from everyone. Separated and alone, and utterly abandoned. The ambivalence I had felt toward the moon shot, the accomplishment of it all, the waste of it all, was now directed, of all places, right at them. Silently, my involvement had turned to anger and blame. They had lost interest in the adventure so soon. They were already resuming their regular summer routine, the landing on the moon having become part of that routine. It had been taken in step by them just as it had by Armstrong himself, at least so it seemed. There they were, walking away, finding new objects along the sidewalk, new interests, new minutes, new hours. They were as they always were, returning to their work and to this day, preparing then for tomorrow and that day, and so on.

But why hadn't they prepared me for the inevitable changelessness that in truth each of us knows before and after all the moon shots in the world? It was, after all, the same feeling we had shared in reminiscing over Red Sox victories, even the unimportant ones.

The feelings hadn't lingered that long, just long enough to urge the boys to stay after the game to get a peek at the players coming out to a private parking lot to fetch their cars. Long enough, too, to help them recognize famous men, for maybe they'd get a look at Reggie or Carl or Rico or Big Jim, and maybe, too, they'd even be looked at by them, and by this touch of eyes meeting together be reborn. But the feeling soon would find no home and so it would vanish. Tomorrow would be another day, another game, another go at memories and wishes.

Gino and Israel had turned. Walking away from their bunch they came at last toward me. Gino started, "My mother said that Senator Kennedy is in lots and lots of trouble. She said that Americans like to make trouble for the Kennedys because they [the Kennedys] could do what they [the Americans] couldn't do. So she said he's headed for big trouble."

"Have you talked with your mother about Kennedy, Israel?"

"Unh-Unh."

"My mother also said that rich people can get away with anything and not get caught. Even murder. And she said that if what happened to Kennedy happened to me I would go to jail for ten years." They looked up, searching perhaps for confirmation, perhaps for sentencing. "She told me that if it happened to Israel I'd never see Israel again. Is that right?"

For a long moment we just stood there, the two of them in their specially initialed couches looking out their windows beamed upward to the moon, me in my high-back chair peering through the window emanating radio waves back to earth. Throughout Gino's words, the boys had stood together holding hands.

Now suddenly they wheeled about, breaking into a gallop, craning their heads back in my direction and thumbing their noses, waving, jabbering and cackling, yelling all kinds of happy jibberish. "Hey, Tuesday night you said you would referee our game. Bill Hartigan left for New Hampshire, so you have to now."

"He went to Rhode Island, you ninny. Don't you even know where Rhode Island is? I'm teachin' him Tom, don't worry. I'm teachin' him."

chapter 2

Leo's Child in the Age of Aquarius

Philosophy makes us ripen quickly, and crystallizes us in a state of maturity. How, then, without "dephilosophizing" ourselves, may we hope to experience the shocks that being receives from new images, shocks which are always the phenomena of youthful being? When we are at an age to imagine, we cannot say how or why we imagine. Then, when we could say how we imagine, we cease to imagine. We should therefore dematurize ourselves.

Gaston Bachelard, *The Poetics of Space*

M arty Ballam looks almost exactly like her mother. Even at fifteen she has the same mature, wise face, the same widespread eyes, pale white skin and, as everyone has noticed, the same long blond hair that on special occasions she will pile as high as she can on her head and then tuck under and clip with a shiny silver medallion her grandmother had made into a pin.

"She always looks so nice that way," Marjorie Ballam said. "But try to get these youngsters to wear their hair like that to school. The younger generation! You'd think we were suggesting they go in evening gowns. Everything has to be so casual, so unkept, so cool. Isn't that what they say? Got to be cool, man. Do your own thing." She laughed. "Seriously, Marty's really a wonderful girl, though. She always was. We never had any trouble with her. Never. She always did like she was told. Not one of those kids who you have to say something to twenty times before they even give you a 'huh?.' Marty's a very fine young lady. We're very proud of her. Yes. Very proud of her. She's going to be all right, too. She's not

going to set any school on fire or break records, you know. But
she's going to be, you know, like they say, solid citizen number
one, and this country could sure use some people like that. It's
getting to be you don't know what's going to happen next, or
who's going to be breaking into your house when. Don't you think
that's true?" And she sighed deeply.

Marty Ballam was born about two and a half miles from her
house on Michigan Street, the only house in which she has ever
lived.

"What's really neat about that is that my mother was born in
the same month at the same hospital. And guess what? The same
doctor who delivered me delivered her. No wait. Wait. I just
learned how to say that. No, you have to say the doctor who delivered her, delivered . . . no, the doctor who delivered her mother
delivered her. He was the same doctor. Oh, you know. Dr. Ryle
is about eighty-five. He's still alive. We see him all the time. Mom
calls him up on my birthday. Teddy had a different doctor when
he was born. Dr. Ryle had retired and he got us Dr. Abelson. He's
really cute. In fact, he's a doll. Some of my friends always try to
figure out ways to hang around the hospital just so we can see
him maybe. He's very tall and has very strange, dark eyes. He
looks like an Arabian but I'm sure he's Jewish. Anyway, that's
Dr. Abelson. Maybe I'll be a nurse. Not really; I'm just kidding.

"Anyway, what I wanted to tell you was that every day Mom
and I get to read our horoscopes together since it's the same one
for both of us. We're both Leo. I don't know so much about it.
We don't really take it all that seriously but you'd be surprised.
Like last week, Wednesday, it said you had better be prepared for
something like bad. No, they said upsetting but not long-lasting
sadness. You're not going to believe this, but that very afternoon
I got a D-minus on a French test which I took, you know, before
then, and Mom got a bill so large from Sears she practically hit the
ceiling. Dad had to write the accounting department because there
just had to be some mistake made. So they were right. It's really
eerie."

But how does one feel in this the age of the "impulsive now,"
as "the kids" squirm in their places, fight the establishment, and

find themselves, at fifteen, glowering up at nasty old authorities whose words they cannot trust, whose hypocrisy they no longer tolerate, whose purpose they will no longer condone, when one receives a D– on a sophomore French II test? A D– on a test designed to "examine our capacity for managing the uses of pronouns and direct and indirect objects?" How exactly does one feel in this age of dropouts, freak-outs, teach-ins, moratoriums, debates over bussing and that oozing uncertainty, and that "lack of identity" business that, like an itchy fabric, has fallen down on students of all ages, suffocating and scratching them and rendering them fish, heaped together in ragged, outworn nets? How exactly does one feel when one's paper comes back loaded to the very edges with *la*'s and *le*'s, *celui*'s, *elle*'s, *il*'s, *ceci*'s and *celui-la*'s, and none seems to align appropriately with the sentences written in that absolutely impossible language? How does one feel when an inability to come up with answers produces a test booklet displaying emptiness in the most frighteningly conspicuous places? How does one feel in this the exalted age of Aquarius when you get a D– on a French II exam on personal pronouns and direct and indirect objects? "I mean, you know, does it even matter anymore, Marty?"

"I felt this high." Marty lay her hand perfectly still, flat out, palm down, parallel to the ground an inch above the top of her shiny loafers with the dull "lucky pennies" stuffed into the little slits on the tops of them. They're still worn to fetch, perhaps, the same luck that came to us. "I could have crawled into my socks except they were too high. Poor grades do something to your ego. They make you feel so small and unimportant. Then I'm afraid . . . well, you know, what's really the worst, well, not exactly the worst, but you know, what's hardest, is that you kind of hate to show people how you feel. 'How'd you do, Marty?' 'Oh, so-so. All right. Good enough. I didn't really study that hard.' You know. You just don't rush down the halls yelling, 'Hey, you guys, I got a D-minus! I got a D-minus! Aren't you proud of me? I'm living up to your expectations.'

"Then I know I have to tell Mother and Daddy. Dad seems to take it easier. Mom is harder. She just can't understand why I'm not doing better. Maybe I should say why I'm not smarter. We all know I'm no genius. But of course I don't always get D-minuses. I do B's and C's. Teddy's going to be real smart, though. He's only in fifth grade but you can tell already. His teacher told Mom he's going to be real smart. I'm glad, in a way, that he's got the brains in the family. It's more important for men to be smart than women. I can always get a job or, well . . . someday I'll have a husband. But Teddy, men have to make money and they have to be brainy to do that.

"Actually we're just like Mom and Dad. I look like Mom and Teddy's got Daddy's brains. Teddy's going to be a doctor, I'll bet. Daddy never says anything about it but once I heard him talking on the phone to Uncle Phil. Phil's my mother's brother. And he said something about the real Dr. Ballam, or waiting for the real Dr. Ballam to take care of him. I felt that, like, well, maybe he didn't really care what happens to me just as long as I look pretty. He loves it when I cook, for example. He and Mother act like a king and queen. I cook and Teddy waits on them. We don't do this very often because I have homework. That's the lousy part. Every night during the week, that is, and Sunday too, they all get to watch television but Marty has to go upstairs and do her homework. Dad lets me watch like maybe one hour on school nights. He never believes it when I tell them I'm finished. He probably would if I started to get good grades. Pretty soon Teddy will start having homework and he won't be able to watch either, that little rat.

"I suppose Dad's doing the best thing. He works hard for us. He wants us to have good lives and to be happy. He always says, 'If I have one wish in life, it's that I know that you and Teddy and your mother are safe, happy and well protected.' You met Daddy. Didn't you like him? He was much better looking when he had hair. You should see the photographs of him when they got married."

"As good as Dr. Abelson?"

"No, not really. But don't tell him I said that. Promise?"

"Promise."

Three days after graduating from pharmacy school, Martin Arnold Ballam quit his job at Simeon Drugs where he had worked for years, first in the stock room, then as a delivery boy and finally, in his last years of school, as salesclerk.

"Those jobs, as much as I hated doing everything, except the selling part, kept me alive. They had a funny system in those days. When you came they gave you a job where you couldn't see the customers and they couldn't see you. Now they call them consumers, but in those days they were still customers. Anyway, then when you got better and had some experience, they'd change your job to delivery. Then you'd see the customer but not in the store, you see. By the time I was finishing with school they let me do a little selling. For a while there I was making more money as a salesman than I did as a pharmacist later on. As soon as I became a pharmacist, 'course I moved to a different place then, but anyway, what with the expenses of being married, I got married exactly one week after graduating. We didn't have much money. Marjorie, Mrs. Ballam, she worked with this sewing machine outfit. What the hell was their name?"

"Singer?"

"No. I know Singer; this was a small outfit. They ran a business in Columbus and Indianapolis and here. Well, in those days, no one else had money but we had a little. Finally things worked out. We lived in an apartment in a building right around the corner from here. Just last month here, they tore it down. They're going to build one of those apartment spreads with stores in the bottom. The whole thing. Marjorie and I took the kids to see the place. Funny, that place had, well, really, if you want to be precise, it had what they called two and a half rooms. The smallest bedroom and the tiniest kitchen. Lucky for us it was that small though. I don't think we had three pieces of furniture to our name in those days.

"Funny how things change. You know, really, I knew things were going to work out, just about as they have. I mean, really, I just knew somehow we'd stick it out and someday we would be living in a nice home. You've been in our home. It's a nice home. Nothing special, no castle. It ain't no Camp David or Onassis, but it's got all you really need. Modern kitchen and all. I've got a beautiful basement, stays dry as a bone.

"But what I wanted to tell you. I just knew like Goldwater said, remember, in my heart, it was going to work out just about like it did. Some guys worry themselves sick about it. Marjorie and I didn't even talk about it. We just knew. Maybe I read it in a horoscope somewhere like Marty and her mother read every day. I've always worked in the pharmacy and drug business, and of course it just had to get bigger. So now, like the story says, I manage this whole affair. Still, you know, it's funny to see that apartment come down. It's like, you know, a bit of your life taken away from you. Even though you still have better things and you wouldn't want to go back to those times for a million bucks, there's still a part of you, like they say, that comes down with all the brick and wood and plaster. You've been talking to Marty a lot, eh?"

Marty and Marjorie Clausen Ballam are more than a bit proud of the head of their household. They speak of him often, never sanctimoniously, as thoughts of him return and return again in their reflections on life, its meanings, or just simply in the day-to-day processes which, after all, constitute one's own private identity, as well as one's grasp of the entire world. Both wonder where they might be if it weren't for him, or where other marriages, other matches, or an impetuous step might have taken them.

Frequently, but on weekend evenings especially, this one handsome and strong mother, her sleeves folded back, a clip-on apron embracing her middle, sits across the kitchen table from the daughter who everyone would agree resembles her, and against a silence broken only by the soft grinding purr of the great kitchen clock, they dream aloud and to themselves of men and women together and alone, of families and of all sorts of marvelous futures which like trays of Christmas cookies, are spread out before them, over the counters and tables of their working spaces. They think, too, about means, finances, money, bills and balanced bank statements or allowances which properly saved or smartly invested might even take them to New York or California or Hawaii, Australia or Paris, London, Singapore, or Mexico. They imagine the world's majestic, rich and glamorous ladies: "Jackie" and Elizabeth Taylor and Princess Grace, the Queen of England, Mrs. Kennedy, and speak in a tone not of severity, really, but of sober maturity and reasoned daring, of possessing great wealth. Their voices dropping, the room's light dimming, they share a fantasy of limitless resources, literal wells of resources and constant replenishment.

"You know the kind," Marty will say, "with slaves carrying you around and four cars in the garage. You know like that ad on TV where the man has nothing to do so he keeps pushing his car over the cliff. And then he and his chauffeur walk back to his mansion and inspect all the rest of his cars?" Wealth would bring bushels and bushels of new shoes and gloves and purses and closets with so many dresses they would have to be filed by some complicated sorting system.

"No, you know what they'd do? They'd computerize all your clothes for you. Then you could push a button telling what kind of dress you'd want and there would be those revolving clothes racks like at the cleaners. Then the dress would appear. Plop."

But so often, their thoughts, their night dreams aloud are swished silent and motionless by an interrupting sense of communal allegiance and thankfulness. Then they honor the man of the house, the rightful head, and together appeal to God, perhaps, to let him stay with them for a good long time, at least for a time beyond that which anyone dares to contemplate. They might also speak, in these rare moments in which time becomes the happy victim of flirtations with luxury, of the poverty they have seen not only in sections of their own town, but in the ghetto neighborhoods of the large cities to the north and south which they can't help but observe from time to time when they ride the trains together as one single, substantial and interlocked family.

"Seems like they always build the tracks right along those poor people's houses. It must be terrible all that noise and dirt. That's what's nice about airplanes. It's all so clean, and you come down in such lovely areas." Marjorie Ballam.

"My social studies teacher once told us that whenever we take the train we should be very careful to watch for the different regions of the city. Like the slums and the business districts and the residential districts. You really can learn quite a lot just by riding the trains. Planes are faster but you don't get to see anything. But I like them better." Marty Ballam.

By anyone's terms, the homes around Michigan Street are comfortable, lovely, "as much as anyone needs." Always a bit of space
shows between the houses as well as between the house fronts and
the street. Always a bit of space. Address numbers are clearly
marked and shortened driveways or concrete runners make it possible to park an extra car or two. Usually a screened-in porch pokes
out from the front of the house, and often too "old-fashioned"
double seat swings are suspended from the plank board ceilings, a
bicycle or two leaning behind them, and firewood stacked, waiting
for winter, behind them. The porches and swings are first to feel
the seasons change. The thin bamboo-textured shades tacked on
to creaky rollers, wound up above the window openings, collect
the frost. It's easier just to pull them down during the winter in
order to keep the snow off the porch than it would be to replace
the screens with windows, which because of their size would be
terribly costly, not to mention heavy. The rest of the windows in
the houses typically have aluminum sliding storm windows and
screens, all part of one single assembly. They make the winterizing
of houses simple and quick. And just as simply, the houses change
back, opening themselves to the sun, breathing deeply again, and
welcoming the spring and summer.

"All you do," Martin Ballam was saying as he crouched beneath
the large window on the stair landing between the first and second floors, "is pinch in these two little fellows here and that
releases the . . . come on baby . . . that's it . . . then you push
it up to the top, a little farther, as high as it will go. There. Like
that. Now the other window comes down. Pinch the things. They
always stick. I just can't get them . . . they work so goddamn well
when they're new. There it is. Easy as that! So! I often think it
would be nice if everyone in America could live in a house like
this. You don't need more space. You don't need more than this.
Those big houses with all that ground are just a headache. You
gotta have twenty men working for you just to keep your house
up. You can have that! Me, I'll take this.

"I'm going to tell you something which you don't have to believe. If today, right this minute, a guy came to the door and says
'Ballam, on the spot, I'll give you forty thousand dollars for your

place, lock, stock and barrel,' you know what I'd do? I'd laugh in
his face. Where am I going to get something as good as this for
forty, for fifty thousand dollars? You know the way they build
buildings today? You know what that junk is made of? I'd like
to see everyone in a home like this. Maybe a little smaller, maybe
a little larger. It'd be very nice. Don't get me wrong. I don't mean
tract houses, like when you come in drunk and you end up in
your neighbor's place 'cause they all look so damn much alike.
That's a goddamn funny thought, though, you know? You have
this guy staggering out of his car and going in this house, waking
up the next day surrounded by people he's never even seen before.
He's looking at them. They're looking at him. Didn't Carol
Burnett do an act like that one night? Maybe, it was Dick Van
Dyke? No, I think it *was* Carol Burnett.

"I'll tell you something else. I wouldn't mind a bit who moved
into this neighborhood. Black, white, green, blue, yellow, red. If
a man's got the money, he's got the right to buy whatever he
wants. We got colored people living right around the corner.
Right over here on . . . a . . . what's its name . . . on . . .
Wayland Place. Right over here on Wayland. You wouldn't want
to meet finer people. They got a daughter who goes to school with
Marty, they're in the same class. No problems at all. Marjorie
always says she wishes some of our white friends were as nice.
Were as polite."

Passing the Danforth family's house on Wayland Place on their
way to school is by now rather routine for Marty and Teddy
Ballam. When the Danforths moved there, "Was it one, two, three
years ago already? Where does the time disappear to?", Marty
still accompanied her younger brother, this despite his protestations and desires to pick up as many leaves as he could carry in
the fall, or to make mounds of diminutive snowballs with his heavily mittened hands during the winter. They would trudge along
slowly, she bundled up in high boots and a navy pea coat, he with a
six-foot muffler of even wide blue and gold striping wrapped what
seemed to him hundreds of times around his neck and shoulders.
Then, as in a loyalty to ritual, he would stoop to examine a stone
or wrapper and she would yank at him to continue. Twenty little

steps further on, humming a child's score, he would find a newly
shoveled driveway which would mean sweet, fresh snow, or, in the
autumn, raked heaps of crisp and satin leaves. Then of course, as
is the reasoned way, he would have to bolt from her unexpectedly,
and with a charging whoop settle bottom first on the soft, downy
pile. And together Teddy and the leaves would crackle with unexpected delight.

Marty came to hate it. At twelve and thirteen it was kind of
fun actually, to show off your baby brother. She could almost use
him, especially when there were older boys around. It seemed to
her that Teddy ignited a sort of fantasy in them of playing mother
and father. They would come to treat him like their own son, then
act, in that wondrous way, as parents themselves, even though it
might only be the first time the young man had come around.
Naturally, Teddy would ruin everything. Naturally. Not only the
fantasy, but the way the fantasy helped these two others to find a
means of moving together and avoid, in the beginning anyway,
the honest sharing of private parts they might never have dreamed
one shares "with a boy"! Or, "with a girl"!

"Stop acting like Mom and Dad," he would scream at them.
Maybe, too, he would even cry or run from the room seeking either
of his parents and through them some vestige of justice. Marty
and her friend would laugh, like parents laugh, although they
felt some shame as well.

In those early September days three or four years ago, when the
black family first arrived, and the thirty new Negro children were
for the first time delivered to the school in the large, yellow busses
with the wide black stripes down the side, Marty didn't mind so
much when Teddy found something to do in front of the Danforth home. She would move nearer to the street and then halt,
very casually. Watching her brother snatch at a squirrel running
a hundred feet away, or stomp acorns under his heel, she would
gaze unobtrusively over his head at the porch and windows of the
Danforths' white house. It was, she so often mused, almost a car-
bon copy of their own home. The same front porch with the
shades, although the Danforths' did not have a swing, the same
double-dormered roofs on either side and the identical criss-

crossed windowpanes on the top, top floor. Did the Danforths'
have an attic with junk like theirs in it too? They even had a tree
on the side of the house where she guessed the kitchen was located,
exactly where the small maple she had helped to plant stood on
their own property. It was kind of funny, "eerie" as Marty would
say, this Danforth house filled with its special tingling mystery.
Several times she tried to speak about it with Teddy as they
trudged on to school.

"What do you think it's like in there?" she would ask her ward,
who by now was totally camouflaged with leaves although he
seemed unaware of it. "Do you think they have a dog or cat or
something?"

"Where?"

"In there, in the Danforths'."

"Who are they? Do we know them? Hey, you're always telling
me to come on. Now you're the one who isn't coming." But the
mystery about the house remained for this young woman on her
way, back and forth, five days a week to the junior high school.
She thought about the house from time to time each and every
day. She thought about it hard when she saw Susan Danforth in
English or social studies class. What happens to Susan when she
goes home? "Maybe she gets all swallowed up in a big cave or a
dark pit or something. Or maybe there are funny things hanging
from the ceilings, or, I know, staircases leading to secret rooms and
tunnels.

"Then again, I used to think if the house is so much like ours
on the outside, maybe they're the same on the inside too. So you
know what I did? I decided that the best way for me to see the
inside was to wait for Halloween and then I'd take Teddy trick
or treating. He really comes in handy sometimes. That's what I
did. When I think of it now, it's so embarrassing but you wouldn't
believe how we all used to wonder about it. Everyone used to
talk about it all the time. You know. We knew it was just like all
of our homes. Someone even said he'd watched Mr. and Mrs. Danforth move their furniture inside. But, I don't know, I still had
to see for myself. After I did it, I felt like a fool. Then I wanted
to get one last peek so I planned to take Teddy home again and

change his costume so we could go there again. I stopped 'cause I began to feel that Mrs. Danforth was either going to call my mother at that point, or the men in the white coats would be coming for me."

All of that "silliness" ended several years ago. A hundred years ago as far as Marty was concerned. For now, eons later, the walk by the Danforths' en route to the senior high school only occasionally brings forth memories of those first autumn days, that one peculiar Halloween night, the sense of eerie craziness, and through it all, Teddy's ingenuousness and impeccable lack of comprehension.

"You know I often wonder whether people have the same thoughts that I have. Like whether Teddy ever knew what I was thinking. We talk now a little about the Negroes; there are some in his class. But I wonder whether other people have those crazy thoughts. Like you know, on Stapleton Avenue where we walked that other time, there's that fence, remember, that long white picket fence, and I let my purse rattle on it? You know why I do that? It seems so silly to even talk about it. I once saw a movie where the girl always walked to school. I think she was in college, and she used to do it, or something like it. So I do it, not because I like the sound especially, but it's kind of like I'm a movie star. I pretend there are lots of cameras and lights and people and things in the street and they're watching me do this scene. Oh, and it's all going to be very romantic. I'll meet some boy and then we'll walk by the gate together. It's all silly isn't it?

"Once my Aunt Lorraine, she isn't really my aunt, she's a friend of my mother's, they always go shopping together. They used to play cards or something and they got married at the same time and all that. Anyway, she came by on Stapleton and I was actually talking to myself. Out loud. Like a nut. I was in the movies and talking away like I was going to the funny farm. I was so embarrassed and she thought I was absolutely out of my mind. You should have seen her. She looked like she was going to faint right in the middle of the street. So you know what I said? I said something like, 'Oh, I'm sorry Aunt Lorraine. I saw you coming, but I've got a test in English and I had to memorize a big speech from this play. I keep thinking I'm going to forget it.' And I went on and on like this and she actually believed me. I think.

"Sometimes I think that I can't tell lies without being caught at it. Once I lied to my father. It was so embarrassing. He knew darn well I was lying but he never said a thing. Never once. It had something to do with money. It would have been better if he did say something. I felt that big. But sometimes too I feel that I could tell really important lies and get away with it, like that time with Lorraine. I mean, you know, really big lies, like about crime and murders. Sometimes I imagine I've killed someone. No one has seen me do it. I'm the only one in the world who knows I did it. Then all sorts of strange little people question me and I look them right in the eyes and lie between my teeth. I even fool the lie detector by keeping real great control over my breathing and heart. I just sit there perfectly still. Sometimes this happens in my dreams. It's a lot stranger there but it's like the same thing. I know something or I've done something and people are asking me and I'm lying and they're taking it all in. They believe every word I say. Is this normal? You didn't believe me when I told you the men in the white suits are going to be coming for me any day now. If they see you with me, they'll take you too."

Later in the fall of her sophomore year, with the trees bare of leaves and the earth bracing once again for the winter's first snows and long frost, Marty and Mike Arnenstein went out together. It was at night. Marty passed it off as a date, but Teddy, "damn him," insisted on calling it "an affair." With Mike waiting on the porch, clapping his hands together to keep them warm, Teddy ran around the living room jabbering things like, "Marty's getting married," "Mike and Marty," and all sorts of greetings about loving and kissing.

"Mother, make him stop it, already." Then to Teddy: "I'll get you for this."

"Teddy, come upstairs. Come upstairs. I want to show you something. Come upstairs, now. Right now. This instant, young man. Come home early, Marty. Have a good time at the movies." Then together they walk to the Century Theater about ten blocks away, talking a lot about school, grades, Mrs. Gralie's stupid tests and the dress that Miss Donovan wears every Monday, Wednesday and Friday without fail, and Mr. Langton's combing his hair downward over his forehead in order to cover up the baldness, and Mr. Belden, the gym teacher, who is so tough even the police force would probably reject him.

"I hate that man with a passion."

"What a bummer."

"Becky says if he bothers her once more in the halls about anything she's going to stab him with a scissors."

"Then we could drag him into the furnace and the whole school would stink."

"The whole city would smell. Ugh. He's such a horrible man. Why do they keep him?"

"I don't know. Somebody must like him. He's probably old man Harney's right-hand man."

"I don't like him either. You can't trust him for a second. He'll tell you one thing one moment and say something entirely different the next. I know some teachers that don't like him either. Sometimes they'll tell you."

"He's really a bastard. My Dad's got stories about him. He's just lucky to keep that job of his."

"Why don't they fire him?"

"I guess the school board likes him too much."

"Hmmm."

And there is college to talk about, and jobs, the importance of getting good grades right from the beginning, the fear that junior high marks might already be hurting their chances, the fact that extracurricular activities really make a difference and "things like that." But they speak as well of their animosity toward some of the older kids in the high school, like Mike's brother's former best friend Stephen Mackler, "who used to be such a nice guy but who now is a hippie with beads and all that, smoking marijuana and thinking he is really something big. You can't believe it, Marty, he used to be the greatest guy."

Mike told Marty that his father said that "all this business of blaming all this marijuana on the parents is ridiculous. Something just went wrong with Steve's brain. It's as simple as that!

Just like people suddenly go crazy or jump off a building or get a gun and think they can just go out and shoot all the goddamn people in the world. Something goes whoof, like that, in their brains, and you gotta lock them up. You lock them up for their sake as well as for innocent people just walking around like you and me.

"Between you and I," Mr. Arnenstein had said, walking home from a Saturday morning high school football game that autumn, "when I see these kids playing football and marching in the band, I feel proud of each and every one. Like Mike's friend Marty. You know her. Now there's a perfectly wonderful girl. If I could, if I had the power in my hands, I wouldn't change a hair on that girl's head. She's a wonderful girl. Wonderful girl. But if you've ever seen these others with the hair down to here and without the shoes. Thirty degrees outside, they're walking around without the shoes, without the coats, without gloves. They're nuts. If this is supposed to be cute, or rebellion, or hate the establishment . . . I think they're nuts.

"But I'll tell you something as long as you're so interested in them. The parents who make such a fuss about them and say how dangerous it is that long hair and bare feet are walking around under their perfect children? They're nuts, too. Believe me. They're just as nuts. People should let people alone. A man with a gun, that's one thing. I'm not talking about that. But a bunch of rich kids who want to look poor, who they hurting? Themselves! It's nobody's business. They want to catch pneumonia and die, let them catch pneumonia and die."

Coming out of the movie, Mike and Marty walked quite a while before the talk came freely to them. Walking almost a full block in silence, they peered in the small shop windows on Washington Avenue, watching with fascination the breath steaming from their lips then disappearing into the night and soon, up, high into a sky that peered down upon them, their town and their state — the sky which dangled down at them, the moon they long ago had agreed could no longer be the same.

"You want to go to a party?"

"Sure. Where?"

"Buddy Wilmick's sister's house. Near you. You know. A whole bunch of kids are going."

"What time is it?"

"Ah . . . nine-thirty."

"O.K. But, I'm going to have to get home pretty soon."

"Sure. All right. We'll make it."

The walk to the party takes these two friends past the Ballam house, where Marty, walking to the inside of Mike, just as they had learned once somewhere, dares to peek through the windows at the dancing gray and white shafts, the metallic lights of television. A casual glance, unnoticed certainly, but for an instant, a time which, as it happens, seems so long and so reluctantly urged into a memory and a no more, the wish to end the date right then, right then, and be home again with her parents and the silver glow, explodes. In that instant, the wish explodes so loudly it must be heard by all the world, but surely by him. Then, still in that same enduring instant, at long last, slowly dying, the wish disappears. But where? Into the sky, into memory, into a later instant? Maybe all three. Maybe so.

"Sometimes at night I feel so frightened. It's hard to say, really, what I feel. I don't feel it every night, of course. But like that night with Mike that I told you about. I don't know. It was like I was scared of something. Sometimes I feel I know what's going to happen in the future, like what was going to be happening at the party but . . . I don't know, I just get scared.

"You know what it's like? It's like, you're going to laugh at this, it's like when I know my period is coming soon. First any day now, and then any hour, and any second. I'm always convinced it's going to come in bed. Or sometimes I'll be talking in class and I'll think, I'll bet I get the curse right now. Janet and I used to talk about it a lot. She said she wasn't really scared but if, no that's not it. Someone told her once that when you're very late it means you might be pregnant, but when you're late but not *very* late, it means you almost were pregnant. It's like a warning or something like that. Last year we went and asked the nurse at school about it and she said that there were a lot of stories about getting your period and that girls ought to know if there is any reason for them to be pregnant. No. Is that right? I can't remember. She said: 'Janet, Marty, no one can tell you that you are pregnant without you knowing first.' Then she looked at us as if maybe we were pregnant. She asked whether we had something to tell her. I thought I'd die on the spot.

"Want to know how silly I was once? When I was about twelve or thirteen, there was this big picnic, and everybody messed around and ate near this lake. Then a bunch of kids went swimming. You know. And a whole group of guys came along and they dunked the girls and all that. That was kind of fun. Really. Then they started doing these things where, you know, the guy lifts the girl on his shoulders and you try to pull the other girl over the guy's shoulder."

"Cock fighting."

"Is that what they call it? Well, before they started, I heard these guys talking about let's have some whatever-you-call-it fights 'cause it's the cheapest feel in town.' They're right, too. By the time you get up on the guy's shoulders he's put his hands all over you. And these other girls thought it was just so great. I thought it was sickening what they were doing. I even told this one awful boy who kept pestering me to take his hands off or I'd call my father. Do you believe that? I actually said I'd call my father. These kids couldn't believe it. They looked at me like I was nuts. I felt like, remember when I told you about the time I lied to my father. That's how I felt. I wanted to drown on the spot."

Sandra Wilmick's party that one winter night had been wild. "Damn, it's really wild, huh, Marty?" Almost like a television drama's conception of what parties are like, is the way it was at Sandra Wilmick's house on "I can't even remember the name of the street now. Oh, wow!" The rock records and the throngs of people pushing and being pushed, and everyone loving it all. To walk by someone meant to touch them and be touched all over. And there were smells, familiar, but heavy and exaggerated. Young people and old people were there, yelling, whispering, mouths so close to ears, hands so close to hands, and Mike seeming so tall suddenly, and so old. What was worse than that, was the girl so young, moving about, thanking her youth and two special, special parents, and praying she might never mature at all, or that she might bypass the entire clump of years out there in the living room, or stay forever exactly where she was just a few moments before.

In a room beyond the entrance hall, on top of a pile of coats, the lights aglow, a couple is making out, and with horror Marty recognizes Janet. "I mean, you know, it was all right for her to be doing that but I always thought . . . I mean . . . this all must sound so perverse. God, it sounds like a novel."

Six months later, now in the heat of the summer months, Marty Ballam, nicknamed after the man she had resembled so strongly during childhood, reminisces about that party and her inexplicable feelings of fear and forewarning. "That horrible den of iniquity. All I could think about was coming home and getting into a hot bath. It's so dumb really when you think of it. I wasn't born yesterday. But seeing Janet. She looked like she was being murdered. Once I walked in on a cousin of mine. She was babysitting for Teddy and me. I must have been about ten or something. And she was making out with her boyfriend on the couch and I giggled. I ran up the stairs and jumped on my bed and bounced up and down and giggled. I wasn't even embarrassed about it. I sound like a real prude, don't I? I'm not really, at least I don't think I am."

What comes out of these moments of talks and reminiscences is precisely that question: how does one know if he or she is a prude? How does one learn what practically amounts to hard sociological data, about sex, about making out, about potency and impotency, about beauty and ugliness? Each of us carries on that drive to be this much bigger, this much ahead or that much behind the next one, and then the one after him, and after him. What comes out of these moments is how one learns that he or she is doing all right, what in fact is "all right"; and how what is "supposed" to be happening at fifteen hasn't already happened at twelve and should have, or won't happen until seventeen and should have way before then. But how is one supposed to know when she cannot confess to the fright and nausea and physical illness lasting until the following Tuesday, when she must go back to Janet and lie. The feelings come out, because embraced and fed by that one enduring instant, none of the memories have retreated.

"Were you sick, Marty? I was going to call you last night to see if you needed something, but then Billy called and I think that stupid thing is on again."

"No. I just had you-know-what. I had such unbelievable cramps, I thought I was either going to die or give birth right on the spot to some monster."

"Oh, I know, don't remind me. Hey, there's going to be a groovy party Saturday night . . ." And they're off again, their psychologies and physiologies no longer charging them or running them or being them, but rather racing to keep up, never daring for a moment to break down or protest for respites.

"Sometimes I run around so much I feel like I'm never ever going to get sleepy. Crazy isn't it? I'll probably drop dead at thirty with a heart attack and I won't even know it." But everything else is left so far behind; that last weekend, and most especially last weekend's date when "everyone was making out like mad, you shoulda seen them, Marty, Oh, wow!" is either forgotten in the rush of new plans and fresh intentions, or stuffed like stained laundry into the bottom of a hamper where it is buried alive in the mess of yesterday's and last winter's. Who, after all, in times like these, admits to fear or to a sense of empty inadequacy? At this precise and ecstatic instant, confession surely begets banishment, so you bolt on, blame it on the cramps, and borrow just enough from a culture which has itself come far enough (that is to say, really, not far enough) that the packets of fear and insecurity come to be saved for and, even worse, described for you by psychiatrists, school counselors and endless cadres of "trained professionals."

All of life, just about, is coming to be seen by some of us, not all of us of course, as a series of packets, of television shows, of denials followed instantaneously and without fail by dramatic presentations and unadulterated pretense. Tab A is put into slot A and night follows day. Tab B is put into slot C and before your eyes is enacted the dissolution of a language and a history you had not only depended on, you had by fifteen years of age come to

believe were the only language and the only history there ever
were and ever would be. Certainly they were the only worthwhile
language and history. Who would contest that? Those silly German, Latin, Spanish, French and Russian teachers with their
posters and photographs, marked-up short stories and novellas,
and everything printed on that cheap foreign paper with the uncut
pages.

Walk past the vaporous silvers and purples of television and the
warmth of a home, the model her father had wished everyone
might own, and the three of them sitting inside like dumb fools,
like immaculate saints, and step from the cold into an oozy, tex-
tured warmth. Then at last innocently insert tab B into slot C
and watch them collide together. Molecular people in the most
prime of all prime time. Watch her, Janet, from English and
French and social studies and from after school and weekends and
telephone calls, and from the showers after "PE," and from all
those intimate eons, watch her bent backward on that pile of coats
and gloves and scarves, her skirt half off and "the funny little
design on her pants so visible, so close and touchable," that it
keeps you home in your own bed for two more days.

" 'You're just out of it, Marty. If you don't realize that stuff's
going on, man, you're really out of it. You ought to keep your eyes
open once in a while. What the hell do you think school is all
about, anyway?' That's kind of what Mike told me. He thought I
was a child. I wouldn't dare for a million dollars tell him that I
had spoken to my mother about some of the things at that party.
And I was glad I didn't have another date with him that following
weekend. I don't think I could have stood it. I trusted Mike. We
once agreed that it was a good idea that kids shouldn't smoke and
that we'd tell our parents if we smoked. Or drank. And we talked
about how far, you know, you should go with a girl. And he
agreed that you can pet and all that, but that, well, you know, the
rest can wait till marriage. He agreed and I thought he was just
great. What a sucker.

"Then, I don't know, something happens to boys. They all get
together and do whatever they do and ride around and all that,
and they decide that you can't be a big man until you sleep with
a girl, or lots of different girls. I'd like to know what he'd say.

I wish you'd ask him if he wants his wife to be a virgin. I'll bet he says yes. Oh, I don't care what he says. I was such a fool to trust him. He probably thinks I'm some kind of a basket case walking around wishing sex hadn't been invented. Maybe girls are the same way. Who knows. Who cares."

Most of the conversations of those three cherished summer months came around to the same themes: boys and sex, popularity, clothes and appearance. But it is almost as if the language itself contained pockets of feelings often having nothing whatever to do with what was being spoken about, or for that matter, with the feelings that popped up here and there: the anxiety with the willingness, the fear with the daring, the reservations with the plotting. At some level we know so well about these pockets, because we have put them there ourselves, hoping, perhaps, that someone else might find them, and might speak of them and to them.

"You really have to get to know someone a long time before you really know what he's thinking," Marty said once. "Even when they say one thing, they might be thinking or wishing something entirely different. Did you know that? Oh sure you do. That's why you're a psychologist, or social . . . or whatever you are. I always think that's really the way I want my husband to be. He should be able to tell when I'm saying one thing and meaning it or saying something else and meaning something different. You know what I mean? 'Course, he's got to be good looking, too."

"Naturally."

"Naturally."

"Like William, maybe?"

"Well . . . I . . ."

"Just a little?"

"I guess more than a little."

William Garrison Rinehart had come from out of the blue early that September, absolutely brand new. Before then, he simply never was. But on September sixth at precisely four-thirty P.M. he was among the living, socially born. Mr. Ballam had introduced them at the drugstore and, "Oh wow! He looks just like that ad. You know the one? 'I came back.' Before I left the store that time I whispered to Daddy something like, 'You sneaky man,' and he blushed. You should have seen him." William Garrison Rinehart. He couldn't have come at a better time. Surely God-sent. Just what the doctor ordered. Just what the horoscope predicted. "Do you believe that? Unbelievable. All true. All true. I kid you not!"

The time, or the sense of time or whatever it is of fifteen-year-olds, can anyone describe it or feel it again? Are we ever able to know just how it is that eight months can "zing" by so quickly, and, at the very same time, crunch along so slowly? Is the experience of that special time identical to how we perceived it immediately in retrospect, that is, at the moment when that eight-month period concluded? And is that immediately retrospective calculation, such as it is, the same as when we look again, in retrospect, but from a time, say two, three, five years hence? Naturally, it's not really the same, but is it close? Close enough? Is it now at all like it was, and does everyone think about time this way? In other ways? What really do we remember of school? How slowly or quickly this part or that part passed? Or is it maybe that we recall the time of the recollection, the feeling of time moving quickly or slowly, rather than the actual events that filled all that time? Or is it not this either?

William Garrison Rinehart. In fact, he helped along the very time, the very adolescence of a young woman. He didn't start time moving again, as some will say. How foolish. Time was moving. "My life came alive. You can't say that. Can you say he made life come alive?" A private, totally personalized time was clicking off its markers again. It was in her eyes, in that appearance they, the girls, spoke so much of, and in the dance that was her motion in and around the house. The lights and cameras and stardom followed her about.

But in the corridors of time, in and among its narrow slits and on its generous and expansive plains, were also tucked away eight months almost exactly from the time of the party and the wish to return home. Then the two days in bed, the wish fulfilled perhaps, with what it seems so many young people diagnose as trauma. (How the word often sounds more deadly than the events it describes!) Those eight months were there too, deep, deep inside time's pockets. The descriptions of life, the accounting, reporting, confessing of life in and of time, as, after all, a diary is, contain all sorts of these pockets. Some stretching from Monday till Friday: "Thank God for Friday afternoons." Others from Friday until just as late as one dares stretch it on Sunday night: "Why don't they make us go to school on the weekends and let us stay home the rest of the time? Or better yet, send our parents to school and let us stay home." Then the pockets of seasons, autumn or football, and the months, the periods, and summers: "God, I wish we lived in California. But then I'd never see snow again and I love the snow, too. I would miss it, I'm sure."

William Garrison Rinehart. Tall and rich. Handsome. Publicly gruff, privately gentle. "He's conceited, but who cares! All men are, really. But he's earned the right. Even Jan is envious."

Like a wondrous revolving disc, the seasons turn, and in the astrological space given over to September and October sit school, more Friday night dates, and more locker by locker conversations. There's the time they try to petition the administration to permit them to wear pants. Certain they will lose; they sneak their skirts into their lockers, and when Mrs. Minelli, "that old fish," orders them to "change back into clothes or go home," they march to the lav to resume their uniforms and talk about socks and stockings and panty hose and mini-dresses and maxi-coats. They speak about the boys, too, of course, who helped them with their pants crusade, and, even more, about the boys for whom in part the crusade was launched.

But even these conversations, as animated and absorbing as they seem, remain but fillers. Fillers between weekends, between football games and, for Janet, cheerleading practices. For Marty, classes drone on. Time is homogeneous, a hunk, or maybe school has finally stopped it altogether. Nothing seems vital, nothing important. "I always get this funny feeling when I leave school and see the Negro kids piling into their busses, I should say bus. I always wonder what they get out of school, or like, do they date? They don't come to our parties but they probably have their own parties. They're probably better. It really seems a bit silly but you don't know what to say to them.

"Sometimes they frighten me. Like this morning I saw a whole bunch of guys walking down the hall. They seemed to be looking for a fight or something. I mean, they kind of walked like they

owned the place. Actually, I knew one of the boys. He's in my
English class. We talk a lot together after class, but when he gets
in with his friends he acts tough and important. I don't say anything. I mean, I'm sure they know what they're doing. Sometimes
when they're all together and talking very fast I don't even understand them. I used to think they did that just to bother us and
that they couldn't even understand each other either. They just
did it to annoy us. Like when Teddy was real little, my girl friend
and I, you don't know her, she moved away, we used to speak this
crazy make-believe language. Teddy would think we were talking
about something. He'd get furious and start to cry or call for
Mother and we'd die. That's what I think, used to think when I
heard those kids. But they *are* talking. They can talk like us but
outside class they talk that other way. Fast and all that. It's like
they're foreigners.

"Oh, you know what I dreamed once. I dreamed that . . . well,
I have to tell you something before so you can understand. There's
this boy in social studies. He's a Negro and his name is Calvin . . .
Calvin Marks . . . no, it's not Marks it's something like that. Anyway, he's on the football team. He's a great athlete. Basketball,
baseball and everything. Well, he always wears those tight pants.
Every time he moves you can see all of his muscles move like right
through his pants. The funny part is that I knew I always watched
him, especially when he wore these orange, they're . . . they're,
pumpkin-colored pants. It was like he was naked. I used to wonder what would happen if anyone ever knew I was watching him.
Can't you just see it: Marty Bellam, sex maniac, carried screaming
from social studies class. So anyway, one day in the locker room
some girls are talking about boys' clothes and how they like to go
to the football games because the boys' pants are so tight. And I'm
just bursting. I'm going to explode. And Jane What's-her-face
says, 'Do you guys know Calvin Mingus?' Mingus, that's his name.
'Do you know Calvin Mingus?' and she goes into this thing about
Calvin in social studies class with his green and orange pants. Oh
wow! It was really wild! Just about every girl had noticed him and
everyone was so surprised that everyone else had too. We just died
laughing. I love that part.

"Oh, I almost forgot, the dream. I don't remember when I

dreamed this but I was in social studies class and Calvin came in, this is part of the dream now, and said that he had heard all about our discussion in the lav about him and his pants. So what he wanted me to do was sit on his lap so I could feel his pants. I told him something like I really didn't want to, but I really did. And he said, 'Oh sure you do. Come up here, little girl, and sit on old Calvin's nice old lap.' And I wanted to. Then he said, 'You sit up here this minute or I'll come over there and murder you. Very slowly like, too.' I told you, I'm ready for the men in the white coats."

A funny feeling sort of overtakes one, or maybe it just slips through some sense of our adult defensiveness, when the meetings and walks with Marty and the kitchen conferences around the white formica table with all the Ballams assembled continue into a second year. The feeling has to do not so much with the increasing fuzziness between friendship needs and "research requirements" as with being implicated in a sense of drama or dramatic occurrence that one wishes might soon come to pass. Rather suddenly, we want life to take a magnificent turn in a direction no compass would ever comprehend, no astronaut be able to retrace. As silly as it sounds, we want people who are close but not really honestly close to become famous, rich and famous. Maybe they could become movie stars, Western heroes, great ladies of the world. Through some combination of their words and our words, we want all of us together, all of us who have shared the movies and parties and walks by a black family's home, to become special, special and immortal. That's probably what it is: we wish to make the others and ourselves immortal.

"Maybe, who knows, we might live forever," Bill had told Marty one night as they rocked on the porch swing and through their graceful motion together transported themselves backward to the freest childhood and then forward again to a point in time where they dared look back at themselves and their own futures, or so it seemed that night. "I know one thing for sure; I want to die before you."

"Oh no. I before you. I before you. You're the more important person."

"You're great."

"We're both important."

"Thank you. I think so too."

"That's nice."

"So are you."

And yet, the wish to bestow all of this immortality and specialness seems cruel in its condescension. Every poor black, "working-
class" Catholic, Appalachian, Jew, has to make it upward to the
top, higher than the top, then, impossibly, over the top to a place
of absolution and sacredness. Nobel Prizes aren't even enough,
and surely they're pretty close to immortality. Everyone is meant
to be lifted up, higher, higher, just as a father swoops down and
lifts his somewhat frightened child, the child with his father's eyes
and his mother's manner, way up into the smoky air, so that his
back scrapes against the ceiling and the light gleams dangerous
inches from his hair. Then the relief, the utter collapse of tension
when the child is released, excused, and he sinks back, partway,
to the height of his father, their faces as close as faces dare be, a
musical rest before the descent back to a child's height, a child's
space and a child's topography. The child, tottering, looks about,
and that large giant whose head surely would crash through all
the ceilings of the world if he cared to raise himself to his fullest
height, if, as they say on report cards, he ever extended himself to
his fullest potential, straightens up. The moment coughs, catches
its breath, then clicks on, the child down there, the adult up here.

That part of society down there, this part up here. And in-
stantly, everyone is living in a house just like Martin Ballam's,
like Mr. and Mrs. Danforth's too. Is that what it's all about?
Maybe so. Part of it, anyway, at least at this point.

But whose job is it to shovel away the condescension and un-
easiness from partings and completions? Or should they remain,
intended as they were? Who is supposed to say, "It's all right if
we don't see one another as often as before" or, "I'm as good as
you, you're as good as me"? Who is to say, "we're both important"?

"So?"

"So what?"

"Will you write this up, all this stuff we talked about?"

"If I do I'll send it first thing to you and your parents so you
can all check it over."

"Check it over for what?"

"Well, you know, there may be mistakes or things you don't want me to say."

"You don't have to do that. There's nothing you can say that wouldn't be all right."

"I wouldn't use your real name, of course."

"But you can. Why not? I don't have anything to hide. I really don't. I'm not ashamed of anything. Like remember when we talked about things like sex or drugs or marijuana or politics. All those juicy little topics. I'm not ashamed of my feelings. A lot of kids feel like I do, so what's there to be ashamed of? That I don't get drunk or make out under the stairs of the boys' gym? I told you right at the beginning, remember? I told you we were just like everyone else, and that you weren't going to find anything interesting. Remember? That's what happened, didn't it?"

"Hardly."

"You remember all that stuff about the fence and the movie camera with the lights and all that? You know why I do that? Look at me, I'm starting to analyze like you psychologists. Maybe that's what I'll be. A psychologist. Then I'll go around analyzing people like you do. Right?"

"Right."

"No. That fence thing. I think a lot about that. I know I'm not going to be any movie star. And I know that I'm never going to be anyone special. Not in the big world, or the little world either. I'm not going to be the President or famous or anything. If you wrote something about Nixon that would matter, 'cause he's famous. He's somebody. He's, no, that's not what I really wanted to say. He's somebody but I'm somebody too, like Bill. But he's more important. I'm not that important or special. Like if he were killed, like President Kennedy, it would be horrible and everyone would know. But if I got killed, you know, my parents and my friends would be all shook up, but who would come? If I were young it'd make the papers and all that, especially if I got raped or murdered or something. But, well, you know."

"Hey, I've got a question for you," Marty began. "Just for once. If I got killed. I know. Really. Listen. If I got killed, what would you do? Would you feel sad?"

chapter 3

The Children of Nine Lives

today
is mine (I claimed)
(to) a man
a voice
I sent
you grant me
this day
is mine (I claimed)
(to) a man
a voice
I sent
now
here
(he) is

A Teton Sioux song
by Shell Necklace

When you come to think of it, they all were ex-
ceedingly brave, even suspiciously loyal to stay together, to stay as a
group for as long and as intensely as they did. Every Tuesday
afternoon at four o'clock, at four o'clock precisely, they dragged
or bounced or hunched into the little seminar room on the second
floor, flopped their coats on the backs of the chairs, sat down,
jumped up again to jabber about food, and then settled in for two
hours of talking, joking, thinking and hard work.

There were eight of them. And to hear my descriptions, my
categorizations is to know the unavoidable prejudgments I brought
to them. Boys and girls (in that order), blacks and whites (in
that order), all young, all from desperately poor families. Every

Tuesday for almost two years the nine of us sat down together at that old grainy brown oak conference table, our feet propped up on its horizontal leg supports, to speak about a life, about nine lives, rather, which, as they say, seemed to funnel deeper and deeper into time. It wasn't really that the accumulation of hours together caused our utterances to concentrate about reminiscences. Rather, it just seemed as though the accumulation of whatever it is that remains after hours and hours of the all-of-us-together brought forth expressions of profoundly deep trust and friendship as well as hurt and glory, and all of it set in a wholly private, sacred and unique vessel of time. For as the months breathed slowly on, the Tuesday afternoon hours sped by. Like pearls, one by one, fastidiously strung together on a single silken strand, the Tuesdays began to stretch out over a new and special time, and if it doesn't seem altogether crazy, in a totally new and wondrous direction in space as well.

Nine lives together, nine lives apart; five together, four apart, the boys together apart from the girls; the blacks together apart from the whites, the white boys together, the black girls together, all together, all apart. The one rich and older apart from the eight poor and younger. All finitely apart; all permanently together. Nine lives permanently together. It was like a round, a children's rhyme one might sing in an exclusive nursery school, or maybe in a day-care center somewhere. Nine lives together. Evanescent. Permanent.

As in a round or nursery rhyme, there was in fact a gentle but still sturdy ritual about the meetings. We never spoke in the idiom of organizations and capital government, using words like "having a dialogue" or "confrontation sessions," but there were modestly protective rituals, linguistic and otherwise, a concatenation of preparative actions, somehow necessary for our integrity, if not actually religious in manner. All were purposeful and seriously intended, if not obsessively transacted. For example, there were, first and always, food arrangements. Someone had to bring the pizzas or roast beef specials, the dogs and milk shakes and French fries. This meant procuring money in advance, or even better paying out a "wad" and then getting repaid by me. Best of all was to be paid by check, for checks implied big business, adult business, trust and reliance.

From the beginning, Kenny Morris was the carrier of food, the provider of a nourishment and sustenance he had for more than ten years consciously wished he might receive from the transitory bands of people setting themselves up as his family, almost like circus attractions in those weary, swaying canvas tents. When the preordained circus "run" was concluded, the bands shifted about. Disassembling their unity, their collective alliances dissolving, some moved on, some stayed, most left. Grandmothers and grandfathers left, father left, then a new father came and left. ("Is he a stepfather? He's not a stepfather 'cause my father's alive. No. *Is* he a stepfather?") Then still a third father, a third provider in a surely finite genealogy came, but in months he too departed. Departed for somewhere nearby, or is it faraway? It has never been too clear just where all the fathers go to.

"But who cares anyway," Kenny would say five months later, as snows and vacations and beautiful, tall evergreens pulled along atop car roofs reminded the nine of us and our families, constant and changing, that our second Christmas together was approaching. "Who cares about these other guys? It's my father I'd like to meet. Just once . . . again."

"You never even met him, man?"

"When I say met, I really mean remember. I met him. I just can't remember him. I just can't get his face up in front of me."

The meetings would start first with Mr. Morris's first child and first son, Kenny, bringing the food, waiting on each one of us. What had been the group's wisdom in selecting this one among them who carried out his duties in all weather, with all hardships, or so they seemed to us, with an honesty and gaiety one attributes only to make-believe people, like, well, like Santa Claus, or as Beverly would say, speaking for us all, like "the best father in the world"?

"That's what's really funny about you, Kenneth." It was as though Beverly and Kenny, in a more than imaginary way, were married. Or so it seemed, especially when everyone else called them Kenny and Bev. But for themselves, they insisted on that formal intimacy, that fragrance of sweet respect, so often noticed among marrieds: Kenneth and Beverly. "That's what's funny about you, Kenneth. Sometimes I think you'd be a great father. Then I think, don't laugh," — and they wouldn't — "you should be my son. It's like you're a little baby sometimes. A hungry little baby."

Kenny would bring the food, and the others in their thankfulness would tease him. "I said rye bread, man." "Where the hell are the anchovies? Where did you buy these anyway? Sears?" "How many times'd I tell you, 'black and white frappe.' Black and white! Make a list the next time, will you." "Je-sus!" Then there were the drinks. "Change for a dollar." "Two dimes and a nickel for a quarter. Who's got it?" "Loan me a dime, beautiful." "Kiss off, brother. Get your own bank loan." Bottled drinks, pop, tonic, orange, purple, clear, white milk, chocolate milk, shooting the thin paper straw casings about the room, or better yet, into the ear of your neighbor. The cups of love would pass about the room. The cups of love, bottled love and psychic fuel sustaining them for those hours, carrying them perhaps over to the next Tuesday, and the Tuesday after that and the one after that as well.

"I can't make it next week." It's Johnnie.

"Oh, no!"

"Why not?"

"Basketball practice's starting late that day."

"Gee . . ."

"What time can you come?"

"Ah . . . I don't know. Five maybe."

"O.K."

Then the furies answer. A wild chorus of pizza and roast beef eaters respond to this alteration, this wedge among them. And mouths full:

"Well, be here at five. Five and no later."

"Change your practice time. Hey, I miss two hours of work to come here. So you can come too."

"You're looking for a way out, John Hurd. You're scared. That's why you never talk in here anyway. You're scared. Right? Am I right?"

"Let him alone."

"If he can't come on time, I don't think he should come at all. We made, like, a deal, and there's always something else happening. I'd like to go shopping or have a taste, or something, so I think you should either come or not come. We spent two whole wasted weeks figuring out a time to meet. It took forever. We made a deal. There's eight of us having just as tough a time."

"There's nine of us here, Janie."

"Oh yeah. Tom. Well, that's what I feel, John. Come or don't come, but don't give us this basketball jive. We're all busy people."

"And terribly important." Moonie.

"Yeah, real important. Your mother know where you go on Tuesday afternoon, Ronny?" Kyle.

"Sure. Kind of."

"Mine doesn't. I don't think so."

"What do you mean, kind of? Does she know or doesn't she know?"

"She knows. Ronny just ain't confessing."

"She thinks I'm at a tutorial session."

The pace picks up. Introductions have vanished. It's as if the talk has suddenly been transcribed, musically transcribed by someone else, orchestrated not by any of them individually, certainly not by me, but by the group. It's partly that, I begin to feel, and it's partly an orchestration that comes from all of us being publicly together and privately among the others all at the same exact time. It becomes extraordinarily difficult to describe, much less explain. The "deal," as they call it, implies that the private and public, the strictly personal and the something to be shared with them all at that proper moment which now waits its turn must somehow be addressed, or alluded to, or thought about, or folded together and crushed back into silent musing and memory.

The group's orchestration means different ranges and tonalities of discussions and moods, at times percussive, at times lyrical. There are rhythms in their speech for dancing and loving, rhythms for marching and slaughter, rhythms for women, rhythms for men. There are solo parts, monologues going on and on, and duets, like Kenny and Bev, trios, quartets, and finally the tutti; all of them together, talking altogether if not all at once, as an entire family or society or culture. And always there are the nine of us, who an hour before were literally light years apart, but who now are together, our thoughts and utterances coming neatly together, wondrously orchestrated. Then at last, the finale, the meeting's end, reviving not only the themes of the earlier and earliest discussions and movements, but of all prior themes from all prior movements, and still all of it anticipating the themes and the structure that will constitute the shape of next week.

"God, school's getting worse and worse. I'm going to quit." Kenny.

"Where were we?" Kyle.

"Do I owe you any money? Don't I owe you for tonic?"

"What were we talking about last week?" Bud.

"You owe *me*, smart guy, not *him*. *I'm* out a buck. Remember?"

"You, Kenneth. Your mother getting drunk every night. 'Member you spoke about the times you opened the closet door and the beer cans fell on your head."

No one laughs. The pace is right now. The pace is right now for work. In their way, in their inimitable way, impetuous and persevering, they have saved John, reiterated the contract, a contract not only of allegiance but of purposeful work, and have sewn together the hours of this week and last week. They're resuming not only from where they left off but from their individual and collective beginnings, and from secure and insecure starting points. They are a group, for whatever that means, each one at times more with the others than he is by himself, at times alone even in the presence of the others, at times considerably (and noticeably) less isolated. In their work, the work which proceeds as quicksilver on the outside, around the grainy old table, the work which comes so slowly from within, the memories and associations, themselves also not unlike pearls strung on invisible threads of time and brilliant situation, move them, move us. We are thrown backward and forward all in one stretched and dazzling instant that houses a dream, a joke, a happening at school, Kenny's bad grades, or more likely, the mention of family or friends, living or dying.

Many would say it's just good old "rapping." What is rapping, after all, other than important talk amplified by deep involvement? Is it close to what the analysts call cathecting? But the group, not that it has to be, is doing something more than rapping, for there is at least one additional chore, one additional level of experiencing about the group. We speak to one another and the words mean what they mean, although it is remarkable how the most common and silly words take on such great stature and personality within a group. The words become like little fifth grade boys, all at once so decked out in football equipment that they become recognizable and unrecognizable at the same time. Examples? The words "us," "they," "here," "group," "teacher," "person," "brothers," "close," "feelings." All recognizable, never found on vocabulary tests, of course, but now inserted into a slightly new, marvelously vibrant rhetoric, a rhetoric yielding direction and purpose if not identity itself. Or maybe it's a grammar. "Touch" is another such word. "Friend" another.

So there is first the level of just plain speaking to someone and then speaking in response to what one has heard. Naturally, one hears what the others hear, as well as what none of the others can hear. One hears, too, what in fact was never said. One hears, therefore, differences in sounds and differences in silences, and particularly when wishing, anger, guilt, loneliness and loss are involved.

The response, then, is perplexing, a question bathed in antipathy, a fear in the midst of statements of indecent conceit, a battle won among a barrage of unthinkable curiosities. We speak to one another. But before we begin, a contract is offered. Here, then, legitimated by the outside and probably hiding behind its shapes and sounds, I claim authority and hence speak first to these eight fourteen, fifteen and sixteen-year-old students from the two public high schools no more than five blocks away from our university offices.

The group is to meet regularly to speak about the kinds of things that truly interest them, perhaps too, about those things which bother them, frighten them or especially please them. The discussions will be a bit different from the sorts they might have known before, as from time to time we may want to dig a little deeper into matters, whatever that means. Maybe we'll try to figure out why things are upsetting us, and maybe we'll be able to make things in the world a bit better or easier for us. Perhaps the language of the group may aid us in defining a purpose. Well, we'll see what happens.

It is an absolutely foolish speech. It's genuine, to be sure, but as in all contracts people smartly rush to find the small print, the kicker, the hedge. In our own group, the students have been chosen because they are having an especially "tough go" at home, at school, somewhere. How exactly they differ from all the rest of us is hard to say, but they would have ideas on this. Usually "tough go" means something like the existence of "performance problems"; the "child" is causing strain in those who guard him, clothe him, feed him, teach him and scold him. Kenneth is flunking just about every one of his sophomore courses. Where he evidences exceptionally poor performance is in Spanish and French. His teachers are bewildered, his mother is bitter. Within the stretch of one year he has started the one language, switched to the second, switched back to the first, and then, for two weeks, dropped math so that both languages might be studied simultaneously. Now he is flunking both languages. Four months into the group he tells us that his parents spoke French because they came from Canada, but they refused to teach it to him so that they could continue to use the language without him or his brothers and sisters understanding. Words are also walls.

There abound in this age of the mind and everyone's new and slick access to it fabulous cerebral connections to be made. Bev makes one. Maybe the flunking of French and this new information are enjoined in some form. I haven't opened my mouth, but all the other times I did this may be what I was teaching. Now I wonder whether it is any good at all, this "third ear" business, or if that's not what it is, this selective linking of one pearl with a pearl that seems to lie so innocently way down the line, separated by so much space and time that it is remarkable that anyone might want to connect them. Even then the connection seems so chancey, so accidental. And yet, for the moment I kind of like it, the game, the drama, the connections, the linguistic calisthenics they unveil before my eyes. They are in a new workshop, listening.

"Hey, that's damn good, Bev. That makes sense. Don't you see it, Ken? Everyone knows you're bright enough to do damn well in French, but you don't want to learn it because then you'll be like your parents." Johnnie.

"I don't get it."

"Wait, wait, wait. That's not quite it. Dig it. If Kenny learns French, he gets to find out what his parents were saying about him all those years. You said you knew somehow your parents were talking about you. Right?"

"Right. I remember that. Did I say that in here?"

"He said that in here. I remember it."

"Hey man, if you can't remember and I can, you're worse off than I thought." (Everyone laughs.) "Now dig it. You don't want that French jive because you don't want to find out what they were saying. So you switch to Spanish, which is stupid 'cause it ain't going to help you with the French. And somehow, I ain't got this part figured out, you're just working against yourself, and everything's mucked up."

"Maybe that's why I'm flunking German." Bud.

"Sock it to 'em, doctor, you're starting to sound like Tom. You'll probably come out of this thing looking like him, too."

"I wish someone would help me in English."

"Ugh! Shut up, man. This is Kenny's hour. Kenny baby, this is your day. Help us out."

"Lord, Lord, help us out."

Regardless of the contract, regardless of the expressed purposes or strategies or techniques, my own reservations or confusions, or for that matter their techniques and doubts, the group comes to mean psychotherapy, with a definite emphasis on the psycho. But it is my doing; my personal culture's doing. Not from time one that marked our initial session, but from a time before that, in the selection procedures, when, like fraternity rushees, they were "tapped" for a spot in the group, the communication is "psycho" and "therapy." Come on Tuesdays and see the "shrink." Come on Tuesdays and try someone else on for size. Come on Tuesdays and see how your fellow man suffers too, and how you're not the only one.

"Hell no, man. Nothing special about me. I'm just like all the rest of you. Even you honkies! We're all a bunch of loonies. Ain't that right, Tom?"

"Can he tell whether we're really nuts?"

"Hey, are you a psychiatrist or a psychologist?"

"Is he a *doctor?*"

"What the hell's the difference?"

"If you think I'm bad, you should see my sister!"

"Well, I mean if he's a shrink, then . . ."

"Man, I *know* your sister. She *should* be in here."

"Man, are we talking about Kyle or Tom?"

"We're avoiding the issue. You ever notice that whenever we really bring up something important, something really big . . ."

"I'll tell her to come next week."

"Really big show!"

"Shut up."

"The hell you will."

"Whenever we get to something big we turn on Tom. Why do we do that, Tom?"

"Yeah. Why do we do that?"

"Don't answer her."

"Why not?"

And they shelve it. They're not quite ready, apparently, for this one "digression," but in it they recognize a second level, a second use of that rich and penetrating language of theirs. They know it full well, so it matters little for the moment whether they have it thoroughly reasoned out, or whether their knowledge is spurred by conscious, preconscious or unconscious processes, by monsters, machines or even balloons. They know at that moment that their very language, while running along in one direction, linearly, along a slithering but still well-defined canal, has quietly trickled away and found new beds into which it dares to flow. They know, in a group's way, that just as they have rested their hands upon that long, grainy oak table, so have they allowed the words and grammar of each of the others to flow into them and to seek a new level. They know, and how colossal and utterly human this intuitive task has been, that there are other languages, other grammars, other vocabularies and expressions which, like living organisms, burrow within heaven only knows what part of their

bodies and their stored experiences and now respond on their own
to assist them in responding in a way which will forever seem
to them larger than life.

They are learning in this sensitivity, empathy, encounter, T-
group, therapy group, rap session, or whatever, that all these wondrous languages within them are not in their secretive demeanor
evil nor even foreign, but natural, biological maybe, cultural
maybe, fantastic and hopeful. They are learning that the others,
too, have these languages, possess them as sure as they're sitting
there. And, just as they once wondered whether they might catch
the mumps from one of their classmates, or why they couldn't
wear an eye patch like the one Preston Singer wore in the second
grade, they now begin to feel that this deliciously private nation
of dreams and sounds, while not exactly owned by the others, certainly is trespassed upon rather frequently.

They have, in a word, found a new presence, not really new,
but new to them, and that makes it new. They have unearthed a
presence and with it, most probably, a rather engaging new notion
of immediacy in which this presence mightily strides. Some of
them, moreover, are able to make two more miraculous connections. The first is a recognition that this new presence, this new
recess of their soul may be not unlike what the "druggie kids"
find when the days get dark before dinner and everyone kind of
glides together, sharing their stuff, their pharmaceutical syntax
and magic matter.

The second connection is that somehow, still ambiguous, of
course, this newly isolated presence represents the secret side of
the druggie's treasure, for they are in space, purpose and style very
close. This fact they teach me. But we are all able to make an
essential differentiation between the two.

Essentially, it is this enlarging sense of self and humanity that
leads the group to propose after-session sessions without me in
order to try out for themselves or simply rehearse experiences that
seem to them foreboding. It is this presence, moreover, discovered
partly from this new group privacy and partly from this new
group publicness, which suggests to them that perhaps their problem is a fear of my not being there. It is not so much perhaps that
they wish to try out dirty, frivolous or creepy material in my

absence. Rather, how grandiose the thought, it is living together without me that they wish to try out in my absence.

But even this proposal fails to reveal precisely what this presence is all about. For as all the languages of this newly found little nation scream their noise, the pearl way back on the strand jingles again, and the poignant issue they chose before to shelve is reopened. The after-session sessions, also as a ritual, come to be a routinized cadenza not merely tacked on but provided by their composers as unwritten measures to be filled with new and untried music as well as new interpretations (that sacred word) of familiar music until the mystery of the notes is yielded up at last. When the one issue got hot, they tabled it. Now, not really so much time later, they stand ready to take it on.

An after-session session means living without me, the nine minus the one. It means an investigation, research deliberately undertaken to know autonomy and virtue, aloneness and wisdom, separation and desertion. It means "making it," staying up late past normal bedtimes, bending the rules, tampering with what should be an implacable sternness, and catching the night before the day might recede. After-session sessions mean tinkering with the mechanisms underlying the notion of forever, for they render each of the members immortal. Time has at last been extended in their favor.

Suggested in the wake and haze of a discussion involving Kenny's foreign language problem, discovered in the hunt for translations and totally restructured pasts, after-session sessions mean acting out in a protected zone the knowledge they all have held from the moment consciousness was born to them: they without me, me without them. Children telling *parents* to get out. Children without parents who never wanted the children in the first place and let them *know* it. Let them *know* it. Not by intuitive secrecy or through hushed calls. They let them know it just like that!

"My mother told me right out."

"My parents used to say I was an accident. They were glad to have me and all that, they said. But that was a lot of horseshit. Man, if they'd wanted me, I'd be with them right now. I'd need the goddamn FBI to find my father!"

"Hey, just 'cause your mother died doesn't mean she didn't want you."

"I didn't know I was adopted till I applied for a driver's license."

"She didn't *die,* man. She didn't *die.* She killed herself, man, with all her little children right in that house. All sleeping away in their little beds. It's my day today. Today's my day. I'm asking for this day."

"The man said, 'Hurd's not your real name, son. You better go home and talk this over with your mother. If she's your mother.' "

"It is your day, Moonie." At once the room becomes still, as though Moonie for that instant, in a perfectly crazy but yet appropriate game of "show and tell," were about to wheel in his entire past, baked in its hot darkness, drenched in its syrup tears. They all have stopped eating.

"Get this now. I go home and ask my mother about it. She says she better tell me the truth. She ain't my mother and she's sorry she ain't. And that my real mother is the woman, my Aunt Helen, who visits us about once a month. So there I am, and there you are."

"It's your day, Moonie. Anyone as brave as you."

"Hey, what about Johnnie? How about Moonie and Johnnie?"

They have found then, in this presence, a nexus of languages, some their own, some clearly not, which all told offer them three forms of communication. First is the linear communication each of us depends on to remain in-life or, as philosophers have written, to exist in-the-midst-of-life. Next, there is the language, ostensibly linear but actually quite intricate, what with all its rivulets of expressions, turn-abouts and eddies of form and semantics. Here is where diffidence lurks, where moods are hidden in dreams, and where fears are packed on the ice of casual talk. Alive in groups like this, if one can ever reach it, is what almost amounts to the meeting's agenda trapped inside the busy-little-everyone-talking period that precedes the actual "work." Here, in the midst of all those greetings and renewals that mark the moments before commencing, are the headlines of the stories they are about to tell or read, stories bred in a prose of anticipation and trial. The group members know it; hence the swirling directions of language, the rivulets and the turning back, and hence this second level.

Because of the work they cannot turn out from their minds, not at this point anyway, they speak at a level of controlled, purposive but diffused thoughts. Layers of ideas run on top of one another. Kyle once likened speaking with the others in the group to hundreds of clotheslines strung out between trees. Moonie thought it was more like a musical staff, the notes bouncing about on top, between, above and below the steady black lines. The person knows what he's saying in this mode, but he knows, too, of all the other "stuff" accumulating there that he wants to get out as well. But still he stays superior to, on top of, all his messages. He garbles them, perhaps, with a code only he may decipher, but if it isn't metaphorical beyond recognition, he provides the rules for deciphering these messages as an encoding process right with the utterance. Without making it explicit, he informs the others, work with this, forget that, ignore the facts, ride the mood, avoid my words, let them tell you instead of what I was last time, or what I've been wanting to be all my life. The words may be a warning to disregard everything, or to put everything away somewhere until the sender can retrieve it. The words proclaim that one is dealing with life as best one can. They are a pledge of allegiance to the group as well as pronouncements of struggle.

Linear messages, diffused messages, and then the discovery of still another layer, perhaps the brainy bedrock of it all, the unintended, possibly uncontrollable layer of instinct and confession. Now, like lava, the interior pours out, and the person is first covered over then transported by his own words and by his own subjectivity as well as by an indescribable substance which holds the words, images and illusions together and guarantees their succession and endless origins. The interior pours forth: icons with impulses; poetry with recriminations. The experience is an evisceration, the dissolution of all rules, social and grammatical, the end of ordered and orderly action. It provides a cleansing, a glance too long and too straight at one's own organs, and, to some extent, a redefinition of self and well-being. The group has become the localization of a new consciousness and a new continent. But for some it signals the onset of a sometimes gaudy, often gorgeous insanity.

This is the level the group often seems to crave with an intense apprehension. Its sounds and shadows are alluded to at every single prior session. This is what they might have hoped would come from the contract. This is the irrevocable richness. And again, they know the "druggie kids," too, in their mode and medium flirt with just this sort of experience, fish for it, ride it, juggle it and call it, absolutely rightly, a trip. It *is* a trip. It has motion and jangling action, new sights, lurching vistas, latenesses, on times, ambiguous escape, discreet flight, all places in all spaces. It has come down, been derived from one's own cells, one's own muscles, one's own guts, and one's own majestic, profoundly sad but always proud life space, now seen for the first time publicly.

Here, then, amidst the instinct and confession, a conceptual level seen both in our "materials" and in the nine lives roams the flexible, porous boundaries between the single self and the exterior nation. Here are the boundaries amidst this layer of most primitive and most advanced language, the boundaries and markers which keep the one from the others, the person from the group, the one from himself. Or, in those moments of utter malleability, even invisibleness, here is the final suffusion and distinction of the self and the others, the simultaneous ability and inability to discern where I end and they commence. What is most confounding is how this sense of the group contributes to the formation of the personalized boundaries of oneself. Do we know, can we tell just what part the language of the exterior, the listening to them talk to me, the listening to them speaking among themselves, not to me directly, plays in the birth of my own eternally private and uniquely human sense of interior? Not just my thoughts, but interior.

Irrespective of the strategies which any leader, by his intellect and apprehensions, wants and ideals, imposes upon it, the group image reminds all its members of the most fundamental image of society, the family. This is, after all, the unit, the matrix, the biological insistence, really, that human beings abide by. The family is unity itself, a constellation of persons transcending the irrevocable ties to interpersonal space and personal history, portions of which, naturally, will forever remain secrets to the other members.

Primordially the family stands allied by name, blood and temperament, and this can only produce a special unity.

A child does not know his parents' past, yet he still may learn to resent it, not so much, as it usually seems, because it was a time of his father's or mother's suffering or achievement ("Why, when I was your age . . ." they will say) but because it represents a veritably endless chunk of time which is merely heard about through fragmented reports. And, because it is barely recognized though certainly not shared, this other past, the child's past, takes on the quality of separation and desertion. Father was there then, but I was only indirectly there then. Father as reporter, child as seeker. So, almost as if in retaliation, the child, now alive with his parents, or with one parent, or with an aunt, discovers, first, that the experience of time is not the same for him as it is and was for parents or brothers and sisters, and, second, that he requires a time, really a time within a time, belonging solely to him. Maybe he must share some of it with his brothers and sisters. He may leave his family, therefore, in order to shape this time as well as his ways within it. Or, he may stay around when the one older person leaves, also in order to shape this time and address still newer ways. Now he may rightly claim ownership of hours to which only his brothers and sisters share access and minutes whose location and potential only he knows. After-session sessions grant to their originators a mastery over birth, destiny and demise, all of which represent the very roots (routes) of any group.

But just as the family, the seed of society against which all nations someday must be evaluated, provides a basis for this presence and for these days of public attachment and private expression, so does it initiate the most primitive as well as the most advanced notions, self-conceptions really, of public and private health.

"Baby, when you hear what I got to say, you're goin' to think I'm crazy." Moonie.

"I always thought you weren't all there."

"Not a chance." Janie. "You know how many times at night I think I'm going out of my skull, and I turn the lights on just to make sure everything's still there?"

"Trouble is Janie, you miss us. Ain't that right? She misses us."

[2]

The family, the enactment of all its members one to another and all of its members each to himself define, in some yet to be explained process, sanity and insanity. The language of these several people fits together. The words fall into proper order or proper disorder and therefore emerge as creativity, maybe. The words of one interlace, marry with the words of another, or refuse to marry at all. Then someone is reviled or repulsed by the words of another. The pearls now are in total disarray, separated, dislodged, and the silken strand is severed in a million places, well, in nine places. The family is the strand not only holding language and thought together, but holding consciousness together. Holding together, in the early days surely, the "instruments" of subjectivity, perception, assessment, and pure knowing, holding them together to the extent that one need not fear running up against, turning away, or begging off from any reality, be it the reality of the external or the interior. The internalization of the family, not merely the connotation of family, is for some the internalization of social integrity and cognitive order. For others, however, it is disintegration and psychological collapse.

This is the accomplishment and the challenge: that a group of people would find almost at once the peculiar equipment that makes them believe that they together possess the power to drive each and every one of them back to the scenes of urgent despair, grief and insanity, and simultaneously the equipment that, at long last, might relieve them from what had always seemed an inexorable intimacy with dissolution. Equipment that might restation death at the end rather than at the beginning of life. Equipment which puts their life into focus and separates out the breath of the others.

A group of people has discovered no magical source or tool invested with a spirit of the supernatural. They have discovered that in and among themselves lie the very fabric of trust and care and the soil of disclosure. It is because of the disclosures that the preparing and transporting of food, nourishment and nurturance matter so centrally to any group, and especially to a group of young people who often are deprived of the right of giving just such nourishment, or to a group of lonely people, for whom the mere possession of food means a hold on life, a fortification against today, an opportunity for tomorrow. Food means chance and luck. But it is the disclosure, ultimately, which carries as its energy and cargo the instinct and the confession.

Groups have a power to achieve the level of instinct disclosure, partly because of the additive sum of each member and the presence he projects, and partly, perhaps mainly, because of the reality of the memory, screened or unscreened, of the family. Groups are able to formulate the shape of the collective, and the position of people standing, sitting, eating, sleeping, moving, talking, in the midst of which a solitary self is reared and launched. Groups truly comprise the architecture in which a single person claims living and working space. They are the beams and support on which one predicates immodest ascendancy as well as pedestrian recognition. The attachment to family is permanent. To introduce the dynamics of group, of nation, of microcosm, therefore, is first to replenish the past and then to resurrect a lasting continuity with it. For it is in the family that tradition is personalized and myth comes alive.

To speak about "here and now" limitations on groups, as many practitioners do, or about herding group revelations into an arena of the "here and now," is of course a bit foolish. Just to sit around an oak table, eating and speaking, with a single authority figure, a single man whom they (we) all have claimed, overseeing it all, is, in a way, to be at the dinner table night after night. It is to be at the dinner table some never knew. It is to be-in-the-world day after day. It is to-be-there as well as being reminded of being there, although at some language levels, this difference isn't worth applauding. The dinner table, the symbolic joining of care and nurturance must be the arch holding the single body upright and aloft. It is now that food is served and that the events of all time, up to and including this instant, are recounted and as genuine gifts presented to the others and hence to their descendants. Here among all the millions of meals the metabolic spirit of groups survives. And only out of this spirit and the communion that derives from it can pure action hit its goal and self-possessed leadership its target.

What gives groups that special quality that has made them and groupings and groupies so dazzling in their appeal that they now scintillate their smooth messages everywhere? Essentially, it is that wondrous union of sensory data which may be noticed or noted for the first time, with, second, the insistence by leaders that these data be noticed and noted, with, third, the recognition that there is an honest-to-goodness eternal recurrence within each instant such that groups make people do things just as much as people make groups become things. Each second of group activity both repeats earlier seconds and prepares us for later seconds. In this way, as Durkheim observed, society exists exclusively in the minds of its members.

More exactly, groups produce information, experience and data coterminous with their arousal or reminders of earlier experience. That is why, it would seem, a "here and now" orientation exists more for the group's safety than for its efforts. Residing undeniably within the here and now is the recurrence of a lived succession of "here and now's," as well as an inferred succession of yet to be "here and now's." Indeed, one function of groups may be to teach persons that the notion of eternal recurrence, that the existence of all time compressed into a single second which when examined has already vanished and become the next second, need not be static occurrence or eternal repetition. Life need not be a series of separations from fathers nor a series of maternal suicides. Again, death may be restationed in a more "proper" time, at the end. Furthermore, recollection, reverie and remorse themselves possess temporal parameters which are intended to keep them in appropriate zones, zones intended, moreover, to communicate appropriate moods. But recollection and report must not overflow their albeit precarious dikes and lead to inference, anticipation, expectation or assuredness. The future cannot be nothing more than the past reenacted.

One side of the coin, therefore, is the knowledge that aging means time means change means futures distinct from pasts. It appears to the nine of us almost as a formula. Yet on the other side of the coin, and not at all the unforgivable side, change need not be equated with progress, maturation or growth. There are times, after all, when we must noddingly concur with those who say, in a temporarily stilled tempo, I am what I am, and this fact and its recognition give me comfort as well as courage, identity and adventure. Tomorrow is new and unknown, but not totally so, and certainly not foreign, unimaginable or shocking. The group gives to its constituents these presents, too, for them to take away.

What, then, groups are about remains a not yet answerable question. Maybe this is good, or maybe someone simply has to proclaim now when group life becomes, as it unquestionably has become, so shrouded in a knowing and wizened certainty that we do not know the richness or the poverty, the public or the private, the "primitive" or the fantastically advanced languages that constitute this form of social enterprise. At bottom, it would seem that groups deal with issues no less profound than life and death. They start, they live their lives in their appointed time and space, and they end. And each of us does the same. Our families of origin and procreation, as Linton called them, also do the same. Maybe, too, cultures and nations do the same. The food that Kenny brings affords life-giving nourishment to each of us, but some wonder, too, whether he has put poison into the sandwiches. The marriages of members, not just symbolic, imply permanence and endurance, artificiality and make-believe. To begin is to conclude, to conclude is to begin again. To be certain is to have arrived at a nowhere. This we know. But how often do we overlook the ramifying meanings that these "birth-rebirth," "fantasy-reality" themes have for each group member. Associations know no rules. First come first serve; there remains an endless supply.

But each thought, each utterance, probably takes each member closer and closer to the gates of a feared psychic death as well as to a cathedral of freedom and emancipation. Just as the days and months, the roadbed of any and all experience, move in one direction toward a future holding out finitude, so too do the group's utterances safeguard a potential for actual life no less than a womb holds the presence of a breathing, heart-beating, experiencing life.

chapter 4

Of Youth and the Time of Generations

In the long enslavement of childhood I knelt on hard wood in
cold churches, striking my breast at each mea culpa, and
resolved to confess my sins, do penance, and amend my life; and
so I do; I have forgiven my parents all their care in rearing me.
What I pray for this year is not the remission of my sins, but the
wit to remember them when they come back to me as my
offspring's, and grace to see the luminescence of things lost in
things present. The breath I want now is simpler, only to live,
which is to be hurt, which is to love. . . .

William Gibson, *A Mass for the Dead*

The action of the secret passes continually from the hider of
things to the hider of self. A casket is a dungeon for objects. And
here is a dreamer who feels that he shares the dungeon of its
secrets. We should like to open it, and we should also like to
open our hearts.

Gaston Bachelard, *The Poetics of Space*

Not too long ago, an attractive college senior gently
asked whether she might speak with me a few minutes. Her manner was marked by that timorous politeness that symbolizes how
ably school systems instruct students to avoid pestering their elders.
The contractual acknowledgment "only a few minutes" always
seems so sad, implying, as it must, an unforgivable presumption
and a taking one away from activities so unalterably more important.

Jenny sat across from me, her hiked up miniskirt, her youth, a
sorrow in her eyes all compelling me to attend to her. She had
come with "no particular problem." She spoke about her courses,

her job, the few hours each week left for schoolwork, and her two male involvements. One, she explained, was a boy from the mountains of Utah, someone who knows of the poet's world, yet someone at present dreadfully caught in the scary, exhilarating cacophony of the "drug scene." The second, a young man, "straight," good head, "my parents like him," "his father is a noble man."

Although Jenny concluded almost every other sentence with the words "it's funny," nothing she said was ever funny. She had known sadness; indeed, as she continued I felt as if she were speaking as the burdened parent, herself as her own child. "It's difficult to stay healthy here . . . I don't know if I can pull my life together. . . . I don't know if I can make it. I hope so . . . I'm not sure."

We spoke quite a lot more. Periodically she would ask whether I was sure I had the time. I tried to convince her of my commitment and interest, but somehow her perception of the teacher's role, together with the institutionalization of "office hours," screened a deep concern.

Then, suddenly, Jenny produced the kind of frightened confession I have heard from nearly every young person who has come to me not necessarily for help but for some hoped-for strength in friendship: "When I was thirteen, I became my father's confidante. He was having an affair with a twenty-year-old girl, and I was the only one he could speak to. . . . Later I went to the prep school she had gone to. He thought I'd like it there."

The moments with Jenny resembled so strongly other hours spent with students troubled by their experiences with drugs. Often with these students I found an absence of any fundamental strength; it just seemed as though some last-ditch power to fall back on was gone. Like Jenny, these other young people were not sure they were going to make it.

Months before, in a hospital therapy session, John, a fourteen-year-old boy living with his mother and his four brothers and sisters in a low-income Boston housing project, had spoken of his parents' divorce, a damaging separation that had been preceded by his mother seeking his counsel. Although only eleven at the time, John was, after all, the eldest of her five children. She had been thinking of getting a divorce and wanted his advice. John looked away from me before he spoke. He rubbed his forehead so that I could barely see his eyes. It was difficult to understand him through the nasal sounds, the sniffing, the Boston-scented words which remain for me an accent. "Why did she ask me? Children don't want to know about things like that! Why did she have to ask me?"

Will is a tall, very pale young man, a high school drop-out. He lacks poise but shows honesty along with despair. His very gait is a plea for help. At the time I met him, he was inextricably dependent on Methedrine, pot, LSD, cough syrup, anything that could be popped, dropped, sniffed, smacked, anything that could produce that coveted ecstasy, "the high." My first and only meeting with him lasted for about an hour. No therapeutic or ritualized rules of time had stopped us, however. Will had opened himself, perhaps too quickly. Having plunked down several chapters of his life, he had begun to frighten himself. There had been his questioning of homosexuality; was he wrong not to want to "make it" with girls; his poetic sophistication about the inexorable realities of lower-class life styles and dreams; his lack of anger, his domination by anger, and a missing father: "When my father left, my mother turned to me in a special way. It was as though she wanted my help. It's like she wanted me to take his place. She made me sleep in the same bed." He held his head in his hands and turned toward me with a look some mistakenly call a smirk. But it is not a smirk. Time and the supreme awareness of this "new" youth have transformed both the context and meaning of expression and expressiveness and what sociologist Erving Goffman has called "face work": "I guess I must have an Oedipal thing, huh?"

One last person. Janet, a college student and a friend of a friend of a friend, somehow "found herself," as she said, in my office. She had been "busted," and the court had placed her under the care of one of their psychiatrists. Because the relationship had become perfunctory, Janet now refused to see him for even the prescribed once a month. "He's not interested in me." And soon the blame had shifted inward: "How can he be? I don't spend enough time with him. I'm just another 'monthly.'" Four years before, when she was fourteen, Janet tried to commit suicide. She swallowed all varieties of pills, a total of more than eighty: "I wanted to go to sleep." The precipitating causes were many, but for her the most fearful event occurred three days before the attempt, when her mother took her into the kitchen and closed the door so that her father and brothers would not hear. " 'I know you're young,' she said to me, 'but maybe you can help. Your father and I are not having sex. Have you learned anything that might help me?' I swear to you, these were her words." At the sound of her own words she wept.

The theme of young people's involvement with adult authority is an old theme, hammered to life almost daily in studies published on parents of adolescents, hippies, drop-outs, druggies, militants, etcetera. Recently I have noted that some writers "on youth" have openly chastised parents for failing to assume assertive roles with their children. Even some psychiatrists now argue for parental toughness, perhaps as a reaction to an oft-blamed emphasis on permissiveness.

Authority implies an inequality, or what some prefer to call an asymmetry, between the old and the young. The term asymmetry is rather telling as it implies quite unequivocally that there is no even exchange between generations, nor for that matter is there ever a possibility for it. Parents are by definition not peers, and their concern for children does not even imply that "good" families yield loyal colleagues. Yet the asymmetric structure of authority is not all bad, although parents and children are more than a bit ambivalent about it. Longing for the taste of adolescence, parents in many instances overstep the bounds which the asymmetry purports to guard. In some cases, as in those described above, their intrusions turn out to be nothing short of disastrous. For some young people, a quiet inner strength vanishes when their parents trespass on the property of time belonging strictly to youth and destroy the very same asymmetry which they themselves once wished to destroy.

The theme of authority is complicated, therefore, because the young and old alike often wish to tamper with the time defining generational separations but come to realize the potentially devastating results of such an escapade. The asymmetry means restraints on behavior, and the young, being today so profoundly aware of the facts of life, recognize these restraints as well as anyone. Generally, the young seem more open than ever before, or is it that social reality seems more translucent? Perhaps there are fewer secrets today than yesterday, and perhaps too our society presently honors revelation, and the supposed absolution it yields, more than confidential trust.

To a great extent, my concern here is with the breakdown of asymmetric authority and the effects and meaning of parents trespassing upon the property of the young. For there are quite a few highly sensitive young persons, mostly students, not necessarily "disturbed" (that ubiquitous word), who have experienced the rattling of their very souls when a parent chose not to preserve the asymmetry quite possibly required in authority relations. Often I think of the troubled pasts and equivocal futures of these persons living in a society so riddled with thoughts of death and insanity that the spirit of death and the fear of and fascination with insanity pervades their explorations into sex and drugs. But our topic is not *all* young people or the universal causes of mental illness, drug taking or school problems. One cannot generalize about "youth" from a few encounters, nor indeed would one dare generalize about all the hours in another's lifetime on the basis of but a few hours of friendship. Still, from even these few hours, a few pictures, a few concepts however dim, emerge and they seem worth remarking on.

There is little doubt that young people extend, prolong, or simply react to their parents' demands, be they uttered or silently passed on. As Erik Erikson has said, one generation revives the repressions of the generation before it. But equally important, adolescents have become brilliant readers of parental intentions. Or perhaps adults generally — and I include here parents, teachers, ministers, deans and psychotherapists — have too frequently become predictable or transparent in their dealings with young people. High school students now portray with ease the "shrink scene."

They anticipate with frightening accuracy the words and moods of churlish school administrators. A fifteen-year-old Negro boy told me that he could not get help from his school guidance counselor: "I wouldn't say this to his face, but he doesn't like Negroes. He may not even know this, but we know it." I spoke to the counselor in question. Not only had the student correctly interpreted the man's attitude; his impersonation of the man's behavior, right down to the speech patterns, was perfect.

All of this suggests to me that the cat of the authority relationship is out of the bag. The young understand and appreciate more of adult motivations and, significantly, the sociological rationalizations for so-called adult action in authority contexts. While they may protest against school principals and programs, the young will also confess a sympathy for their elders' plight of being trapped in the policies of some greater bureaucratic establishment, the "system." Yet they can recognize what they call a "sell-out" or "game player" a mile away, and a heady college freshman, if the matter concerns him at all, can learn to differentiate between the "authentic" liberal and the "institutional" brand from the last row of a lecture hall. Their language simplifications like "smarts," "head," "cool," "cop-out," are illustrations of an almost social-scientific terminology, and, more significantly, they function in reducing complex action patterns to levels succinct and manageable, at least for them. Their language shows, moreover, the swiftness and clarity with which they can first interpret and then act upon personal and institutional demands. (Many students recognize that their parents' social class is still the best predictor of their own school success, and that the poor and particularly the poor blacks cannot hope to compete even with the omnipresent mediocrity found among the "advantaged." Hence, while their understanding of local school competition and the mobility channels school generally offers may be profoundly true or totally incorrect, greater society seems to become more and more disillusioning and uninspiring.)

Perhaps the best illustration of language reflecting social sophistication and the apparent translucency of social reality is the expression "psyche out." A college junior assured me: "It's so easy to know what a teacher wants, or what he'll ask on a test. They never change. Give 'em what they want. You make them happy and you win." Even modest Phi Beta Kappa students claim they have "psyched out" their teachers and their college programs and have emerged superior merely because they were the better game players. The fact remains that to "psyche out" something or someone is to stay one slender step ahead even of expectation. It seems to be the ability to perceive the expression on the face of the future.

While it is progressively more difficult for young people to be duped by authority figures, it is as easy as it always has been to be damaged by them, a result so common when the superordinate, the elder, the parent, the teacher wants to equalize and make perfectly equitable what might better remain as an asymmetric proposition and relationship. Again, asymmetry refers to relationships wherein the commodities exchanged are of unequal and therefore incomparable content; hence the behavior of one person is not a call or demand for the identical behavior in the other. In its most fundamental form, asymmetry describes relationships in which one of the members represents unquestioned authority in a particular context, and thus it refers to interactions engaging parents with children, teachers with students, doctors with patients.

Several years ago, while leading what some of us call a self-analytic group, something not unlike the popular T-group, I was invited to a party given by the members of this group. As it was early in their history, it seemed reasonable to them that an informal evening together might loosen up and simplify all relationships. I was sorely tempted to go, but a wiser man suggested that I not. The asymmetry, he urged, ultimately must be preserved by the person holding authority. I may have lost something by finally declining, but I probably protected a valuable tension in the leader-member relationship, a tension which added to the learning and enhanced the members' chances to attain a sense of autonomy in the group. The symbolic nature of my refusal, moreover, reaffirmed the asymmetry, or inequality, which some of us working in groups feel is essential, and which members in their way often confess is preferred, especially during the early hours of the group's evolution. The leader (or father) must in some sense forever remain the leader, and while this angers many, particularly those in groups, kindness, gentleness and care are in no way automatically precluded by such a philosophy and by the strategy which derives from it.

More recently, members of a self-analytic group observed their leader's participation in a political demonstration. At the following meeting they spoke of him with a newly discovered reverence. How good that he shares the same values and that he exhibits the courage to speak out against administrations, local and national. But they spoke, too, of a disgust for their mothers wearing miniskirts and for parents generally who act like kids. Anna, a mature young woman, told of a feeling of actual nausea that came over her when her roommate's mother discussed the college courses she, the mother, was attending. Upon returning to her dormitory, Anna made a long-distance phone call home and luxuriated in the relief that her own mother still was pursuing what she called "mother-type" activities: luncheons, museum visits, and food budgeting.

The ambivalence is evident. Young people want to attack authority and I suppose this is probably the way it must be, and always has been. But in matters of human dealings, although not in issues of strict ideology, authority is not to "come down" to the child's level, as parents once so perceptively felt it necessary to kneel down, if only to attain a spatial equality between the generations. Authority is not to give in; it is to remain firm in its commitment to preserve, among other things, that essential asymmetry and the corresponding indelible generational separation, even if this means being seen as a "square" or "straight-arrow." This last statement, however, must not be construed as my suggesting that only authoritarian authority is functional or practical or healthful. This is not what I have in mind.

When a small child orders his parents out of his bedroom, he necessarily fears the enormity of the act. So, in a tearful rage, he can only pray that the parents will go no farther than the living room. Similarly, when members express the intense desire to kick out the leader of self-analytic groups (in symbolic reenactment of the primal horde story, perhaps), invariably they want to know if, should they be successful, he would really go, and if he would return.

There is, then, a primitive core that develops out of interactions with parents, a core that pleads for the overthrow of authority. Yet there is also a hope that one will be unable to do just this. There is a hope, in other words, that the superordinate's strength will resist any attempts to be overthrown. This notion, of course, is paramount in Freud's explication of the Oedipal relationship. Parents simply cannot break down or retreat. They must prevail, and no one wants this more than the child himself. In terms of this infantile core that stays with us, parents are perfect, without problems, immortal. Relationships with them, therefore, preclude both equality and peership. A college student said it this way: "No matter what I do in the face of authority, I end up a child. It happens even when I don't know the authority. Are we forever children to older or more powerful persons?"

When children are born a series of events almost ceremonial in nature takes place, whenever possible, in which the mother's mother lives with her daughter for the first weeks of the newborn's life. Though serving a highly functional purpose, this ceremony tends to reinforce, at more latent levels, the new mother's bond with her own mother. Thus in no way does the arrival of the infant place the mother and grandmother on an equal plane. In a sense, the birth reaffirms the existence and concept of not only generations but history as well, for regardless of one's activities as a parent in one's most recent family, the family one has created, one forever remains a child in that other family, one's first family, the family into which one was born. And this causes more than a few problems.

For example, for children to outachieve their parents, an event not uncommon among college students (and let us not forget, as some would urge us to, that women are confronted with career aspirations and the ensuing competitions as much as men), means that they, the younger, must delicately initiate revisions in parental relationships so that the older generation will not interpret the younger ones' accomplishments as indicators of their own dismal and unprogressing ineptitude. What an incredible task it is for these young and talented students to return during Christmas and summer vacations to the rooms and persons of their childhood; to return where all of us know we cannot again return, then to battle the very essence of what seems to be an unjust but still unstopping passage of time.

Why is it in these times that each of us believes in the development, yes, even in the successes of our surging expectations, but sees only aging in our parents? Perhaps the eternal danger of the immediate future is that while it guarantees reports on the outcome of our most present investments, it brings first our parents and then us closer to some inexplicable end. But for the handful of "right nows" that constitute our involvement with the present, our youthful preoccupations make only our own movement in the life space visible. All the rest, parents and teachers included, remain unchanged, timeless: "It's like they've all stood still. They bring me back to my childhood 'hang-ups.' They know I've grown up, they know I'm at college; but they're used to me as I was when I was last there."

These last expressions and sensations are so clearly not the sensations of regression. Although we all have fought back urges to feel once more, for even a bittersweet interval, the winds of childhood, returning or wishing to return must not be mistaken for regressing. On the contrary, returning is often resuming. This is what is meant by bringing one back to childhood "hang-ups." It seems like regression, for only in our direct involvements with our family does "family time" again move ahead. In our separations from a family, that certain time stops, and the stillness augurs death. But the student returns and the time of the family altogether jolts forward again, alive, just as the family itself becomes vitally alive, although life now becomes a bit more cumbersome. The sensation is precisely the same as seeing someone we haven't seen in years. Almost at once we pick up our conversation exactly as it was at the moment of our separation. Now, because both of us have experienced so much in the interim, we cannot really fill in the spaces, and so we are obliged to disregard the interim and the maturation and change it obviously contains and seek a resumption of those earlier days. Whereas we may feel that we are regressing, in fact we are following reality's dictates right down the line, and doing our level best to resume prior action. And while it is stupendously exhilarating in the first few minutes, or hours, or even days, it sometimes becomes dreadfully cumbersome and, even more, discouraging and unbearable. The time of separations may be that significant, for people once so closely knitted together may find that apart they drift in different directions toward different experiences.

The predicament confronting the child at these times is to help his parents resolve some of the problems that occur when the young outachieve their elders. Variations in accomplishment must be reconciled in ways that legitimately reinforce parents' ultimate authority and special superiority. Irrespective of attainments, son and daughter want to remain in the child's role, at least in this one context and at least in this one home. The parents know the child's task and, like the vaudeville joke, the child knows the parents know, and the parents know the child knows they know.

It is in interpersonal dilemmas and gestures of this sort, gestures made and carried out in such public yet at the same time secretive ways, that families reaffirm health. The gestures imply the mutual recognition and trust of which Erikson has so poetically and firmly spoken. By these gestures, the social and temporal gaps between people, even those who share a treasured intimacy, are preserved, sociologic and psychologic genes are somehow passed from one generation to the next, and one is, in Erikson's words, able "to see one's own life in continuous perspective both in retrospect and in prospect." [1] The division made first by time permits the evolution of the adult and sanctifies the appropriateness and truth of the confirmation and the Bar Mitzvah. For sociological reasons, the gap between the generations stays open. But it is all right because distance need not be construed as distrust, nor separateness as desertion.

There are no such gaps, presumably, in the family histories of those young people presented at the outset of this chapter. In their lives, sociology has been tricked, and time has been placed, as it were, behind itself. By being shoved into unbearable roles, these certain persons were asked to overlook generational intervals which must appear to them to be at least as long as eternity. As the parents despairingly sought to haul in the nets of time in order to make the space between the generations smaller and smaller, they thoughtlessly or impetuously or unwittingly coerced their children into caricatures of marriage counselor, therapist, and, worse, buddy. Jenny *is* the burdened parent; she is as herself, her own child. Her father's confession, the information, the content were all unwanted by her, absolutely and desperately unwanted. In what vessel does one possibly store such information? Time alone should have prevented such utterances, but a "proper sociology" would have guarded against such a "friendship."

In a highly speculative vein, the unquestioned obligation to live sanely through these provocative, seductive and terrifying engagements in which the generations are nakedly slammed together is perhaps the first exposure to what later on becomes the psychology of the drug experience and the basis or content of the drug reaction. The searching for advice, the confessions, and, importantly, the collision with revelations, are without doubt experiences to "blow one's mind." They are the inevitable contact of ageless and recurring dreams and unshakably psychotic moods. They remain almost as a cause of the cerebral explosion pre-LSD and speed. They are "freak-outs" par excellence, and grade school flirtations with insanity.

For two years I saw a girl who is now thirteen in a hospital therapy setting. Kathy's language and psychological test performance indicated a possible psychotic diagnosis. Her recurring dream and one which, truthfully, intrigued us both was of her in a forest being chased by a large bear. Up on its hind legs, it pursued her and quite regularly caught her. The dream had become so terrifying that Kathy had resorted to magical powers invoked through some ritualized bedtime behavior, just to prevent the bear from appearing. How terribly symbolic the content of this is: the personification of impulses at the same time sexual and aggressive. Yet, with more examination, how literal is the content. Kathy's father, an alcoholic for all of Kathy's life, returns home at night from work pitifully drunk and staggers toward her, his shirt off, the hair on his chest, his muscles and his skin exposed, with his smell, with his pants open. Pleading for sex at a locked bedroom door, he is continually rejected by his wife until he promises to "grow up and behave like a man." And so he falls on the sofa, and in the dim light, and with heavy breathing, he masturbates as a little girl watches, bewildered and horrified. Thus the dream evolves, appears and reappears, and never fails to produce an agonizing fright.

Like Kathy, too many children have been "freaked out" by some form or some speech of the family's drama. Now, the strategy of many of these children, although nascent and unconscious, is to get out of their homes, get out of their own lives and out of their minds. What a miracle it is that some do stay, conjuring up reasons for the necessity of their remaining close to suffering parents and a damaged family unit whose mechanism is shattered. But the muffled aggression in their renewed loyalty is unmistakable. The children and their parents are like the envied lovers in the old story who never stopped holding hands until just once, whereupon they beat each other to death. Holding on to a mother's skirt, after all, may be more than a wish to remain near and in touch. It may be playing the boxer who by staying in a clinch prevents himself and his opponent from manning battle stations at arm's length. The act of caring, as gracious and humane as it is, often masks a desire to destroy and cause pain.

When a thoughtless and angry Cambridge mayor's purge on young people led him to chastise "hippies" for having run away from home, I reacted by thinking that on the contrary maybe the parents ran away first, in some fashion, hence the children merely followed suit. Now, after examining life stories like those of Jenny, John and Will, I wonder whether, like the most domesticated of pets, some young people, "pre-hippies," ran away because their parents rushed them, frightened them, and got too close in an uncomfortable way too soon. I wonder whether it was the feeling of being emotionally crowded by their parents that caused them to "split." Or maybe it does in fact have to do with parental and school rejection or derogation, or the constant threat of parents getting a divorce. Maybe the rejection, the running away from children, is more powerful and disruptive than the running toward them. Still, even in unabandoned escape and angered protestation children may be responding to or fulfilling some communicated need or directive of an authority somewhere. Maybe outbursts of anger and "misbehavior" are the only things some parents and some teachers feel comfortable dealing with, as their response to them appears so clear-cut and reasonable. Perhaps they provoke the very outbursts they claim they are seeking to avoid in order to bring about these interactions. How curious the thought, therefore, that protest and escape by the young represent an obeisance of older people turned upside down.

Equally curious is the observation that the familiar need-to-forget-or-escape-from-it-all explanation of alcoholism returns in serious drug taking as a desire to repress. My friend Mickey is a handsome young high school drop-out with an exceptional literary talent. When Mickey was eleven, his parents fought so savagely that he would find his mother lying in pools of blood. Becoming the man of the family, Mickey would have to call for the ambulance, and days later, as it always turned out, after nursing his mother back to health, he would turn his attention to reuniting his parents. This very same pattern was repeated at least six different times in one year.

During one cryptic account of a drug experience, Mickey practically went into a swoon. Then he caught himself, along with the heels of another truth: "But when you come down, man, you come down hard, and that taking each moment one by one dissolves into that rotten other present, the one where you say, I gotta go back to my job. And you ask yourself, why do I do it, and you know, you gotta feel responsible. But it's O.K. because you think about the next high." I suggested to Mickey that coming down means having to think about tomorrow. "Wrong, man," he smiled, for he had one on the shrink. "It's the past; it's on your back like you know what! . . . You say why did it have to happen to me? Fuck tomorrow, baby. It's yesterday I've got to beat!"

In speaking with Mickey and young men like him, one senses an ironical and twisted searching for, most amazingly, what seems to be insanity. While the shocks of childhood were merely flirtations with craziness, by sixteen they have reappeared as an open willingness to consider steady dating with it. At first only a couple of times a week; later on, every day and every night, then all the time. The apparent psychotic quality or "way-out-ness" of the drugs is at once terrifying and exhilarating. The downs hurt but serve to affirm the lingering presence of sanity, or at least the ability to call upon it one more time. Then, if the user is sure it's still there, he goes back up on top all over again. Or so it seemed to me once.

Not ironically, the very same strategy of "blowing one's mind" is sometimes used as a way of keeping out of memory or consciousness the mind-blowing experiences which might have urged persons toward this intimacy with drugs in the first place. But just as drinking fails to induce forgetfulness, drugs seem to be failing many persons in their efforts to "repress" the past and keep it off their backs, or so say many students. If Timothy Leary is right, the next state may just be electronic brain stimulation, hence when pharmaceutical repression fails, attempts may be made to actively engage in a fantasy of total memory ablation. At that time, a metaphysical present will evolve, free of any recollections and expectations; free of all regrets and despair. At least some might wish this as they commence a new era of experimentation.

Failing to understand these complicated and gifted people, I often forget myself and remind them of their futures as adults and as parents. It's not that easy. For one thing, their very sense of future differs from mine. The option to "start again," moreover, as in marriage and career is highly problematic. Many fear they will repeat the desecrating scenes of their childhood: "I'll ruin my kid a helluva lot more than the drugs I take will"; "Are you kidding man, can you see me as a father? You gotta be nuts! And you a shrink!" "A freak kid's gotta better chance than I did!"

If starting again were possible, some, assuredly, would opt for total recommencement. Knowing full well that their parents never wanted them in the first place, some almost cannot go back far enough to reach a time when their own histories might have started off on good footing. Few admit it, however, for this would be to proclaim absolutely one's non-being. It would be to break the slim and delicate threads that now barely hold the generations pridefully together. Kathy told me that her mother was informed by doctors that she could have no more children after the birth of Kathy's nearest older sister. In fact, two more children were born. The mother admitted that she had not wanted either one. Her "not wanting" became the daughter's description of herself as the "unexpected surprise." Kathy and I knew that she understood the conditions of her origins and the facts of her life. Indeed, I felt that her rather tardy inability to comprehend human anatomy and how children are born might have symbolized an even more profound reluctance and self-protection, a very understandable self-protection to be sure.

But there is even more, for, regrettably, the concept of insanity pervades the worlds, however expansive, of many young people. What many want to know is utterly predictable: "Just tell me one thing man, am I crazy? I mean, you know, am I crazy?" The word "crazy" is ubiquitous. It has lost some of its primeval jolt, perhaps, but it holds on to an unmodifiable message. There is so much insanity in television scripts and movies and newspaper accounts. Insanity is even feared when one is witnessing the inexplicable behavior of those around us as they do nothing more than fight aggressively for social and private rights too long in coming. The blacks are called insane, the poor are insane, the "kids" for sure are insane. It it also feared when one is witnessing those well-meaning men who seek to control persons who protest. The cops and the National Guard and soldiers are insane. The young hear the President called mad and the war insane, and they puzzle over insanity's bewildering function in excusing murderers in jury trials. Partly because of this the young may even seek insanity as a way of getting out of the draft. Insanity or a belief in it seems to be able to immobilize some, liberate others. It's a natural resource to be harnessed.

In my day, not so long ago, a "joking" admonition for guaranteed military deferments was simply this: when the army doctor examines you, kiss him. Now it's insanity. Naturally, the worry exists for these young men that they might carry forever the brand of insanity on their sleeves just about where the private stripe might have gone; but still, to be crazy is to avoid military service. Like kissing the doc, it is also the ineluctable avoidance of maleness. An often cruel society rubs this in: a real man fights for his country. Ideologies and spirit react against this of course, but the doubt, however slight, stays. American socialization patterns, normally instituting strict sex role differentiations, take care of that. There will be a lingering doubt, although in much of their questioning and concern, perceptions and anguish the young find older persons who will support them. Many of the "knowing class," they come to learn, now prefer to think of "business as usual" as the real insane course, and jail as an undesirable but still honorable and healthy way out.

Earlier I spoke of a resistance to bearing children and the feeling that one could not successfully assume responsibilities of parenthood. In some cases it seems as though the diffidence some young people display in "going on" masks a wish to start anew. The present urge to keep the cycle from repeating and the intention to keep fresh life from beginning must be considered from the point of view of sexuality. Although the language remains unchanged, actions of "procuring" and "scoring" today refer to drugs. The prophylactic, its slick package dirtied by months in the seams of an old wallet, has been replaced by the nickel bag: "Always be prepared." A funny reversal, furthermore, concerns sex role functions in a new economic market, as girls now solicit funds to pay for their boyfriends' stuff. I was stopped by one of these girls in the street on a beautiful October afternoon: "Excuse me, sir," she began her proposal, "how about a quarter for a cup of God knows what?"

One cannot be certain of the sexual habits of the persons of whom I speak. But anyway, it's no one's business until they mention it. The subject, however, is close to the conversational surface. It is as intimate as it ever was, but seemingly beginning to be freed of its irrational ties to some mysterious and primordial secrecy. As with much of their behavior, many of the young merely make overt what their elders do covertly. In so doing, they seem much more honest and far less foolish. The conspicuous consumption of products and styles by other youngsters, however, is often little more than a mimicry of their parents.

Like Will, many young men on drugs confess their apprehensions about homosexuality. It is not simply that they fear their impulses. This pattern, ironically, seems to be more common among those actually engaged in heterosexual relationships. Instead, they tell of a lack of sexual impulses and a concern that perhaps hard drugs have destroyed the sex drive. Because of their sophistication, they comprehend the possibility that their activities generally could be interpreted as homosexual, but about this they manifest little panic. Some admit that they are able to "make it" with girls only when "high." They confess to fright, but it does not compare to the fear that they may be (going) crazy.

This is the supreme danger, as it suggests again, the complex reversal of not only competence in drug work and sex work but the associated interchange between the organs of sex and the "organ" of drugs, the mind. One almost wants to assert that a phallic phase of development has been temporarily supplanted or postponed by a "cephalic" phase. All life comes to be fixated in the mind, and Leary spoke for the generation at least once when he advertised that each brain cell is capable of brilliant and repeating orgasms. Whether scientific or metaphoric, Leary's words were not forgotten.

Is it then too farfetched to draw parallels, first between the act of getting high and sexual foreplay or the eventual sexual excitement; and next between the actual mind-blowing experience with its visions and thresholds of exhilaration and the orgasm in which the person is exquisitely primed by his own powers; and finally between the depressing down, the returning to time and reality, and the detumescence and resumption of normalcy and normal size? To be sure, the reasoning is dangerous in its analogical foundation, but the symbolic orgasm of the drug state as occult sex seems to have both homosexual and heterosexual aspects.

This then leaves one issue, namely, going mad from a drug experience, the "freak-out," the ultimate reward, the ultimate punishment. It builds to total destruction, at once implosion and explosion. In students' own words, it is brain damage and disintegration. Simultaneously, it is conception, pregnancy, childbirth, castration and death. Some continue to believe that from the

womb of the mind a new child, a freak child is born, and it all is
supposed to happen in the longest-shortest instant that time ever
knew.

By some students' own admission, the freak-out is also a premedi-
tated "cop-out." To take drugs is to willingly step out of the natural flow for a moment or two. In a way, it has much of the quality
of living with a sexual partner unmarried, for there is an anticipation of an end coupled with the preparation for some later recourse. Demanding no commitment, or less than common commitment, drug taking is an out permitting the luxury of retiring as un-
defeated champion. No one can fault the last-minute term paper
writer or the patient hospitalized with an overdose or from a bad
trip. Both have their excuses and reasons for being remiss and,
like little children, excuses for being out of school. Yet both wonder, presumably, about what their competence might be like void
of recourse, void of excuse. Both wonder, too, about the lack of
preparations for an equivocal future shrieking death, and the
minimal confidence already displayed in present endeavor.

Depicted in so many of these notions is the mass communicative
society in which we survive. The accomplishments by so many are
so great; the knowledge and awareness so swift in arrival and so
deep in meaning that in a way we leave the young no excuse for
failure other than severe illness and total collapse. Adlai Stevenson once confessed relief that career decisions were behind him.
It *is* hard to be young today as so many good people are already
so advanced in practically any area that one might choose for
himself. And so many new areas have already become crusty. Perhaps this is a reason for so many "dropping out," if only temporarily.

In sexual relations, the excuse that probably maintained the
sanity of frightened generations of men no longer exists. Girls
have "the pill" or other devices, and aggressive action now swings
both ways. Students offer apologies for not smoking pot and ago-
nize over an inability to get excited, much less involved, in political enterprises. To be straight is to be square, and like it or not the
straight become defensive and tempted.

Our televised and instant replay society also allows few secrets.

We see the war; we see men murdered; and we become frustrated
when we cannot discover the exact frame on which is recorded a
President's death. And as if that were not enough, our newspapers
pry and reveal, our movies reveal, and so too, apparently, do some
parents. While many children fantasize that the secrets they safeguard for their parents preserve some mysterious family integrity,
others are, in fact, maintaining this very integrity by keeping all
family secrets safe and locked away. It is these persons who sometimes bite a quivering lip in fear that exposure of their treasured
secrets will cause their families to unravel.

In truth, there *are* young people responsible for the knit of adult
involvements, a knit that sometimes fails to include even themselves. In the long run, Jenny's silence helped to keep her parents
together, but she has paid a price. It has taken one great effort!
For her, living moment to moment is not the medium in which
experience fits. Living through the day is both the medium and
the experiential essence. Day work matters. One must keep the
glue of sanity from softening and walk on, no matter what.

So one keeps in his head or in his diary what he heard Daddy
say to that woman, or what he saw Mommy doing in the restaurant, or what he heard Mommy and Daddy say to each other on
those nights when their anger exploded so suddenly that no one
took the precaution of closing the bedroom door, as if that really
made a difference. This is the stuff that stays inside, sealed over
until it pops out in a doctor's office, in a creative writing course
short story, or in those first poems written for no reason during a
Thanksgiving or Christmas vacation.

Then, while all of this goes on, performance demands shriek for
attention. One must compete and succeed often enough, make it
on one's own, and react to the war and the fact that he or a boy
friend will soon be drafted and, not so unlikely, killed! One must
be good in school, good at home, good at sports, good at pot and
good in bed. Life becomes unmanageably meaningful. It is enough
to make one (want to) go insane.

Most make it through, however, even with the knowledge that
their culture warns of belligerent Chinese, overkill, communism,
and an equivocal future. One cannot know when the next and

final war will come, nor when past experience with drugs will suddenly reerupt in the form of a grotesque child or one's own psychotic demise. But most make it through, and ten years later they look in disbelief on their own pasts. "I couldn't do it again," they often will say.

Unmistakably near, death becomes a real reality. Less fuzzy than ever before, its shape and sound hover about self-analytic groups, rap sessions and coffee dates. Damn the future and the inevitable! It was better in the 'Thirties when gravelly throated heroes sang into megaphones. It was better, too, in the last century when men wore frock coats, beards and long hair. It was better and easier because it was the past, and perception of the completed proves the validity of survival, if not of achievement. At very least, the past means having gotten this far. It also means the seat of much of the trouble that many just cannot shake.

Some young people reveal a peculiar attitude about the past. It is not merely that chunk of time that was, but the series of events that once were and yet somehow continue to remain as a lining to the present. Not exactly recalled or retrieved, the past has become the stuff of moment-to-moment encounter and the routine of day work. The past has not yet become past, therefore, in the sense of being over, because its foundation, like a child's body, remains soft and unfinished. There are no completions yet, no triumphs, no guaranteed deferrals or subsistence.

To be sure, youth cries. Sometimes it is out of sadness for its own past, sometimes in reaction to the two societies, the one encountered and the one held as prospect. Some observers insist that more often than not in much of its activities youth cries to be heard, or for help. It is too difficult to know for certain whether this is true, particularly because out of the concern, guilt and solipsism of an older generation grows the presumptuous pride that youth, when it speaks, must always address itself to parents and elders, or that speaking means crying or begging. This simply is not true. Attacks on society are not merely hatreds of parents which have gone productively astray. To the contrary, it often seems as though the questionings of those who *precede* us are simultaneously pleas for recognition and directives intended to justify prior decisions and behavior. Adults want a bit of attention and do a little crying and begging themselves.

No one as yet has studied the notes written by parents to their runaway children in New York's East Village or San Francisco's Haight Ashbury district, a district which seems to have faded. These pitiful missives document so well the lack of generational space and the confession of failure in parenthood and adulthood. They could almost be the letters of children who, wishing to come home, promise never again to misbehave. If they did not cause guilt or confusion in the recipients, the young people who screen them would have little need to prevent them from reaching the runaway children. (Those people, young and old, whose self-appointed life task it is to maintain the separation and lack of communication between parent and child must fear, I would think, the fruits of love's temptation, the very philosophy they often profess or at least once professed. Moreover, they are reminiscent of professional mourners who continually remind the congregation or family of the recent loss by crying and collapsing when others attain momentary composure. It is almost as though reconciliation, equanimity and peace are destructive to their sense of a social order.)

The "Come back home — all is forgiven" notes stand as a testament to what must be seen by the young as a crumbling structure or a tragic reversal of intentionality and interpersonal competence. They reflect adults' pleas for help and forgiveness, and as such they represent a far worse social fact than "hippie" farm colonies or pot parties. The notes only document what the poets know so well: of all rewards, youth is a supreme ideal. The old might wish to be young, but the young seem happy exactly where they are. This, too, is an asymmetry.

Few parents are able to accept the passing of adolescence, especially when their own children dramatize more vibrantly than ever the former gratifications and projected incompleteness of their own lives. It is inconceivable to think that young people have ever been simultaneously idolized and despised, worshiped and envied as they are presently. But without doubt, the problem of age grading is now of paramount significance in the United States. It is one of *the* dimensions: whether it is good or bad, the old are preoccupied with the young, and the young so often seem preoccupied with themselves. Another asymmetry.

The period, moreover, has become so erotic. Previously, when the activities of the young were more secretive, adults were compelled to deal with their own imaginations. Now, when sexuality in particular screams at us from advertisements, fashions, television, movies and magazines, it becomes increasingly difficult to decline youth's unintended invitation and accept the process and reality of aging. We almost forget that many of these invitations in fact do not originate among the young. Nonetheless, adults must work hard to avoid the eternal seductions of the young, for these affairs simply do not work out. Time inevitably chaperones such liaisons, and the primordial strain which comes about through the separation of generations never does permit a successful consummation of these two hearts, the young and the old.

The seduction does not stop with parents, however, for the succulence of youth is dreamed of each day by teachers, counselors, therapists, ministers, etcetera. A most dangerous tack for any of these persons is to be uncritically won over by youth's stated demands and ideologies or interpretations of them. Let me give an example of this point.

We are emerging from an unfortunate era during which time psychotherapy was viewed as either panacea or black magic. Psychotherapists themselves finally have undertaken critical self-examination, and for the most part attacks on theory and procedure have resulted in clarifying statements for the practitioners and their clients. Still, there are some critics who expend a suspiciously great amount of energy communicating to youth the evils of psychotherapy and, even more, the harmfulness of any benign adult interventions. By acting this way, these people purportedly signify their "stand with youth," a stand normally introduced by some phrase which seems an apologia, but which in truth is more of a boastful pledge to be like the young, or even younger.

Frequently these critics demonstrate a striking accuracy in their realignment of youth's goals, ambitions and philosophies. Just as often their arguments are indecorous and evil. Many young people in fact do find illness in themselves and do seek help. They despise the proverbial "shrink scene" and rightly so, but in their quest of a "hip shrink" they wish for a modification or, better, modernization of the psychotherapeutic relationship, but not its annihilation. They know it is no panacea, but in anticipation they feel it has worth and are willing to try. And that's a lot. The best adults may be able to do, therefore, is experiment with the helping apparatus and not discourage the trying.

So those of us who aspire to speak for or understand youth must be aware of the seductive nature of our interests so that we will not reach the point where speaking for youth means no longer needing to listen to it. Genuine representation, after all, does not require reliving; it requires recalling.

One final point regards the heightened sophistication of the young, their eagerness to speak, their facile access to recesses of an experienced childhood, and their poignant observations of adulthood.

While longevity statistics indicate that with each generation human beings may expect to live longer, much of society, as Erikson points out, demands that individuals be allotted less time for youth. Earnest young protoprofessionals, especially, uphold this ethic. Scattered not so infrequently about, however, are those whose parents have denied them even this minuscule tenure. For Jenny, the kid stuff ended at fourteen and was succeeded by what appears to her as an anachronistic awareness. For most, the awareness is simply a function of a precocious curiosity and creative need to experience. For the ones knowingly in trouble, the most immediate and pressing action resembles an attempt to complete some poorly understood mission started long ago by someone else.

That time repeats itself is but a comforting saying. The concept of a family cycle, moreover, is misleading, as it tends to slur over the individual cycles unwinding at various tempi within it. Individual cycles never repeat themselves, for in progressing or carrying on in any guise, "healthy" or "sick," the young, as ingenious as they often are, do little more than obey the wishes of others and the demands that time imposes. Typically, the directions given by

those who were here before us are to wait patiently and not walk
so fast.

Sociologists have written that a major function of social structures is to direct its members to appropriate goal states, means of
attaining them, and attitudes that are best assumed in evaluating
goals and means. The desire to become a doctor or lawyer, indeed
the need to achieve, does not come from out of the blue. It is
learned. So too is the desire to rebel, make love, take drugs, escape
and even "freak out." In their way, all of these actions are creative
because they develop out of social forms of, as well as private needs
for, expression. But they have not "sprung up"; like instincts, they
have evolved.

For many today, the evolution is not satisfying, and the internal
excursions and elaborations have become (and probably started
out as), in David Riesman's terms, "other-directed" movements.
Knowing exactly this, many young persons continue, nonetheless,
in their other-directed patterns, and thereby show themselves most
willing to listen outward and upward. And considering much of
our adult behavior, this fact is remarkable.

part 2: Education

chapter 5

The Mosaic of Creativity

> It is Work and only Work that transforms the World in an
> *essential* manner, by creating truly *new* realities.
> Alexandre Kojeve, *Introduction to the Reading of Hegel*

In every child who is born, under no matter what circumstances,
and of no matter what parents, the potentiality of the human
race is born again and in him, too, once more, and of each of us,
our terrific responsibility towards human life; towards the
utmost idea of goodness, of the horror of error, and of God.

Every breath his senses shall draw, every act and every shadow
and thing in all creation, is a mortal poison, or is a drug, or is a
signal or symptom, or is a teacher, or is a liberator, or is liberty
itself, depending entirely upon his understanding: and
understanding, and action proceeding from understanding and
guided by it, is the one weapon against the world's
bombardment, the one medicine, the one instrument by which
liberty, health, and joy may be shaped or shaped towards, in the
individual, and in the race.

This is no place to dare all questions that must be asked, far
less to advance our tentatives in this murderous air, nor even to
qualify so much as a little the little which thus far has been
suggested, nor even either to question or try to support my
qualifications to speak of it at all: we are too near one of the
deepest intersections of pity, terror, doubt and guilt; and I feel
that I can say only that "education," whose function is at the
crisis of this appalling responsibility, does not seem to me to be
all, or even anything, that it might be, but seems indeed the very
property of the world's misunderstanding, the sharpest of its
spearheads in every brain: and that since it could not be
otherwise without destroying the world's machine, the world is
unlikely to permit it to be otherwise.

In fact, and ignorant though I am, nothing, not even law, nor
property, nor sexual ethics, nor fear, nor doubtlessness, nor even
authority itself, all of which it is the business of education to

cleanse the brain of, can so nearly annihilate me with fury and
with horror; as the spectacle of innocence, of defenselessness, of
all human hope, brought steadily in each year by the millions
into the machineries of the teachings of the world, in which the
man who would conceive of and who would dare attempt even
the beginnings of what "teaching" must be could not exist two
months clear of a penitentiary: presuming even that his own
perceptions, and the courage of his perceptions, were not a
poison as deadly at least as those poisons he would presume to
drive out: or the very least of whose achievements, supposing he
cared truly not only to hear himself speak but to be understood,
would be a broken heart.*

For these and other reasons it would seem to me mistaken to
decry the Alabama public schools, or even to say that they are
"worse" or "less good" than schools elsewhere: or to be particularly
wholehearted in the regret that these tenants are subjected only
to a few years of this education: for they would be at a
disadvantage if they had more of it, and at a disadvantage if
they had none, and they are at a disadvantage in the little they
have; and it would be hard and perhaps impossible to say in
which way their disadvantage would be greatest.

                                                    James Agee [1]

With all of its mysteries and incomprehensible
nature, there remains a rather comforting feature about creativity:
it is that we can speak about it, study it, or study those who "seem"
to possess it and still not really be able to make too much sense of
it. And that, in an era honoring technological exactitude and certainty, is rather nice. What is more, the history of efforts to understand the creative process, the creative mind or the creative spirit
is long and marvelously filled to the brim with suggestions and
theories, anecdotes, vignettes, first-hand reports, and all the signs
of real data, hard data and soft data, true data and maybe less
true data, and still little is understood. So we are hardly the first
ones to wonder about creativity and its sources, directions, intentions, and its presence in every man and every woman.

This too is rather comforting, because it means that observers
of the creative process, particularly as it emerges in students, offer
us little more than tentativeness and hypotheses. They offer us the

---

* It may be that the only fit teachers never teach but are artists, of the kind
most blankly masked and least didactic.

worth of what they know, but this can never be enough until we find those who offer us, besides, what they see and feel. That is, think they see. But what others see is necessarily personalized, perhaps overly private or solipsistic. So in the end, when others' voices and words, visions and expressions sink in or die away we still have to confront ourselves, our private and public selves, our working, playing, aging and childish selves, and, of course, our own creativeness and sense of what it meant and what it means to be students.

What is comforting and exhilarating yet humbling is that a secret, magical darkness inside each of us can suddenly spring forth to produce what we feel as newness, innovation, surprise or what some choose to call the spirit of creativity. And no one, absolutely no one can take that darkness away, neither by force nor by knowledge, by greed nor by guile. We know and see and feel a potential for even the actualization of creativity. Yet, while no one's words can bring it forth, for that is our task in pure aloneness, the words of all people somehow put us in touch with what a beautifully wise young man has called the humanity inside ourselves. Then, at last, all of the voices are heard together; for creativity remains a bit more than a metaphoric child of ourselves to be delivered by ourselves to a humanity without.

Still feeling, I guess, the anger, petulance and rebelliousness or just generally that crunch of dehumanization which characterizes so much of school, I have attempted in this chapter to interlard the concepts of some rather important essays on creativity with the words of some extraordinary writers and scientists who for one reason or another stay on as heroes. Though the writing manages to capture but a fraction of a sacred darkness which at this point remains for me creativity, the ideas underlying the chapter come directly out of the works of Jerome Bruner, Abraham Maslow, Robert Coles and Paul Goodman and a small book by Michael Wallach and Cliff Wing.[2] Most handsome, perhaps, in these essays is the authors' generous and unabashed confession of uncertainty and doubt and their essential and eager reliance on artists, poets, playwrights, professors, friends, anyone who might help in the greater task of comprehension. Here truly is the commencement of creativity's religiosity, for as one goes about his adventures with it, he comes to feel wise and ignorant, dignified and humiliated, satisfied and eternally incomplete. Then, as the very foundation of knowledge unravels, and the laws, theories, conventions and traditions slip out of one's hand and head and heart, one is left with oneself, one's knowing, sensate self. And often this is quite a lot, profound and enormous.

Striking in these essays, too, is the repetition of the belief that creativity inspires or is characterized by mysterious but unmistakable dichotomies, antinomies, as Bruner refers to them: detachment and commitment; passion and decorum; freedom to be dominated by the object of creativity; deferral and immediacy. Creative persons, moreover, seem selfish and unselfish, spirits of the heart and head, wish and fact. They are workers and players, hedonists and altruists. And, so humanly, they seem mature and childlike all at the same rich time. They let emotion flood over their bodies and actions, they let themselves perform as children, and they exhibit little fear of the interior and its often illogical linings. But they discover that when all is said (or painted or danced or sculpted or acted or sewn or cooked or recited) and done, creativity, founded on technique and inspiration, takes them somehow, if it isn't too prosaic, beyond their own "normal" experiencing of the world.

So, as some have argued, if school's most egregious crime could be articulated, it would be that students not only are prevented from going beyond this so-called normal experiencing of the world, they are constrained, perhaps, in their desires to approach even the "normal" experiencing of it. Maybe all those extracurricular activities are more important to a person and a society than it would seem from their present status as frill for college entrance applications. Maybe "even C students" safeguard talents and interests and more importantly, worth and humanity, which schools and some parents in their relentless push for academic achievement first deny them and then claim were never there at all.

"The Mosaic of Creativity" is, I suppose, as much confession as exposition, as much despair as "analysis." I hope it speaks to a certain silence in each of us bidding to be heard. But if it fails to explicate even a thread of creativity, perhaps it serves to extend a hand of communion, "human contact," to those unique ones who every day crash against their schools only to find themselves being spun away from their own insides, from their own divinity, as some call it, just as they are brusquely ushered down homely corridors by commando hall guards who fear the results of lingering and solitude. If there is a fuzziness about this chapter, an ambiguity or diffidence, it is partly because that is the state of knowledge, and partly because in not a purely metaphoric manner that may be the way some human beings want creativity to be.

[2]

Juliette Martins all but squirmed in the uncomfortable chair. She looked about the small office and came very close once to appearing satisfied when she let herself see the few Japanese prints on the wall and the other little objects about the room. Then her body moved as though it had remembered a pain or sadness, and not at all concerned with physical appearance she looked as though she were about to cry. "When I think what they make us do and think. That's really it, what they make us think, I could puke. And I don't care who hears this! There are so many people around here with so much energy and there's just no place for them to shunt it. It all just builds up inside of them and they seem better off when they just forget everything and go crazy."

From far across a grassy meadow and down the most gentle slope over a wide boulevard that might be the dream of students somewhere, of Paris or Brasilia, hulk the concrete towers and low, lugubrious dormitories of still another university. It's a giant plant, the factory, some of them call it. Worshiping it, despising it yet depending on it, too, they plot first to own it, then kill it, then wish, as in a children's storybook, it might all fold up like an accordion and disappear between the covers of great colored shapes and objects, its words and writings trickling down the side of the shelf and off the table then under the office door to the granite corridors. Vanished.

"Goodbye, energy of my soul. Goodbye, childhood. Goodbye, anything good."

"Hey, little boy, you see anything of me just walk out of here?"

"No, sir."

"You been here long?"

"Four years, sir, although I thought of leaving once. Maybe even for good. But then I thought of the army and I thought, well, this is bad, but that army thing, it's got to be worse."

"Well, if you see me coming by, stop me. I'm wanted somewhere."

My friend Paul sat on a curb, not far from our home. He carried books by André Breton and Franz Fanon. He carried his oboe, too, in a black leather case, neat and tidy, its delicate white stitching holding it together. Musician going on a house call. Maybe he carried life in that oboe case, or don't the students speak so foolishly as that now, as they used to? Are they truly more poetic than before?

Paul spoke of pulling his life together. "I've got to get it together. I'll get it together. Then I'll get back to the writing. Maybe poetry, too. I'd like to be back in school. Maybe in a year. I'll pull it together."

"I have that too, Paul. I can't always get it together. I do the best I can. That's all I can do."

"Is there someone inside us?" Paul asked. "I wish I could tell whether to wrestle him down or just follow him somewhere."

"You still on drugs?"

"No."

"Is that good, do you think?"

"Yes. Is this your home?"

"Yes."

"Now I know where you live. I'll come by. I promise to come by."

I was about to ask, just then, how does one really come to know the spark or energy of creativity in college students? I was about to ask how one even approaches that angry defiance, or that sullenness or lethargy, joy and bounce, or the depressive anguish, even as one tries to get close to a friend by sitting, as grown-ups, not as children, on curbs where the drivers glare at the wasteful sight of people seeking to get close? How does one get to the long hair, the short hair, the long skirts and short skirts, the wide pants and thin pants, the unmarked books and marked-all-over books, the posters and accoutrements, charms and memorabilia, the childhoods on the desks, on the walls, on the lips of the hundreds of thousands of students, exploding, shot like arrows, being reborn or rekilled in classrooms by their specters, teachers and parents? And by their history. How does one get close to that kind of creativity, whatever it might mean?

Student, Mischievous — Fire at the Architectural Institute

The Architectural Institute's on fire!
Through the halls, the drawings,
Like an amnesty through jail it flies —
Fire! Fire is roaring!

Along the somnolent façade
Mischievously, shamelessly,
Like a gorilla
    red-assed
It thrusts through a window flamingly!

And we're already graduates
Ready to defend our theses.
In that sealed iron safe
My reprimand's scorching to pieces.

Wounded is Watman *
Like a crimson autumn.
Flame my drawing boards,
My city flames and roars.

Like a can of kerosene
Five years and winters fly . . .
Krasilnikova Kareen,†
See how we're on fire!

* A fine quality drawing paper
† A fellow student

Farewell, architecture!
Blaze away blueprints,
Local co-ops in rococo,
Little cowsheds with cupids!

O youth, O phoenix, so foolish,
On fire your diplomas and degrees!
Your crimson skirt you flourish,
With your red tongue you tease.

Farewell, period of borders!
Life is ruins and ashes in turn.
We are all flaming and burning.
To live — is to burn.

But tomorrow, in the fingers a-buzz
Angrier than a bee will thrust
And sting the point of a compass
Out of a handful of dust . . .

. . . Everything's burned to a cinder.
Exhaled to nix.
Everything's finished?
                    Everything's beginning!
Let's go to the flicks!
                              Andrey Voznesensky [3]

Is it their politics or drugs, or their music? Is it rather our politics, drugs and music? Can these things, these activities which often seem to own students, which pull the young around and which, as an irony, possess true life, cause students to taste their first tastes of death? How does one come anywhere close to that sense of the creative child's absolutely total digestion of objects, particularly those with which he works and which simultaneously make his work and play come to life? And how should we react to the inseparable resistances to life and death and the ambivalent infatuation with the perishable and imperishable all about them and all about us?

Life burns within that creative casing. The students suffer from the very same burning within whose midst they pool some magical and unknown energy or turn utterly hollow emptiness into the forms and stilts of their being on the "outside." Their work starts, their work ends, and deep within the marrow of their work the cells of a most ingenious, expansive but inexorable stain make their way to the surface of our collaborations and friendships with them.

How late so many of us come to our insistence that creative students know a place of consciousness whose tracks we can never trace. Their existence is within, more on the slopes than on the concrete, more along the tissue and dripping on the brain than in the lecture hall or seminar room. The students admit to the drippings and even to their tumbling under a bombardment of trafficking currents and cellular stimulations. They hear the sudden explosions of their impulses. They see the aftermath, the craters left as clay and words and designs from the firing of invisible nerves. Theirs is a world, often, of the darkness, of the turning within, and the authenticity of coldness, impersonality, exhaustion and the cradled refuse of lifeless life. They can never speak of it, nor write of it, nor even sculpt nor act nor scream of it. Yet they suffer the very aloneness they require and despise and the breathless fright they've never forgotten from childhood, nor perhaps wished to forget.

My work was created only by elimination, and each newly acquired truth was born only at the expense of an impression which flamed up and then burned itself out, so that its particular darkness could be isolated and I could venture ever more deeply into the sensation of Darkness Absolute. Destruction was my Beatrice. I can speak of this now because yesterday I completed the first sketch of my work. It is perfectly outlined; it will be imperishable if I don't perish. I looked upon it without ecstasy or fear; I closed my eyes and saw that it existed.

But I am not proud of this, my dear fellow; in fact, I am rather sad. For I have not made these discoveries through the normal development of my faculties, but through the sinful, hasty, satanic, easy way of self-destruction which, in turn, produced not strength but the sensitiveness that was destined to lead me to this extreme. I can claim no personal merit in this; on the contrary, it is the fear of remorse (because, impatiently, I disobeyed the natural law) that makes me take refuge in the impersonal, as though indulging in a kind of self-vindication.

The most important thing for me is to live with the utmost care so as to prevent the sickness which, if it comes, will inevitably start in my chest. Up to now, school and lack of sunlight have been very bad for me; I need continual heat. Sometimes I feel like going to Africa and begging! When my work is completed, death won't matter; on the contrary, I shall need that rest! Now I must stop, because when my soul is exhausted, I begin to complain about my body or about society, and that is sickening.

I think the healthy thing for man — for reflective nature — is to think with his whole body; then you get a full harmonious thought, like violin strings vibrating in unison with the hollow wooden box. But I think that when thoughts come from the brain alone (the brain I abused so much last summer and part of last winter), they are like tunes played on the squeaky part of the first string — which isn't much comfort for the box; they come and go without ever being created, without leaving any trace. For example, I can't recall a single one of those sudden ideas I had last year. On Easter day I got a terrible headache from thinking only with my brain, after I had gotten it going with coffee, because it can't get going by itself, and my nerves were probably too tired to respond to any outside impression, I tried to stop thinking that way, and with a tremendous effort I braced the nerves in my chest so as to produce a vibration — still holding on to the thought I was then working on, which became the subject of the vibration, that is, an impression; and so that is the way I am beginning a poem I have been dreaming about for a long time. Ever since then, whenever the crucial hour of synthesis approaches, I say to myself: "I am going to work with my heart"; and then I feel my heart (at those times my whole life is undoubtedly centered in it), and the rest of my body is forgotten, except for the hand that is writing and the living heart, and my poem is begun — begins itself. Really, I am shattered. To think I have to go through all that to have a unified vision of the Universe. But if you don't do that, then the only unity you feel is your own existence.

Stéphane Mallarmé [4]

There is a spirit in that suffering and all about the burning piles of their books, clothing, prior knowledge and future time. Most especially that future time. There is a spirit that says find in your teacher and all his assignments the entrance to internment camps, the gates of hell, the incarceration of all goodness. There is a spirit flaked with that delicious and poisonous anger of theirs toward authority, toward demands and scripture. Curses on the academics. There cannot be teachers in their life, not unless their teachers would climb inside them and hold clandestine tutorials at the foot of their brain stems. For the unknown, they might acknowledge, has no place for teachers. It has no place for anyone — not even themselves, they're forced to admit on stronger occasions.

The unknown is not the incorporation of history nor combinations of contemporaneous facts, nor even anticipations of yet to be found facts. The creative unknown begins with the atavistic combination of temporal portions. It is the child with the boy, the boy with the man, the old man with the old child. It is also the tormented bliss of relinquishing no time, anticipating no space, and praying that childhood's energetic form might be melted down and used again and again and again in nothing but work-life. That is why teachers fail to discover even the property lines of the creative one's sources. It is because students and teachers at best coexist in different times and in different energy systems and worship opposite temporal ideals: the old go forward toward inexorables; the young diffuse backward and forward, inside and outside of time.

Nothing new happened to me. I found intact what I had acted, what I had prophesied. There was only one difference: without knowledge, without words, blindly, I carried everything out. Previously, I had depicted my life to myself by means of images: it was my death causing my birth, it was my birth driving me toward my death. As soon as I gave up seeing this reciprocity, I became it myself; I was strained to the breaking-point between those two extremes, being born and dying with each heartbeat. My future eternity became my concrete future: it made every instant trivial, it was at the core of the deepest attention, it was an even deeper state of abstraction, it was the emptiness of all plenitude, the light unreality of reality; it killed from a distance the taste of a caramel in my mouth, the sorrows and pleasures in my heart; but it redeemed the most trifling moment by virtue of the mere fact that this moment came last and brought me closer to it; it gave me the patience to live; I never again wanted to skip twenty years and skim twenty more; I never again imagined the far-off days of my triumph; I waited. Every minute I waited for the next one because it brought the following one closer. I lived serenely in a state of extreme urgency: I was always ahead of myself, everything absorbed me, nothing held me back. What a relief! Formerly, my days had been so like each other that I sometimes wondered whether I was not condemned to experience the eternal recurrence of the same one. They had not changed much; they still had the bad habit of slipping away with a shudder; but I had changed: time no longer flowed back over my becalmed childhood; rather, it was I, an arrow that had been shot by order, who pierced time and went straight to the target.

Jean-Paul Sartre [5]

No, the creative student seeks no new combinations of that healthy and sick, insulting and penetrating reality on the outside, if he can just manage to manipulate his own senses into erotically and sardonically new combinations and, best of all, noncombinations. How, he asks, can he arrange to have that certain and secure cognitive apparatus of his collide head-on with that vast unknown, and then save and savor the child-man that in the colliding copulation most certainly is conceived? How can he do that? Certainly not with teachers! Maybe with poetry. And with music? Guaranteed!

Charleville, May 13, 1871
Dear Sir:

So you are a teacher again! One's duty is to Society, you tell me; you are a member of the teaching body: you're running in the right track. I too, follow the principle: I am cynically getting myself kept. I unearth old imbeciles from our school: the stupidest, rottenest, meanest things I can think of — in action or words — I serve up to them: I'm paid in steins and ponies. *Stat mater dolorosa, dum pendet filius.* My duty is to Society, it's true — and I'm right. You too, you're right, for today. As a matter of fact all you see in your principle is subjective poetry: your obstinacy in going back to the pedagogic trough — pardon me — proves it. But you'll just end up self-satisfied without having done anything, not having wanted to do anything. Not to mention that your subjective poetry will always be horribly wishy-washy. Some day I hope — many others hope so too — I'll see objective poetry in your principle. I shall see it more sincerely than you will do it! I'll be a worker: that is the idea that holds me back when mad rage drives me toward the battle of Paris where so many workers are still dying while I write to you! Work now, never, never; I'm on strike.

I'm lousifying myself as much as possible now. Why? I want to be a poet, and I am working to make myself a seer: you won't possibly understand, and I don't know how to explain it to you. To arrive at the unknown through the disordering of all the senses, that's the point. The sufferings will be tremendous, but one must be strong, be born a poet: it is in no way my fault. It is wrong to say: I think. One should say: I am thought. Pardon the pun.

I is someone else. So much the worse for the wood that discovers it's a violin, and to hell with the heedless who cavil about something they know nothing about!

You're not teaching for me. I offer you the following: is it satire, as you would say? Is it poetry? At any rate it's fantasy. But I beg you, please don't underscore it, not with pencil or too much with thought either.

Arthur Rimbaud [6]

So is it, as some have alleged, the expression of infantilism that finds air, life and breathing room in the creative student? Is it regression to the distant past, or resumption of what must seem like near past, or the constant starting all over again as in a sketch or verse that constitutes this energy? Is it the order of a secret motive or direction of an impulse that drives the student into and unto himself and makes him seek the omnipotent turmoil of the child as lining to his manhood? Is it that sexualized demon screaming to be both released and imprisoned forever just at the time when one's very soul smacks, eyes open, against society's granite toughness? Is it the "unmakable" quality so many students feel? Is it the immutable and the inevitable? Is it the deaf, the soldiers or teachers? What can they do in the face of faceless administrators, teachers, and governments crying accomplishment and achievement? What sense can they make of today's confusion, indecisiveness and utter lostness becoming tomorrow's exceptional and adventurous history? And what about us on the other side? And what really constitutes the "other side"?

There remains and always will remain for these students the most precarious sense of boundary. Where, they question in their naïve brilliance, can I make a mark that might for even a night proclaim the edge of me and commencement of them? When may I know that it is I with whom I commune and not with political marauders seeking to eclipse their voracious hunger for control and tradition? How, they ask, can I be permanently freed from any intervention, any incision yet still be protected by the arms, breasts and hair which creep within those not so arbitrary boundaries of my definitions of self and being? It is the conflict of outside and inside, the unique person and the seemingly contrived group. Then there is the obligation, held over from grammar school, to hold everyone's hand while marching to the playground, all the while cracking under the anger and sense of injustice of bigger brothers, older sisters, upperclassmen, and taller adults.

Creative students often seem so preoccupied with the unfairness and lack of gentleness of social orders and the stresses on cohesiveness and coherence. Propelled by their mysterious motives, they slam into worlds of graded regulations and biased restrictions. To be taught law and discipline is to be fed poison, for never in their schooling are they permitted to peek at the glass exhibition cases that someday, when they achieve fame, may just house their very own works. Stymied by systems within systems and that unfilled childhood that suddenly stopped, fearing an adulthood of insanity, boredom and the certainty of an inner death, they retreat momentarily from the demons and from the motives, from the impulses and sensuous disorder and disarray inside and take on, of all enemies, the world with all of its warring aggregates and all of its legalities and illegalities. They take on the rich and the poor, the black and the white, the yellow and the red, the living and the dead, the possible and the impossible; and they work while their elders sigh at the first glimpses of youth's inevitable period of idealism. But their special politics affords them life, and like a white-hot iron whips across that private unknown of theirs and scars more than a few passing years and what soon may be more than a few products of creative joy as well as discomfort.

Looking back through the last page or two, I see that I have made it appear as though my motives in writing were wholly public-spirited. I don't want to leave that as the final impression. All writers are vain, selfish and lazy, and at the very bottom of their motives there lies a mystery. Writing a book is a horrible, exhausting struggle, like a long bout of some painful illness. One would never undertake such a thing if one were not driven on by some demon whom one can neither resist nor understand. For all one knows that demon is simply the same instinct that makes a baby squall for attention. And yet it is also true that one can write nothing readable unless one constantly struggles to efface one's own personality. Good prose is like a window pane. I cannot say with certainty which of my motives are the strongest, but I know which of them deserve to be followed. And looking back through my work, I see that it is invariably where I lacked a political purpose that I wrote lifeless books and was betrayed into purple passages, sentences without meaning, decorative adjectives and humbug generally.

George Orwell [7]

The terror students feel of the boundary between their own ringing self and the groups with which they flirt and from which they take away ideas, ideologies, and, finally, partners comes out of the conflict between the security found in possessing tolerant companions and the fear that involvements with others may mean their being devoured. Loyalty in friendship means competition just as much as recognition. Loyalty means compliance and running away as well as running dry. Loyalty means submitting to systems of evaluation, censorship, and adult persecution, and perhaps anonymity as well. The goal is to be recognized for worth, not by name, nor by face; by work, not by grade, nor by arbitrary number. Better by mood than performance; better by sustained effort than by common deed.

But loyalty also has something to do with one's work. For in the work is the breathing of life into words or sculpture, colors, fabrics or food which but moments ago existed in the lush darkness of the unconsciousness. In the work is the despair of aging and the secret dream to please families and friends and, if possible, everyone who lives or who ever lived. Or best of all, pleasing those who haven't lived yet.

In the work, too, is childhood brought up to date with and socialized by adulthood, and the thunder of hate cleansed by love and kindness. So the creative student hopes his work may be loved and that with it he may be loved. But none dares admit to this, except perhaps in recollecting. For in the exquisite instant of demonstration or production, it always seems as though the demon of anger carries the weight of productivity, leaving love first to fill the crevices between work sessions and then to spray over the people who mill about one's thoughts and blueprints for the future. The work makes time congeal. History now becomes tomorrow, and last autumn, the first autumn of school, means forever. The truly creative work not only turns a man or woman deeply inside himself or herself but allows a diffusion of feelings that no one will ever come close to describing, much less recounting, except, of course, as through reminiscence we regain the primitive sensations of our first aloneness, then our first public presentations, and ultimately our earliest need to be watched over.

And these reminiscences, in turn, being as they genuinely are the creative products of all people, place us intimately in touch with the others and their epochs. They reveal to us our favorites and our inchoate notions of a society watching over us and caring for us. Creativity, then, in a most uncanny but intriguing form, seems never to separate itself from fathers, mothers and schools, be they real, fictive, or bits of both.

In the first composition, I was last. Young feudalist that I was, I regarded teaching as a personal bond. Mlle. Marie Louise had given me her knowledge out of love; I had received it out of bounty, for love of her. I was disconcerted by the *ex cathedra* courses which were addressed to one and all, by the democratic coldness of the law. Subjected to those constant comparisons, my fancied superiority vanished. There was always someone who answered more quickly or better than I. I was too loved to have doubts about myself. I wholeheartedly admired my classmates and did not envy them. My turn would come. At the age of fifty. In short, I was ruining myself without suffering. Seized with barren panic, I would zealously turn in extremely bad work. My grandfather had begun to frown. My mother hastily asked for an appointment with M. Ollivier, my official teacher. He received us in his small, bachelor apartment. My mother put on her melodious voice. Leaning against her armchair, I listened to her as I looked at the sun through the dusty windows. She tried hard to prove that I was better than my work showed: I had learned to read by myself, I wrote novels. When she had run out of arguments, she revealed that I was a ten-month child: better baked than the others, more glazed, crispier as a result of staying in the oven longer. M. Ollivier, who was more sensitive to her charms than to my merits, listened attentively. He was a tall, lean, bald man, with a large head, sunken eyes, waxy complexion, and a few red hairs under a long, hooked nose. He refused to give me private lessons, but promised to "follow up" on me. That was all I asked for. I would watch his eyes in class; he spoke only for me, I was sure of it. I thought he liked me; I liked him; a few kind words did the rest. I became, without effort, a rather good student. My grandfather grumbled when he read my report card at the end of the term, but he no longer thought of taking me out of the lycée. In the following grade, I stopped getting special treatment but I had got used to democracy.

Jean-Paul Sartre [8]

Just as the individual fights to be away from the collective, fearing that he may be devoured by it, so too do his self-love and pride scream to be silenced by socialized modesty and self-effacement. Hear me and answer, he will shout. Know that I'm here, in part, even when I'm not here. Let my works substitute for me and thereby live for me. Let them be my living. He fights as well to know everything and become in this way a leader, and to know nothing at all and to become in this way a follower of those who seem strong. But the students seem at times to wish for both. And why not? School tolerates both these drives toward life and work: the drive to stay behind, and the drive to lap all the runners and be seen, and then vault ahead.

There is a certain fun that comes with all that bookish knowledge. There is a certain satisfaction, too. It isn't creativity, of course, they will argue, but all of the knowledge packed so neatly away, retrievable, forgettable, then retrievable again, makes a rather lovely crown for adolescence as well as something to desert completely so that starting all over from nothing will seem a bit less scary. Knowledge also means competence. But just how much of others' works they permit to enter depends on just how much of themselves they feel to be emerging out of their own quiet search.

At times the reading goes well and they feel expanded, inflated and adventurous. At times the reading keeps them from stories utterly more important and from work so utterly more triumphant. Then for months, as their teachers and prodders urge them to study, they literally retreat under a sacred ground and reappear as leader, painter, writer, or just plain spirit. And in these hours no assignments or evaluations can match the outpouring from the spurts of fluids and cubes that they generate or imbibe from an apparent emptiness or depression. Creativity moans in these times, and the calls of scholars seem coarse and foolish.

Praise of Learning

Learn by the simplest things. For you
whose time has already come
it is never too late!
Learn your A B C's, it is not enough,
but learn them! Do not let it discourage you,
begin! You must know everything!
You must take over the leadership!

Learn, man in the asylum!
Learn, man in prison!
Learn wife in the kitchen!
Learn man of sixty!
Seek out the school, you who are homeless!
Sharpen your wits, you who shiver!

Hungry man, reach for the book: it is a weapon.
You must take over the leadership.

Don't be afraid of asking, brother!
Don't be won over,
see for yourself!
What you don't know yourself,
you don't know.
Add up the reckoning.
It's you who must pay it.
Put your finger on each item,
ask: how did this get here?
You must take over the leadership.
Bertolt Brecht [9]

For the creative ones, all the voices on the outside seem consistent and unequivocal. The battling theme of holding back and plunging ahead, as a redundancy, occurs and occurs again. The limitations and freedom of self-love and self-importance hammer away at them, and the meaning of choice or decision gets buried somewhere, or put away for a later time. Procrastination and wastefulness seem uncontrollable. There's so much to do, so many, many options to scan, so many careers to pursue, so many opportunities to ponder. The potential of success seems just about as scary as the potential for failure. So what's the point of living? Retribution, in its often grotesque cloak, appears either way. For somehow, in the mystery of it all, creativity seems to carry with it the certainty of both success and failure, both retribution and pride.

Still the decisions remain to be made and, as they always say, the various paths one might follow begin to be visible. But where does one take comfort or guidance when the entire enterprise means throwing off the past, publicly if not privately, and lurching into upright independence and autonomy? Where does creativity really permit training and hearing, advice and counsel? If to be creative means in part to accept that inner darkness, whatever it holds — and there's no assurance or promise it holds anything "valuable" at all — how can the creative one find any admissible leader, decision maker, or teacher? Does it not seem as if the creative process demands that absolutely everything should come from the inside? Otherwise it cannot be authentic or right. Otherwise, as craftsmen say, it doesn't work. Is not this the case?

So when college portentously holds itself up as the institution-alized epoch for deciding all of the future, the creative person somehow slides backward, collects what seems to him a vanishing strength, and looks, just as the platitude describes, to his heart. It is this which gives him direction, though very little solace. But he can comfort himself during these momentous years of decisions with the thought that truly wise men could do no better in their humble search for some light outside and, with it, a style of life and a plan for immortality and Godliness. For in the jagged times of creativity, there is no direction, no guidance and rather little else but those platitudes about seeing what is in your own heart and accepting whatever it is that flows from your soul.

The Way

It is impossible to tell men what way they should take. For one way to serve God is by the teachings, another by prayer, another way by fasting, and still another by eating. Everyone should carefully observe which way his heart draws him and then choose that way with all his strength.

Martin Buber [10]

Thus, as frightening as it may seem to many, the message to teachers is clear. Even if they might be able to do something constructive about this fright, they had better stay out of the creative student's work space. But they ought not to keep away from it entirely; they must be around, close and in touch, suffi-ciently close so that they may recognize the creative work, but not so close that they might smother its breath. It is a discreet and honorable role they play, for they must tolerate rebukes and harsh-ness which the creative student, which every student may use as a method of making certain he hasn't yet been devoured by teach-ers, schooling, campus architecture, and, of course, careers. It is an honorable role, for it requires the teacher to separate himself from his students in a fashion that only time would understand. It is not quite the teacher's future the student covets. It is not quite his past that the student fears may be bequeathed to him. It's not quite either of these two possibilities, but it is also not too far from both of them.

But what of their respective presents together? Do the student and his teacher share a time, or are both pulling so furiously away from this and then the next instant in such opposite directions that time comes to be stretched of all its meaning and intention? Where in the teaching present does there exist a moment for change? Where in the teaching present does the instant of exchange, communication or learning take place? For that matter, can anything ever be communicated or taught, or is it always true that the creative student turns his back, and with it his past and his dissatisfactions, in the face of his teacher?

To turn away, naturally, is to be left alone, which means the possibility of rejection. Yet, at the same time, turning away offers the student possibility for industry. To be left overly attended, overly cared for means competition just as much as nurturance, and who knows where either of these routes might lead? They might lead back to the secrets of the creative impulse, if it is really an impulse. They also might lead away from these secrets forever, leaving the once young mind with nothing but self-conscious and repetitive soliloquies about childhood and school.

This then is the magic that teachers must unravel: how to keep that energy alive. How to keep those living-dying, working-playing persons fearlessly and fearfully with and within themselves. How to keep them at one and the same time in and out of school, in and out of themselves, in and out of their work. How to make school a playground, nursery, monastery and church. How one second to make school the figure and the ground of all learning and of all knowledge and then, in the next second, make it all disappear — the buildings and the teachers, the books and the trees — leaving all by himself that single creative spirit. How to do all of this and make it seem real and honest, never contrived. How to make school an edifice of the past, present, and future and hence the cord of integrity for all time, and then reverse everything by yanking it all away: the cord, the past, the present, and the future, leaving all by himself that single creative spirit.

How does a teacher bring this about? By what he does? By what he doesn't do? By his wishes and aspirations if he can liberate them from his guilts and dissatisfactions, recriminations and regrets? By his actions, private and public? By his disclosures, intentional and unwitting? Maybe he never thinks of any of these strategies, but rather concerns himself with the only plausible magic he knows, the calling of his own work. And maybe, too, this is precisely what the creative spirit needs: the reaffirming structure of solitary work. For with work alone comes the response to the student's staging of mockery, namely the refutation of teaching altogether from, of all people, his teacher. At first glance this refutation seems pleasurable enough to the student, but it cuts its way to the very spine of that inner darkness, and now he wonders whether his teacher or all of education, for that matter, is worth the mockery, the anger, and the outrage. He wonders, too, about a war with parents and an image of the future which, good or bad, school has begun to carve. And suddenly, of all things, from still another portion of darkness, his unborn children and their whole generation appear before him.

Dear Miss ———,

I have read about sixteen pages of your manuscript and it made me — smile. It is clever, well observed, honest, it stands on its own feet up to a point, and yet it is so typically feminine, by which I mean derivative and vitiated by personal rancour. I suffered exactly the same treatment at the hands of my teachers who disliked me for my independence and passed me over when they wanted assistants (I must admit that I was somewhat less of a model student than you). But it would not have been worth my while to write anything about my school life, still less would I have liked to be responsible for anyone's printing or actually reading it. Besides, one always cuts a poor figure if one complains about others who are struggling for their place in the sun too after their own fashion.

Therefore pocket your temperament and keep your manuscript for your sons and daughters, in order that they may derive consolation from it and — not give a damn for what their teachers tell them or think of them.

Incidentally I am only coming to Princeton to research, not to teach. There is too much education altogether, especially in American schools. The only rational way of educating is to be an example — of what to avoid, if one can't be the other sort.

With best wishes,
ALBERT EINSTEIN [11]

Surely the teacher finds himself in the student. And surely the student wonders whether he, too, has not seen some anticipated reflection in his teacher. Will their times ever cross? Or is it perhaps not age which keeps them apart, but, instead, the essence of authority, the control of one over the other? This is the logical but hated inevitability: that one should have and the other should want, and that one dares to be there before the other and thereby earns what invariably each generation perceives as the single reward. When you look at it, it seems right that most of the "information" should be passed on genetically; the hard part is just speaking together honorably, the parent and child, the teacher and student. But here again time has intervened and renders friendships so trying and painful.

Sometimes it seems as though the creative student treasures the tradition he shares with wise men and idols, but all at once he changes his mind and rejects any time he has not encountered face on. He rejects his father's dreams, or he masks them by erecting his own realities in their place. But his attachments to the prior are always in evidence. Soon he cannot find the truth or fantasy of any authority, until, of course, that authority comes thundering back to him with the strength of a monster god. Then, as in nothing short of a biblical flood, the words, deeds and, finally, the secrets of that authority just explode over the land on which the younger one walks, or someday, like it or not, will have to walk.

Poetry readings, dramatic presentations, graduation ceremonies, perhaps eulogies heard too early, and always letters — they're all words, clusters of man's words held together by iron. Words and music shackle people together, then bind them all to history. The words don't teach, really, they launch creativity, slap at it when it finally arrives, and often brutalize the soul whose fear of work, or war with it, or just plain idleness prevent the next wave, the next movement of creativity from appearing.

Sometimes the storm of words from the old and accomplished to the young bounce away in meaninglessness; sometimes too they sting the recipient and everyone around him. The old demand effort, work, more effort, returning from failure, resistance against the seductiveness of success, fame, wealth and all of that. The old see only the past, so the young think; the young only the future, so the old lament. Yet both struggle and struggle some more with their respective childishness and self-love. Why the old have the upper hand, at least in the creative enterprise, is that they have begun to live with but a few rewards, not of creativity, necessarily, but of the work that supports all those sparks and all of that darkness. The truth they dare push on their children, their children with the fresh eye and unformed heart, is work. Work, work, the litany, work: "When I was your age . . ." and the young run away from the adolescence of their parents and in so doing prevent their special elders from regaining the unregainable.

Adolescence and childishness are not creativity; let no one think that they are. Let no one think, either, that they couldn't be if it were not for a society so ambivalent about letting its precious children grow up at all, that the children, too, begin to doubt the values of maturity. The stuff of creativity is all there, however, in the child's body waiting to be brought forth. The darkness inside is there too, glistening, waiting to be discovered. Dip into the well and see finally what's in the deepest deep of your insides — this is what they ought to teach. But it's not so easy a request to make; it's not so easy a lesson to teach, for it means that the teacher too must accept an inside and have disclosed to himself by himself what heretofore has remained merely the secret potential of his own creativity and health.

Fathers can tell their children about creativity, especially when they themselves dared to hunt for that glistening darkness. Finding it or not, they still safeguard a bit of love in reserve. Fathers can push for the work, the solitude and the aloneness which they know have given birth to creativity right out of their marrow. Their lives practically on fire, their dreams all but fallen away, their futures practically useless and timeless, they cling to their work, the source of their every breath. As the strictest of autocrats, they order their children to look to themselves and not to the vicariousness and deception of others. Work, work alone with and in yourself, they scream in a rage and with an almost primordial certainty. Turn away from the capricious and work, or make the capricious into work. Short or long, words or notes, life or death, work alone. Here is the truth. Here, here where you work or ought to work. Let them teach that and nothing more, say some fathers.

July 7, 1938

Dearest Scottie:

I don't think I will be writing letters many more years and I wish you would read this letter twice — bitter as it may seem. You will reject it now, but at a later period some of it may come back to you as truth. When I'm talking to you, you think of me as an older person, an "authority," and when I speak of my own youth what I say becomes unreal to you — for the young can't believe in the youth of their fathers. But perhaps this little bit will be understandable if I put it in writing.

When I was your age I lived with a great dream. The dream grew and I learned how to speak of it and make people listen. Then the dream divided one day when I decided to marry your mother after all, even though I knew she was spoiled and meant no good to me. I was sorry immediately I had married her but, being patient in those days, made the best of it and got to love her in another way. You came along and for a long time we made quite a lot of happiness out of our lives. But I was a man divided — she wanted me to work too much for her and not enough for my dream. She realized too late that work was dignity, and the only dignity, and tried to atone for it by working herself, but it was too late and she broke and is broken forever.

It was too late also for me to recoup the damage — I had spent most of my resources, spiritual and material, on her, but I struggled on for five years till my health collapsed, and all I cared about was drink and forgetting.

The mistake I made was in marrying her. We belonged to different worlds — she might have been happy with a kind simple man in a southern garden. She didn't have the strength for the big stage — sometimes she pretended, and pretended beautifully, but she didn't have it. She was soft when she should have been hard, and hard when she should have been yielding. She never knew how to use her energy — she's passed that failing on to you.

For a long time I hated her mother for giving her nothing in the line of good habit — nothing but "getting by" and conceit. I never wanted to see again in this world women who were brought up as idlers. And one of my chief desires in life was to keep you from being that kind of person, one who brings ruin to themselves and others. When you began to show disturbing signs at about fourteen, I comforted myself with the idea that you were too precocious socially and a strict school would fix things. But sometimes I think that idlers seem to be a special class for whom nothing can be planned, plead as one will with them — their only contribution to the human family is to warm a seat at the common table.

My reforming days are over, and if you are that way I don't want to change you. But I don't want to be upset by idlers inside my family or out. I want my energies and my earnings for people who talk my language.

I have begun to fear that you don't. You don't realize that what I am doing here is the last tired effort of a man who once did something finer and better. There is not enough energy, or call it money, to carry anyone who is dead weight and I am angry and resentful in my soul when I feel that I am doing this. People like —— —— and your mother must be carried because their illness makes them useless. But it is a different story that you have spent two years doing no useful work at all, improving neither your body nor your mind, but only writing reams and reams of dreary letters to dreary people, with no possible object except obtaining invitations which you could not accept. Those letters go on, even in your sleep, so that I know your whole trip now is one long waiting for the post. It is like an old gossip who cannot still her tongue.

You have reached the age when one is of interest to an adult only insofar as one seems to have a future. The mind of a child is fascinating, for it looks on old things with new eyes — but at about twelve this changes. The adolescent offers nothing, can do nothing, say nothing that the adult cannot do better. Living with you in Baltimore (and you have told Harold that I alternated between strictness and neglect, by which I suppose you mean the time I was so inconsiderate as to have T.B., or to retire into myself to write, for I had little social life apart from you) represented a rather too domestic duty forced on me by your mother's illness. But I endured your Top Hats and Telephones until the day you snubbed me at dancing school, less willingly after that . . .

To sum up: What you have done to please me or make me proud is practically negligible since the time you made yourself a good diver at camp (and now you are softer than you have ever been). In your career as a "wild society girl," vintage of 1925, I'm not interested, I don't want any of it — it would bore me, like dining with the Ritz Brothers. When I do not feel you are "going somewhere," your company tends to depress me for the silly waste and triviality involved. On the other hand, when occasionally I see signs of life and intention in you, there is no company in the world I prefer. For there is no doubt that you have something in your belly, some real gusto for life — a real dream of your own — and my idea was to wed it to something solid before it was too late — as it was too late for your mother to learn anything when she got around to it. Once when you spoke French as a child it was enchanting with your odd bits of knowledge — now your conversation is as commonplace as if you'd spent the last two years in the Corn Hollow High School — what you saw in *Life* and read in *Sexy Romances*.

I shall come East in September to meet your boat — but this letter is a declaration that I am no longer interested in your promissory notes but only in what I see. I love you always but I am interested by people who think and work as I do and it isn't likely that I shall change at my age. Whether you will — or want to — remains to be seen.

DADDY

P.S. If you keep the diary, please don't let it be the dry stuff I could buy in a ten-franc guide book. I'm not interested in dates and places, even the Battle of New Orleans, unless you have some unusual reaction to them. Don't try to be witty in the writing, unless it's natural — just true and real.

P.P.S. Will you please read this letter a second time? I wrote it over twice.

F. Scott Fitzgerald [12]

The irony of the creative spirit is that sooner or later it seems to brush up against, perhaps even collide with, school and, even more, with education. Here lies life for some; here lies poison for others. They all crash together here for a short time, all of those mysterious furies, intelligence, ingenuity, innovation, creativity, learning. They crash head-on producing the roar of grades, to be sure, but merely the whisper of newness or the bare wisp of art. The very halls and floors of the school, painted as they are with politics, verbiage and aggrandizement, exude poisonous oils that spread over creativity's pores, yet somehow the fresh words, notes, models and movements push their way up, up to the outside and freedom.

School plays a funny trick, it seems, on all of those creative ones. It holds them back; we all know that. But in that holding back, in that attempt to make them all comply and conform, some just have to break their necks and, like colts, gallop away. Their attachments to the prior, however, are always in evidence. They fight the ropes and the tethers, they fight them right down to the very end, and even beyond the end. Maybe it is precisely the knowledge of it all, the feeling of being constrained, of being hemmed in that at first drives them inward and thereby far away from all the ropes and tethers and then launches those secrets of theirs into the molds of action and production that light a sleeping darkness. Could it really be true that school protects the creative spirit by at least providing a ground, a foundation from which to erect a dream or vision, or a gate from which to run away as fast as one can? Somewhere in the ground of learning, after all, are the seeds of ethics and goodness, even among all that poison. Somewhere in the ground, too, is the scent of freedom; freedom with restraint, but freedom, even among all of that conformity and obsession with respect. Let's be honest. There are times when total individuality and aloneness, aloneness with work, especially, are frightening, and we run to the side of anyone who may be walking there. Just to talk.

All of this, naturally, has more to do with people than with creativity. School is truly good when they all run away. If it's only hard work, it's incomplete. If they only think it, it's insufficient. Whatever it is, that creative thing, it requires pacing and moving, moving away, coming back, moving away again. Not only the dancers dance; not only the sculptors sculpt. There must be movement, enormous, wonderful, swirling movement in colored and colorless space, all at the same time. The space on the outside must pour like white-hot iron into the space on the inside, and then be able to pour out again so quickly one can see the steam. School ought to be that, too! The outer space, the inner space, the movement of arms and legs and bodies along with ideas and plans, anticipations and reworkings, groups and singles, movies and stills. There has to be pacing room, running room, room to run away.

But there has to be, as well, a tower or a person right in the middle of the school to stand as a beacon or glow. There has to be something that offers a return to the runaways, to the idlers, the knowers and the seers. There has to be a root, a setting, a constancy, a whole. These the creative spirit and the creative darkness in each and every one of us needs from the world. Without them, the thoughts of perishing and impermanency would simply overwhelm us and there would be no energy left over for pure and unrelenting work, much less surprise.

In that beacon or that person, and again, ironically, in school, is just enough of what they call religion to justify, probably, our using words like creative soul or spirit. The religion need not contain the ritualization which for many gives it purpose; it fits nonetheless alongside the mysterious and the incomprehensible out of which the many languages of expression and expressiveness breathe creativity. Where, after all, does a poem or sketch, a recipe, design, joke or play or altogether new sensation come from? Does anyone know? More importantly, will some of us who seek creativity destroy it by finding it, or is that the same old unwarranted fear that always precedes exploration and discovery? It seems now as though the creative spirit and those who work with it and abide by it have a way, not intentionally of course, of covering up the tracks of their work, the footprints that might make the experience of their innovations and industry fathomable, even compatible with our own ingenuous life-styles. "I don't know where it comes from," they say. "I change my mind every ten minutes." "I turn mistakes into purposeful alterations." "I don't think about what will happen to it when I finish it. I just want people to like it when it's done." "What are you trying to do," they ask, "psychoanalyze me?"

A lot of "I's" in all those descriptions. A lot of narcissism and egocentrism, some would say. What does one make of the statement, "I can't bear to part with the pieces I've made"? Wouldn't we say that's kind of infantile, holding on to everything, thinking every note, every word, every gesture should be finalized and made immortal? "Hey Mom . . . Mom . . . Mom. Watch me swim under water." And then, "Did you see that? Did you see me?" Remember those times? "I drew these pictures in school today and I'm going to hang them here in the living room. The ones I made last week aren't good now and they're coming down. I don't like them anymore. O.K.? But you won't throw them away, will you?" Surely that's infantilism. Or is it, rather, the beginning of work and recognition, genuine industry and public honor that know no particular age or starting point, but only changes in the form they ultimately find and agree to over time? Even at the end, our freshest pictures still go up and the old ones of a week before come down to join the batch in a withered portfolio. Still more of the attachments to the prior.

What then of school and the individual child, the individual spirit and the single creative darkness it dares to embrace? Are there better schools and lesser schools? Lighter schools and darker schools? And what of the sadness and fear that the very buildings proclaim? What really has a school to do with education or with learning or, for that matter, with creativity? Anything at all? Do they correlate in some complicated human statistic? And does it matter whether they do or they don't?

Let us be certain of one thing. Creativity comes out of a core of dimness and miraculous human mystery. We touch only its shadow, only its reflection, only its production. It comes out of a core of dimness with the suppressed fury of anger and love, sexuality and hate, poison and blood. (The antinomies again.) And it lasts but moments, not only in its own life-force, but in the life cycle of those who urge its birth or watch its growth and demise. More serious than its evanescence is its impermanence. Sadder than its unintelligibility is its swift passage and suddenly resumed indivisibleness. Work holds it all triumphantly aloft for some hours or for some lifetimes, and then it's gone. But it has left life in its wake as well as the chance for others to be born, and this, after all, is realistically more important than rebirth, which belongs properly to mythology and literature.

If there is a sadness or shame about the passing of even a few creative spirits, it is most certainly that human beings prevent one another from reaching that ground, maybe even the school ground, where creative work often is, well, played out. This is the sadness, I think. All of these perfectly human constraints continue to keep us from knowing just what about creativity comes from genes and what from God, what is really there and what exists only in our descriptions and impressions.

What then of school and the single child, of Juliette and of Paul? Simply this. If there is to be a sacred earth under learning and therefore under creativity, it is made so by the single child who walks upon that earth. Education, then, some would say, is little more than a prayer. But even as that, it would be enough.

chapter 6

College and Career Night in Bristol Township

When I look at American education, I do not see schools, but
young Americans who deserve the chance to make a life for
themselves and ensure the progress of their country. If we fail in
this, no success we have is worth the keeping . . .

> From the speech "For Excellence,
> Freedom and Diversity," delivered
> by Richard M. Nixon,
> October 20, 1968

For many people in and around Pennsylvania, the
name Bristol means backwater flats, the bottom, the pit of Pennsylvania, "The kids in Bristol are sharp as a pistol/When they do
the Bristol Stomp," or just plain America. Once upon a time during Revolutionary days, the elite of several states came to Bristol
to luxuriate in its hot spring baths, but for the majority of modern
tourists, Bristol just sits there as the inevitable town adjoining the
inevitable toll booth on the Pennsylvania Turnpike. For the men
and women of the town, however, and particularly those involved
in education, it's quite a significant sample of "just plain America." For it is their own. Moreover, being America and thereby
connected to Watts, Harlem, Trenton and Philadelphia, Bristol
Township feels all too well the swells of dissatisfaction in the land,
and the fervor and reverence that constitute education.

My tour through the township was guided by a gentle man, strong and big, with a firm handshake and a knowledge of his community quite remarkable and told with pride. We were about to share a few days of our lives together in his community with its population now exceeding sixty-seven thousand. It's a rather spread-out township, one almost requiring you to have a car and, at first visit anyway, a guide who knows the facts of the township as well as the problems it faces. While the guide's mission might have something to do with public relations, a role he'll also play from time to time, there aren't too many aspects of the town he'll hide from the tourist or reporter, and not too many facts he'll withhold. "We've got a lot of problems here," he'll say, "but in the main we think we're doing damn well."

He might tell you that Bristol Township, not to be confused with the town of Bristol, whose boundaries start just beyond this road on the other side of the Bristol Motor Inn, is what they call a bedroom community, for a sizable number of men work in Philadelphia to the south and Trenton, a mite closer, to the north. Some will drive down the Pennsylvania Turnpike to jobs in smaller cities, while others will park their cars in the Trenton railroad station and commute all the way to New York City. "What we have here is homes and kids." More precisely, over thirteen thousand children attend public schools in the township.

Driving in his car down the Levittown Parkway, a handsome wide drive separating Bristol Township from Tulleytown and Falls Township, my guide helped me to locate Bristol Township on the Delaware River near the giant bridge which north- and east-bound commuters recognize as the last monument before New Jersey. He spoke, too, of the Pennsylvania Main Line North where the Metroliner flashes through each morning on its way to Washington, and about Levittown. "That's really a baby farm," he chuckled as we circled its enormous shopping center, then on past Sears and Pomeroys and the seemingly endless lake of parking stalls. There are about twelve thousand homes of three major varieties in Levittown, he explained. There's the Jubilee, which has four bedrooms and a garage; the Levittown, a bedroom or two smaller; and the Rancher, which has no garage and often lacks a finished upstairs as well. But they are all well kept up, and the streets and lanes, each named with the same initial as its district, are lovely to travel through.

Now we were driving along Stonybrook Drive, coming out on to Newportville Road. Then on to take a look at Bishop Egan High School, the large Catholic boys' school which stands impressively as arch rival to Woodrow Wilson, the single graduating public high school in Bristol Township. Across the street from Egan is the modern, low-slung technical school, operating sixty trades for grades ten, eleven and twelve, and administered by the combined efforts of six counties. Built in 1957 and 1958, the technical school is supervised by its own governing board and principal, but all local superintendents sit on this board.

Moving on past the new two-and-a-half-story apartments of Orangewood Park, my guide described the county's opportunity class, comprised of pupils separated from their regular schools for having committed physical violence of one sort or another. Presently housing about fifteen pupils, the class is taught by teachers who maintain access to all educational facilities in the school district. "Our goal is to return these kids to their regular schools. We don't want to lose kids." In fact, the data testify to this as well as to the district's own philosophy of education as expressed in a recently written research proposal: "We think the United States is still an 'open society' in which it is possible to rise in social class and achievement provided that the tools needed to do so have been acquired as a result of education." [1] Since 1952, Bristol Township has expelled one student. Last year, however, three girls were suspended.

To travel through Bloomsdale Gardens, a housing project predating Levittown, then past the 3M Corporation down Fleeting Drive, is to be reminded of the social class differentiations about which the township recently has come to be troubled. Though separated from one another, the houses here are not quite as handsome as in Levittown. Their residents are black, and probably they would be called working-class. Their recreation facility consists of eight swings and a basketball court. At the end of Fleeting Drive stands the hulking 3M Corporation itself, a bastion overseeing

Bloomsdale Gardens from where once it drew most of its employees. Now, however, the management has sensed an inadequate proportion of blacks and adjustments are under way in the company's hiring practices.

Crossing the Pennsylvania Canal where flat barges transport the coal from the mining regions to Bristol, across Route 13 near the Holiday Inn and the elevated turnpike at the Bristol toll booth area, down some unpaved roads through Green Lawn Park, we entered Kingswood Park. Still called "the Terrace" by most Bristol Township citizens, Kingswood Park changed its name to honor Martin Luther King. For the most part, it consists of rows of single-level housing projects built during World War II for factory workers. The buildings need refurbishing, the ground needs replanting. The interiors of the barrack houses are small, cramped, dirty, barely livable for the sizes of the families they protect, and the writing on the walls outside, the slogans and names of heroes and boyfriends, and the nearby Job Corps training building and day-care center mark this surprisingly spacious plot of earth as American slum. The residents of the Terrace, more than two-thirds of whom are black, send their children to schools miles away, which pleases some of the parents, as recreation facilities adjoining their homes are totally inadequate. There's a lake nearby; actually, it's an old quarry, but the contaminated water prevents it from being much of anything save a murky hole where boys in gym shoes, dark pants and striped T-shirts stand giggling over the sounds made by rocks as they arch them high into the water from a sandy ledge. "Some people wouldn't show you this area. You have to have a tour by someone who likes the place."

Now we were doubling back past the township's municipality buildings, police station and tax collector's office. They seemed rather new. We drove by the Brittany Spring Apartments and a row of Catholic, Lutheran and Christian Science churches, through the Plumridge Section of Levittown where a small creek accompanies the flow of the road, past the Abraham Lincoln Elementary School and then on to the Newportville area and the Clymer School, where portable classrooms hunch behind the main building. An existing ruling demands that when new apartments are built, and the population naturally increases, an elementary school too must be constructed.

Moving on to the Croyden region — Croyden Acres and Croyden Manors — my guide remarked on the distinction well known in the region between the upper and lower sections of Bucks County. The lower area, closer to Philadelphia than the upper, is older, and contains Edgley, a handsome stretch of homes in Bristol Township facing, if not directly fronting on, the Delaware River. The upper section, containing Levittown, is newer; that is, it was built after the Second World War. For politicians like Joe Grundy, whose old home still stands enormous where the road to Croyden follows Neshaminy Creek, the distinction between old and new, lower and upper still has great significance. It means differences in who votes and what you have to do to get them to vote for you.

Originally called Shank's Station after a revered stationmaster, Croyden blends rather comfortable residential sections with the region's most poor white neighborhoods. Unlike the rows of barracks at the Terrace, Croyden's poverty stands as single housing units, some in pitiful disrepair. Next to one home is a totally dilapidated shack, and alongside a modest Chevy a beat-up Volkswagen practically heaves from exhaustion as it leans against the wall of a frail hut like a tired horse flaked out over a hitching post. The car's bumper is latched on with bailing wire and clothesline rope.

From the outside, the Mary Devine School, named after a late and beloved principal, seems pleasant enough, but all the published statistics attest to its poverty and inadequate status. Still, the residents here are content, hopeful, and almost religiously engulfed in a pride, in an atavistic loyalty and aesthetics which keep them, even the young marrieds, at home. The people here will not settle for housing projects like Croyden Acres, which rises from the dry soil and loam on the other side of Route 13. Nor do they want Head Start and Upward Bound programs, although the county offers them. They have no intention, moreover, of tearing down from the fronts of their homes the cracked painted signs and shingles which reveal the most important statistic of all, their names. Maybe it's hard-headedness or ignorance; maybe, too, a precocious sophistication and self-esteem which caused the residents of these blocks to protest, to actually demonstrate against a grant from the federal government which, while requiring individual house inspections, would have made it possible to rehabilitate much of the area. Maybe in their seeming recalcitrance these residents of Croyden proclaimed a handsome and righteous militancy that "the boys in Washington don't quite yet understand."

But the tour was almost over. Driving along curving roads edging slightly downhill, passing the Medicenter Nursing Home on the right and emerging at the rear of the Lower Bucks County Hospital, its giant maternity wards bespeaking the county's incredible birthrate, my guide explained the Community School program. In it, parents and teachers together devise, develop and conduct projects for the entire community. After regular classes conclude at three-thirty, the school remains open for activities like movies, Black Studies League meetings, sewing classes and roller skating. Even students attending schools in other districts come here and help to knit together a community, itself feeling the urgency of personal drive, competence and exploration. Twelve months a year, this one community school stays open to its people. "We're proud of our schools," he was saying as the tour ended. "The district has a lot of problems, but we think we're doing a darn good job."

[2]

Even with all the educational programs, eventually most of the students in Bristol Township will conclude their secondary education at Woodrow Wilson High School. Coming from any one of a dozen elementary schools and three or four junior high schools, they will spend their last two years taking courses in the gigantic plant of the high school. Here, where almost two thousand students attend classes, about thirty-five percent of the graduating seniors will choose to go on to some additional educational institution. For some it will be four-year colleges; for others, two-year colleges or perhaps vocational schools. Yet, while the stated objective of the school's principal is to get people into college, it is going to be a while before the "working-class" parents of Bristol Township do "much better than send on thirty-five percent."

All the same, these figures are not "so bad" when one compares this school with comparable graduating high schools in Philadelphia and Trenton, the larger cities just to the south and north of Bristol Township. Indeed, in many respects Bristol Township speaks for much of nonurban America. It has, as the sociologists would say, a small middle class, a scattering of ethnic groups, Protestant, Catholic, and Jewish communities, and its black and white areas of saddening poverty. It has its racial tensions sometimes erupting into fights in the halls between classes and on the streets where black and white bodies collide under political and erotic frustrations, and it has its citizens who realize that there are "problems in America" but who add quickly, "We're no worse here than anyone else."

Like so many communities and the social scientists who feast upon them, Bristol Township becomes confused by the personal and statistical interactions of race, sex, and social class. It is difficult to know, really, when the source of reported tensions is an openly racial matter, and when the so-called ruling or powerful groups are acting in ways to exclude the poor and the dirty. Interracial dating and marriage, moreover, seem rather frightening fantasies to some who right off might refuse a date with a person who previously had dated someone of another race.

But these kinds of issues and certainly the geography of this community were far from the minds of those of us who stood in the high school auditorium on that one Wednesday night, pledging allegiance to the flag and the United States of America, for it was College and Career Night, and everyone's focus clearly was on the final educational objective. The turnout was fine. Parents and children had come to speak with representatives of almost thirty state colleges as well as some local industries. Most of the schools were four-year Negro and white colleges originally founded as teachers' colleges but recently having dropped the word "teacher" from their names. Liberal arts programs have assumed a new status at most of these schools, although teacher training still represents a prominent portion of their programs. But if col-

lege is a possibility, or if these schools are popular with black
students, one could not tell it that evening, as nowhere near the
ten percent black population of Woodrow Wilson High School
was present. After a moment of prayer, College and Career Night
commenced.

In the literature of social psychology, one finds a rather intense
insistence that middle- and lower-class persons may be differen-
tiated by their orientations to time. The middle class, it has been
said over and over again, plans, makes preparations, and generally
lives for the future. The working class, in contrast, prefers to "live
out its impulses," worries about food and work for today, and lets
tomorrow come when tomorrow comes. Supposedly, necessities
overshadow aspirations and dreams. I thought hard of these notions as Principal Frank Daly welcomed the parents, commented
on the turnout, and then spoke of the need for students to plan
and prepare their lives right now: "Our sons and daughters as
tenth and eleventh graders must learn their strengths and weak-
nesses earlier than we had to," he said. "They must make final
decisions as tenth and eleventh graders, not just as seniors. Spe-
cialization means starting earlier, and we must all have special
skills." (On a street of crushed stone in Jerusalem, Gadi Rosen,
my twelve-year-old friend and guide, told me of the examination
he would take the following year in the seventh grade, which, in
an inexorable way, would determine his entire life. If he performed well, he would continue on to a high school geared for
college preparation. If poorly, he would switch to vocational
school. The chances of reaching college after a "slip" on that
examination seemed to him hopelessly slight.)

"Make your decisions now. Parents, you can help your children
by acting as guidance counselors. You can play "one on one" with
your child, but the emphasis must be on deciding right away,
before your senior year." ("I can't really decide what to do," Jona-
than Martindale had said a day or two before I left for Pennsylvania. "I don't really want to go to graduate school right away
and I don't really want to teach high school or grammar school
students.")

"The draft?"

"Yeah. I think what I'll do is apply for a traveling fellowship. That will give me a year to think it out and do some reading."

"Are there no longer chances to get Fulbrights?" I had asked.)

"Now, parents, this is the time to ask all your questions of these representatives. Don't be embarrassed to ask about financial aid. There are no more athletic and academic scholarships. They depend only on need. Many circumstances may qualify you to get aid. . . . Our primary objective is to get students into college."

With these words, Principal Daly turned the meeting over to one of the school's guidance counselors, whose own introduction contained a reminder to the parents of some bleak school statistics: There are some nineteen hundred students in Woodrow Wilson High School, and five guidance counselors.

"Parents," the counselor went on, "you must encourage responsibility in your children. You must think about colleges with them. Be interested and concerned with your children and their plans. But, and this is important, don't use your children to fulfill your own needs. You know that parents often will unconsciously push their own ideas on to their child. So make sure the decisions being made are your child's. Help your child to help himself. Show your child you want the best for him. And if it's possible," he was concluding, "take some time to visit some colleges before applying to them. You should look them over. After all, you don't buy a house without looking at it."

Frank Daly and his staff had planned long and well for this evening. Only a few hours before the proceedings commenced they had made several adjustments since a few college representatives had encountered problems in reaching the school. Some representatives had not arrived even by the end of the preparatory ceremonies. Nonetheless, Daly was laboring to reach his foremost objective.

Suddenly, everyone was pouring out of the auditorium, checking the lists which announced the colleges and the classrooms where representatives would be stationed. Mr. Daly had explained to the audience how the evening program would work. His statement was brief, for he appreciated their needs and, perhaps more im-

portantly, the worth of their time and especially of this one evening. Many, many people held especially tightly to the sheets he
and his office staff had prepared. It was as though these papers and
the gummed name tags worn by the college officials and high school
teacher chaperons had become documents of magic, or perhaps
admission slips to the very schools to which parents and pupils
were about to be introduced.

The wide corridors of Woodrow Wilson High School seemed
endless, labyrinthine. It was a trek to get to the Cheyney State
College representative. Fred Kanter, a high school science teacher
assigned to Cheyney State for the evening as a guide, and I must
have peered into twenty rooms as they slowly filled up. Surprisingly little noise could be heard about the school, but a noticeable
anxiety hung in the rooms and halls. These young people and the
parents who would now have to put even more money away for a
not fully understood educational proposition were confronting
the actuality of college for the first time. In these representatives
they would strain to find some shaft of light, some thread of an
inexplicable but ultimate destiny. In its peculiar way, the evening
had become, if only momentarily, a ceremony of adulthood, a
coming of age, as it were, a time for two generations to join together in an alliance that would launch one of them up and beyond the topography and history of the other. Their presence in
the halls that night, as in a child's game they hunted for their
first- and second-choice schools, only sanctified this alliance and
the thankful agreements it implied.

The chairs in the classroom we entered were arranged in a large
rectangle. Two young women and, presumably, a mother of one
or both of them sat beside one another, their backs to the door. I
met one of Fred's colleagues, a recent graduate of Cheyney State.
Then we nodded to Mr. Burton, the college's representative, himself busily stacking piles of papers demonstrating facts about
Cheyney State. Stuck on Mr. Burton's open briefcase were baggage
labels and stickers of all sorts and colors. He had traveled a lot,
for it is his objective, too, to fetch good students for the college he
serves.

Alone, the six of us waited in silence. When he had finished arranging the sheets in their appropriate stacks, Mr. Burton closed his briefcase, clicked its tiny locks, moved slightly around to the left of the rectangle and began. He had given similar talks before to others, to many others. Throughout the talk, in the pauses and at the end of poetic measures, the woman to my right nodded politely. Often, too, she would smile — just barely, though, and I would hear her "hmm," ever so quietly.

"One simply must have a good education," Mr. Burton was saying. "You know, years ago a high school education was sufficient. But no more. Now you must have at least a college degree and, pretty soon, if you really want to stay ahead of the game, a master's and Ph.D. degree as well. You know that people with college degrees live so much better; they travel so much. The other day I spoke to a man who had just come back from Rome. Think of that; he had been to Rome for only one week! Today you can just fly anywhere. One day in Philadelphia and the next day you're back from Rome. I traveled in Europe in 1956." Behind Mr. Burton on the bulletin board, along with several pictures, the words LE POUVOIR DES FLEURS were written in the shape of the letter V.

The woman smiled gently. "Hmm."

"Cheyney State has changed a great deal since you were there." Mr. Burton spoke almost entirely to Fred's colleague. "It is no longer merely a teachers' college. There are liberal arts programs and science curricula, but you must decide your major soon. In fact, it is a good idea to know what you want to study before coming in September.

"There have been many changes at the college." He moved behind us to the blackboard and drew a small model of the campus. "Now you remember the library? They've added this large addition to the old section and they're thinking about rebuilding the old section to make it as large as the new one. Now this building," he cited a name and pointed to a square he had drawn, "is no longer a girls' dorm. It's an office building. And this building over here is new; it's the new girls' dorm. And a new science building is going up right alongside of it. The boys now live here in this new dorm." He pointed to another square.

Again I heard the woman, "Hmmm."

"Now, and this is going to surprise you, you remember that large farm area across from the entrance?" I found myself nodding. We were all nodding. "Well, we bought that farm and have moved the road which used to separate the farm from the front of the campus to behind the farm way down over here." His eyes alive, Mr. Burton made gestures like a man reaching down to pull his bed covers up over his head, as he described the changes in the placement of the road. He was smiling. "And we got the land on the other side of the new location of the road, too, for a student parking lot. You wouldn't recognize the place anymore. In order to get into the entrance, you gotta do one of these things here": his right hand drew a large (backward for us) S, starting at the bottom. All of us were nodding our approval of the campus's progress. Mr. Burton seemed proud.

Fred's colleague wondered about a stoplight that had been near where the old road used to be. "It's still there." The question reminded Mr. Burton of the fact that the campus is lit each night automatically. "No one has to turn the lights on or off. It's all done automatically." He looked at the six of us, one by one.

As he continued speaking, we passed around sheets from his carefully stacked piles of information. The papers indicated that everything at Cheyney State was on the rise. More buildings, greater endowments, more students, more faculty, indeed the faculty had more than doubled in size in a very few years. More buildings, more academic programs, more students in liberal arts and non–teacher training programs. Most importantly, the school was physically expanding. It had come to occupy more land and seemed to be taking greater and more frequent breaths as it embraced more and more space, more and more earth. Of all accomplishments, and of all the graphs and charts, it was the changing of that road which seemed to touch something so very, very deep in this Negro man. No longer were this campus and its people confined to a certain plot of land, a certain sacrosanct geography, its limits etched in the same iron they might have used in forging the shackles for slaves. This school was moving! It was bursting out, and in flooding its estate over farmlands which for years it had merely spied on, it now audaciously dared to change the very flow of human traffic, its own and everyone else's.

"Now let's get to the details you obviously are eager to hear about. First, admissions. In order to consider you for acceptance, we look first at your rank in class. We feel that if you're not in the upper three-fifths of your class, we cannot be too encouraging." The one woman nodded. It all seemed reasonable enough. "Let's say there are five hundred in your class. If you are two hundred ninety-ninth you're still going to be considered because you are in the upper three-fifths." As he spoke, he wrote the numbers 500 and 299 on the blackboard.

"Now for grades." The few people present moved slightly in their chairs. There was something in the room reminiscent of a jury about to announce some portentous decision. It was as though in that instant admission decisions would be made, and if it were ever to happen, society would change. "We're looking for B's. I can always remember this, as B is for Burton. If you have A's, fine." He smiled. "We don't want D's. C's are O.K., but we're looking for B's. On the college boards, we want a sum of eight hundred, mathematical and verbal combined. If you get five hundred on verbal and three hundred on mathematical, that's fine, because we want eight hundred combined. . . ."

"The expenses for a year break down something like this." Mr. Burton mentioned some figures about room and board and miscellaneous costs and then announced a total of about one thousand dollars. Once again the woman nodded. A moment later, as my own mind wandered a bit, Mr. Burton had finished speaking. Having returned to his original position around the corner of the rectangle, he asked for questions. Silence. The men had deferred to the women, but they seemed contented. Then I asked about the availability of scholarship money.

Mr. Burton smiled. "This is going to surprise you. About twenty-one percent of the state's funds for students went unexpended last year." * We nodded, our heads moving now side to side. The women sat perfectly still.

* At the time, no explanation was made to us of the fact that in the Pennsylvania state college system no scholarships are given since the low tuition is itself considered a grant. The tuition at these institutions, as Josephine C. Knapp has pointed out (letter to the Education Editor, *Saturday Review*, March 21, 1970, page 58), is "about 75% lower than at nearby private institutions."

"What you have to do is find out about how to get the money and then be sure you get your application in on time. This is one of the major reasons students don't get this money. They find out about it too late, or don't meet application deadlines. There are, of course, some special problems with the banks, because they must deal with you individually in setting up loans. You must do this by yourself with a bank, but there *is* all of that money."

The three women were eager to get on with it, but Mr. Burton's words had hit Fred and me identically. We almost smacked foreheads in turning to each other with the same interpretation. We were the only white people in that brick and linoleum classroom, lit as it was by a metallic fluorescent glow, but all at once we both felt that perhaps only we, we on the "outside," were the single ones to catch the exclusiveness and the truly sullen areas of misunderstanding and what seemed to us to be utter betrayal. There had been no mention of pure scholarship monies. It had just been assumed that these people would qualify only for loans. But then loans might be stopped at the banks if individual students could not show proper credentials and prove in some way that they were not credit risks. Up against the bars or plastic windows of cashiers' booths, the dream that I had imagined for them would come to an end. In their entire lives and histories, in all their days, they would be able to come up with nothing for collateral, I thought. If the grades and board scores did not stop them, it just seemed that money would.

But all of this "elitist" reasoning and superior politics belonged to our private stock and culture, for the three women for whom the reality had been unveiled were squirming with excitement. Mr. Burton approached them. He stood inside the rectangle now holding loosely to those sacred forms, the application blanks. How familiar they looked. The woman to my right spoke her first words. She was alive, excited. She spoke to Mr. Burton: "Give her the forms." She directed her eyes to the girl sitting next to her. "She's going to sign them and give them right back to you tonight." The girl held tightly to a light blue ball-point pen, her hand in place, ready.

"Oh, no," Mr. Burton chuckled. "This can't be done tonight.

This form takes two whole days to fill out." He riffled through the pages. Questions and statements, lines for addresses, names, dates, lists, history, and for all sorts of information passed before our eyes. Then he was flipping the pages one by one only inches in front of our faces. In front of our faces, black and white, feminine and masculine, poor and rich. "There's an information form," (flip) "a medical form," (flip) "an academic form," (flip) . . .

When the bell sounded, Fred and I left the classroom, but the women lingered on a bit. Two rooms away we sat again among a new group of parents and students as this time they and we together listened to two representatives of another college. There were no black families here. The talk was essentially the same: the growth of the school, the stress on early decisions, the requirements, tougher than Cheyney State, the expenses, more than Cheyney State. A parent asked the meaning of room and board. "You mean three meals a day?" "That's right." Then there was awe; the enormity of higher education; traveling to Rome for one single week; my recollection of the ten black students who mentioned that before being bussed to a nearby elementary school for desegregation purposes they had never ridden on a bus; the girl who inquired about transferring if she did not make it the first time around; and the explanation of early acceptance for those students possessing outstanding records and a willingness to pledge to the school that it was their first choice. This announcement had made more than a few swoon. To have the future splashed in your face so soon, it was almost illicit or obscene. But it was great, just great.

All of this was in those rooms, in both of those rooms in that enormous high school. And only now could we recognize that we had been fooled, absolutely tricked by the racial matter, or so it appeared. We left, stunned, really, by College and Career Night, swearing to some hidden strength of the past that we simply could not make it in today's college competitions. Over and over again we muttered words about how glad we were that college applications were behind us and how good it was to be finished. But this was not the issue. Indeed, walking through the parking lot, Fred almost laughed in telling of the way he had reached his college decision: "My mother told me the names of the three best colleges in the United States, and I applied to them."

[3]

Almost all graduating high schools sponsor some form of college and career night. As the guidance counselor in Bristol Township had recommended, many students will take trips to prospective new "homes" before they select one. Some, in fact, will bed down for a couple of nights in order to see how the "kids" there live and work, what they eat, where they go, what they say, how they devise a future, and where they deposit a past. But for the majority of young Americans, with their "working-class-present orientations" and their parents' special accounts in small tidy banks neatly stashed away for their education, there will be no visiting, no sense or realization of "the best," no sense of the often greedy and competitive forms of tradition and legacy that college graduates and their scion treasure and perpetuate, no trips to the city on shopping sprees for freshman wardrobes. Yet all of the dreams and fantasies of trips and homes and fraternities and possibly the commencement of a magically new tradition to be born in a city over a hundred miles away are alive, glowing, warm and special to these people as the lights at Cheyney State which automatically turn on in the evening and turn off, as if by magic, early in the morning. The dreams and aspirations are there, make no mistake about it. The "studies" "prove" their existence. Without them, there would be no gripping tightly to a paper announcing the one-night-only stand of a college representative, no anxious reaching for pages and pages of applications, and no desire to sign up, quickly but legibly, proudly and permanently.

But while some students literally will take off in all directions toward an open future, approaching colleges with confidence and good grades, politically sound and dutifully written letters of recommendation, not to mention a list of extracurricular activities halfway down your arm, most students will sit silently in their classrooms some one evening and pray that they might forever preserve those slim moments with slick representatives from what must seem like heaven itself. On the spot, even in the hardness of their chairs, and amidst the crass coldness of high school architecture and building materials, they will fall in love with a college and the faceless people who teach and study there. They'll fall in love, too, with the buildings that watch over small acres of sacred college land, and with roads which have not even been dreamed of yet or maybe already have been built, and moved out beyond an imagined farm, to a parking lot, and still further out to unplanted earth, to the end of America, and to Europe itself. For them and the chunk of society they recognize at least partly as their own, in order to locate that future spot, in order to make it to some narrow pinpoint of destiny, they are going to have to hit a keyhole absolutely perfectly, with the precision of a computer-driven rocket. For there is just not that much space reserved for these people, and not that much room for slipups, or out-and-out failure.

So, on this one night they have been reminded, as they have their entire lives, just what stands in the way and just what can go wrong right down the line at each and every interval of social and personal evolution. They are hardly the chosen people, these inheritors of the earth. There will be little patronage coming to them. Higher education is going to put a mighty depression in that special bank account, but never in their strength, so they say. Once again they will have to start doing without for still another period of timeless years: "My daughters are going to have to learn to live with what they have," a parent said. "They've got these fancy ideas in their heads, but they're going to find out different very soon. You have to make do with what you have, that means with the bitterness, too. There's not going to be any miracle coming to our house, today, next week, or any week."

It is just a tiny keyhole they must hit; it is not open sky. In fact, the very thought of openness might repel some people. It is so tiny, that keyhole rimmed with rejection and defiance, that merely to tap at it, much less swarm around it, cannot help but call forth the primeval aggression and sorrowful turbulence of the powerful excluding the powerless, or of the tall shoving back the short, or of the big man goading the small man to shoot from the outside, from the top of the keyhole, or perhaps letting him dare drive cocksure and naked right down the line to the hoop he himself guards with a ferocious strength. Maybe, too, it is the father keeping the son away while envying him his strength and his irrevocable hold on an unseen future.

Back in the motel that evening, I walked about my room examining the furnishings, the wide bed, and the reproductions of Utrillo and Van Gogh. The following day I would leave Bristol Township. For some reason, although inhibited by the pluralism of contemporary racial politics, educational strategies, and social class data, I kept repeating, as a litany, the words which earlier I truthfully had not perfectly recalled, although Fred had recited them with a diligent obedience, if not an educated loyalty: "I pledge allegiance to the flag of the United States of America and to the republic for which it stands, one nation, under God, indivisible, with liberty and justice for all."

With all this and so much more in mind, the ride to the Trenton railroad depot the next day went quickly. Inside the station, alone, the train from Philadelphia to New York still ten minutes away, I met Butch, one of several aggressively competing shoeshine boys. We spoke a little, Butch and I, about his twelve brothers and sisters, the father he's never known, and his aspirations to become a boxer. He showed me the James Brown split and smiled broadly. Then, because my shoes were of an unshinable fabric, he begged me at last to give him a dollar, promising that he would pay me back when I would again pass through Trenton. I was embarrassed and he knew it, but we walked to the train side by side, our hands close together, me dragging a suitcase, Butch clutching his shoeshine kit. We waved to one another through the window. Then I with the others was moving, and he, alone on the platform, was still, then out of sight.

On the train I read a few pages from the *Bristol Township School District Program:* "Our situation is one of social class, not race, although race is the surface manifestation of the problem." Then passing through the New Jersey countryside, past farmlands

and backyards, I thought I heard the voice of a teacher from the
Mary Devine School in the Croyden region. Suddenly we were all
back together in a group, listening to someone recount his childhood of poverty, his parents going without dinner night after
night but standing proudly above their children watching them
munch on some bread and sip coffee. And the teacher who sat
across from me, listening to these words and conjuring up, no
doubt, his own experiences with hunger and visions of exhaustion
and hopelessness, had dropped his head on to his arms which lay
crossed on the table. "Oh my God!" he was saying, "Oh my God
Almighty."

It's a very tiny keyhole, and there is no reason under the sun
why, like Mr. Burton's road, it could not be pushed back so that
the sky, as enormous as it seems, could be made that much more
spacious, truly endless and truly free.

chapter 7

Simple Words,
Simple Deeds

In the short time I have been at this predominantly white
school, I have found a small minority of racists, equal groups of
frauds and interested persons, and a majority of apathetic,
uninterested ones. To me, the most contemptible group is the
group of frauds, strangely composed of the professed liberals and
the ones seeking understanding. It seems odd to me that a once
class of racists change due to the presence of one
Afro-American.
  Yvonne Criswell, "Mixed Emotions: My Year at Wellesley" [1]

Maybe the easiest way to get from the campus of
the University of Illinois to Urbana High School is just to walk
south on Lincoln Avenue to Washington Street, and then east past
handsome homes to Race Street, where the large educational plant
stands, its entrance facing Carle Park and the arch on its western
boundary, its athletic fields in the rear, and its carefully trimmed
lawns and evergreens on all sides. The high school has an older
substantial section, and a new wing marked 1955 on a white foundation stone. Inside, the corridors are wide and long, exceptionally
long, and lined with hundreds and hundreds of numbered lockers,
1407, 1408, 1409, 1410 . . .
  At 11:16 in the morning a bell rings. Students pour out of classrooms and study halls and suddenly the corridors are alive,
crackling with young people "talking shop," teasing, shuffling
papers into their notebooks, admiring clothes, snatching at books
or long hair or at ideas somewhere. The band rehearsal has
stopped, and the small society of about fourteen hundred students

in this three-year senior high school are in motion, practically in flight, except for those who drag to the next class, to the next assignment, to that evening and to the next day. Homecoming Friday is two days away, October 17, 1969. The football team isn't winning too regularly, but a homecoming queen and her attendants have been selected, and students mutter something about floats and demonstrations.

The bell in the corridor rings again at 11:21, and where moments ago the very power and music of young people, their exhaustion and elation, relief and mischievousness had splashed down the long lockered corridors, now there is that familiar sanitary silence of school. The band has reassembled, and even inside of Principal William Fromm's office their practiced scales may be heard, tidy and precise. Classes have resumed. The thirty minutes devoted to America's first Moratorium Day are over. The day may now move ahead, as usual.

In his new-wing office of painted cinder blocks, his desk placed beneath a three-box cartoon showing an ingenuous hunter devoured by a wizened lion, Principal Fromm speaks of the over two hundred students who had failed to come to school that morning, and who now, presumably, were engaged in "that peace deal" sponsored by their university brothers and sisters, their models, their idols: "It's too bad the kids aren't creative enough to do something on their own. They always go to the university where they follow the university students like sheep. . . . Well, maybe it's better than something being upset here." Maybe so. No occurrences in Urbana High School on October 15. Like most every other American high school on that day, it is peaceful in this "liberal" community where "occasionally we'll have a teacher with a beard."

The official policy of the school on Moratorium Day is political neutrality. One administrator confesses his opposition to the moratorium: "I can't support it if Hanoi's government and groups who want to overthrow America support it," but the same man honors the 10:45 to 11:15 period ordered by Urbana Mayor Charles M. Zipprodt "for the commemoration of the dead of the war." For Principal Fromm, neutrality, not neutralization, is the word. "If teachers are honest, the students will know their political beliefs. But indoctrinating kids is unethical and probably illegal."

Earlier Fromm had publicly announced that "any student who leaves the building Wednesday for reasons other than illness will receive an unexcused absence." On this point, the so-called "political" students, most of them, presumably, now marching on the "quad," have bitterly opposed him. They have fought back just as they did on the student newspaper censorship "business." "They get elected to the student senate and lose their interest in better education, painting student lounges and dress codes. They're interested in moratoriums and students' rights. They want what they can't have." Then, turning his face away so that he speaks in profile, "it makes it tough on administrators and sponsors."

But they are intelligent, these "activists," these "want-what-they-can't-havers." While Fromm cannot with good conscience, or any accuracy for that matter, characterize them or the homes from which they come, he is certain of a correlation between "getting along at home and getting along at school." This is for him the control part of the story. There is a sadness part of the story as well, for there are students, he relates, who, finding home impossible and money available, move to apartments near campus in order to be closer to the souls and spirit of what at this moment seems the best next step and the best alternative to building a sane society. And "if this isn't sad enough for you," then maybe the case of the boy who hasn't seen his father in three months even though they live together in the same house, because the father finds the son's long-haired appearance too ugly, is.

William Fromm's goal is to prepare high school students "for a successful, happy, and productive life when they enter whatever segment of society they enter after school." This means that regulations and norms like dress codes are set by the styles of employees at local banks, businesses and Carson, Pirie, Scott & Company. College-bound students, almost seventy percent of the approximately four hundred twenty-five UHS graduating seniors, must be prepared for achievement and scholastic aptitude tests. They must move ahead in science, foreign languages and math. In this regard, the university helps the high school by accepting superior students in regular freshman and sophomore courses. "Society seems to think that everyone should go to college. We know they won't. Some can't. So you have to get some students prepared to go to work." And just like that, just as though the words had unleashed lightning, the conversation turns to the racial problems in the school. And just like that, one feels, in a sickening metaphor, that fresh sutures have again been ripped open, and that few other topics of conversation will be pursued that day.

"When a student has anxiety about something and wants to hit someone, he'll hit someone of the other race. . . . It's the biggest problem we have . . . and there are fewer immediate solutions we can make." And so there are! And it is the biggest educational problem we have, for this school like so many others on moratorium as well as non-moratorium days, on all days, must, in William Fromm's words, "teach what communities want students to learn." And there is no way of knowing what communities want, even with citizens advisory committees working diligently and honorably on vocational education and school finance. And even if there were ways of knowing a "group's mind," consensus could never be reached, especially on racial attitudes, for these attitudes reflect what they call, and what we call, American pluralism. Good or bad, left or right, center or extreme, rich or poor, there's not going to be consensus here, especially not in a community of working-class blacks and whites, professional whites and blacks, intellectuals and all the rest of them fighting for what they believe in, fighting, perhaps, against what others depend on. There's not going to be consensus here in the lockered corridors, in the social studies class, in the gymnasium, not even in Carle Park, where occasionally students may escape for a few moments to eat their lunch on the grass and smile at the young mothers who push their children on the swings or who dream quietly to themselves as their children find an enrapturing industry in the sand boxes. Indeed one probably would do well to treat consensus on race as Whitehead advised treating simplicity in philosophy: "With doubt."

So the evening meetings about education and economy and rules and styles continue, and the caucus discussions grow in intensity with each faction certain that it must resign itself to four steps forward, three steps back. Four forward and three back, and that, as they say, is the political tempo of the times, here in Urbana, likewise in Boston, Philadelphia, Chicago and Oakland.

But the race issue is what is always there before and after homecoming, Moratorium Day and the World Series; after Washington's and Lincoln's birthdays and Thanksgiving and Christmas and Halloween. It's race that powers the busses bringing the black students from "the end" (the community's north end) every school morning to one side of the building and white students from the rest of the Urbana area to the other side. It's race that silences the men who drive these busses and who argue that their job is to collect the children once in the morning, deposit them once in the afternoon, and not have to see them on the weekends. The race issue says ten trips per week and no more. And it's the race issue that revs black students in the halls and keeps on the tip of their tongue, ready, handy, the anger and data of racial oppression and injustice. To be sure, some spew "the words" as if they had memorized lessons rather than recalled experience; and others hammer out the rancor and rhetoric in an attempt to achieve a militancy that may catapult them to a selfish yet still useful leadership; and others may slip and refer to themselves as Negroes while their friends lash back and teach, "Black, man, black. Don't forget it. Black." But even to strangers, the crying fright, the recognition of powerlessness and that uncomprehended bitterness stay on, and by their presence announce the state and status of race in this one institution:

"The treatment of whites and blacks is unequal."

"When black girls get pregnant they send them home, but the white girls get to stay. You shoulda seen that Nancy What's-her-name with her belly out to here. Ain't that right?"

"You better believe it."

"The administration doesn't know how to discipline blacks. They let us go too far and then they cut us off."

"They won't let us elect a black homecoming queen. They think they've done enough when the attendant is black, or if there's a black cheerleader."

"That's right, man."

"You know what this is?"

"I'm not sure."

"It's integration and separation at the same time. You dig that?"

"They keep bringing in all of these indigenous paraprofessionals."

"They bring in who?"

"They put us in the dumb tracks, that's why we don't go to college."

"They're trying to teach us that we're dumb."

"Right on."

"You know about tracks? Well, that's what they do."

"They won't let us tutor the black kids who aren't smart. That's why we don't go to college."

"That's right. That's right."

"He's right."

Several students pity the administration for its inability or refusal to perceive, as they say, that whereas whites wish to be treated as individuals, blacks want to be treated as "one black, large group." At least, so these certain students say. Still, even with a functioning Black Student Alliance, there's no "black consensus" either. But why should there be?

"Why should we all agree? We're all different, aren't we?"

"You think we all look alike, man?"

"Hey man, let's get out of here."

"Naw. I want to stay and talk."

"I don't trust him. Let's get out of here!"

"Wait, wait, wait, wait, wait."

"Come on, Raymond. We're shuffling."

Like explosions in a steamy tunnel, black voices, histories, proposals and attitudes literally scintillate in the corridors and small office rooms, even as the peace procession to Champaign's West Side Park grows in number and purpose and floods its human tides quietly but persuasively over those "vapid" flat lands many in the East and West continue to dismiss as "the Midwest."

"Is there interracial dating?"

"Who's this guy? He from the college?"

"Sure, they still got some Toms around here."

"Yeah. Like Jo-jo."

"What do you mean, man; I'd like to find me some rich white man with lots of money . . ."

"She would, too. She would."

"You better believe it, baby. I would."

Random interviews with students and faculty reveal white groups who would side with blacks right down the line, on each and every demand, on each and every complaint. They might even join the corridor skirmishes and join the students who march with a ferocious pride and arrogance and then, unexpectedly, slam up against one another in an anger and eroticism that not too many hall guards, young or old, are about to restrain. But there are also groups who, as though we didn't know, given half a chance might bolt from the constraints of public demeanor and spoken promises and fight the black students, their alliance, their names, their habits, and their homes and origins everywhere, and particularly those who live in "the end." There are also groups who reveal what a university chaplain on this first Moratorium Day decries as the greatest sin of all, outright indifference. There is no consensus here. But it also must be known to most by this time that the sophistication and knowledge, alertness and drive found and accepted in more and more young people cannot yet characterize the millions of adolescents who continue to get lumped together as the "younger generation." A Boston area social studies teacher recently told me that while marijuana usage is rampant among his high school students, seventy-five percent of a junior civics class had either never heard of Eugene McCarthy or could not quite place his name in American political history. So sophistication, style and codified knowledge often come to be subsumed in adventure, rebellion and compliance and thereby mislabeled.

In his old-wing office, Assistant Principal Taylor Thomas, himself a black, admits to the lack of an educational orientation in a black community where night gun battles bring terror to thousands of local citizens and headlines to urban newspapers hundreds of miles away. Last night two more shootings, two young men dead. Tonight again, perhaps. One of four black staff members, two of whom work in the physical education department, Thomas differentiates between ghetto savvy and academic attainment, knowing full well the label of Tom some would throw at him because of this. While he insists that one cannot be proud or ashamed of things "he can neither cause nor cure," in truly primordial tones he understands the fire and message of black power, black rage and black pride. And if he could ever let himself go for just a moment . . .

If ever racial justice or its determinations fell to anyone, it has fallen to the few black high school administrators who find that they cannot make a move without criticism from one side or the other, old wing or new wing, left or right, black or white, young or old, rich or poor, top or bottom. They must admit, finally, to the lack of equal opportunity and the built-in "inferiority complex," as they call it and know it, which, as the students will tell you, schools teach along with history and mathematics. But there are also black parents, themselves more knowing in that new way and probably prouder or angrier or more confused than ever before, who, like their white counterparts, insist that their children be taken out of remedial and tutorial programs and inserted at levels where the status is better and the air cleaner but where, Thomas says, "They're not going to make it." There are also white parents, some more silent, but others more daring than ever before, not at all newcomers to "civil rights," who fear that splotches of publicity may render that political tempi four steps forward, five steps back. Four steps forward, five steps back, maybe because too many people everywhere are still interested in battles, explosions, failures and setbacks. The fragments of success and peace don't seem to carry the impact, the pizazz they once did. Every day there are more and more facets of being stigmatized and oppressed, and they all seem reasonable, significant and, of course, worrisome.

Essentially supporting his principal's goals, Taylor Thomas adds "societal change" as one of his educational ideals, along with a permanent end to that inferiority complex. "You don't get over this overnight, but I got it whipped now." Getting this far has allowed him to see how inefficiently institutions are run, and this can only enhance his constantly precarious sense of self. The game can be played by "their" rules and still they can be beaten. But the entire swatch of society is going to have to open up and, as they're saying more and more now, whatever it means, "let it all hang out." Black people are going to have to drive the big machines on construction jobs, assume foreman positions and find offices in new wings as well as in old ones. And, really, that's all that is meant by playing them at their game, and winning.

Perhaps it isn't race so much which preoccupies this one school or this one man, for if the world were truly clean and truly free, and Assistant Principal Taylor Thomas could have his way and his rightful power, he would "get rid of faculty members who can't relate to any students" with a decency and integrity that being human ought to imply. After all, as dean of male students he learns more about the teachers and parents who bring in students to be disciplined than he does about the frightened and repenting students, black and white, who daily stand before him awaiting his rulings. But then again, perhaps it *is* race and the hour-by-hour, day-by-day feelings which come without respite, without moratoriums, from something no one can cause nor cure, from something that hovers all the same in each and every space through which he and about one hundred fifty students pass five days a week: "You don't get rid of it until you walk into a white gathering and you're the only black thing and you're not uncomfortable."

How often had those same words been spoken. But was it not true that the age of the invisible man and what Joel Kovel calls "thingification," [2] had passed, slowly, finally, and was now truly out of sight? All of those wretched confusions of being liberal or not liberal enough, and the inability to speak with a man of another color without the feeling that, like the thin strip of material the photographer slips in and out of his big box camera, race won't slip in between the words only to veil the complicated hates, attractions, antipathy and sensuality.

Every day, it seems, someone is able to state so precisely, so wondrously, the condition of the blacks or of the whites, or of the whites and blacks together. But then by that night, when that other one's words have dropped back into the mist of history, we frightened ones who work our work and hope that others might be free to do the same, are left with that haunting bewilderment and the stack of pledges, resolutions and promises made to an unborn generation, not to mention to our own residual futures.

But then again, what can one man do? What is one woman supposed to be able to do? Or five people? What can they produce as a contribution, as a collective statement, first dreamed up then initiated then acted upon and supported right down to the very end? What can they do to let history know that change is possibility and that despite its human armor, time remains vulnerable? How does one crack not the political positions of those with whom he works, nor the political apparatus that veritably drives the artifactual institutions he and his colleagues and their predecessors have contrived, but the politics of his waking and sleeping existence? How does one alter the stuff of consciousness, even, to such an extent that eventually the materials of dreams are reordered and imagination is recolored, as it were, and everyone is made to feel less angry at night, less frenetic in the day?

How might a person or a group of persons, not celebrities but ones you know really well, become so courageous or daring or just so committed or fed up with it all, that entire communities would come to know of their actions and presence, and all of history learn the exact date on which they have chosen to commence that singular action and that shiny new collective presence? Where exactly do these people come from? And what happens when racial conflicts or the deaths of great men or something we can never know drives them to make a move, drives them to push an institution or a generation, drives them to slap at routinized traditions and stale conventionalism? And do they contemplate or attempt to previse the results of their actions, or is it the case that more often than not they simply cannot play out tomorrow until tomorrow is delivered, even when they believe that ideology and not impulses and racism and not rage direct their interior moves and circumscribe their public behavior?

At times it seems so unreal. At one moment simple persons do little else than teach their classes, check their profits, direct their plays, await their babies. And then, at the next moment, totally unprepared, somewhat unwilling, momentarily helpless, then gathering strength and resources, clutching at the law and at those same artifactual institutions, he or she is caught in the middle of a scrambling of passions and a fury of indignation and indulgence. It all comes together as horror, scandal and war. Everyone connected with it can recall exactly the details, horrid and comical as they now may seem, of each succeeding event, and those in the middle of the hurricane have at last triumphed in penetrating history. For although it may not have been their intention or even in any realm of imagined possibility, they have made single days and nights, the whiteness and the blackness, iridescent, and they can now with but the slightest natural reminders urge their memories to linger on the dates of events which they created and on those days and nights when they in fact helped to turn the world and brighten the moon and the sun.

[2]

On Friday, May 31, 1968, Wellesley Senior High School, Wellesley, Massachusetts, devoted one-half of the school day to studying racism in America, partly in an effort to enlighten students of the then recently published *Kerner Commission Report*. There were panel discussions, movies, speeches, dramatic productions — the works! I went to the high school that morning to participate in a panel discussion with students, hence my presence at most of the morning's events. Upon entering the school, I encountered a rather powerful-looking man. Standing at the head of a corridor, his face somewhat in darkness, his arms folded across his body in an almost self-comforting posture, he looked down at me, shook his head from side to side and uttered the one word "smut." I smiled, a bit terrified, and moved past him, wondering, naturally, what he had seen or heard.

What he had seen and heard had taken place in the gymnasium where bleachers had been set up on both sides of the basketball floor. Students occupied one set, the set facing the entrance. Sev-

eral of us stood at the entrance, viewing the backs of actors playing to an absolutely spellbound young audience. Four actors, presenting segments of plays, poems, even a dramatization of the
sociological study *Tally's Corner,* had the audience enthralled.
They were so enthralled that at one point, during a scene from the
Marat/Sade, in response to an actor's plea for people to stand up
for their rights or something like that, a group of black students
did exactly that. They stood up, looked about rather sheepishly,
and sat down. No one laughed, however, even in embarrassment.
In the main, student seating was segregated predominantly by race
and, less significantly, by sex.

Throughout the performance, the faces of the students, as they
say, told the story. They were utterly involved, swept up in the
fire of black and white dramatists, poets and actors. They laughed
at times; literally squealed with excitement at other times. They
were angry and frightened, perplexed and relieved. School was
good. And I thought, reluctantly, if it takes a *Kerner Commission
Report* and the assassination of a great man, well then, that's what
it takes.

When the dramatic performance ended, the students exploded
with applause. They leaped out of their seats, many wanting to
get close to the actors, perhaps even to touch one. Their spirit was
just as vibrant during the lecture and panel discussions. They
argued, listened, argued some more. They were polite and respectful, but a political restlessness could be felt in their rhetoric. They
wanted in, even though some of them might not have been too
certain of what that meant. They weren't self-conscious about their
status. They just wanted a piece of the action, a piece that had all
at once been promised to them.

The black students, especially, seemed as though some systemic
emergency brake had been released. They had been lurched forward, almost as in a convulsion. Were they actually speaking about
race for the first time publicly? Was this really the first legitimate
open forum on race in this high school which received a few bus
loads of young Boston black pupils each day? It couldn't be the
first time, although there was the account of a teacher who had
taken his class on an excursion to see the movie *In the Heat of the*

Night but had rejected these same students' wishes to speak of their reactions to Martin Luther King's assassination on the grounds that this activity wasn't appropriate for that moment in the year's curriculum. Well, they were talking now. In fact, they refused to stop even after the panels disbanded and the actors and visitors had returned to their city obligations.

Outside the gym in the concrete and brick corridors of the school the atmosphere was electric. This was what is really meant by being turned on. The school had shuddered from the onslaught of movies, plays, lectures and panels, and one could only envy the teachers who would confront those wonderful mobs after lunch. The senior high school of Wellesley, Massachusetts, had taken a courageous leap. I took back all I had felt about suburban high schools, and promised to work a little more on my prejudices. Schools like Wellesley had their problems, but they did the best they could. The school had been turned on, and indeed it had stayed turned on for the rest of that special, special day. I hated to leave the place; it seemed that good. Several teachers, upset by the dramatic presentation, had stomped out of the gymnasium before its completion. They had felt the language to be obscene and inappropriate for the children of the senior high school. But in the main all was fine. This too would pass. Sadly enough for the students, classes would carry on and "normal" curriculum would resume for the last few weeks of the term. But the year had been made, at least for some.

However, the people of Wellesley had other ideas. The fire of the theatrical production and particularly the language from a segment of LeRoi Jones's *The Slave* had ignited the town. It was as if an atomic reactor had blown up, or a low-rent housing project for blacks had been proposed, accepted, built and inhabited in the time it takes to say "Up against the wall!" A school committee meeting the following Monday brought bitter, almost violent discussion, but still reports indicated that the majority of those in attendance supported the May 31 program, movies, panels, LeRoi Jones and all! A few cried "obscene" and wrote letters to newspapers, but a Wellesley College philosopher and town resident represented the other side by writing that poverty, racism and Vietnam were America's genuine obscenities. Most significantly, hearing only secondary reports, the superintendent of Wellesley schools publicly announced support for the entire program. There followed a day or two of silence, and then it started.

All at once the Wellesley *Townsman* became essential reading matter. Letters to the editor came in from the left, right and most oblique center. Parents and teachers wrote of scandal and horror as well as of a community reawakening. Some of them questioned how the program could have been approved, others how it could have been so long in coming. To read the *Townsman* was to hear the frightening roar of a community doing its level best but unable to tolerate this most recent event. In response, two resident families known by many for their "liberal activities" invited the theatrical company to perform the play again in a public place. They suggested the town library. The town selectmen (three elected officers who together fill a position analogous to mayor) voted no, feeling it would only cause unnecessary trouble. The *Townsman* also reported that one parent, a hospital custodian, had contacted the local district attorney's office. Criminal complaints were to be sought and with them the "Wellesley incident" would be born. There would be investigations now, and a court case, perhaps even prison sentences, although this last outcome seemed highly unlikely.

Then came the night of Senator Robert F. Kennedy's assassination. Like so many we commenced our television vigil disbelievingly. Wellesley, too, had heard the news from California, but the incident over *The Slave* had now gained too much momentum to be silenced even by national tragedy and mourning. Machinery moved, people talked, police investigated, and before Senator Kennedy's body had been transferred to St. Patrick's Cathedral five people were notified that applications for criminal complaints had been filed. They were instructed to appear in court the following Tuesday morning for a show cause hearing. The charge was introducing an obscene and indecent play to minors in a place of education. In Massachusetts, the maximum penalty for this crime is five years' imprisonment and a five-thousand-dollar fine. It must be noted that a good bit of precedent, tenuous as it is, stands in the law courts for obscenity charges for literature. The clause, however, that strengthens this precedent is introduction to minors in a place of education.

The five people charged were the drama company's producer; the director of the company's actors; the chairman of the Wellesley Committee to End Racism (having grown up in response to the King assassination, the committee had openly supported the Friday morning programs and had incurred the company's expenses for the performance) ; and the two teachers who seemingly were responsible for inviting the company to the school. One of the two was my wife, Kay.

Upon receiving the notification Kay had gone to the school's principal. He confided that he had misunderstood what the police had said they would do when he turned in the names; he had not expected the part about a criminal complaint. Still underestimating the gravity of the case, he advised Kay that lawyers would not be necessary.

At once the community was split on the issue, although not at all down the middle. With the exception of the students, the majority of Wellesley's population stood opposed to the theatrical production, even to the extent that criminal charges were felt appropriate, apparently, since no one moved to have them dropped. The students indicated slight majority support for the May 31st program. Their support would not be very loud, but loud enough to demonstrate that social and political attitudes now separated the generations of Wellesley by entire lifetimes.

On Saturday morning June 8, following the issuance of application, a surrealistic drama unfolded. It was a Warhol happening, a Mailer movie. Our friends Jerry and Christina had rushed to our home to give support and counsel. Their son Lucas was at once into the candy jars. As it was a hot, dry day, Lucas begged to play outside with Ian and Edie, neighbor's children, in a small plastic wading pool. Arrangements for the Kennedy funeral train were being made. People were flocking to New York, and as I phoned unknown lawyers whose names had been suggested, Kay made coffee for all of us.

I never have been able to fully understand whether one hears various sounds simultaneously, or whether the sounds in fact are heard individually, linearly that is, as one attends to them. In recalling sounds, I always get the feeling they have occurred simultaneously. This one Saturday morning, the surrealistic montage of sounds contained the voices of announcers at St. Patrick's, descriptions of plans for the funeral train from a New York railroad station, the mature voices of unseen lawyers, Kay recounting facts of *The Slave* and, above it all, the giggling chatter of Lucas and Ian. Standing naked in a shallow pool of water, they spoke of their genitals.

There is a totally helpless feeling that comes over people when they become implicated in events like this. It is mitigated somewhat by speaking with lawyers, but like a recurring muscle twinge or thunder, the helplessness and fright return unexpectedly, and too frequently. Sometimes the feeling is comparable to when we lie in bed and think about death and, in a childish way, we can't help but fixate on being no more. Being no more. Then comes that cold, deep shudder that scintillates throughout our bodies, and we must physically jolt the feeling out of consciousness. So it was during those days. Complainants received no news from Wellesley except that an open school committee meeting had been announced for the Monday evening before the court hearing, primarily so that feelings might be aired and details explained and justified.

On Monday morning, June 10, a Boston radio station broadcasted an editorial condemning Wellesley's excessive reaction. It started with a sentence like, "The suburb of Wellesley is a quiet, college town, with large homes and well-combed yards," but its strength was apparent. One had to marvel, moreover, at the speed with which people hear, react, commit themselves, and then make available copies of their commitment. But this was happening on all sides as the community's polarization took on the proportions of a giant nuclear physics experiment.

On Monday night it rained. When Jerry and I arrived at the school auditorium only two people were present. A man sat across the aisle from us. He sat sternly erect and perfectly silent except for the sounds of his heavy breathing. Then he turned to the woman, the single other person in this large hall, and said something like, this time they had gone too far and that they had to be stopped. She agreed. Kay had felt the meeting to be too complicating so she had stayed home to grade papers.

After long moments of silence, the auditorium began to fill. Students rushed to sit in front. They would have camped on the floor had they been allowed. Handsome students poured down the aisles, some dressed in the costumes we associate with hippies. This took special courage that one particular night, but many young people don't compromise themselves, and their styles clearly are a fundamental part of their sense of self. Television reporters, too, strutted about wishing to be observed perhaps. Their recognizable faces momentarily took many of us out of our political moods.

The long, sloping aisles were kept empty, but along the perimeter of the auditorium and in the exits, students, parents and teachers were everywhere. The hall was jammed. The noise swelled, then diminished suddenly as television lights splashed on the stage where the Wellesley School Committee, led by the Superintendent of Schools, paraded, single file from stage left. At the time of these hearings, one woman sat on this committee and served as its chairman.

The exciting although anxious proceedings of that Monday night meeting might best be described as a rather grotesque fugue, its inner voices audible only to those sufficiently aware politically to listen for them. *The Slave* contains words some had felt to be obscene. In the particular performance in question, it also contained a scene in which a standing black man leans over a seated white woman, nuzzles her a bit as she modestly resists, and, according to the actor who did it, gives her a small kiss on the side of the neck. In the play, the two are former marriage partners and the parents of two children. This scene became known as the "chase and rape" scene. The so-called obscene word, "fuck," to be precise, became abbreviated and known simply as "the word."

Along with segments of other works carefully selected and integrated by the theatrical company into a continuous performance depicting black feelings and philosophies over the last twenty years, a portion of *The Slave* had been presented on the gymnasium floor of a white, upper class Boston suburban high school. About twelve black families live in this community. Three years before, Boston's METCO (Metropolitan Council for Educational Opportunities) program sought to gain rights to bus twenty-five black students from the Roxbury district into Wellesley Senior High School with its population of about thirteen hundred pupils. There was at the time some protestation. Convening to oppose the METCO proposal, a small group calling themselves Operation Abolition METCO had instituted a town vote. However, a sizable majority of the ten percent of voters going to the polls only for this one issue had voiced their acceptance of METCO.[3] After this rather difficult go, Wellesley had consented, and in the fall of 1966, twenty-five blacks rolled in each day, hung around the local METCO office, went to class, hung around the METCO office and were bussed home. There was tension, but mostly a distressing bewilderment remained. Many white students at the time confessed desires to be helpful, and large numbers of Wellesley homes opened their doors to blacks. Some students dated in Wellesley or spent weekends in Wellesley homes. Rarely did this pattern reverse itself, however, as very few Wellesley students made weekend night drives to the homes of their new colleagues in Roxbury and Dorchester.

Still, accepting even these few black students in Wellesley was no mean accomplishment. As recently as 1969, METCO had abolished its programs in several Boston suburbs where resident opposition had proved to be too much to overcome. More generally, the strategy of bussing now hangs in the web of the federal government.

Wellesley survived, however. Indeed, the busload was doubled in the second year of the METCO program with no further town protests. Students were not necessarily encouraged to speak about the racial "merger" during class time, although for different reasons more than a few, understandably, were unhappy over those two black faces in the rear of the classroom. The issue, as they always say, was swept under the rug except for the blacks who, even today, receive gawking stares and long looks as they move about the town, as shoppers, moviegoers and sight-seers. For the principal it all seemed to be working out just fine. We even got a new end on the football team, he told reporters.

Many fears, fantasies and brutalizing problems are awakened when school integration of this form takes place. These problems typically are not known by the critics of segregation who stand on the sidelines rooting for change. They are, however, more than a bit familiar to those who find themselves in the middle of racial scrimmages, and locked in to the point where social and historical precedent folds up, comes undone, and then reappears in bold new costumes and stunning modern masks. It is feared, for example, that blacks will become the favorites; that they will receive special attention; that the "good" teachers will have less time for the whites; that blacks will bring drugs, dirty music, sex and immorality into the high school; that they'll befriend the whites, or ignore the whites, or intimidate the whites, or kill the whites. And it is feared that blacks will want to date the whites, and that the whites will want this as well. And then one day, you'll see, a black man is going to lean over a white woman and kiss her, and we'll be sorry we started this whole thing.

In the year before the *Slave* scandal, Wellesley had had a drug scandal, a short skirt problem and a long hair problem. Its history was not unlike that of other American suburbs. Each case brought the community's venom and fear up to higher and higher levels. Some felt that the drug case had been poorly handled by the school's administrators, particularly after some students had been suspended for confessing that on occasions during the summer vacation, literally months before, they had experimented with marijuana. At the time of the drug case, students' anger had been unleashed and many openly protested the administration's action. But others formed a vigilante group and waited after school one day to cut the hair of a "hippie-looking" boy who by his appearance was disgracing the school and the entire community.

Each time, with the skirts and the hair and the drugs, parents, naturally, had intervened. Punishment was demanded and punishment was meted out. And each time, Wellesley, to the discontent of its residents and surrounding neighbors who necessarily receive the overflow of guilt by geographical association, had made the headlines of the Boston newspapers.

LeRoi Jones, therefore, was just the unfitting end to a perfectly traumatic year. This time, as the man in the empty auditorium said, they had gone too far. But who exactly were "they"? For that matter, who ever is "they"? Well, "they" were the teachers who supported the program. The parents knew about "them" as a sizable group, but, in fact, hardly a majority of the school's faculty had signed a letter in the *Townsman* supporting the play and the program, apologizing for the furor, and hoping, almost pleading that future programs of this sort would be presented.

"They," however, were not among the large list of signers of another letter from teachers opposing the play and pressing for censuring action of some sort. Several teachers were themselves barely able to tell which "they" to join. One teacher, for example, confessed his appreciation of the program but felt he could not sign the support letter in that he had neither seen nor read the play. This seemed reasonable enough until his signature appeared several days later on the published opposition letter. (This act is reminiscent of the following line uttered in the midst of the crisis by a distraught parent: "I haven't read the play but I've read just enough to know it shouldn't be read.")

"They" were the school committee as well, and more than anyone else the Superintendent of Schools, who had advocated and maintained METCO from its inception. Knowing no more about *The Slave*, its performance at the school on May 31, or black literature generally, than any of the people urging censure, this man had officially proclaimed his support of the entire program.

"They" were the local residents who had sponsored the program through the Committee to End Racism and then had proposed that the play be performed again in Wellesley. Along with the superintendent, these people seemed the most pernicious, as they were locals, neighbors, the very people with whom one shopped, voted and stood on the sidelines of the high school football games. They at least should have known better.

Last, and most uncomfortably, "they" were also students. Literally hundreds of them had instituted and signed a petition arguing for the success of the May 31 program and urging that similar programs be offered in the future. Like their teachers and parents, these students had responded with quick, penetrating action. Notice of their petition was reported in the *Townsman* while the petition itself was being prepared for presentation to the school committee. Political action, we learn, belongs in rough and smooth hands alike.

All of these voices, all of these interests had produced a resentment often diffuse, always unsettled, always confusing. No public incidents meant no reason for direct action, but the anger persisted, and on the night of Monday, June 10, as the rain pelted down on this one suburban Massachusetts high school, the anger, in its most grandiloquent and ignominious form, burst out. It was an evil catharsis; the instincts had discovered the objects of their energy, and the fugue commenced.

The school's principal spoke first. He claimed responsibility in one area, this being his decision not to intervene in the second performance of the production as emotions were running high after the first. (One of the actors stated that had anyone requested *The Slave* to be deleted from the second performance, the company would have either consented or canceled the performance altogether. They would not have gone against the wishes of *any* official school representative, including a student.) The principal showed sympathy for the anger expressed on both sides and voiced support of "free speech." But he provoked wild applause with the words: "But I go on record that the type of language used in that portion of *The Slave* should not be used before an audience of high school students." Moments later he nearly brought the house down: "I believe the young men and women in high school today should be made aware of the problems they will be facing in their world of tomorrow. But these problems do not have to be voiced with four-letter words, and I can pledge you a repetition of such a performance as *The Slave* will not again be given as long as it is my privilege to be the principal of Wellesley Senior High School."

Following the principal, several representative persons of the community spoke briefly. A teacher association official hoped that the issue now might be dropped, as did a gentleman of the clergy.

Both expressed misgivings about the play's language but seemed content that the matter had played itself out. But it hadn't quite; the second voice of the fugue was just audible.

A woman was now speaking, reminding the audience first that she was not an American, only married to one, and second that she had not prepared a speech. Her point, however, was well made. Teachers should maintain total control of classrooms and not permit pupils to have their way in discussions. Where she came from, teachers permitting freedom and open discussion of this sort "are investigated." Like the principal's, her words were well received.

Next a teacher spoke. He was an opponent of the performance. Invoking the names of John Fitzgerald Kennedy and Lyndon Baines Johnson, he described the early days of his career at Wellesley High School and utter amazement at the changes that had occurred in the school during his brief leave of absence. There had been significant changes, clearly instigated by an easily recognizable group of recently appointed young teachers.

His was a difficult speech for those students and teachers who either emotionally or intellectually honor and obey the principles of academic freedom. Teachers accusing teachers or testifying against them seems to go against the ethics of many educators but, more importantly, depicts for students the cracking of an authority structure in which they might like to believe. Most everyone admits that the pluralistic nature of society must be taught in school, but witnessing the bare knuckle fighting of one's parents or parental figures as they bid for divorce and settlement of a political and social estate is a trifle more shocking than one cares to admit. For many it is far more frightening than the language of *The Slave*. Equally frightening for many students during those weeks was the performance of their parents, both that Monday night and from that night on in the privacy of their homes. Many were to see their parents, as they said, for the first time, in a way, and while some would be more proud than ever before, others would be wounded by this the first collision with hypocrisy.

It is inconsequential that the teacher speaking himself resorted to four-letter words both that night and in the press to emphasize the intensity of his feelings. It is not inconsequential, however, that his speech introduced the fugue's third voice, an attack on the school committee and, especially, the superintendent. In its way, it was the preamble to a speech by the local state representative whose words were forceful and comforting to parents, if not a bit platitudinous. He couldn't stand idly by, he walked together with Negroes, fought arm and arm and marched shoulder to shoulder with the founders of METCO. Some of the students groaned, but only a few seemed aware of the purpose of his political enterprise. For his talk served to remind the audience, the adult audience, really, that they alone possessed ultimate control over their schools, the students, faculty and all guiding committees. The speech also roused the drowsy bitterness toward the METCO decisions of two and three years back, and the unhappy failure, for some, of Operation Abolition METCO.

A housewife-parent spoke next. She felt the play was important, but when she told her fellow residents to take their heads out of the ground and listen to the world of poverty and despair about them, the audience, like the furies, chanted, "Speak 'the word,' " "Speak 'the word,' " "Speak 'the word.' "

Next, a psychiatrist-parent gently assured those assembled that according to his reading of scientific literature, nasty language had no lasting effect. "Cool it, Wellesley," he prescribed, and commented upon the gravity of Senator Robert F. Kennedy's death and the relative insignificance of a town's uproar over a few words in a play that had already been produced on the New York stage. They had to applaud him, partly because he was a doctor, partly in appreciation of a slain Senator. But many didn't like it. I thought he might have been crying as he walked, heavily, up the long aisle and sat down.

A black woman was recognized by the chairman and with her words, finally, came what was to be the fugue's final voice and abrupt conclusion of the evening. From one of Wellesley's few black families, she commenced by recounting that she had quietly told an earlier speaker, the woman advocating teacher investigations, that she hadn't liked her remarks. The woman had responded, "If you didn't like them then why don't you go back to Africa where you came from?" With this, many students gasped, horrified. Years ago, the woman was continuing, remarks like this went unchallenged, but no more.

Directly in front of me, a white man leaned over to a black man and asked, "Who's that speaking?" The black man didn't know. The white man seemed surprised and annoyed. How was it possible that this black man did not know that black woman?

Now, with the woman's talk concluded, and with the excitement and anger truly at fever pitch, a young man, and recent graduate of the school, stood before the packed audience. His posture spoke of the many battles raging within him, some perhaps rather private. He waited for silence. His youth anticipated his support of the program. So far, the sexes seemed fairly evenly divided on the issue, but the young seemed consistently on just one side. At least on this one night, among the young primarily supporters of *The Slave* were in attendance.

The boy stood almost contentiously, still waiting for silence and the right moment. No necktie, no sport jacket. "Some of you have objected to the program and its language," he started. These were approximately his words. Well, he was going to quote a line from the play. A pause. He waits again, looking at us, his sense of the dramatic rather acute. Then he speaks again. "Sit the fuck down." Days before, the roof of Wellesley, Massachusetts, had blown off. Now the walls had collapsed. "Stop him!" they cried. "Get him off of there." "Who the hell is that kid?" In grief, women placed their hands over their mouths. Men shook their fists. Students shrieked. It was a furious score, the instruments blaring to some incredible but unwritten finale, but this one young man wasn't anywhere near done. Again he was standing there, serenely, quietly, waiting for silence and a second chance.

Well, while some object to it, "I first heard the word 'fuck' when I was five years old in Wellesley, Massachusetts." There was something else about by people who go to church, but this was lost in a frenetic din. "Kill him!" "Drown him!" "Fire him!" "Suffocate him!" "Where the hell are the cops?" "Why don't they do something!" The walls of Wellesley were totally razed now, and it seemed as though the very foundation had given away. Wellesley seemed to be no more. It was as if it was all gone. Screaming and yelling, dismayed, threatening, angered, crying, frantic, they piled out of the auditorium. At once, a policeman entered from the front, spoke momentarily with the committee chairwoman and hauled the youth from the auditorium, his arm twisted behind his back. (A reporter later explained that the police had requested a decision: would she stop the boy or should he, the policeman? In her fear and horror, she approved of his intervention, and in one hysterical moment the boy was gone and the auditorium was up for grabs.) Unbelievable. Unforgettable.

Behind me a young girl had begun to sob inconsolably. Wanting to comfort her, I led her through the crowd and out of the auditorium. We started to go outside but the driving rain forced us in again. Returning, we saw the boy, held by the police and calling for help, being dragged down a corridor. It was the proverbial movie scene. But I had assumed responsibility for the girl. Then an elderly woman appeared from the crowd with a face, really, of all of our grandmothers', our white grandmothers, loving, kind, accepting. She saw the young girl's tears and my own desperation and the boy in the distance. I motioned to leave the girl in her charge so that I could go down the hall when she spoke: "What the crap is bothering her?"

Absolutely stunned, and, I must admit, a trifle amused, I left the girl, totally bewildered, and chased down the hall after the boy, the police and the press. By this time they had all returned. As I rushed by an office I heard and saw a lawyer demanding the youth's rights, and from my left, disbelieving, I heard "the word" spoken again from the auditorium. As it turned out, the evening's final address, made by one of the school's assistant principals, had contained it. Then, running into the rain and the night, I saw them all exiting. Everyone was bundling up, seeking his car, dashing for home. The meeting had been adjourned and the real drama of Wellesley Senior High School had concluded.

What followed in the subsequent days and months is much like the actual court hearing, details within, rumors, pieces fitting together without. The confusion at the police station that Monday night and the attempts made by many people to reassure a sleepy and frightened father that his son was courageous and supported by large groups of neighbors were resolved in a public apology by the boy the following morning just before the show cause hearing. The machinations of the court lessened the burden on this young man and his town, but one always wonders what such outcomes would be if all events were just as they were except that the protagonist was black. This is unfair, perhaps, but surely many "unfair" thoughts tease one's sensibilities in these times.

As for the hearing involving the two teachers, the theater personnel and the chairman of the Committee to End Racism, a continuance was issued on the evidence that, as a Boston newspaper reported it, one of the complainants, a married teacher, my wife, was expecting a baby. The decision for a continuance was made behind closed doors. Lawyers and reporters tried to interpret the moods of the prosecuting police chief and judge, but too much was inferential and nothing concrete could be discerned. More confusing was the separation of teachers as they milled about that morning, waiting for court to convene. The teachers acting as witnesses to the performance stood here, the complainants there. Several people carried messages back and forth. It was an unpleasant scene, particularly as the morning papers were filled with reports of the previous night.

One purpose for a continuance, we are told, is to let combatants cool off. In this instance, a second continuance in fact was issued as the birth of our daughter prevented Kay from appearing at the announced date. The hearing was then rescheduled for September 11. At the time it seemed like a million years off. Apparently the cooling-off period worked. When the million years had elapsed and September had come, the town seemed eager to get on with life and "repress" the thoughts of the previous spring.

As in all legal cases, this one too possessed its share of events implying psychodynamics, people's frustrations and urgent needs to retaliate. Too frequently lawyers must take all the aggression, righteous indignation and fear and transform them into legible, legal, admissible briefs. Often it is done brilliantly, much to the dissatisfaction of outraged and flamboyant clients like myself who scream for issues and ideologies. In law courts, however, issues don't assume precedence, and ideologies are hidden in the woodwork and balustrades of legal chambers. While it clearly has its third and fourth gears, the engine of the courtroom, for uninitiated observers, seems to clump along at a snail's pace. Still, snails by their very pace show a certain dignity, thoughtfulness, and a special natural steadfastness.

The court procedure again required waiting and deliberation. Before commencing, the women teachers, witnesses and complainant, conversed for the first time in months. These particular witnesses, however, were never called. Two male staff members only were asked to recount their observations and impressions. Both had been troubled by the performance. One found it, along with other sections of the dramatic presentation, "disgusting," and had walked out. It was he I had encountered in the self-embracing pose muttering "smut." The other, a young guidance counselor, was eager to have matters resolved. One sensed his desire to reunite the faculty and be done with the *Slave* affair forever. Neither wanted harm to come to anyone, not to the students nor to the complainants. Importantly, both stressed the socially redeeming nature of the play and the entire performance generally. Importantly, both denied that anything had been sexually arousing. These two features, the infamous socially redeeming and prurient interest clauses, are fundamental requirements for legal rulings on obscenity.

But the criteria proved to be insufficient in this hearing as the judge first refused to consider *The Slave* as part of a continuous presentation of segments of dramatic works arranged in historical sequence and then ruled the play obscene for minors. He did, however, excuse the complainants on the grounds that given the witnesses' testimonies, they could not be charged for introducing the obscene play. His definition of introduction meant simply "Ladies and gentlemen, boys and girls, I would like to introduce the actors and actresses. . ." And since no one does "introduce" dramatic performances as one would acts in a variety show, all five people were excused. In summary, then, a crime had been committed, but these were not the criminals, although newspaper and television reports left the latter fact somewhat ambiguous.

To say the least, the decision was a complicated and confusing one. "Even liberals" questioned the fact that the judge would claim that a crime had been committed but not convict the complainants. "Either you say no crime, or crime and convict." Many declared the ruling should have been contested, if not clarified. Did the judge mean that he still wanted to make arrests, or was he placating all the involved parties? The police, after all, had unearthed a crime, but the lawyers had successfully "defended" their clients. So, for the moment, no one would be legally injured. The judge did say, however, that if a criminal could be unearthed, he would entertain the case again.

But there are other types of injuries, and, predictably, the most vulnerable in these cases are those persons residing in the community, the ones who cannot so easily move away from the heat of the action. The two families who had advocated repeating the dramatic performance were pressured to leave. Indeed, one story had it that their landlords ousted them: The wife of the chairman of the Committee to End Racism began to receive cold stares from those she once counted as friends. Possibly because of this scornful pressure, but possibly not, this family, too, left the community. Several faculty members resigned. Others pledged to do the same the following year, and when the time came they honored these pledges. Black families also threatened to pull out. The former chairman of the history department, who worked on the May 31 program, departed for a neighboring high school, but final approval of his job was detained during the long ordeal. Reasons for the delay still are not clear.

Months, years later, the school continues to clean up. Few persons, apparently, speak about the episode during class time or any time, for that matter, when students are around. Students have reported that all has been swept under the rug. In September following the incident a severe pass system was enforced by which students had to show written permission to be late to class or linger in the halls. To prevent and control future scandals, several school custodians were deputized by the local police chief. A proposed field trip to see the movie *Romeo and Juliet* was prohibited by an assistant principal on the grounds that its nude scene might provoke reactions similar to those occurring in the

spring of LeRoi Jones. The male teacher complainant sought
public exoneration and the principal seemed eager to authorize it,
although earlier he had uttered "No comment" in response to the
judge's decision. Exoneration, of course, implies absolution of an
admitted guilt. Rumor had it, too, that a liberal school committee
member would soon resign. If he did, his resignation would be
filed on top of the one submitted by the superintendent soon after
the scandal had receded. How these events connect remains uncertain, although some bits are well known but not reportable.

All the events are important, however, as the authoritarian responses to *The Slave* and the dramas coming out of Chicago tend
to turn some students overnight into revolutionaries and anarchists, or so it seems. In times like these, the world seems so terribly unjust that a transitional period of "becoming political" is
junked, and students are brilliantly transformed from readers of
politics to outright warriors. This is what some people mean when
they talk about "becoming radicalized." The phrase, however, is a
bit overdetermined, for often what it implies is fighting vigorously
for a short term against the establishment on one explicit issue
that deeply matters. Thus, many so-called conservative residents
"were radicalized" by the government's handling of the oil leaks
in Santa Barbara. But these people, most probably, would not at
all identify themselves either in style or politics with "notorious"
campus radicals whom presumably they oppose just as vehemently.
Yet whether or not radicalization of this sort enhances one's sympathy for the purposes and intensity of campus politics is not
known.

Like its local high school, the town of Wellesley has also been
cleaning up. In a way it is like a young woman caught in a compromising position having to adjust her hair and straighten her
skirt and stockings so to appear properly innocent. For one brief
instant it looked as though Wellesley would again make headlines after the first court hearing when a sailor sought sanctuary
in one of the town's churches. The crowds returned and rather
hurriedly the sailor was led away. Days later, students recounted
the obscenities they had heard on this occasion, and shook their
heads in recalling the relative mildness and absolute safety of *The*

Slave. Reconsidering the town's one-year history of tribulations, one student registered his vote for the year's one really obscene event: the afternoon some Playboy bunnies "took on" some local men's group in a softball game on the field of the high school.

On the night of the court hearing, Boston's educational television station produced "The Wellesley Incident." The program contained the entire dramatic production including *The Slave*, performed as it had been on the gymnasium floor, and with one exception, by the identical actors. Several words, however, were bleeped in accordance with television regulations. The performance was followed by separate discussions, first among some parents and a history teacher from a neighboring community, and then among students from Wellesley and Roxbury. The program concluded with the adult group returning, now having listened to the students. Depending upon one's point of view, the program was a success or failure, interesting or foolish. Depending upon one's age and point of view, it was the adults or students who really spoke to the major issues. Some local newspaper critics wrote that the students treated the issue of race, whereas the adults got a bit too engrossed in sex. Even Sigmund Freud was brought into the argument as one parent, apropos of something, questioned the teaching of psychoanalytic theory to high school students. One got the impression that psychoanalytic theory might have meant sex.

The "Wellesley incident" once again provoked more negative than positive phone call reactions. Some Wellesley teachers complained that the "chase and rape" scene had been toned down. Others felt that in the presence of soft lights and a theatrical set the scene had more impact on television than it had had in the gymnasium. But in comparing the present and past, one juggles immediate perceptions with recollections and reconstructions of perceptions, for each has its unique history and context. Thus, not only do aesthetic distinctions become blurred; one wonders whether external reality can ever hope to meet the standards of excitement and unrest erected by one's fantasies. In some cases, moreover, fantasies preclude perception. A Roxbury teacher, for example, explained that a colleague of hers had refused to watch the program, or even read *The Slave*, for, having seen a picture

of the female teacher complainant in the newspaper, she reasoned
that given that short skirt "the play was obviously obscene."

The play, however, is not so obviously obscene. For that matter,
very few aspects of the Wellesley affair are obvious. Most clear,
perhaps, is the raw power of a community. In Wellesley this power
necessarily affected a court decision as well as the personal decisions and destinies of several individuals. One such individual, the
high school principal, chose to obey the demands of the community's louder voices. To some, the reported fact that he gave the
names of five people to the Wellesley police chief before an investigation had been made is no more egregious than his reluctance
to uphold academic freedom, support his faculty, at least until
details had been articulated, and assume responsibility for that
entire day in May. No official faculty meetings were called to discuss the case. And yet, while he might have intervened at crucial
times, he cannot be blamed, for the case is but a paradigm of a
community controlling its public schools. As one parent argued,
paying taxes gives parents the right to have a say in what goes on
in their children's education. The tax legitimates parental intervention; hence the principal, like all school employees, becomes a
servant of the taxpayers. In many respects, therefore, the Wellesley affair represents a profound tragedy, maybe even *the* profound
tragedy of contemporary secondary schools. Although there has
been little or no precedent for it, there comes a time, alas, when
teachers and principals must be honored as professionals and not
viewed as indentured servants or hired tutors. If taxpayers insist
on teachers earning credentials, it would seem that they must begin
to honor the privileges and duties that these credentials adjudicate.

Furthermore, there must be some consistency in the rationales
for interventions, since it is empirically true that parents normally
intervene in school socialization functions but rarely in academic
ones. Parents' brigades, therefore, seem to march to the call of
socialization procedures and public scandals. It's pot and hemlines
and haircuts and LeRoi Jones that bring them in and oblige principals to act as sheriffs. For the teachers involved, irrespective of
their political position, these interventions would seem degrading
and emasculating. As all of these points require elaboration; spe-

cial treatment is given them in Chapter 8. Yet one last point must be mentioned now because it demonstrates a serious inconsistency in parental interventions.

The decision of the hearing, marking as it did an end to the Wellesley case, failed to make front-page news, although *Playboy* magazine picked up the story only to treat it inaccurately and insensitively as one might a dirty joke. The case, which initially had occupied the front pages, was at the end preempted by the stories coming from Boston's Roxbury and Dorchester districts where black residents had begun a battle to insert black principals in predominantly black schools. During the time of the Wellesley hearing, five white teachers had been fired by the Boston School Committee for supporting protests in favor of black principals, a move calculated to help this community gain some say in the determination of their children's education. And so these distinctly different communities, distanced from one another by a short bus ride made ten times a week now by about seventy-five black students, carried on their simultaneous wars of autonomy and self-determination, as racism and maybe total annihilation as well hung in the balance.

For everyone involved, cases of this sort generate one heartache after another. One doesn't know what to do with his anger or sense of helplessness which so rapidly turns to futility and despair. Over the summer, complainants received threats, hostile phone calls and viciously obscene letters. Yet, as funny as it seems, the playful jibes of friends like "Do they have a place for babies in prison?" and "You'll be able to visit your husband once a month," hurt us more than the incoherent letters and calls of the anonymous which literally reek of an indescribable illness of which they have little knowledge and appreciation. Then again, it may not be their illness at all.

How often during the hot July and August nights did we wonder together whether our feelings, for even these tender moments, could possibly compare with what some blacks feel every moment of their lives? Were we too extreme, or was this *their* helplessness and *their* objectless anger and abject rage? We wondered too about intellectuals, whose satisfaction, it so often seems, comes about through being informed and whose action so often ends at the point of being informed. Were *we* in the end the supreme danger of the black revolution? Were *we* the unmarked minefield of their battleground, the impediments on those crusty surfaces they call their earth? Can *we* be trusted to be there when the going is tough, and when nothing less than life and death issues and not eroticism or impulses or psychopathologies or social structures warn us of the danger that tomorrow might bring?

In retrospect, the Wellesley affair now seems a rather large hump on the plain of the past. My own thoughts keep returning to the voices of a man and a boy. The former, a lawyer, came out of the hearing despairing. Too often had he experienced what he termed the irrelevance of the law and the unnecessary fright of naïve clients. The boy, a member of the student TV panel on "The Wellesley Incident," had, as I recall, sought alliance with a fiery black student. He had wanted in. He had wanted to join the struggle. The black youth told him something to the effect that you need us but we don't need you. So there they were, as together and apart as the entire masses of black and white America.

Perhaps this is as it must be, but we too reject America if we ignore white problems, the only problems really, to which we maintain open access. Out of anger, "decent" people were urged to leave Wellesley, the community where surely the racial plague of the 'Sixties had metastasized. But this must not be the result. People must not leave. Too many rich, white suburban high school students "want in"; they want to be a part of a viable, honorable America, and only schools will provide that opportunity, however limited, if families fail. The students don't necessarily want revolution or scandal, they merely want teachers and administrators who will help them to pull back society's rugs and examine everything that has been swept underneath.

It is nothing short of a denial to say that the language of *The Slave* is street language. It's also home language. Moreover, it's nothing short of a denial to focus attention only on ghettos if this means forsaking large groups of extremely talented students who, as tomorrow's inevitable leaders, will truly be "disadvan-

taged" if educators revolt and leave them restless amidst their inherited opulence. Yet even their restlessness, as trying and choking
as it soon may be, cannot take proper account of the world one
thousand miles to the west in Urbana and twelve miles to the east
in Roxbury. With simple words and simple deeds, groups of Americans are always working to transcend a level of existence that has
forever rendered them "objects" and "things" in a land where freedom and possibility were known to launch their foreign brothers
and sisters to stations in a social space as far away as the moon
and the sun.

chapter 8

Dressing Down the Naked Ape

The repressiveness of the whole lies to a high degree in
its efficacy: it enhances the scope of material culture, facilitates
the procurement of the necessities of life, makes comfort and
luxury cheaper, draws ever-larger areas into the orbit of
industry — while at the same time sustaining toil and
destruction. The individual pays by sacrificing his time, his
consciousness, his dreams; civilization pays by sacrificing
its own promises of liberty, justice and peace for all.
                    Herbert Marcuse, *Eros and Civilization*

In referring to sixty-four years of his work Salvador
Dali observed, "Happy is he who causes scandal." Presumably the
kind of scandal Dali had in mind implied the powerful impact of
artistic expression on communities less than prepared for the shock
of aesthetics and sociology. Scandal, then, had something to do
with changing what was once agreed upon, what was once con-
sensually appreciated, once morally valued and ultimately settled.
One assumes, moreover, that witnesses of scandal are psychologically bowled over backward, and that in their collective reeling for
equilibrium, parts of a greater culture jolt forward a bit, in some
temporal, social or spiritual wave.

So it was with the Wellesley scandal, with its words judged to be
obscene for minors and that morsel of sexualized nuzzling that
through time and with the bowling and reeling grew to proportions of a "chase and rape." Almost predictably, the town had
swung hard to the right with the force of a power sweep. People
were cut down if they got in the way of the so-called "conserva-

tives," and rather than try to disrupt the interference many simply galloped away. School rules, regulations and rituals became omnipresent and sacrosanct, and while the students surreptitiously whispered the rhetoric of radicalism and revolutions, administrators, faculty and custodians monitored the locker rooms, lavatories, and parking lots more assiduously than ever before. As if this were not enough, some of the heroes of the end sweep against *The Slave* announced their candidacy for town selectman and school board member. Several "infamous liberals" resigned and departed. It appeared that townspeople no longer were reeling but instead affirming the temporal and spiritual stakes of their ground and of their civilization. The stakes appeared to have been driven into a cement of social permanence and irrefutability.

Then suddenly two rather remarkable events took place, one totally unpredictable, the other seemingly unprecedented. First, the two outspoken opponents of *The Slave* lost in their primary bids for election as selectman and school board member. Although they possessed qualifications, knowledge and long-standing professional experience, they were beaten. So, borrowing language of an irresistible metaphor, the sweep had been detained if not stopped by the sidelines. The town had changed its mind a bit; it had, in effect, ruled against end sweeps in either direction.

The second event represented the culmination of a history remarkable but becoming a bit more commonplace these days. Early in their senior year two or three students approached their young history teacher with suggestions for a reading assignment. Over the summer each had read Desmond Morris's *The Naked Ape* and felt it to be ideal for the senior social science course. Respecting their advice, the history teacher read the book, only to become equally enchanted with it. The class then took a vote and decided to read the book, but not as a regular required assignment. Indeed, even discussion of the book was not going to be mandatory. These options seemed best, as the students wisely feared that the second chapter, entitled simply "Sex," might prove an obstacle difficult to overcome. True enough. The department head disregarded the students' and teacher's thoughtful proposal as well as the book's excellent reviews, and ruled it off-limits. Sympathizing with the constraints placed on their teacher and anticipating the negative decision, the students had already suggested that the potentially scandalous chapter need not be officially discussed. It was to no avail, however. The book was deemed too provocative for seniors, of whom most would move on to college and others to military service and jobs.

Receiving a second disapproval from an assistant principal and still a third from the principal, who had not read the book, the teacher chose to take his case to a "higher court," the school committee. The heat went on again in Wellesley. For a time it looked as though the previous spring's open school committee meeting dealing with *The Slave* would be repeated. At that time, the townspeople had argued the merits of such literature, and in so doing had displayed for contemporary ghetto warriors like Kenneth Haskins [1] what real community power looks like stripped to the waist for fighting. The *Naked Ape* meeting, however, was closed. No one was invited. No members of the press, no outsiders, no visitors. The decision came out three to two in favor of the teacher. He could assign the entire *Ape* with all its nakedness, providing students brought in letters of permission from their parents.

The following spring an interesting development took place. For unknown reasons, the history teacher's contract was not renewed. As of the next September, he would have to find a new home. But, as he himself wrote, "due to the ineptness of the administration and anti-student atmosphere of the school, I would have left anyway."

These stories, these scandals are not apocryphal. Neither are they especially sensational. They are, however, paradigmatic, for they depict the structure of many suburban high schools and the relative power of the public school's four major constituencies: parents, administrators, teachers, and students. They symbolize, furthermore, the nature and philosophy of education, for certain suburbanites, anyway.

Truthfully, one cannot state flatly that all schools kill students' spirits or destroy their minds through a resolute insistence that irrelevant curriculum programs be dogmatically pursued. In literally thousands of American classrooms one finds students who love their work, worship some teachers *and* administrators, and lament the swift passage of high school's gentle time. Too many students express an excitement and involvement in their schoolwork to convince me that all is bad and that nothing is salvageable. (My wife, now on leave from her English teaching assignments, is visited by her students of one, two, and three years back. And the gleam of respectful reticence and adoration in their eyes, along with a genuine but not obsessive openness, assures me that something wondrous took place in her classroom. Partly it came about because of her, partly because of these young people; but mainly it evolved because of all of them together. Something wondrous took place, often, if not regularly, something predicated on all of them being there.)

This is not to deny, however, the fundamental purpose of schools, which presently seems to focus about the processes and implications of socialization. Like most all schools, suburban high schools emphasize dimensions of behavioral appropriateness on the one hand and the management and evaluation of present activities primarily in terms of their future meanings on the other. These two aspects, appropriate demeanor and the task of shuttling people on to college, career, and ultimately "civilization," constitute the school's socialization function. When education is defined in this way, it is only natural that parents and administrators assume ultimate control. But as neither constituency physically enters the classroom, their role necessarily is limited to the regulation of behavior on school grounds and to the control of ideological references and intentions in publicly announced curricula.

By stressing behavioral appropriateness and career preparation, suburban high schools give the impression of suspending adolescents between what should have been the goals of childhood and what clearly can wait for adulthood. The very concept of high schools, therefore, first symbolizes then actualizes the periodless, timelessness, or "nowheresville" of adolescence. Schools, in fact, may be a major cause of these well-known adolescent sentiments. As school activities come to be attached at both their past and future borders to such ephemeral reminiscences and anticipations, students begin to lose the identity of their own present sense or life force. The act of thinking about joyful pursuits like singing, acting, politics, journalism and athletics in terms of their usefulness on college applications (the so-called extracurricular activities) demonstrates the temporal suspension and alienation experienced too often by high school students and their teachers.

Nonetheless, the model of many schools remains the kindergarten, the garden of children, the place where spirits are taught to behave and to pass the time with a smidgin of fun and a mite of disciplined routine. School keeps children off the streets and provides mothers breathing room. As one woman confessed, "Eight o'clock in the morning means the start of my only daily freedom. It's awful to admit, but without school I'd go crazy. I know they're safe and they're probably learning interesting things. And I'm free."

Recognizing the erudite babysitting features of high schools, many students now seek the freedom of individual tutorials, work-study programs, ungraded seminars, and encounter groups. Good or bad, whatever their choice, the significant fact is that they not only emulate political strategies of their college brothers and sisters, but they internalize the university, or their impressions of it, as a model for high school reform. In part what infuriated so many students when *The Slave* and *The Naked Ape* were drummed out of classrooms either was that it was done because of obscenity rulings, or because the students were deemed to be insufficiently mature to read about sexual behavior many of them already discreetly practiced, or because of belligerent "civil rights" attitudes more and more of them boisterously uphold. To be sure, students offer the familiar yet sanguine argument "If we're old enough to die in Vietnam, we're old enough to read about how babies are born." But this is hardly the reason why those Wellesley students chose *The Naked Ape* in the first place.

They also might argue as two young girls did: "Our parents are threatened by sex; we're not." Or, "What sense does it make to keep good literature which happens to have sexual references out of the classroom when nothing prevents us from buying utter crap in the supermarkets, drug stores, and airports, not to mention taking it out of the public library?"

All of these arguments make sense as well as reveal other, less conspicuous sentiments. But students put forth the strongest point, perhaps, when they ask what cognitive, social, psychological or natural magic is performed over the summer following high school graduation that "permits" them to study sexuality, philosophy, psychology, LeRoi Jones and Desmond Morris as college freshmen but not as high school seniors? The answer is, no magic at all. The change is a sociological one. It is not chronological age that matters as much as the definition and nature of the school as an institution. It is important, moreover, to those who live by the regulations and rituals of these institutions. For understandable reasons personal change is not so easily made.

What many students now seek is a university model for high school, a model which at present most suburban high schools, naturally, seem reluctant to adopt. But who exactly is it in the high schools who disapproves of this model and continues to perpetuate custodial schools? The answer: some administrators, some teachers, some parents, and some students. Maybe even everybody, to one extent or another.

For administrators and parents, behavioral control might be seriously shaken if the so-called university model were adopted. Students might be too free to come and go; hence too great an emphasis on "premature" responsibility and autonomy might result. Right now schools are "fine," for they are designed primarily for the people who professionally run and financially support them. "Management is for managers," one student said. Through employing some universities' concept of freedom, albeit limited, administrators and parents might lose control. In the university model, parents, after all, play a rather silent role. Indeed, if truth be known, a surprisingly small percentage of many private universities' revenue derives from the presently exorbitant tuitions paid by parents. And, too, parents feel they must forfeit certain rights to the behavioral control feature of university socialization, even to the extent that many students treat the autumn of their freshman year as the time when parents must relinquish total rights to authority altogether, even "at home," wherever that might be.

Where parents hold on in both high school and college is in

the channels of career guidance and opportunity, although frequently this hold is insecure if not invidious. It is said of elite
men's colleges, for example, that getting the boy in is a minor
problem, as a good prep school presumably can handle that. More
difficult is assuring him a position in the eating club, fraternity or
secret society which offers him a direct and exclusive link (almost
as an underground railway) to financial, business, even law firm
positions. During high school parents need not recede quite as
much. They may even dare bring their grievances to a school committee or esteemed headmaster, as one father did recently during
a dispute with his son's school's Dress and Appearance Committee.
In attempting to protect the sanctity of his son's hair, he wrote, "I
am sorry for you because I am afraid you are trapped: meaning to
teach manners, you will find you foster cynicism and hypocrisy."

Yet even for such a father high school represents a time of sus-
pense as well as temporal suspension. Given the established order
of many contemporary high schools, the honoring of socialization
functions normally legitimates parents neglecting their children's
needs altogether. Or, if this is too extreme, it permits them a reasonable justification for abdicating their part in socialization and
learning. "It's too late now," the father of a high school freshman
lamented. "You know as well as I their personalities are as good as
formed in the first few years, and as for teaching, I'm hardly
equipped to teach literature. I couldn't even teach a six-year-old
new math." Sadly, then, as parents bequeath these questionable
rights, high school teachers come to define their purposes as part-
time guidance counselors, part-time nursemaids, part-time disci-
plinarians, part-time therapists, and, if a piece of time remains,
teachers. In large measure, teachers have become caught between
the instrumental chores of pedagogy, irrespective of how they
might interpret them, and the so-called expressive core of their
involvements with students, typically represented by discussions
and counseling after class.

As much as teachers might resent these obligations, although
one does not know for certain that they do, they cannot refuse
them, since the social structure of most all high schools makes it
almost impossible for students to bring their problems, much less

their person or personality, to administrators, whose very purpose connotes judgment, disciplining, permission requesting, etcetera. Because of the school's structure, students cannot freely approach administrators with problems other than academic ones, as they feel, and maybe rightly so, that administrators are in collusion with their parents. Administrators represent their parents' agents in the school; hence teachers are the potential source of genuine, although cumbersome, friendships.

Guidance counselors and high school psychologists, some might think, would be the logical resource in these times, but many students complain that these people, too, tend to be influenced by the ethos of the administration (their bosses) or, if not, to orient their advice too much in the direction of what is suitable and adaptable for the school rather than for individual students. What many students wish to communicate, really, is that guidance counseling essentially means one of two things: behavior problems in the realm of mental illness or advice on improving records for college admissions officers. In a real way, students cannot "afford" to engage counselors if they fear that psychological diagnoses will appear on college letters of recommendation. So in the end counselors, too, tend to embody the school's socialization functions.

More tragically, and not so incidentally, in most high schools and colleges there is not a soul with whom (not just to whom) students may speak about personal needs, difficulties, or problems who remains free of some mental health, disciplinarian, or counseling stigma. To get a little help or encouragement or advice — and this is not as exaggerated as it sounds — students practically have to break rules, flunk courses, or "crack up." Then, precisely because they sit face to face with the dean or "shrink" or "cop," they become obliged by the situation itself to play the role of student in academic, psychological, or legal trouble. The definition of the situation or the encounter demands that students play out the "misdemeanor" as well as the behavior and feelings publicly associated with it. It all relates somehow to giving "them" what they want, but not what the students feel or feel that they are, and this in turn always seems to come at a time when they are really not quite certain they could give this sense of their identity to anyone, anywhere, ever.

(A rather unusual side of this same problem was described by Lisa Peattie in a talk entitled "Youth of Today: Different from Yesterday's?": "A couple of years ago one of my daughters, then in junior high school, thought about failing a little bit. Her school district straddled two areas of different social class, one of upper-middle-class families and one of lower-middle-class and blue-collar families. Sara enjoyed the more rambunctious style of the latter group but found it hard to get to know them, since in most of her courses she found herself exclusively with young people of her own social class. She proposed to a friend, a teacher at the school, that she might let her grades slip so as to land in some of the other classes. The teacher told her not to try. 'If you get bad grades,' he told her, 'we'll worry about you; you'll be an underachiever, not doing what you are capable of. First we'll talk to you; then we'll call your mother; then we'll get you professional help.' ")

What saves many students and provides them the strength they require to make it through the day, and what resiliency they do exhibit, are the prolonged bull sessions or "hard rapping," as now, for this moment anyway, they are called. Ironically, though, these sessions are discouraged both by the regulation of students' free-time socializing, and, more subtly, through the architecture of the buildings. So, to keep their sanity and pursue their interests, students charge furiously into after-school intimacies, and when dinner hours terminate even these, they spend the rest of the night on the telephone.

Given these exigencies and the absence of almost anything resembling an educative community, the suburban teacher remains the single school authority to whom students may turn, albeit uncomfortably. Their emerging relationship is hardly free of complications, but in a genuine school way each is all the other has. Even a glimpse at some of the features of this relationship shows how complex is this "hidden curriculum" notion of which educators speak, and how high-powered is the school business being transacted five days a week.

Often hopelessly "strung out," some students veritably wince from the swishing of an iron chain of constraints swung at them by parents, administrators, school board members, teachers and fellow students. While their work hours involve straightforward as well as not so straightforward learning procedures, naturally with the assistance of books but now more and more with what they call "visual aids," other happenings occur "on school property" that also shape their existence. As Theodore R. Sizer [2] wrote, "Many significant things that children learn are untestable and may be affected by the political structure of a school or school system. The attitudes of teachers, the pride (or lack of it) that parents have in a school, the extent of accountability of the staff — all may have subtle but important effects on learning." And there are other untestable happenings, some less conspicuous but even more pernicious.

For example, students see more clearly than ever before the battles waged by teachers with their "superiors" whom the students and teachers feel are inferior to them. At times teachers invite students to join them in their campaigns; at other times they try to keep them from "the kids." Nonetheless, when they cause polarization of schools and communities, scandals do little more than expose the various tensions which sizzle and foment each day and foster the budding of teacher-student alliances. While the scandals may possess what some would call cathartic value, they can hardly be described as joyous celebrations for either group. This is important to remember, for there is an incorrect belief that political and social upheavals are initiated purely for sport or expressive delight. To be sure, self-indulgence and aggrandizement, as Peter Schrag [3] noted recently, adhere to such missions, but they are not necessarily fuel supplying a life power for these political turbines.

In their sophisticated awareness of college programs and in their attempts to initiate the ideals of these programs, high school students recognize that, given present conditions, administrators openly infringe upon a sacred realm when they enter classrooms either physically or spiritually. Students feel the infringement through their teacher's self-consciousness particularly when school officials reeking judgments come to observe a "class in action." To assist their teacher during these watched moments, and to demonstrate an uncanny and often unpredictable loyalty, students put on especially good performances for their silent but hardly innocuous visitors. When the visitors enter into the discussion, hoping perhaps to prepare a miniature educational community, the relief is noticeable and the experience rewarding. Authority has for a moment receded, and equality seems believable. However, when visitors refrain from communicating on the grounds that involvement is "inappropriate" and necessarily implies spoiling the "objectivity" required in teacher assessments, their silence is construed as judgmental, if not disapproving.

As if this were not enough, the educational experience is complicated further by the abdication of many parents of supposedly home-based socialization functions, by the eager willingness of many teachers to take on such functions, and by the pervading social class phenomena underlying these functions. To be more specific, in speaking with high school teachers, particularly those in English and social studies (the curriculum areas requiring, in addition to prescribed materials, expression of feelings and discussion of controversial issues), one gets a sense that the parents with whom these teachers meet are essentially concerned about their children's daily behavior and their future careers. Parents ask questions like, "Can you get him to discipline himself?" and "Can you get her to stop biting her fingernails?" Many parents, therefore, not only abdicate much of what also belongs at home, but sometimes give the impression of denying the fact that teachers have any worth, talent, or purpose beyond that of grooming adolescent personalities and then hitching these personalities to some appropriate social tramways. Who knows, maybe knowledge for knowledge's sake is a wasteful goal after all, although it probably is not articulated quite this way by those men and women whose work is knowledge and whose source of joy is in this work.

In fact, very little discussion between teachers and parents of classroom philosophies, exercises and assignments ever takes place. From the teachers' perspective, this omission is degrading, as it implies that they are professionless employees, or, more accurately, the man and woman servants of the parents and hence of their children as well. Recently on a television talk show about education a bitter man with knowing justification screamed exactly this point: "Don't forget for a moment that you administrators and teachers are the servants of the people. We pay the taxes that make up your salary." So teachers (and administrators) have no alternative but to be the servants, and the more they accept this profane and harsh contract, the more schoolrooms resemble anachronistic kindergartens, if not plantation estates, and the more students and their faculties may feel alienated from anything "relevant" (that ubiquitous word) or valuable. Now, not only suspended in time, students' very lives dangle on the teeter-totters of adolescence and childhood. Even worse, they come to see their elders teetering and tottering on the very same playground.

In most suburbs, the explicit class differentiations between the local families, on the one hand, and teachers *and* administrators, on the other, at times render the school almost unworkable. As students seek a natural and honorable emancipation from their parents, often exhorting cries of intellectual superiority in the process, they discover that teachers do much the same with administrators. Each group, then, has its unique conflict with authority, its own special brand of "generational gap," and its own experience of oppression. And this is only one of those "subtle but important effects on learning" alluded to by Sizer.

What prevents teachers and students from allying themselves in a truly Homeric (or is it homeroom?) battle for freedom is more complex. It transcends the fear, however, that teachers who "get in too tight" with students or assign what students have suggested in the first place, actions seen by some as acts of communion if not of student take-over, may be relieved of their duties. In part it has to do with expertise, age, and experience, all natural obstacles, and probably importantly so, to a consummate alliance. What prevents the teacher-student alliance in the suburbs has to do with the fact that the majority of teachers can neither socially nor economically identify with the families of their students. Simply, their origins and life-styles are not on the same continua, or if they are, then too great a disparity is felt. As a result, and although for some it may involve intellectual and professional compromises, teachers are forced to acknowledge their sociological and psycho-historical ties with administrators.

Neither free yet from their own understandable ethnocentricity nor sufficiently aware of these ephemeral continuities and social continua, students cannot fully comprehend the dynamics of this social class business. It is but one of many cases where student sensitivity and insight fail to compensate for clearly codified knowledge. In evaluating pedestrian schoolwork and in dreaming of future achievements, students rarely grasp the sense of incompleteness so many teachers feel in their constant orientation toward protection and preparation of the young. Just the impact on a teacher of the term "preparatory" school may never be contemplated by the most brilliant and mature of students until years after their graduation.

In contrast, preoccupied with students' "behavioral adaptations" and their college and career dowries, teachers knowingly guarantee the social and economic factors separating themselves, those in their charge, and the university people soon to take charge. Merely by witnessing the paucity of students who express to them aspirations to become high school teachers, contemporary suburban teachers must wonder about the worth and esteem of their profession and its still tender rank in the American prestige hierarchy, not to mention its relationship to the "betterment" of the already "better" classes. (This problem is not unique to suburban high schools, since one finds university teachers, too, bemoaning their efforts and the costly intellectual investments made in students whom they finally "lose" to law, medicine, business, or politics.)

Surprisingly few high school students recognize the sociological divisions between themselves and their teachers. It is appreciated rather suddenly when one questions them on the degree of association between their parents and teachers. It became crystal clear to one high school junior. The edges of his eyes wrinkled slightly as he confessed, "None of my parents' best friends are teachers." Suburban parents, naturally, have noticed the differentiation and in some instances have attempted to ameliorate, although crudely, the problems it causes. In one suburban community, for example, residents organized a program where on one or two nights a year every teacher in the high school was assigned to a local family with whom he would dine. The proposal's patronizing tone was so painful, however, that teachers requested an abrupt termination. "Take a teacher to lunch," someone muttered. "Let the slaves quit the field and come into the big house," said another. It was true. Everyone, teachers and parents alike, saw the analogy and, worse, they smelled as never before the underlying sentiments. Administrators, incidentally, had been omitted from this particular program.

Something else students often do not comprehend is the cleavage of faculty members over various issues. They understand political polarization and the so-called liberal's versus the conservative's (or what they might call the sensitive versus the insensitive) reaction to issues like LeRoi Jones and Desmond Morris, but they often fixate too strongly, perhaps, on generational and political differences, and thereby miss the substance of adult culture or, more specifically, differential career commitment. This point requires some elaboration.

All school systems, suburban or nonsuburban, like all social systems, experience personnel turnover. Students leave after three or four years; untenured faculty, ironically, after about the same length of time. Tenured staff and administrators stay longer. So do the parents in a particular community. The duration of one's contract with the school, however, may be only indirectly related to the intensity and quality of one's commitment. Career teachers cannot afford to jeopardize their chances for tenure or, if tenure is already attained, the safety and sanctity they have inherited with it. Even if they secretly plan to transfer (or transform) school systems, they, like the students, dare not spot their records with public exhibitions, classroom flamboyance or political muckraking. They cannot, because of their overriding position in the community and the weakening of the very meaning of tenure that results as a consequence of this position.

A certain group of teachers, however, can afford the luxury of pedagogic daring and defiance even to the point that scandals result. Scandal, of course, is neither their goal nor the source of any sadistic happiness. Still, by dint of their marginal position in the school's structure, this group knows it can rely on a freedom held in reserve, a freedom quite handy when in fact entanglements bloom as scandal. Comprised of teachers dedicated to their students but for various reasons uncommitted to a lifetime of teaching at their present schools perhaps, this group remains somewhat immune to the sanctions of control actualized in future job offers and tenure. Professionally, they can afford to take risks, something which shows in their work and in their local reputations.

The marginality of the women teachers in this group is reinforced by their marriages, actual or prospective, to professionals on the "way up" in other fields. While this situation and the rationales it offers exist essentially because of the inequalities of job and social positions between men and women, one result has been that these particular women teachers may excuse themselves from their social class affiliations with regular career teachers and at three-thirty each weekday plug back into society at a substantially higher notch. Accordingly, these women's social and economic identifications, if they materialize, are likely to be more with local families than with the administrators and teachers who stay behind. And most everyone in the community knows this. (An interesting test of these social and economic identifications, not so incidentally, would be to study the positions in the school and community held by those persons known to the spouses of this special group of women teachers. All things being equal — as if this were ever possible — one might find that the higher the social class of a teacher or administrator the more contacts he and his spouse will have with local parents.)

The male members of this special group, typically teachers of English and social studies, have, after several years and often at severe personal risk, achieved such charismatic reputations and personal followings that administrators dare not impose burdensome restraints for fear of bringing "the kids" down upon themselves. In these cases, love literally conquers all, as parents, too, can do nothing but support, perhaps reluctantly, those cherished teachers who may well be ideologically opposed to the ethos of the local school board. Given their age or sex, achieved charisma, associations with the upper middle class or openly self-confident political liberalism, whatever it may be, this group of men and women knowingly predisposes itself to blisters of tension and baleful hostility. These teachers have become the frequent topic of conversation at town meetings, at school cafeteria tables and in faculty lounges. In interview after interview with all sectors of the suburban high school community, their names are among the first to be mentioned, their status among the first to be challenged.

The challenge takes several forms, some of which are confined to social animosities in the lounges and cafeterias but nonetheless are adequately controlled and, for the most part, hidden from students. The hostility, however, often assumes a most ignominious character, one that inevitably destroys the educative process. I am referring to the occurrence of teachers spying on one another or coopting students to become underground sources of information about other teachers' life-styles, attitudes and classroom proceedings. Although they are heinous, if these spying campaigns ceased at the point of information gathering, teaching might still carry on and classrooms might still remain democratic and free. But too often teachers will report the names and actions of their colleagues to principals who then request departmental chairmen to supervise and regulate the classroom and out-of-classroom behavior of these "marked" teachers. Now, whereas university departmental chairmen oversee the spectrum of curricular needs and often attempt to facilitate individual efforts, high school departmental chairmen may be obliged to keep watch on suspected teachers. Because of this onerous dividend, many quit. University departmental chairmen also resign, of course, but usually it is for very different reasons.

An example of this pernicious overseeing and spying is the still pending case of a tenured suburban teacher who has actually been taken to court by his fellow teachers on the grounds that his appearance and dress implicate him as being irresponsible. What makes this case so significant is the twist that could come if it is ruled that his persecutors are libelous for having signed petitions against him on the above grounds. Also at stake, naturally, is the firing of permanent faculty members. But the main issue may revolve around what sociologist Harold Garfinkle calls "the documentation of the preconception." When teachers are threatened or even fired because of sloppy dress, or, as in another instance, because some hemlines were judged to be too short, administrators and fellow teachers may be meting out punishment not for these "noncrimes" but for the political and social postures represented daily by these teachers in their appearance. Nonetheless, appearance and especially those sexual features of appearance, like hair and hemlines, that get people into trouble are only part of the daily policing of values and positions guarded by teachers and their colleagues. Thus, while some have said that the enterprise smacks of fascism and paranoia, others contend that policing is a necessary feature in schools if subversive, destructive and corrupting elements are to be kept out of the classrooms. To criticize either side of this exquisitely tense educational posture is really to remove schools from the greater society in which they merely are members. Moreover, it is to stand above teachers and administrators, parents and students and condescendingly refute the intellectual and emotional worlds these people know and at present quite logically respect.

Yet it can and probably should be observed that much of this policing behavior violently contradicts many university interpretations of academic freedom. But this is exactly the point: little academic freedom and inadequate conception of it exist in most suburban American high schools, or inner city ones, for that matter. Hence, with teachers *and students* left structurally and philosophically unprotected, there can be minimal spontaneity, limited free expression, limited discussion of "controversial" issues and, indeed, ultimately only the barest tracings of democracy in any classroom.

Again, the university offers the model of such academic freedom, a model with very explicit limitations and biases, one felt to be irrelevant by some radical college students but indispensable to sociologists like Talcott Parsons and Gerald M. Platt,[4] who have written: "From all these trends, a type of university has arisen which is relatively insulated from the direct influence of many societal demands and needs. Without this autonomy the academic man could not pursue his scholarly and scientific interests or his teaching of knowledge for its own sake without obstruction or diversion. Without such freedom and the partial autonomy on which it rests the American academic system could never have attained its present level of excellence." But when a teacher knows that his job may be jeopardized by what he might say or wear in class or outside, he comes to know very little autonomy at all. In fact, as actually happened in the *Slave* affair, it takes only one student to go home and report the day's classroom adventures for the machinery of constraint and repression to grind. Ironically and sadly, in these schools without even a morsel of academic freedom, students have joined administrators in their unwitting sanctions of faculty members. Cases of mere rumor destroying a teacher's career or episodes of students exaggerating or even lying about schoolroom conversation to the point that teachers lose their jobs are not as rare as one might wish.

For career teachers, this double constraint of teacher-student surveillance is often too much to surmount. They soon learn that one lives longer by staying in the middle of the road and abiding by the social and pedagogic traditions of the school and community. This, finally, becomes the nub of their adaptation. That many teachers who launched careers in the 'Forties and 'Fifties continue to thrive today in the same school and with the same curriculum only assures their inheritors that theirs is the formula for longevity and a memorable yearbook dedication. The fact that teachers do adapt to less volatile and less politically extreme positions is quite well known. Because of the adaptation or, as some might choose to call it adjustment or, more poignantly, maturation, many young teachers are seen as the proverbial "sell-outs" by the youngest teachers just starting in the school. As always, they are accused of compromising principles and values for the sake of job security and eventual tenure. They suffer inside from these pressures of political activism and the necessity to maintain both their jobs in a good school and their moonlighting employment that, after all, permits them to approach financial solvency with a ray of dignity. But they suffer, some of them, even though they often strike back at the group directly behind them only to emerge among the most severe critics and judges of behavior, appearance and ideologies that only months before they espoused. Some, naturally, have "changed their minds," or "seen the light," but some undoubtedly require this denigration of their immediate past as part of the insurance that the present might flow more deliberately into a logically continuing future.

For that group of marginal teachers who, if they were irresponsible, might dare to flout their present jobs and future employment opportunities, the leverage of administrative and collegial social control is greatly reduced, and the rewards and benefits of academic freedom are noticeably less relevant. So they won't get tenure. So they won't be rehired. So they'll teach in the inner city. Maybe they'll quit altogether! Most probably do not wish to quit. In fact, they very likely value tenure, but primarily in terms of its adjudication of accomplishment and excellence, and not so much in the rhetoric of professional permanence and economic security. For these reasons they are likened by some of their colleagues to invading society matrons donating afternoons a week to hospital volunteer work. In the same way, ironically, their lack of career commitment buffers their own struggle for academic freedom. Empirically it seems to be true that one does not push so hard for freedom in one sector of one's work life if one is guaranteed even a greater freedom ten or twenty miles away in the community one calls home. No one can yet be blamed, moreover, for placing his own future and the future of his kin before the future of anyone else, even with those who once in genuine intimacy and comradeship he shared a bountiful past.

Despite the various degrees and manifestations of professional commitment, high schools, if they are to survive as educational institutions rather than as elegant day-care centers, must at least institute academic freedom in order to protect marginal and career teachers as well as students and administrators. Everything else may best be relegated to facilitating this freedom. The arguments often raised about granting teachers liberty to choose classroom topics are (excuse the pun) academic, or if not, highly political. Teachers continually make choices of one sort or another anyway. They choose to teach this course rather than that one or assign this book rather than that book, this passage rather than that passage, and, consequently, this approach rather than that approach. To question the legitimacy of a teacher's personal opinion, therefore, is academic, because he or she constantly offers personal opinion. But so does a doctor offer personal opinion when he diagnoses illness or prescribes medication. Like a teacher's, his opinion, presumably, is studied, experienced, knowledgeable; but it is still personal opinion. A doctor or teacher may even suggest seeking someone else's opinion; and while the noble terms consultation or team teaching have evolved, it all usually boils down to opinion.

With all the opinions, there remains a precedent for teachers not to advertise their political beliefs. Even though students know their teachers' beliefs, the attempt at neutrality probably preserves a certain valuable ethic for some teachers. Yet one wonders whether this insistence on neutrality and avoidance of controversial issues contributes to an even greater problem for teachers, namely their image of being intellectually weak and personally effete.

Unfortunately, it must be admitted that at present the few public opinions offered by high school teachers — outside of court, that is — do not count for too much. As Joseph Featherstone [5] indicated, relative to opulent university professors and prospering high school consultants, high school teachers' persuasions merit very little credence at all. One hopes but is not yet assured that their word carries more weight in classrooms, where their latent status as servants is either overlooked or made invisible. Yet for the most part, within the tangible structures governing suburban and inner city education, teachers possess practically no autonomous prerogatives and no basis from which to claim absolute authority, much less wisdom. They too are among the victims of education, rarely the sources of knowledge about it. Their awareness and experiences are overlooked or dismissed by so many investigators that in some cases teachers have actually come to believe that these experiences are second-rate and unworthy of being recalled or communicated. In other instances, our overly zealous acceptance, overevaluation and romanticizing of teachers' accounts have caused these teachers to distrust us as well as the data they themselves have presented. But in the main it is the drama and

tension of school that we applaud and reward, and not the drudgery and pedestrian activities that after all constitute portions of
everyone's work.

All the same, we pry information out of teachers and, in oblig-
ing us, their lives stay open for us. Indeed, their very fantasies have
become accessible to public scrutiny and necessarily made account-
able to anxious sorts who fret about teacher inadequacies and their
simultaneously mythical and mundane powers. But when all is
said and done, we have rendered teachers among the poor of our
land, for poverty has many meanings, private and public.

Politically and professionally, high school teachers have yet to
be granted full citizenship. Their growing bargaining powers and
union tactics have grown to impressive proportions lately, but it is
at best questionable whether or not the labor union image is the
one they ideally wish to portray, and the associated political, social
and economic community the one with which they would choose
to be identified. There is, after all, a noble white- and blue-collar
history to high school teaching, but there is also an intellectual
tradition of universities which teachers have directly known and
once admired. And the fact that they may cherish this orientation
means that they must sustain a certain conflict of truly personal
identity and social definition when they take part in or even read
about teachers' union negotiations.

On the intellectual side, the fact remains that teachers' expertise
is doubted, maligned or totally ignored, and in the suburbs, where
teachers' relatively low salaries and lack of occupational prestige
place them "beneath" the social gazes of their bosses, their literally disenfranchised status renders them servants, or at best, paid
tutors. Against the backdrop of a culture that fundamentally
values education for the possibilities it offers in occupational mobility and social opportunity, and where the "teaching of knowledge for its own sake without obstruction or diversion" is reserved
for an elite and insular group, high school teachers too frequently
have become nursemaids or educational and social travel agents.
This fact remains whether or not students recognize it or confess
to it. Over time and through the unrelenting strictness of educational systems normally tolerating only minuscule adjustments and

refinements, teachers now have resigned themselves to performing a great many, perhaps too many, purely socialization functions. Perhaps because of this resignation they presently seek a legitimacy in intervening in the psychological realms of their students where the most arrogant of psychotherapists dare not trespass even with their own patients. And if this were not bad enough, some teachers now argue, literally, that the best "service" they can offer their pupils is psychoanalysis.

Administrators, too, are caught in the locks of socialization enterprises and, like it or not, they have acquiesced to becoming ruthless deputies and clean-up squads. Truly they are the sheriffs, the righteous posse awaiting the brawls and looking for the villains who threaten to shoot up the town. Somewhat obliged and partly willing to be the hunters of young persons, they, by the very act of hunting, contribute to the transformation of a tiny group of adolescents into "criminals."

Like certain representatives of the press, television, and social science, administrators are accused of focusing attention on the split seconds of errors, misdemeanors, or rebellions while permitting the remaining millions of hours of law obeyance and utterly obsessive loyalty to go unobserved. They are the feared judges and censors of a microsociety that students, by law no less, must first taste, then swallow, then digest.

But administrators too remain pinioned by a "community's control" and find themselves obliged to prowl the grounds of inequities certain parents, teachers and students still refuse to acknowledge. We must not forget that administrators' salaries originate in the same purses as teachers' salaries. So administrators are battened down by restrictions on their freedom as well as by the "backlash" of their own expressed dogma. What a complicated phrase it is that goes "I'm sorry, but my hands are tied." As is true for everyone else, the preventions that administrators first impose and then reify reflect the expectations they hold or fear or maybe even secretly wish would come to pass. But what is most serious is that schoolroom encounters have become circumscribed by people living under these types of social constraints and the personal constraints that go along with them. As a consequence, each and every classroom contains the scent of their ideology, expectations, and the secret wishes of which they may not yet be conscious.

Finally, legitimated by that lavish swatch of society cut by most American suburbs, the parents, the rightful rulers, run their schools on a stage of so-called community control that must make residents of Oceanhill-Brownsville in New York City literally weep with envy. As it is elsewhere, the key word in the suburbs is control. Each person, each link asks the next to behave but, contrary to common belief, obvious political issues and ubiquitous racial tensions fail to define the entire chain. For inevitably there are the socialization factors, the behavior inspections and career preparation, all of which for some reason tend to minimize the values of human involvement and restrict the communication of personal worth judged according to criteria derived from a student's own capacities.

Partly this is due to the fact that many school personnel feel that students, merely because of being rich, do not require personal attention, much less encouragement or friendship. "They've got it made," said one teacher. "I need them as much if not more than they need me. In fact, I'll bet if we could all change places right now, the poor old teachers would love to become the rich young students."

"What about the students?"

"I'll bet they'd be happy right where they are."

Fantasy, envies, regrets or whatever they are aside, the day-by-day, year-by-year routines of education insist that periodically teachers and administrators be reminded that while part of their job is to fulfill parental obligations and duties, they neither own nor even share the flocks of students passing through. This is the way so much of school has come to be psychologically as well as sociologically defined: "passing through." The teachers well may be admired, even treasured by some few of their students; but they have not yet escaped from the social fact that at some level they are indentured shepherds who, without their appointed flocks, have no claim to the fields and their fruits. The students pass through the lives of teachers who long ago agreed to claim no rights and no percentage of someone else's presumably opulent future.

The economic argument "I'm in control because my taxes pay

your salary" is a painful one, often seductive and invidious. What makes it so is that no measure of expertise or even interest in schools is necessarily implied. When Norman Podhoretz said of the WASP's that "neither their earlier arrival nor their majority status entitled them to exclusive possession of the national identity," [6] he might well have been referring to the unspoken spirit that now supports the beams and pillars of those few parents who, frequently by their aggressiveness and verbosity alone, tend to control suburban schools.

To be sure, a small percentage of parents publicly demonstrate active interest in their children's education. Or maybe more than a small percentage do and the low attendance at PTA meetings, parents' nights, or silence at the dinner table each evening means that they acknowledge teacher-student priorities and choose to remain discreetly prudent with their interventions into the adolescent world. Or maybe the nature of high school and the essence of adolescence are such that parents cannot afford to trespass on school grounds nor even attempt to discover the paths where their children walk each day. Still, many parents cling to the tax-legitimate rhetoric, and in so doing begin to believe in some misplaced religious decree that makes their bellows and squeals the ultimate "words" on education and their swatch of society the ultimate citadel of democracy.

But — and we come full circle — parental bellows and squeals also are reasonable, to be expected and, as painful as it may seem to some, to be protected. Suburban parents want good things, success and happiness, for their children. They want, in a word, the exact same things all parents want for their children. In announcing their ideals, they employ the very words used by the school administrators they hire, administrators who have learned well and remain constant. Many parents have moved to suburban residences precisely to put their children on the social and educational tramways that they know depart from there, tramways, incidentally, advertising a rather impressive record of safety. Accordingly, the parents keep a careful vigil on their tax monies and a twenty-four-hour guard detail on the politics and politicians of their communities until all of their brood are well stationed in college. At that point, they pack up the old yearbooks and hockey skates, letter sweaters and report cards and move, perhaps back to the city, perhaps farther out in the country. Then a new family comes to take their place, and as these two sets of parents converse, younger children again swarm over the damp autumn grounds and argue over the perfect spot for a hideout or tree house. The memorabilia lie in wait for the college students or young marrieds who for a stolen moment may feel again the pace and exhilarating anguish of high school. But rarely, though, do these reminiscences and possibly unspoken calls for returning in time constitute a substantive interest in education, their own or their children's. Still, the poetry alive in their feelings keeps the spirit and emotionalism of education awake, if not alert. So all of this means that children too, in their way, will someday come full circle.

According to Webster's, one of the origins of the word scandal is "cause for stumbling." Experientially, we do sense a stumbling, a reeling and realigning in the face of scandal. Confirming Webster's definition, scandal does mount tensions in communities, for it does seem to transcend individual outrage and, instead, bleed through the fabric of neighborhoods and townships. But scandal need not cause the shame that Webster's also suggests, for if time and space could just somehow be transformed, the recent scandals in New York and Wellesley could well be the harbingers of entirely new concepts of secondary school education, concepts that might give democracy a chance.

Perhaps the genuinely vital instant of education is precisely that instant when parents and teachers, administrators and students fill local auditoriums or gymnasiums to proclaim publicly, at least to one another, what education is all about, or should be all about. Perhaps in the collective reeling for equilibrium, groups of people of astonishingly different backgrounds and types of intelligence and purposes might come to know the counterpoint of community education and even admit to themselves, as profoundly difficult as it truly is, the hatred caused by their differences. It may seem to some students at these meetings that their parents act like children, or that their administrators behave like officers of a misplaced gestapo, but the fact of the matter is that in these rare and celebrated hours, school ceases to be a kindergarten and in its bumbling way grows up. In their reeling and realigning, all are forced to climb over the abutments and encumbrances imposed by their societies and, even more, by their own psychologies, moralities, personal styles and philosophies. So even if the participants at these forums sound hypocritical, and surely they will to someone in an agitated audience, they nonetheless have taken a crack at empirically defining education and have "expressed" themselves and "encountered" one another in the best tradition of modern sensitivity group practice.

The parents and students have expressed themselves and encountered one another, that is; but as things stand now the social constraints felt by teachers in their classrooms and by administrators in their offices remain operant in open school committee meetings. The oppression of certain constituencies still persists. Administrators still find it difficult to go against the social and political grain of the local residents. And when teachers threaten to strike, local parents and much of society at large still cannot decide whether to treat them as working-class employees appropriately and certainly legally demanding profane rights or as sacred healers who, like doctors, dare not place self-interest before the interest of the community's children. Teachers are not always unequivocal, either, on this last issue.

Equally confusing about contemporary education is that the very same language used in conjunction with school decentralization frequently denotes exquisitely different sentiments and purposes in various communities. When Roxbury (Massachusetts), Watts, or Oceanhill-Brownsville parents scream for the right to run their schools and invoke taxation arguments in this context, their goals may be the same as those of suburban parents uttering the exact same linguistic claims, even though the communities are so separated socially and economically, and geographically. But race is not always the salient factor in suburbs, although more than a hint of tension exists. In this connection, a subtle ramification of bussing black students into white suburbs is the fear among suburbanites that bussing is but a precursor of an inevitable city government control over far-reaching suburban policies, policies having to do with the day-by-day aspects of life apart from racial integration.

There are those people who publicly ask schools to someday be the arena, the community, really, where all four constituencies may meet together regularly and eagerly, at times to clean up and reel collectively in the wake of scandals, at times to cause them. For these so-called "radical" critics of American high schools, scandals presently seem to be a major stimulus for bringing suburban constituencies together. But even their occurrence fails, as the community's and school's social structures maintain the discussions at self-protective or openly hostile levels, and rarely at levels of exploration and daring.

I must confess that for a long time, and especially during the long, long months of the *Slave* scandal, I actually believed without question that violent uprisings of this sort in schools were the solution. In truth, the problem is far more complicated. As wiser people than I knew at the time, scandal can set back as many people as it lurches forward — or maybe it's to one side or the other. The reeling and realignment always seem to bring freedom for some but strict repression for others. Scandals initiate valuable conferences and reconceptualizing, to be sure, but they necessarily frighten so many of us in their story that one must wonder whether the natural defensiveness that necessarily emerges is beneficial or harmful, particularly when no one is ever around to assist us in handling this defensiveness or the aggression that so logically follows from it. There are always times when we would love to do nothing more than throw caution, subtlety, and our senses of humanism and care out the window and bop our designated adversaries on the head. Surely everyone has felt the almost uncontrollable eruption of anger and rage which make it seem that our souls were possessed by demons. Most probably, rage of this ferocity has roots in the social and political contexts igniting it as well as in the machinery of our sometimes concealed, sometimes exhibited psychodynamics.

The question to be asked, however, is: how stands the institution when the violence settles and the attackers recede? How stands the institution for which, presumably, we have unleashed our rage? Has it changed? Can we now draw a line to connect the injured and even dead persons to the events which brought amelioration, progress and a new democracy? It is not merely a theoretical question of whether or not one condones violence or scandal as much as it is knowing empirically whether the scandal has improved the lot of deeply complex people like all of us. How then stands the institution?

Not so simply, the problem arising for many suburban high schools is for the constituencies, in the context of their social structure and the template of history in which this structure breathes, to articulate their respective interests and priorities. This task alone would constitute education. Indeed, the public school committee meetings and hearings, when students are invited, represent archetypal forms of orchestrated community education. Harvey Pressman's concern for the urban school is equally viable for those he calls their "overprotected suburban counterparts": ". . . the schools must allow the experiences, needs, and facts of life within the community to generate much of the curriculum, and they must permit meaningful participation by high school students in governing these schools." [7] But, as is the case in an honest poker game, the suburban players must commit themselves to action before the announcements of the final ante amounts. That is to say parents, administrators, teachers and students must proclaim their commitment to the value of education on a daily and nightly premise. It is not fair that any group may jump on a school political or social issue and then jump back again as quickly to resume the callous indifference so many people display all the rest of the time. It seems a bit unfair, moreover, that the regular, dependable players can so easily be evicted from deliberations and decisions when the ante gets high and be replaced by the ultimately powerful people who suddenly appear when it is reported that big killings can be made.

Too often, small conflicts in school systems become not the reason but the justification for all sorts of people to invade school grounds and demand rights, rule adjustments and personnel changes which might easily have been considered at an earlier time. Scandal makes it possible for the entire suburban community to enter the school, but it also renders insignificant the voices of certain constituencies. Thus the metaphor applies that those who have played every hand of every game are abruptly dismissed when the going gets hot and the stakes rise. Parents, only naturally, should be in on the regular decision-making apparatus which is itself part of the educative process. Yet their role in this apparatus must be carefully examined, for at present they very frequently bring little more to educational pursuits than their socialization and political tenets. And while these tenets bear rather heavily on educational institutions, they cannot yet be said to constitute the entire academic enterprise. In purely functional terms, schools and the societies from whom they rent cannot tolerate parents, or anyone else for that matter, who, acting as police or firemen, rush in at the clanging of alarms tripped off by people like LeRoi Jones and Desmond Morris.

For political reasons, there are times when one does "charge" an institution essentially to highlight or emphasize a particular happening, event or policy. In these times, the so-called extreme or isolated behavior of an institution is attacked, heralded or mocked. But for the most part, the kind of social change almost all school systems sorely require in order to make them democratic, equitable and eternally just would come from the "interruption" of each and every daily activity and an insinuation of new sentiments and philosophies in practically every cubic foot of institutional space.

These last statements are not made in advocacy of destroying inner city and suburban schools. Nor are they meant to imply that no one nowhere does any good at all. This would be unforgivably absurd, condescending, no doubt, and disrespectful of those many persons who every day sustain the constant injury and only momentary glory of educational plants. More importantly, it would be to strengthen the position of those like myself who now enjoy the comfortable posture of social critic or consultant. It would be to exalt those of us who need not bother to rise at six each morning to begin a grueling school day but rather wait until the early evening hours to commence our lists of criticisms and sure-fire recommendations, while the objects of our vituperation enter the last phase of the workday, the paper grading and the endless preparation and administration. And this leaves out the parents who, as much as we might wish to derogate their actions, nonetheless labor hard physically and psychologically to attain that special future they crave and may even feel is earmarked just for them.

How easy it is to believe that if we could but hold a few certain powerful ones in our hands, spank them, or tell them a thing or two, all of society's children everywhere would just, well, would just make out fine. How easy that would be. Still, to possess financial resources and power does advantage people enormously in a variety of ways. One way is by allowing them to stumble occasionally, often, even regularly and still "make, it," whatever that means. Money, after all, may be used as a medium of exchange not only for goods and services but for error, irresponsibility, remission, failure, and even crime. With the social standing it affords, money alleviates the potentially visible and "telltale signs" of all those nasty things that poor people, black people, or foreign people are supposed to do every day in their exotic urban jungles.

The rich and successful can afford to gamble, stumble, and experiment with education. From time to time they may even want to dabble in community scandals, because, like it or not, they are practically assured of window seats on those tramways. It is this same assurance of accomplishment or public success that Russell Baker caught in the bustling but confident ambience of the Harvard Yard. And it is the same self-assurance that Kenneth Clark, Jonathon Kozol, Nat Hentoff and the others just cannot discover in urban classrooms, where students are denigrated and self-contempt boils.

In the end, I think that equity is the goal: all men and all women holding the identical rights and claims on the past, present and future of their nation. All men and all women lovably profane, wondrously sacred. To achieve this, it just seems as though scandal and experimentation are inevitable. One hopes that someday a society somewhere may be able to transform those political, sociological, economic and psychodynamic features that now predispose our institutions and their members to the abuse on all sides of scandals, to instruments of receptivity and acceptance, or at least tolerance. Right at the moment, we are nowhere close to this. While our proven intellectual capacities are nothing short of fantastic, our collective psychology, in an evolutionary sense, is just not up to it.

So if we fear experimentation, or even this word that augurs tentativeness in a culture of such technological certainty, let us take this fear seriously. Let us not forget, however, as many have suggested, that experimentation often means nothing more than required institutional change where the results are already known. And, too, let us not fail to differentiate between the rational and irrational components of this fear and therefore avoid examination of our society and the lavish communities which nourish so much of it. Until that time, all of us will be deprived of so many things, most prominent of which may be that happiness Dali promised.

part 3: Politics

Tutoring for Democracy

Important and new insights often arise when men and women
of imagination accept responsibility for a class of men
previously bracketed, judged, and diagnosed as doomed to
inferiority . . .

Erik H. Erikson, *Gandhi's Truth*

In this chapter and the next three chapters our concern is with students and their political activities. Perhaps we
should say our concern is with that certain group of students whose
political activities arouse us enough to engage in politics ourselves
or write or think about them or just discuss them at dinner parties.
It is almost impossible to believe that so much has changed and
evolved in these last few years on college campuses. By now the
expressions about campus developments are clichés, but still, as in
all clichés, a lasting truth pokes through now and again. There
are indeed differences between our silent generation and their
more audible one, although the differences are not always as profound as we make them out to be. The events of the last few years,
indeed of the last months when campus bombings have occurred,
make it plain that some Americans have at last joined together
some of their most salient fantasies with their ardent conceptions
of revolution and ignited them with rage. The death of a research
worker at the University of Wisconsin is known to most Americans. Kent State, a school not too many of us who applied to east-
ern and western universities knew well at all, is now a household
word. A household word like gun and cop and kid. And this week
as I write, a strange-sounding name begins to be a part of that
household collection. Isla Vista.

The events, then, as almost surrealistically they flood over hundreds of campus towns, have come along hot and heavy. Yet while there seems to be a linear development to them, each one following its predecessor logically, though sometimes violently, there have been recriminations, doubts, and a funny cyclical sort of turning about. Maybe it is ambivalence that drives some students back from the left to grab on to the ladder of democracy for one last time. And maybe it's the same ambivalence that sends them back to the left again when they feel that the establishment is in fact incorrigible or unsalvageable just as they had thought a few months before. So they slam back to the left all over again.

Several years ago, as a student, I was involved with two university organizations whose expressed purpose was to tutor lower-class black youngsters. It was good work, gratifying and worthwhile, but not exhilarating. To be sure, we felt exasperation when things went bad; but I never felt that tremendous surge of whatever it is that one feels in a "good" demonstration. Politics was pretty much an activity of the brain at that point. But with each day it was moving into the blood, another cliché, and it was becoming contagious. People were getting involved not only with campus political activities but with the activities of the Pentagon and the CIA. People were becoming involved with America, and the walls which were meant to protect sacred scholars from their profane college villages, and simple well-behaved towns from frolicking students were beginning to rot, soon to fall away altogether. But it did not happen all at once, at least for me.

The announced purpose of the two organizations was to increase these young Negroes' intellectual capabilities and eventual achievements. The long-term goal of both groups was to boost Negroes into higher educational tracks in their respective schools and eventually, thereby, to better the social conditions in so-called ghetto communities. This was to be accomplished by spending time with students from surrounding neighborhoods after regular school hours and working with them in their courses in which their performance had been considered poor. How much time a tutor spent with his tutee was determined by the particular individual involved, for no stringent rules governed the didactic nature of either program.[1]

A major difference between the two groups was seen in the kind of identity they chose to present to the communities they served. One group acted on the surface much as a community-oriented service organization. Indirectly associated with civil rights intentions and purposes, it allied itself with clear-cut policies of educational improvement. Partly as a response to its interactions and planning sessions with community officials, its programs usually took the form of gentle criticism and of contributing supplementary educational services.

The second group saw itself more as a link in the chain of modern social protests, indeed as one of the very early links of the 1960's. The group's members were not politicians *per se,* nor were they what we now quickly dismiss as "radicals." But they were, in the language of those years, "politically engaged." Perhaps they even symbolized the mood and budding actuality of the revolutionary theater now taking place. Members of this second group unabashedly expressed their interest in the furtherance of and the need for the fight for human rights. (Many of us spoke this way in the early 'Sixties.) Thus, two very distinct images emerged in this university's two tutorial movements. These images were perpetuated, moreover, by the tactics and logistics the members chose to employ in their work, as well as by the qualities they sought in the individuals invited to join their movement, both as tutors and tutees. This politically oriented, or ideological, difference is best indicated, perhaps, by the titles of two articles written by members of the organizations during the early months of their work: "An Appraisal of the Boycott" and "Improving Tutoring."

While the two groups revealed certain substantial differences, they also revealed some identical sociological characteristics. Both groups, for example, were essentially comprised of university students ranging in age from seventeen to twenty-five. The backgrounds of these students were comparable in terms of educational histories, career selections, life-styles, geographic origins, and even in reported social and political orientations and interests. But these facts are no surprise, as to a great extent membership in both groups reflected the demographic features of the university's student population as a whole.

A simple rationale for the existence of both groups was expressed in the following citation from a leader of one of the groups: "We exist because the school system isn't doing its job." [2] Believing this to be true, over one hundred men and women offered their services to one or the other of these two groups in order to tutor young people in most high school or junior high school subjects. Any university student could work for either organization, devoting as much time as he desired and with no obligation to participate in the administrative functions of his organization.

[2]

Like many organizations, tutorial groups clearly perform a major service in community action. Yet the nature of their task, its voluntary membership, and its conspicuous position within contemporary social reform movements make these organizations more susceptible to somewhat different forms of recruitment procedures. In most business organizations, for example, individuals are hired by nature of their talents or experience in the performance of prescribed roles. But in movements such as student government, political reform, civil rights organizations, and these two tutorial groups, the activities and administration of the organizations necessarily appeal to specific kinds of persons not always possessing easily evaluated talents as much as evidencing easily recognizable ideological stances. It is not my intention here to examine the typical tutor personality, as if there were one; but one must understand that inherent in the work of the two tutorial organizations is a tone — a temperament, really — generated by its membership. Thus a large-scale organization may recruit membership on the grounds that certain personalities, as well as one can tell, are most able to adapt to its programs. Or the leaders may believe that several years with the organization will change a person so that he will begin to look and act like all the rest. Need I mention many young people's responses to this? These tutorial groups, however, seemed to derive their identities, indeed their personalities directly from those who happened to be working at any particular time.

More than most organizations, therefore, the identities of the tutorial organizations tended to reflect the energy and purpose espoused by its existing generation.[3] And it was a generation.

It is this last thought more than any other, perhaps, that instigated these observations. The two organizations were observed when both were reporting successes in their programs. What made their positions so intriguing as well as so important was the fact that one goal, "educational improvement," could burgeon into two discretely different tactics, philosophies, and organizational personalities. Particularly striking was the contrast between the political, almost revolutionary policies of one group and the maternal and almost Calvinistic doctrine of the other. Yet both approaches made sense and they both had worth, and they both brought hope and great gains to many young and valiant people.

The leaders of one tutorial group, which we might call the "Reform" group, advanced a position that their "service" was in fact one branch of a major social revolution as they saw it, a revolution which appeared to them to serve temporary personal identity problems as well.[4] This was their observation, indeed diagnosis, not my own. Leaders of the second group, which might now be called "Uplifter," did not define their mission as revolutionary; in fact, they hurriedly denied any identification, as they themselves noted, which made them appear as intruders or revolters. Derived, to be sure, from dissatisfaction with social conditions, their strategies could not be described as revolutionary. It is not hard to see that with these widely differing perspectives the two groups developed different styles of interaction with the communities and the schools supplying children for tutorial sessions, and different announced political intentions, procedures, and, eventually, personalities of the membership.[5]

The groups, then, differed in at least three important ways: first, in their involvements with political factions; second, in their community-based organizations; and third, in their own personal approaches to bureaucratic management. Each of these points requires some discussion.

According to their leaders, the Reform group sought to align themselves with other political organizations also working in problems of racial integration and improvement of the conditions of blacks. They participated in community political action and generally demonstrated a sophisticated political awareness. In a way, Reformers required the evolution and development of Negro protest organizations before they could take their place in the revolution as it existed in the early 1960's. Their rebellious stance, moreover, required strategies of political or pseudopolitical action. On this Reformers all agreed.

Uplifters, on the other hand, purposely played little or no part in contemporary community political action. In fact, Uplifter leaders repeatedly stressed that their interest was restricted to education. Though seriously concerned with the "Negro situation," Uplifters chose to identify with civil rights activism rather than take any active stand outside the classroom. This position, however, did not prevent Uplifter workers from opposing existing community political structures and philosophies. For both groups were vigorous opponents of what they called, perhaps too simplistically, the "power structure," while at the same time being ardent proponents of building grass-roots disturbances, particularly within the then relatively quiet, "politically uninformed" Negro communities in which their work took place. Still, enormous differences existed between their belief systems and the frequency and contents of their pronouncements.

To be more precise, the Reformers' position in the community was one of antagonism, open defiance, and expressed alienation. Feeling that so much of the community was to blame for existing conditions, they (we) could not pretend to act with courtesy or complacency, much less compromise. The goal of helping young Negro students existed alongside the dissatisfaction with a society which allowed people to live in such wretched conditions.

Uplifter leaders reported a very different approach by advocating a positive working relationship with community members and urging their tutors to maintain strong ties with their tutees' families, schools and school associations. Any Uplifters who felt the degree of dissatisfaction with society demonstrated by the Reformers did not permit outward expression of it. Always encouraging the notion of gentle improvement of the community in

which their tutees lived, they worked to prevent enmity and alienation.

It seemed evident to those in the organizations that the identification of the community as a friend or enemy reflected the different degrees to which private aggressions might be managed. It is
both psychologically and intellectually unrewarding to attack just
one particular individual for his contribution to the state of the
"disadvantaged Negro," and consequently there emerged in these
groups varying intensities of hostility toward the community and
anyone who might be associated with it. This orientation of the
tutorial movements anticipated the kind of direction that members ultimately proposed in the establishment of their own organizations, organizations that might well be characterized by the
members' attitudes toward bureaucracy generally.

The dread of bureaucratization and belief in its pernicious ways
were expressed by many members of both movements. I felt it
myself. Nonetheless, fearing a loss of individual effectiveness, Uplifter administrators recognized that their group would have to
become more bureaucratic. They saw it coming and they feared
that the routinized style bureaucracy would bring would mean the
end of spontaneity and worthwhileness. Yet despite all this they
moved to erect what appeared to be a rather successful set of
bureaucratic office operations.[6] "IBM would be proud of us," one
member commented. Some actually liked the business smell of the
whole deal. From the standpoint of tutors, how the movement
survived its administrative demands was, for the moment, imma-
terial. The important thing was that the office was beginning to
"run smoothly."

In contrast to all this, the Reform movement philosophy defied
the insidious elements of large-scale bureaucracies. Reformers
continually stressed the fact that administration had been and
would continue to be handled by informal measures. When the
informal style and its ambience were lost, they said, the movement
would necessarily have failed in its purpose and efficacy. Outwardly, then, the major difference between the two groups was
always in evidence: whereas Uplifter leaders feared that bureaucratization meant fostering organizational growth as well as pre-

venting childlike informalities, Reform leaders insisted that any form of bureaucratization would breed mechanization, and the destruction of the very humanity they valued most in society.[7] If they had to, they would expend as much energy fighting a bureaucratic structure as they would tutoring the community's less fortunate students.

We might expect that the alienation evident in the Reform movement would help to explain why this one group maintained its sentiments about bureaucracies. For example, we might propose that the greater the need to stay individually alienated or socially marginal the more group members stay together and reaffirm their sense and definition of alienation. If this proposition is true, then by establishing a bureaucratic organization the Reform group might be unable to meet the rather volatile psychological needs of many of its members. "People would be walking around too up-tight," is the way it was described to me many years later. As a result of this thinking, the Reform group's organization permitted a great deal of informal exchange and always worked to minimize organizational restrictions.[8]

Two offshoots of these attitudes toward bureaucratization were, first, the differing involvements with community organizations and, second, the varying nature of actual teaching in the tutoring programs. With the emergence of their bureaucracy-like organization the Uplifter group found they had to reduce the kinds of services they could offer to tutees. While their more formal organizational arrangements enhanced their relationships with community agents, it somehow tended to foster restraints in their own educational ingenuity. Although Uplifter members experimented with all sorts of teaching techniques, their programs often seemed to lag behind the more expansive, innovative, and relatively unstructured Reform movement curriculum.

Quite possibly, the freedom and individuality honored in the Reform movement partly through their loosely structured administration worked to produce a free-form type of curriculum, one emphasizing the individual tutor-tutee relationship. Never were tutors asked to pledge themselves to strict philosophies or carefully delineated educational procedures. Perhaps, also as a function of their rebelliousness, Reform people moved away from regular school programs and instituted instead their own novel reforms. Thus Reform tutors attempted to introduce philosophy and political science to high school students failing in history and civics. Uplifter tutors, on the other hand, attempted to explore the contents of courses in which their tutees were enrolled and then, employing the same course outlines and bibliographies, sought educational techniques that might effectively communicate the school's program to the student. They were in this way more oriented than the Reformers were to the immediate pragmatic needs of their tutees.

[3]

Let me now outline four propositions. Let no one take these as experimental hypotheses; they are merely guides for sorting out some impressions and notions.

First, both tutorial groups were controlled by people motivated in part by a hostility directed toward those persons not participating in any activity aimed at improvement of the Negro's condition.[9] In the Uplifter group the hostility was softened considerably so that the movement could establish cooperative contacts with families, schools, and certain community organizations. In the Reform movement, however, the hostility stayed on as a driving force. When it dissipated, the character of the Reform movement appeared to be threatened and many Reformers thought the mission was failing or believed that the organization was in the process of changing its perspectives in order to become more like the Uplifter group.

The maintenance of hostility in the Reform group, therefore, helped to create a movement of alienation. The minimal amount of organization reflected, among other things, the degree to which tutors desired to be collectively alienated or at least set apart from the university community. The alienation, and I think this is the proper term, was perpetuated, moreover, by the phenomenon of "picket training," an action suggesting the indoctrination of tutees into the Negro social protest movement. This type of action did not occur in the Uplifter group. Here the major practice might more appropriately be called "level raising," since activities were directed essentially at educational improvement and social betterment and always without revolutionary tactics.

Second, both groups recruited members by appealing to potential political moods and to that sense of alienation. But while Uplifters gave the appearance of being a cooperating body, Reformers coalesced young Negro tutees first with one another and then with their tutors and thereby furthered their posture of alienation.[10]

The third proposition is highly speculative. In the Reform group particularly, tutees seemed to be unconsciously equated with their tutors' own identities, or so it seemed to me. That is, tutees became the image of what the tutors might have wished to be themselves: active young colts imprisoned by a cruel and insensitive society. This image was enhanced by the fact that Reformers worked primarily with tutees not much younger than themselves. Generally, it seemed as if Reform group tutees held the enviable position of having been oppressed, whereas the objects, means and results of oppression for tutors were far more vague.

Fourth, and equally speculative, sexual identification also seemed to play an important role in one's perception of the attractiveness of a tutorial group.[11] It appeared to me, for example, that identification with what society often characterizes as masculine activities increased one's liking for the groups. Because of their political overtones, tutorial jobs were not at all of the "passive" or "protective" variety that society so often allocates to women. The Reform movement, particularly, demonstrated an assertive and aggressive program, somehow befitting, I thought in those days, a masculine personality. These last two propositions have further implications, incidentally, when we consider that the tutee was taught rules of performance determined in part by a tutor's desire to unite with his compatriots and deprecate specific hated symbols and conditions in society.

While these propositions will be pursued in a moment, it should be pointed out now that it is precisely political movements of the sort we are examining here that alter stereotypical definitions of masculine and feminine. It was in fact the case that many outsiders saw the women in these movements as being, in their words, "manly" or "masculine." Nonetheless, these very same women, by altering their own conceptions of sex roles or "appropriate" action for men and women, helped in their way to transform basic conceptions of reality, conceptions which definitely brought about such a movement as women's liberation which, had it been formed at the time we all worked in these tutorial groups, would have found many of the tutoring women in it. Thus, not so inadvertently, the truly positive contribution made by such tutorial movements may be as much in the restructuring of roles, opportunities and life-styles of university populations as in the reshaping of the children who in those days we unashamedly labeled the "underprivileged."

In *The True Believer* Eric Hoffer has written: "We do not look for allies when we love. Indeed, we often look on those who love with us as rivals and trespassers. But we always look for allies when we hate." And, a little later on: "It is chiefly the unreasonable hatreds that drive us to merge with those who hate as we do, and it is this kind of hatred that serves as one of the most effective cementing agents." [12]

When I read them, Hoffer's notions seemed rather pertinent to the mechanisms described in the first proposition. Then again, in their extremeness they also seemed relevant to a Hitler movement. Hatred did not seem to be functioning as a "cementing agent" in the tutorial movements; indeed, the movements concentrated on many forces besides those which served to maintain intra-group integrity. Tutoring volunteers did not display intense group feelings as much as they revealed a mutual identification. The hostility that was expressed in these movements, therefore, appeared to be far less intense than the hatred observed in a fascist movement, a label thrown around rather loosely these days.

In the Reform group, the hostility and the opportunity to express it through the training of a young social "misfit" or "outcast" was about all that was required to initiate tutorial activity. Publicly displayed hostility, formerly directed at particular objects, usually led to psychological benefits for the entire movement. Thus, when an individual joined up, he seemed to be carrying an anger aimed at an oppressive society, an anger that just might have been employed to ignite his initial activities in the movement. The emotional arousal maintaining this heightened state was not usually dissipated even during a long tenure in the movement. It remained for at least two reasons. First, there was little about tutoring or establishing an alliance with a tutee that produced anything other than a resurgence of rebellious feelings. Through the tutee and fellow tutors, the individual tutor received a legitimate affirmation of his desires to fight the institutions in society he felt to be unjust. So from the vantage point of his own personality, the hostility was reinforced and the emotional arousal preserved.[13]

There were at the time quite a few people who, in observing the Reform group, felt their personalities, that is, our personalities, to be chock-full of infantile urges seeking gratification in an organization providing an opportunity to attack mommy, daddy, teacher, preacher and world. For a long time I wondered about this very same notion (in) myself. But it would seem that, while politics and psychology cannot of course ever be separated theoretically or experientially, in the early hours of political socialization — as, after all, both of these tutorial organizations represented — psychological needs swell, and political requirements and ideologies often ride a few feet behind. Then, about the time that sociologists and psychologists like myself come to study these movements (or our prior experiences in them), the movements themselves are well along toward their political purposes. But for one reason or another the examiners are able to see little more than the psychological residues which trail behind in the path of mounting political action. More generally, it always seems that we are out of time or out of step with the kids: sometimes behind but sometimes, too, somewhat in advance.

A second reason for the sustained emotional arousal had to do with the fact that rarely in the Reform organization was the expression of hostility ever curtailed by fellow members or any persons associated with the organization. The individual tutor, presumably, stood as a member of a movement vis à vis society. Intense relationships and channels of deeply human exchange were established in the tutor-tutee friendship, but not very much personal gratification was received from one's activities in the tutorial setting. It was more the movement that mattered.

From the perspective of motivation, the Uplifter group seemed to transform what we have called "ignition energy," whatever it was, into a more perpetuating level of energy by redirecting an individual's attention toward the major goal of social cooperation. How this was managed is questionable. Psychologically, perhaps, members were made to feel ashamed of personal needs in light of their recognition of lofty work values. They were discouraged, moreover, from indulging in personal feelings of any sort. Perhaps they were just obliged to transcend private tribulations.

From a sociological viewpoint, the Uplifter movement may have unwittingly modified these psychological features by imposing bureaucratic mechanisms which actually turned out to increase the organization's "efficiency." Then again, there may have been considerably less anger among those recruited for the Uplifter movement. Indeed, interest in joining either of the two campus groups might have been predicated on whether the student saw himself as a teacher or as a social reformer. Though not possessing overly strong identifications with members of their movement, or for that matter with its ethos and philosophy, Uplifter members did recognize the prevailing social strategy that their movement would insist on, namely, that the tutor-tutee relationship be the basis by which the student, the school, and the community are improved.[14] Any other strategy was off-limits; hence quite a few constraints were placed on the members' freedom.

[4]

No social movement can continue to run on "ignition energy" alone, as the work proves to be excessively draining and just cannot be maintained. If the daily level of work energy is to remain moderately constant and work output is to be somewhat predictable, a new source of energy must be introduced. Anger or hostility as an igniting energy, drains an individual too quickly, too unpredictably, and often, as many organizations will confess, too unproductively. Thus a psychologically more economical fuel must be introduced after a movement is initiated.

Most campus political organizations, therefore, protect themselves from the uncertainty, confusion and the eventual reduction in strength caused by a sudden influx of persons who are seeking to let off some steam and take on some politics but who just as quickly rush off again, leaving the day-by-day work of the organization to the old standbys. A certain core of people must be maintained if any movement is to remain viable and something more than the dream of a few industrious people. So it is that the transition from an "ignition" energy to a "maintenance" energy has to be expressed and responded to in terms of those hated words routinization and bureaucratization. Genuine charisma, according to Max Weber anyway, lasts but a short time, and only routinization makes it possible for people to become functionally, economically and psychologically involved with their movement.[15]

This becomes a difficult stance to take since the words and concepts presently are so unpopular, but student leaders know what it means to "get their groups together." They know too that they must cleanse their rhetoric of classical bureaucracy language and construct a new conception of organization built along dimensions of freedom and efficacy. It may be as much in their organizational strategies as in the social and political actions they take that young political students propose changing the enormous social institutions we and they have come to know and live within. To visit an SDS meeting, for example, is to be introduced not merely to a strange and powerful political language and intention but to a sense of organizational democracy which, while appearing ragged at times, continually stresses equality among members and an ethic of total inclusion.

Outsiders at these meetings, even those "sympathetic to the cause," may see and hear a leaderless cacophony, disarray and little else but a pep rally form of spiritual coalescence. But this is not what is happening. For just as the women in the tutorial movements contributed to a vital reconceptualization of how the sexes are "supposed" to behave, so have radical groups, as much as one may wish to oppose them, contributed to a conception of organization and, if you will, bureaucratic management. Ironically, and often with great difficulty, I have sat in on SDS meetings opposing what was being offered and yet, at the same time, marveling at this new, sometimes bizarre, sometimes mysterious, sometimes crude manner in which the acting leaders were actually tutoring their constantly shifting membership in what I can only call a democratic style of open forum meeting.

Pure hatred or unmitigated hostility would not have been sufficient to sustain the members of the tutorial movements. Consequently what occurred is due in part to a change of emphasis from psychological gratification to social reform, plus the successful transformation from a heightened emotional state to a more calmed social, political or ideological state in which the earlier forms of power supply the energy required in educational and political campaigns. The transition in energy qualities is reminiscent of the four transitions of social movements advanced by the sociologist Joseph Gusfield.[16] When taken together — and here we enter a rather central realm of sociological considerations — the four transitions describe a progression or transformation of charisma into a flourishing social movement. What is interesting is that each one of the four prior situations in Gusfield's scheme represents a final state of the reform movement, while each final state depicts an end state or at least an ideal end state of the Uplifter movement.

The first transition involves the individual member. In this transition, he moves from the role of agitator to that of administrator.

The second transition refers to a member's relationship with other members. More precisely, the transition describes movement from a state of being disinherited to one of being integrated.

The third transition describes the member's relationship to what Gusfield calls his audience, or what in our terms would be those portions of society addressed by the tutorial movements.

Theoretically, the relationship shifts from one predicated on conflict with society to one predicated on cooperation with it.

Finally, there is a transition in social movements describing a fundamental change in that movement's source of action. What Gusfield outlines is essentially a transformation of the movement from collective spontaneous excitement to regulated and predictable (that important word) behavior.

Now, borrowing Gusfield's language, it seems reasonable to describe the Reform movement during its inception and in its daily activities as being agitating, disinherited, conflictual and excited.[17] Because of the character of the relationships between members and movement, the Reform organization apparently prevents these four transitions from occurring. In contrast, the Uplifter organization forces the strength of its organization upon its members and this, coupled with the psychological predispositions of the members, causes the transitions to proceed.

Besides being useful for descriptive purposes, Gusfield's transitions also predict something about the relative successes of the two groups who, even now, continue to maintain themselves. The status of the Reform movement, for example, would have suggested that either it transform itself into the final stages of a bona fide institution or perhaps die out altogether. In contrast, the Uplifter organization seemed to possess the foundation for greater longevity if only because it had depersonalized many administrative tasks which in fact demanded the attention of only moderately talented administrators. The Reform group, however, seemed destined to survive only as long as highly active people with sympathetic political and social philosophies as well as proper psychological predispositions made themselves available.

[5]

The ideal of the Reform movement was not merely to improve those Negro students lodged in lower education tracks. If it had been that, there would have been little need for the two tutorial groups to remain separated. Perhaps the true ideal of Reform leaders was expressed in the organization's major activity, "picket training."

In the beginning, tutees in the Reform group were selected on the basis of their needs for educational assistance, since without it they seemed likely to remain at the bottom of their classes or leave school. Before the tutorial process ran its course, however, tutees were made aware of the existing political forces in their own communities, their schools' "degrading" practices, and eventually the importance of some kind of revolt. Picket training represented the process of teaching and justifying the techniques for this revolt. It was what we now call outside agitation. Through picket training, the Reform movement organized its tutees into trained political cadres; it brought young people together and taught them the meanings of alienation and reform.

To picket train effectively, Reform leaders employed three procedures which insured the coalescence of members and renewed the sense of angered alienation. First, they selected only high school tutees. This guaranteed them trainees sufficiently mature to commit themselves to an important movement. Second, they established a genuine trust, especially during the early sessions. Right from the start, tutors presented their political inclinations along with their pedagogic wares. During the first meetings, emotional support enjoined with political efforts, rather than a pure teaching exchange, began to shape the nature of the tutor-tutee relationship. Then, third, after establishing a decent, trusting friendship, they "officially" accepted the tutees into the movement, a ceremony reinforced by promoting them to a level of administrative responsibility.[18]

Unlike their picket training counterparts, Uplifter tutors rarely injected political content into their teaching. Moreover, by selecting younger children than the Reformers did for their program, Uplifter administrators discouraged picket training from the outset. Indeed, soon after the recruitment of tutees, the organization functioned much like a public relations bureau: tutors visited schools, met with parents, and worked to prevent socially disruptive action. And significantly, by arming themselves with university sponsors, Uplifters tended to present a more "legitimate academic façade." Reform tutors, in contrast, rarely advertised their university associations, although they hardly could hide them, for an open exposure of their credentials seemed to endanger the marginal position they valued in performing their services.

At this point, the concept of alienation, particularly as we have applied it to the Reform movement, needs further explication. Marx's well-known treatise "Alienation and Labor," [19] which stresses the involuntary activity of the worker, the subsequent separation of man from his work, and the eventual loss of the worker's identity, perhaps expresses best what both tutorial movements were able to avoid. In contrast to an alienation from work, the type of alienation achieved in the Reform group was created by having tutors set themselves apart from institutional or university references. In order to fulfill the standards of the movement, tutors almost had to thumb their noses at those factions taking no stand in the political arena. This meant that tutors were engaged in turning people against one another, or, as we now say, polarizing activist and nonactivist students. A remark from a university student not doing tutorial work at the time illustrates this mood. After listening to a Reform leader's speech, he said: "They make me feel like *I* caused segregation, like *I* was the cause of the Negro situation. It's kinda, well, it's like I hate him for yelling at me because I am not doing anything, or maybe I feel guilt — I don't know."

As I look back over these paragraphs I begin to fear the counter-insurgency label that could be leveled at me. One issue, above all, ought to be clarified at once. While the words "outside agitator," "troublemaker," "community organizer" have been used to describe such social movements, along with the even more extreme term "brainwashing," these labels are absolutely inaccurate and almost comically nonsensical when it comes to describing the tutorial groups. Whereas few could doubt that tutees were being introduced to a movement of social reform — although I would not submit that in actuality they were being used as "fodder for the revolution" — no one could honestly deny the impressive concern and sense of care demonstrated by members of both of these organizations. Underlying all the anger, discontent, the desire for change and at times the belief that America was incorrigible was the very same ethic now being advanced by so many educators — to treat students with decency and integrity.

Thus, what the tutorial movements had in mind when they spoke of reform and improving human rights was not at all in conflict with their members' insistence that schools treat students as people and not as numbers, not as lifeless roles, and not as objects. When all the anger is dissected and tutors' identifications with tutees are finally understood, we may discover that one additional motivation to do tutorial work is the treatment of tutors by their own universities, for they too feel a sense of rejection, dehumanization and an alienation in a society which, when examined closely, has not included them nor valued their talents as much as it might and as much as it should. Saul Alinsky's words about popular education are more than relevant here and very much reminiscent of the recent educational pieces written by such men as Paul Goodman and George Dennison: "The organization is convinced that when people get to know one another as human beings instead of as symbols or statistics, a human relationship — carrying with it a full constellation of human attitudes — will inevitably result." [20]

Let us understand that while differing on their degree of political association and interest, both tutorial movements observed the daily harm that comes to children as a result of the dehumanizing treatment they receive in schools — and, let us be fair, by both white and black adults and children. In light of the myriad examinations of ghetto schools, it hardly seems necessary to describe here the conditions found by these university tutors. If ever a rescue fantasy seemed justified, this was the time. Yet neither tutorial group indulged in such a fantasy as each in its way built an organization and a philosophy quite apart from this fantasy. In defense of the counterinsurgency argument, I have to assert that, when all was said and done and, inevitably, analyzed, it was the need to care for a group not of disenfranchised people, for that word seems so elegant and actually was not that popular then, but a group of people who just were being gypped, set aside, forgotten. The university students couldn't stand it any longer. Maybe they felt guilty, maybe bitter, maybe confused. Who knows? Whatever the reasons, however, they felt that something had to be done, and the development of tutorial groups was the political action they took. Maybe it should be said that politics was growing out of this simple yet deeply complicated urge to help make life better and possible for a small group of people not very much younger than the tutors themselves.

The irony of that whole period is that the attack on the university's role in this gypping process was barely audible. I recall statements like, How nice it would be if the university helped us a bit more or took more interest in us. But I seriously doubt that anyone then, with very few exceptions, had on his or her mind the idea that the university and its riches, and not the slums a few blocks away, would soon be the zone for out-and-out war. This idea was not spoken of in those days; the work of the tutors kept them and their charges off the city streets and out of trouble, so peace was maintained. But let us recall that these were days before Stokely Carmichael would move to throw whites out of "the movement." These were the days when white university students could move about on the "outside" and, possibly because of this, dare to overlook what later on some of them would find unforgivable in their own neighborhoods.

[6]

We return now to the original third and fourth propositions, the highly speculative ones and the ones most difficult to evaluate. We are not in these propositions advocating what Hoffer has described as the "total surrender of a distinct self to a movement." [21] Nor can we confirm his notion that "people whose lives are barren and insecure seem to show a greater willingness to obey than people who are self-sufficient and self-confident. To the frustrated, freedom from responsibility is more attractive than freedom from restraint." [22] Far from it. These processes are not at all representative of the students in the tutorial movements.

Closer to the truth, I think, is the earlier idea that the black tutee may have unconsciously represented a part of the tutor's own self-image. The black youth, for example, was reached at a time when he was experiencing oppression in a way that the tutor may have wished to experience or perhaps was already experiencing oppression. And, too, a deep feeling of oppression emerges from an adolescence where no long-lasting objects of restraint are known or where one finds no support for his urge to attack the usual objects of restraint which have greater relevance for others. Accordingly, desired rebellion might be directed "nowhere," that is, inwards, or everywhere: at home, parents, teachers, friends, the government, fashions, conformity. Speculatively, the tutor, himself sheltered by an often unreal mothering school environment about which contemporary students remain so ambivalent, may have unconsciously redefined the tutorial relationship such that the *tutee* could legitimately rebel against all those forces which never did oppose themselves to the tutor. The *tutor*, on the other hand, could attack a so-called middle-class position (the position of his parents and some contemporaries), which he may have equated with a neutral or opposing attitude toward integration. The fact that Reform tutors dramatized their collective need for revolt may explain some of the hostility directed at nonparticipating university students.

By "legitimate rebellion" and "legitimate opposition" I mean only that there was support for the position to oppose institutions and persons whom tutors felt had contributed to the horrid conditions of ghettos. There was a collective spirit, in other words, a movement. If a tutor, in his aloneness or out of the purely idiosyncratic nature of his psychology, wished to "fight back" but could find neither a cause for rebellion nor an object toward which he might direct his anger, his activity may have been permanently silenced or, more often than not, directed at a central source of the rebellion, himself.

One implication of this point is that some students, though surely not all, after seeking out social and political movements initially to deal with their rage, disappointment or sense of rejection, may quickly leave the movements when they discover, first, objects to which they may direct their anger or whatever it is and, second, that in truth they hold a very meager interest in politics. These people, in other words, have received from the movement exactly what they required: the certainty that they need not continue to direct their antagonisms inward but may finally direct them to the people who rightly should receive them. In this almost cathartic manner political movements on some campuses, according to their own leaders, have played a psychotherapeutic role in teaching especially younger students that they no longer must blame themselves for all the world's evils. Where these students go from there is not as well known.

Through the recruitment of older tutees the "identification" process, if we may call it that, became more credible for Reformers. Tutors, after all, were a mere step away from their own high school years and presumably there would be less credibility in an attempt to identify with grammar school children who are not fully aware of their own potential for social action. In psychological terms, moreover, a very young tutee may be so malleable and so willing to comply that imbuing him with the seeds of reform might also fail to bring that certain satisfaction to the tutor. In the end, therefore, the movement must possess believable intellectual and emotional impacts in order for both the tutor and tutee to experience a social-psychological plausibility as well as, perhaps, the attending unconscious rewards. To some extent, an age similarity brings persons closer together and makes their action and activity credible.

How tempting it is to conjecture that tutors were the children of those proverbial permissive parents. If this were true, we might guess that the greater the degree of experienced permissiveness the more tutors would seek out organizations affording the opportunity to strike back against a passive and seemingly indifferent society. We might also guess that the movement would provide tutors with the symbolic materials of aggression, such as the tutee himself.[23] The revenge that hypothetically ensues would appear to be somewhat free of conflict because, first, tutors would believe they could incite others who felt as they did and, second, because the movement enjoyed such wide acceptance in substantial sectors of the society, or at least in the university community. Conjectures aside, tutorial groups, even in "those days," were not maverick groups. The tutees, moreover, through whom the psychological revenge was supposedly being achieved, were themselves learning to seek revenge. So what existed in the psychological reality of a tutor was brought to fruition in the social and cultural realities of his tutee.

Although it is considerably popular, the permissiveness hypothesis has more than a few failings. Most important among them is the fact that the very concept of permissiveness has come to suggest so many things that it is now practically meaningless. And, as if this were not enough, too little evidence exists to support a notion of parental permissiveness generating student activism. Still, it is true that Reform group tutors characteristically described their parents as political neutrals or as politically disaffected. Remarks from two tutors illustrate this rather clearly: "My parents read the papers but I don't think they really understand what I'm doing here," one said. "In fact, I wonder whether they understand anything I do. All they seemed to care about was that I went to college. So I'm here." "My parents are great," the other responded. "They really are, but they live in another generation, that's all. They won't vote for Goldwater if he's nominated, but they are out of it in civil rights. It is not their concern. In a way, I somehow think I wasn't a concern of theirs either until something went wrong, you know, until I did something that would bother them." How very often are politics and parents aligned in the psychology of those students in whom we have taken special interest.

[7]

Turning now to the last of the propositions, we are reminded of the sociological writings which speak to a difference between characteristically masculine and feminine kinds of behavior, and how this behavior relates more specifically to the ways in which people come to define "appropriate" tasks and enduring life-styles for themselves. In the main, sex role differentiation is understood first in the context of family relationships.[24] Here is where a child learns that, good or bad, right or wrong, there is a rather predictable set of forms governing the division of labor which, however, do not always work out so smoothly. For all sorts of reasons, there arises the problem for some parents and for some children of just who does wear the group pants. There arises as well the more conceptual problem of why someone must assume authority or leadership in almost every group situation. So it is that sex role identification tends to meet, if we may say this, sociological as well as psychological encumbrances.

Unlike most institutions, the tutorial movements provided opportunities for women to assume leadership positions "normally" given over to men. Run almost exclusively by university women, the movements recruited or seemed to appeal to women who, if not desiring so-called instrumental type jobs, then at least felt comfortable in them. Whereas Reform women sought out these jobs, Uplifter women tended to go about comparable tasks in a conspicuously more "feminine" style, that is, as we unthinkingly and prejudicially, perhaps, tend to define feminine style. One might say that they pursued social change in a highly integrative fashion. In their dealings with schools and the community, for example, Uplifter women leaders seemed to worry about bandaging social wounds even before the changes they advocated had been undertaken.

Reform women leaders, however, tended to avoid these emotional or integrative actions—which, again, we think of as feminine — in their affairs outside of headquarters. They made their plans and capitalized on their acts before any hurts were healed. They pushed for integration inside the movement but not outside of it. Furthermore, the conspicuous political orientation of their movement with its scent of quiet revolution marked it as being what society unfortunately considers masculine. Quite often people would ask what kind of women would perform in these ways. (One explanation of female predominance in the tutorial movements would be that women normally had more free time than men to devote to such activities. But this explanation holds primarily for nonuniversity people and does not explain the different representation of the sexes among participating university students.[25]

It would follow from these observations that the psychological perspectives of persons recruited for administrative positions in the tutorial organizations must be minimally congruent with the styles of the organization itself. Moreover, people of either sex demonstrating what society defines as masculine behavior should be more attracted to Reform group positions, where open rebellion and an impulse to shove their group's ideas into society are salient. In this light, there is some evidence, though scant, that the Uplifter group attracted slightly older and usually married women who seemed a bit more content with a tutorial project free from political, revolutionary or even "angry young man" overtones. These women openly expressed their desire to help but at the same time chose not to define their work as political or social engineering in nature. In short, they elected to be helpers, not soldiers.

The Reform and Uplifter tutorial organizations represent two characteristic kinds of student-oriented social protest movements, movements which continue to exist on many American campuses. To understand a part of their identity is to understand some of the social psychological involvements manifested by student populations in their important, sincere and active participation in the civil rights movement. The differences between the Reform and Uplifter movements, I suppose, could be reduced to notions like personal identity versus bureaucratic effectiveness; psychological sustenance versus sociological maintenance; social revolt versus social repair; or even those rather cumbersome terms picket training versus level raising. But this kind of dichotomous reasoning neither honors these groups nor elucidates their programs. More importantly, the processes we have superficially described and speculated upon symbolize many of the social and psychological dynamics extant in modern civil rights organizations and possibly point to some of the problems encountered not just by individual students but by large student groups seeking to maintain themselves. One hopes the observations have some relevance for these groups as they anticipate the difficulties that will continue to arise both from within and outside their movements.

At present there is a feeling among many of those still calling themselves civil rights workers that the intensity and vitality of the modern social protest cannot be extended in this, one of its earliest forms. Should this sentiment turn out to be true, it will be interesting to trace the evolution of both types of tutorial groups, particularly the Reform group, which thus far has avidly refrained from making any bureaucratic preparations for the future. In the meantime, however, there remains the issue of that certain group of students struggling to hold on to American democracy in its most fundamental forms. More precisely, there is the issue of their ambivalence toward national elections and the men who ask these students' parents and perhaps now them as well for support every few years.

chapter 10

Thank God for the Simple People

And I asked myself about the present: how wide it was,
how deep it was, how much was mine to keep.
                    Kurt Vonnegut, *Slaughterhouse-Five*

For the so-called radical students, the presidential
elections of 1968 couldn't have been less exciting or more lacking
in import. Standing firmly opposed to the system that they claim
reinforces unrepresentative government, and having lived through
Miami's pap and Chicago's street wars, they regarded the big
election eve hoopla, which some now barely remember, as just
another bit of ugly America. For the more moderate students, as
they have come to be called, but most especially for the young Re-
publicans, it was a sweet victory, a victory tempered only by the
norms of opulent suaveness and precocious restraint usually operating on most American campuses to "control" their young Republican and Democrat "fraternities."

For large groups of students, however, it was neither victory nor
another political bit. Indeed, it was the crashing end to what someone called a "self-indulgent fantasy" they had been nurturing for
weeks and the onslaught of what someone else saw as a most piti-
able sense of guilt. For large groups of students, that one Tuesday
night's television vigil had convened calmly enough with drinks,
sandwiches and discussions of school and life, women and men,
but had ended late the next morning with hundreds of them on
their knees, exhausted, begging for California, Ohio, Illinois and

Missouri to "come home to Humphrey." As Nixon had pulled slightly ahead and as each early indication of a possible Humphrey breakthrough had turned out to be little more than the wishful reporting of professional but still political announcers, the power of this one election had hit these students on the head like a ton of uncontested electoral votes. "Do you believe this? We were all there, some of the same kids who had been in New Hampshire with McCarthy. We watched TV like boobs, and everyone there with his VOTE WITH YOUR FEET button was literally on his feet, rooting, cheering, crying for Humphrey."

By Wednesday morning university buildings had sagged with the weighty depression of these particular "kids." Rumors of cabinet appointments were on everyone's lips. It was definite: Volpe for Health, Education and Welfare! Romney for Secretary of State! But it could be Reagan or Strom Thurmond! They would have to go somewhere. "When you really have to worry," a friend said, "is when our neuroses turn out to have prophetic utility in addition to the damage they already do." Actually, few of us at lunch on that Wednesday, as I recall, had anything much to say; not enough data were in yet. But, as one sociologist remarked, when has the absence or paucity of data ever stopped social scientists? We laughed and several people most assuredly thought momentarily about the growing precariousness of their federal research grants. Then it was, just as the phrase goes, business as usual.

But it wasn't business as usual for all the students. For now, two years later, with quite a bit of "data" in, it is clear that some students, some young Americans were profoundly saddened or angered with themselves and were openly admitting of the dream they had played out and of the fitful realities they had denied. For many, it took an entire year for that certain "data" to emerge. One girl, for example, confessed to the fantasy that she would awaken to discover Bobby Kennedy running against John Lindsay. Another was convinced that Governor Wallace had stolen votes and that upon their return Vice-President Humphrey would win. For others it was the absentee ballots that would save the Vice-President, and for still others a fantasy was born that the minority candidates were going to pool and collectively transfer their votes. In the midst of it all came "news" that Medgar Evers was really alive! And, for a long moment, it was believed. A few thought that with the election won, Nixon would "release" Agnew. "It's possible, you know." Many held tightly to this last thought, their eyes opening wide as though a revelation had finally released some ponderous anchor.

The absolutely clear and unquestioned belief extant in so many of these young minds was that out of that one November's mysteries would come a savior, a father, a man who would make everything come out all right. For many, the belief or wish or whatever it is persists until this very instant. To be sure, for some psychology graduate students, the whole thing sounded strangely like children expressing a faith in the ultimate omnipotence of their fathers or, as they (and we) say, "father figures." Several students even suggested that similar dynamics might be at work when adults merely enter voting booths. "Who knows what people hope for when they pull that political slot machine handle?" All the same, there were many young college as well as high school students who preserved this rescue belief right to the very end. But in the absence of such a man, they had decided it was all downhill from here, and disaster, as a sardonic hope, became an imminent possibility.

They recall it all now as if it had occurred yesterday, for in fact yesterday, the first Tuesday of a fresh and new November, brought it all back to them. The language and sentiments directed at Lindsay and Stokes and Austin, naturally, were a bit more cautious now, a bit more restrained. "That damn Nixon election aged me. That's what it did. It aged me." Elections age us all, of course, for they seem to clump the years together by fours and then, all at once, even with forewarning, jolt us forward as if someone were seeking to make up missed birthday parties or perhaps, as if time itself had forgotten us, and recognizing "its" oversight, had yanked us out of our already dislocated status.

For some students, the fantasy of being rescued was irrelevant and a bitter petulance remained. Many, after all, had knocked themselves out from McCarthy and Kennedy to California and Chicago. Their idealism and their idols had been killed and they damn well weren't going to give another ounce of sweat for what they saw and maybe continue to see as a sick and rotten society. "America's been a caricature this long; we might just as well keep our image intact." (Strangely enough, just as this sort of language was "properly" attributed to angry college demonstrators, it has popped up again, uttered by, of all people, United States Senators.)

Quite a few people, of course, had felt this petulance, this anger stained with defiance, and had worked to keep the energy levels of the young high. They had done everything to encourage students to transform their energy back into work; into working for local peace candidates; into working to build up funds and political structures. But too many of the "kids" wanted none of it. Perhaps it was their pride or even narcissism that urged them toward a say in the big contest. Quite justifiably, they wanted a voice in the presidency and found themselves unable to get involved with local candidates who too often lacked charisma and confidence. In a way, the lingering disappointments of 1968 had seeped into their contemporary impressions of John Lindsay and Carl Stokes and, to a greater extent, William Austin. For a while their mood was such that even "Big John" couldn't be exciting unless he was running for something exciting. Merely to beat those other two candidates in New York was hardly worth the investment of campaign volunteer work. Nonetheless, with many, Lindsay has always remained the exception to everything and so he emerges, as one student put it, a "more enticing bit of sociology." Still, the disengagement, the extrication from politics was all there, partly demonstrated in the students' bellicosity and irreverence, partly demonstrated in the irreconcilable set of disappointments and setbacks. They had had something, but it had been taken away, and so by their own admission many preferred to choose the route of inactive defiance. They chose to sulk and lie to themselves that they didn't give a damn.

But they gave a great damn, and their unrelenting care masked by cleverly created resistances burst through on that Tuesday night over two years ago, and then gave way once again but a few nights back. To risk a pun, they were inundated by the utter collapse of their own damns. For weeks before the presidential campaign many students had counseled people not to vote. Their grocers, janitors, launderers, postmen, barbers, everyone had been advised, most likely quite rightly, that under either candidate the poor and especially the poor blacks would suffer and the name of militarism would shine like never before. Couldn't people see there was no choice but to vote "no" to the whole blasted democratic way! Then, as Wednesday's early hours came on, these same students found themselves wondering whether the grocers and launderers and barbers had cared enough and had in fact voted. They had parked themselves in front of their TVs — flipping between Cronkite and Huntley-Brinkley; it was all dependent on who seemed to possess the optimistic returns or on who might make a slip and thereby reveal his preferences — and had rooted for America's squares and straight-arrows. And they had cursed the nonvoting public. All this came back to these certain students during those months between the two Novembers.

In interview after interview students told of the late-summer discussions with their parents. With one foot practically out the door on their way back to school, they had fought with staid, incorrigible elders who dared consider themselves liberals and, in a few cases, intellectuals as well. They admitted to the "vague superiority" feelings they held toward their parents, feelings which had been born elsewhere but revitalized on their campuses. They spoke also of tasting the pride of "coming on tough," "like a radical." If only to maintain their student-political postures and that generational distance everyone speaks of today and which students, like the rest of us, buy, they fought against the notion of the better of two evils. They harped instead on the "evil of two lessers" slogan, and then they labored to maintain the splendor and minimize the confusion that grows out of the many roles they presently are obliged to endure: son, daughter, student, political activist, "anti-establisher." Some sheepishly admitted — although the admissions came many months later — to making a case of their individuality and autonomy by arguing with their parents from political positions, indeed radical positions they knew little about and truthfully didn't even advocate.

Some, however, advocate these positions now. They have protested, read, watched and protested some more. Much of the arguing with parents has stopped, but the eagerness to march with comrades, invade buildings, and crash working-class society through the gates and onto universities' private and public land has grown.

For some, that is, it has grown; but it hasn't grown for all. For now, even a few months later, others, having tasted the tastes of "political activism," have turned away from politics and have literally run back to classes, to studying, even to scholarship and classroom compliance. At least, some teachers say that they have; the students aren't yet certain. The war continues to annoy so many young people. The first moratorium seemed so right, so unequivocal, so appropriate. But the molesting of deans and calling the police "cops" or "pigs" is a bit more confusing than it was a year ago. Long times can be that short. Duration that subjective. Early September that different from early June.

But on that one Tuesday evening in 1968 many students prayed that their parents hadn't listened to them but instead had contributed enough to Humphrey's campaign to pull him over the top. For once in their lives, perhaps, the "kids" had hoped their parents might see through the petulance and defiance. For once, perhaps, they rooted for their parents to "make it," just as they would root for Bonnie, Clyde, Butch Cassidy and the Sundance Kid to "make it." "Thank God for the simple people," one girl sighed. "Thank God not everyone's an intellectual." And one year later she would smile at the thought that her words and the bitterly complex philosophy that had launched them would place her, politically that is, or is it socially, not too far from an Alabama governor who makes quite a few students smile. "I'll give him one thing, that sonofabitch racist. He spoke his mind. He's not so dumb, you know."

"I know."

[2]

No one knows for sure the sources of complex feelings like guilt and shame. Indeed, on the basis of even long conversations over long periods of time one hesitates or should hesitate to label people guilty or shameful. In this instance, however, a sizable number of students were themselves willing to label their own feelings. And this is just as it should be.

"I'm glad I didn't have to face Humphrey," a college junior confessed. "I feel as though I've committed some incredible crime which the whole world knows about but no one can catch me." Others were actually impressed by the fact that they had somehow managed to keep their feelings from consciousness, and thus from themselves throughout the entire campaign. Only recollection brought the feelings back from time. They spoke of an irritable neutrality during the last weeks of that October. They recalled ridiculing all of the candidates and remembered a final contentment when Senator Kennedy got jeered in Boston for playing party politics and doing his best for "Hubie." But by that Wednesday morning it was a different story, not only for the Democrats but for those who had teetered on the very rim of an abused democratic apparatus.

It is foolish to reduce these political attitudes to psychological processes, just as it is dangerously absurd to speak of the anger and disaffection of radical students purely in terms of a displaced hatred of authority or of a reaction to permissive upbringing. If truth be known, sociological processes too must be taken into account when one is speaking of the political attitudes and intentions held by individuals. Study after study indicates that most adults commence and conclude their voting experiences in the model of their parents. Even contemporary radicals often seem to be continuing battles with their society undertaken what must seem to them eons ago by their very own parents. So something is being passed on, even if one must wait a while for its appearance. (Is this what they have recently called the hereditability factor?) More important, there is at some point in the development of attitudes and beliefs the internalization of other's beliefs along with the incorporation of ideologies prevalent in one's society, in another's society, or in the perceptions of this other's society. This too we know.

For the students in question, indeed for most students, political attitudes (or, in the case of radicals, becoming politicized to the point that one can speak of "my politics") hardly represent some esoteric currency one could easily get along without. Political "activism" or more precisely, devotion to politics, campaigning, revolution, social change, isn't an extracurricular routine sought by students to clear their minds of book learning and lectures. The effort is too great, the task too hard. Politics is for many the central core of their very souls; it is the single reason for their "staying on" and the fulcrum of their identity. It is, in a word, their work; possibly it is their religion as well. All else comes second. Whether we admit to this or not, it now seems to be a cold, hard fact.

No doubt the transition from high school or college campus political preoccupation to politics as occupation disturbs many people in the "establishment," whatever that is. But if ever there was commitment to or solidarity with a cause or purpose, albeit an evanescent or transitory one, the students, like those they have wittingly aroused to oppose them, make this commitment. They work at politics. They work hard at it, finding in it themselves, as they say, along with the oppressed, and finding a serious identity along with a dedication to progress, change or even revolution. If their entire political enterprise were to stop tomorrow (as some wish it would) or make an inexplicable about-face, one could never rightly call that enterprise a psychological displacement or social moratorium. Indeed, with so many of its features, it now possesses the characteristics Robert Bellah (in *Religion in America*) [1] has described as being an American civil religion. To hear America, now in a time of open fighting on political issues, react is to hear, perhaps, the unabating antipathies toward a logic and a reverence that once dominated national religious wars: "What I don't yet have figured out clearly is how all of this connects up with what's going on in Ireland," a graduate student mused, "but I will. Give me another week." And someone scanning the Pittsburgh mayoralty election returns of 1969 responded: "I wish there would always be someone around to guarantee us each day that we always had another week."

For the silent student Humphrey supporters, politics or its religious images lay somewhere between their soul and the world of

what is amusingly termed "extracurricular" pursuits. The images
lay at the periphery of the field over which one romps and plays
in his attempt to find what he must keep from his childhood,
what he must shed, and what of adulthood he can honestly and
permanently reconcile and protect. Politics, after all, symbolizes
much of that ugly adult world made and perpetrated by "them,"
but gradually and inevitably falling into younger and softer hands
and now, although hardly to any overwhelming degree, to a few
black hands as well. But of course on this last point the students
continue to reinterpret the evidence and continue to debate.
Progress yes! Progress no! Hoffman versus the Supreme Court decision to get tough with segregated schools in the South. Justice
Burger versus Mr. Mitchell. Stokes's win, Bradley's loss. Charles
Evers's win, "What's-his-face's loss in Minneapolis."

"The blacks aren't getting anywhere at all."

"You can't say that anymore, man. You can't say that!"

But some still do, while others live so deeply inside the bowels
of this country they cannot hear the debates at all. Or, if they can,
even without being filled in they're already tired of them.

As Kenneth Keniston,[2] among others, has indicated, the remarkable psychological adjustments made by the majority of radicals have not yet been made by the majority of students. Most students continue to internalize politics partly for its function in
effecting change and distributing power in society but partly, too,
for its function in effecting change and realigning values within
their private personality structures, private geographies and fantasies. At various levels, therefore, politics is not only keeping a
bigot out of the White House; it is an attempt to resolve one's
relationship with authority and response to rules and outright
repression everywhere. Thus, while one cannot reduce political beliefs and attitudes to simple psychologisms, although the temptation to do this grows, one is wrong, I think, to suspect that purely
psychological processes play no part at all in their evolution, and
particularly during adolescence. It is at this age when, as so many
social scientists and critics have pointed out, society insists that
schools keep the children out from under the mature feet of hard-

working adults who themselves are either trying to make it or, sad as it is, have already made it.

"It ain't this way in Israel," a Rhodes scholar roared over a beer. "Man, at thirteen they tell those kids, 'Today you are a man,' and that kid had better believe he is. They'll hoist him up into some four-wheel-drive tractor made in South Bend or make him pick olives, and he can suck his thumb or finger his pimples, but he'll work ten hours a day and shut up about it. Or get out."

"Sure he will, those militant bastards. They think they're Westmoreland incarnate."

Then, for an ever increasing but still chosen group, college comes along and predictably, as in most academic experiences, the internalization of knowledge or the exposure to political matters as well as the involvement (dare I say identification) with the dispatchers of knowledge again means reconciling social politics with what R. D. Laing poetically calls the "Politics of Experience." [3] With books and teachers as well as with academic regulations and rituals, students try on politics for its social and personal size. Some will buy in, others not; but not fully aware of the psychological consequences of their investments, the great majority will need more time and more contact with admired men and women from whom they can borrow political wraps. They will need time to pretend, time to romp, time to attack and time to decide. They will employ politics and politicians as weapons against whole societies, one another, their parents and teachers. They will be confused and troubled by young contemporaries who having successfully completed, it would seem to these students, their trials and pretending now proclaim themselves fulltime political animals — no, political humans, if not revolutionaries. In fact, one can go further and say that at times they will feel troubled and bullied by the radicals.

But even this too may be changing. Students now have discovered new objects against whom they must fight in order to keep themselves in schools and to preserve their sanity. Indeed, it appears as though the challenges and taunting they have for months leveled against known and unknown commanders are finally being answered. For, in a frightening way, as in the war games of children and adults alike, every player who makes a claim to some bit of America has suddenly sprung out of his darkened trap or fox-hole and with guns and words firing streams of ammunition has begun to yell: "All right, you guys. Here I am. You better come and get me or I'm coming to get you." That's what many students say they hear right now in their land. And they don't know whether to make believe it's an old Cagney or Garfield rerun and laugh, or whether it is the beginning of a national psychotic break-down and quit, only to die.

[3]

In the case of Humphrey's silent generation, what seemed to have troubled students more than anything else was that the lead and support of trusted intellectuals seemed momentarily to vanish. Like petulant children, many adults, as with derision we are called, threw literate temper tantrums and surrendered after Chicago 1968 never to be heard from again until our deans were physically disposed of and extraordinary faculty meetings demanded our re-appearance into that world we dare call political. Several students remembered the learned scholars and journalists who presumably could afford to write of America's need for a vacation from pol-itics and of the black revolution's becoming a "drag." So it was that some of the very persons who had been teaching the young to "turn on" to politics suddenly were seen throwing the switch the other way and retreating to the darkness, to the traps and the foxholes. The public petitions and statements stopped and already tenuous campaigns collapsed. Everyone was "pulling up stakes," "despairing," being "wiped out," and unprepared students were left holding nothing but their "VOTE WITH YOUR FEET" buttons.

Wanting to be fair to both sides, for there always seem to be two sides, many professors in fact switched alliances and went right along supporting the better of two evils — that is, they voted for the 1968 and 1969 models of democracy. Actually, some of their signatures appeared in rather conspicuous places. Because of this action, this consistency and loyalty, they suffered public abuse.

But the students denigrated all of this and labeled the whole bunch of "them" "sell-outs," apologists for "the system," or institutional liberals, racists or cowards. But for the most part, in pursuing public and private political ends many of us, however briefly, forfeited our genuine political shares and in so doing abandoned the students and the country they hold in such adoring contempt.

But, still wishing to be fair, it is difficult to understand, much less explain, this need for men, for saviors and fathers, this need for other men, that the rest of us too maintain. Why is it so hard to admit to the students that the loss we feel at the death of Kennedys, Malcolm X's, Everses, Kings and so many others, even those who die, as they say, "natural deaths," destroys a part of us too and, in a sense, drives us back to our work, to our "business as usual–ness" with a new brand of fervor if not exceptional parochialism? Why is it so hard to explain to them that abandonment can make us abandon? The various forms of losses in politics, ideological concessions, campaign defeats, jailed students, crying policemen, battered human beings and the assassinated all pull us out of one form of existential alliance and slip us into new forms. And how often do we not even know what's happening to us or feel the slippage that surely occurs. As for the students, the prevailing abandonment either cannot be articulated or is so disturbing it just is better left in silence.

In no uncertain terms, many students were abandoned, forsaken, and thereby compelled literally to mill about the grounds and playfields of college campuses. Afraid and unwilling to go home, unable to express their anger and gloom to their once revered abandoners, they sat on their anger, made themselves vulnerable to the bullies on the outside and to the guilt (or is it shame?) on the inside, and, as if in a dream, played out the long weeks of Octobers and the early days of Novembers.

Dreams, however, always come to a bewildering and unequivocal end. For a moment one lies there quietly, looking about, seeking bearings, reorganizing, rearranging, and then wham — it's ice-cold reality! It is this way with assassinations, the defeat of minority planks, and the apparent conclusions of unsuccessful campaigns. And it is this way in awakening each morning. Just for an instant

one is peaceably drowned in the illogical mysteries of a seductive
and terrifying unconscious only to be doused suddenly by an implacable reality. In that instant we say that we feel numbness.

This, in part, is what so many students felt during those days.
Sandwiched between their ongoing battles for autonomy and the
abandonment by teachers against whom retaliation seemed impossible, they sought were dreams, wishes, fantasies, anything that
might have prevented the inevitable awakening. They denied their
preference for Humphrey and with their denial renounced an im-
permanent ideological (and familial) alliance with their parents.
They tried to lock the entire campaign away but again and again
it exploded out of its psychic shackles and probably it continues to
smolder. One reason it does is because very recent political and life-
style conversions of many young faculty have brought new hope to
many students and a fiercely new vision to various sectors of some
universities. In a way, these conversions and transformations re-
kindle the same spirits lost during national and local elections. Yet
these very same conversions have contributed to a drifting back to
scholarship and a social compliance evidenced by some of the more
quiet students. But here too a problem arises, for, as Daniel
Ogilvie has pointed out, deciphering students' silence becomes an
awesome task. Always, it seems, students manage to find means
and methods for introspecting themselves to the point of psychic
death. They fear, Ogilvie writes, "that they have no insides, and
this fear is countered by a fear that they *do* have insides that they
don't know what to do with."

Most distressing about all of this, perhaps, is the fact that so few
of us during these last years were able or willing to see through
the students' and our own denials. Certain ones among us actually believed that none of us gave a damn. We agreed of course
about Governor Wallace, but that issue was an easily managed
decoy. For a while it seemed as though only the radicals maintained their principles and equanimity, but this may have been
because they had previously articulated the pieces of America's
puzzle that they wanted to replace or destroy. They have not nor
will they be concerned with or seduced by the same old pieces that
invariably remain after national political conventions, both truly

effete campaigns and out-and-out street warfare. But what too many of the rest of us did during the time between the last November elections was first to reject the pieces offered to us and then, because they weren't exactly the pieces we wanted, to pretend that all the remaining pieces were equally intolerable. When we lost the first step we canceled the whole parade and thereby deprived thousands of students who, although they weren't necessarily proud to admit it, would have been quite eager to march.

Now, with what might actually be described as a year-long tantrum unpleasantly behind us, the confessions and waning sadness of Humphrey's formerly recanting supporters who had urged others not to vote and their symbolic successors caution us to return to political work. A time of waiting and exalting the "simple people" to inaction has ended, and the age of the "silent majority" has apparently been born once again. Something broke down during that one year, something which, not at all ironically, was almost reestablished by the "simple people" but which now requires considerable repair and commitment. It does seem ironic, however, that America's President offers us a model of someone who has also trespassed upon a rather shaky world of denial and defeat.

[4]

A final implication of the ambivalence toward so-called democratic procedures and student involvement in politics requires brief mention. Of all the surely hundreds of studies made of the origins of and reasons behind so-called student activism, one point rarely receives proper underscoring. It is that one of the best predictors of a student's participation in political action of any sort is his prior experience in political action. The point seems almost too simple to be true or valuable, but considerable evidence stands behind it. The high school students immersed in all types of social agencies and organizations undergo priming as well as gratifying experiences. They may not conceive of these experiences in this way, and one hopes they don't, as schools generally emphasize preparation to an almost destructive and certainly dehumanizing extent. But the fact remains that, having taken their first public political steps, these students are now predisposed to seek opportunities, situations, people who might provide the next step. And the next step, even if only the machine of time is at work, should be more intense, more involving, more committing, more serious. But this step, like the one before it, also possesses its preparative and teaching functions.

The students who went with McCarthy not merely to New Hampshire but to America waited for, hoped for or simply surmised, if they didn't actually initiate, the arrival of events like Moratorium days. Similarly, many of the students who went to Chicago in 1968 or saw a televised Chicago or heard first, second, third, tenth-hand warrior accounts of Chicago pledged that singular event to be their first preparative act and then waited for the next shots. In three or four days, literally thousands of students (and probably many of their elders) felt a jolt which resulted in their swinging several standard deviations more to the left of a fluctuating political center. There were, after all, the dove plank, the Daley machine, the police and anything else they might have wanted to include in order to amplify their case. But above it all was the decision, made with greater deliberation than most of us seem to recognize, to abandon long-standing democratic processes and appropriate attitudes. And, to repeat, while some political conversions take place almost religiously on the spot, most require a preparation and personal reflection that often go unnoticed. So it was that many of the defeated in the two Chicagos and in the two Novembers returned to their college campuses to wait for that single event, that single "confrontation," that single shot which would not only provide for the taking of the next step but which would simultaneously legitimate its ultimate actualization.

Young people more and more choose to enter the pools of politics as members of movements and organizations. They enter, reasonably enough, at the shallow end but soon, finding the air outside so crippling and cold and the comradeship inside so deliciously invigorating and healthful, they make their way, in the habit of genuine achievement and mobility, either swimming or by crawling hand-over-hand along the edges to the deep and deepest end. And the process goes on. More and more entering, more and more working their way to political depths in which they'll either sink or swim. And more and more, to the surprise of practically no one, the pools expand until gradually they threaten to overcome the land in which originally they were built and which promised to support as well as delimit them. It has become a time of political inundation and flooding, a time of splashing overflow and displacement which will no longer grant immunity and safety to the "simple people."

There can be no doubt now that new and different means are being experimented with as young people bid to make their peace (or war) with American democracy. For some, being on the edge of "the system" provokes a mood of uncertainty which seems as though it cannot last too much longer; it is to these people that this chapter has been devoted. For others, the regular steps and even recently invented ones fail to bring gratification, and hence they require much more; it is this group that the preceding chapter was concerned about.

But there is a psychological as well as a historical evolution to be told in these chapters and in the next two as well, an evolution that right now seems to be pitting the generations against one another, or at least putting them in range of fitful combat. About to occur, quite obviously, is a tension far greater than what bubbles in Urbana or erupted finally in Wellesley or manifested itself in organizational strategies in a university's tutorial movements. Because the ambivalence felt so deeply toward their nation and its government by so many young Americans cannot be sustained, it may have to be resolved either by an almost ludicrous about-face yielding a timorous obeisance or by an increase of bloody violence "on the streets." The friction, confusion, sense of betrayal and anger to be found in students described in this and the next chapters make more and more real, more and more prophetic the terrifying words written by those who, in examining the United States, wonder about the tension between an old or traditional culture and a counter culture which recently has made itself militant and imposing.[4]

The battles waged outwardly by young people with their parents and inwardly with themselves over the American elections of 1968 and 1969 stand as a significant historical fact. Presaging change as much as evoking defiance, they lay bare the question of whether informed young Americans are going to be able to get through college (and soon maybe high school as well) without taking one really wild shot at American society, a shot that more likely than not will add to that bloodbath. In writing this sentence and in recalling certain events that occurred over the last year or two, I cannot truthfully be certain whether I am scaring myself by resorting to words, mine and others', like "bloodbath," "genocide" and "wild shot," or whether those of us who have witnessed the intensity of disapproval and dissatisfaction of young people are now genuinely frightened and resigned to the coming of a revolution, even if it is only an abortive one, or a shabby one, a messed up one, or unadulterated theater.

If nothing more, revolution means a complete reordering of one's memory, present plans and safeguarded intentions. To those of us who cannot really count ourselves among the revolutionaries, it demands that we think and read, speak and hear, remember and dream in an entirely different way. It's almost as though we must use a different brain if we are ever to be able to understand what in God's name is happening to the simple people of our land.

Unfortunately, for most of us this reordering, this changeover and this new brain will not come easily, for a protracted period of uncertainty always seems to intervene. So the hope we might, with embarrassment, experience one moment is extinguished, totally ablated by the moods of doom that come upon us like thunder and nuclear war, the next. I had this experience of my feelings being twisted, not played with but entirely turned about, as I read from Susan Sontag's *What's Happening to America*. In a section titled "As Much Experience as an Idea," Sontag attacks a colleague for his apparently inaccurate and possibly crude slandering of the young. I had not read the piece she was referring to, but I felt good because the forceful position she had assumed and the words she chose led me to regain that belief in America, that hope, that strength, that same sense of possibility that had hung just slightly out of reach of all those students, us, engaged in the tutorial movements. Everything had come alive through her language. In a funny way, it seemed as though a string of lights had burst on, like footlights lighting up a country, as her intellectualism and her wisdom carried a banner for all of us.

But that was the first moment only, for suddenly the stage of America had been thrown into darkness again, and I was reading: "This is a doomed country, it seems to me; I only pray that, when America founders, it doesn't drag the rest of the planet down, too. But one should notice that, during its long elephantine agony, America is also producing its subtlest minority generation of the decent and sensitive, young people who are alienated *as* Americans. They are not drawn to the stale truths of their sad elders (though these are truths). More of their elders should be listening to them." [5]

chapter 11

Voices in the Yard

Even if perfect social justice and complete freedom from want
were to prevail in a world at peace, rebels would still be
needed wherever the world is out of joint, which now means
everywhere. Rebellion permeates all aspects of human life.
It originates from the subconscious will of mankind not to
surrender to destructive forces.
René Dubos, *So Human an Animal*

Eternal youth is impossible, for even if there were no other
obstacles, introspection would make it impossible.
Franz Kafka, *Diaries II* [1]

The rain, which had threatened for hours the morn-
ing of the bust, finally came about eleven o'clock. Being inside the
courthouse, no one could tell, but the straggly hair and soggy
clothing of the people who ran inside into the ugly safety of the
giant lobby made it clear that the sky finally had opened.

There's always a feeling in a courthouse that all the people
bustling about, disappearing behind and reappearing through the
padded swinging doors with the oval window, are all involved in
and deeply committed to your case, even if it's just a parking vio-
lation. Certainly, that morning, everyone must have been concerned with the Harvard and Radcliffe students locked up somewhere in the iron and concrete basement of the East Cambridge,
Massachusetts, Courthouse. Certainly everyone knew of the SDS
take-over of University Hall on April 9, 1969, and the Harvard
University administration's decision and the bust in the stillness
of the early hours of the 10th. Certainly, too, everyone has a clear-
cut and distinct political knowledge and position from which he
cannot be budged, a sense of camaraderie, and a definition of the
enemy from which his very life takes meaning. And everything

and everyone and all the words and rhetoric, expectations and deeds are sweetly and undeniably political or legal. Certainly that's all true.

In the courtroom itself at about nine-thirty, amidst the steam and mugginess of a saddened weather and ritualized order of the law, a tall man spoke of the car accident he had sustained at the intersection of two nearby streets. Arresting police officers listened along with a judge and bailiff and the others. The important case had not yet come up.

"Where are the kids? I want to speak with the kids."

"They'll be up in due time."

Somewhere behind a thick, black metal door, young people waited for arraignment proceedings. Only one's fantasies spoke of their condition: if only you could get to them.

"Why can't we see them? I've got brothers in there."

A bevy of lawyers hustled around before the judge as four young men were led upstairs at the back of the courtroom and took their places on hard benches. The proceedings had begun. Those in attendance strained to see them and hear even a word of the rehearsed and linear mutterings of functionaries. The pattern was soon evident. The students would ascend from the jail by fours, men first, women to follow, in alphabetical order. Each case, each human being would be arraigned for criminal trespassing and put into the care of his own recognizance or issued a bail fee if assault and battery charges had been tacked on. Then, in a staggered line of people, they would be set free to find rides back to Harvard and to their homes, temporary and permanent. It seemed a reasonable procedure, the only one, perhaps, allowing each case to be assessed individually, but, as one student explained, it also had the effect of preventing a mass disorder or demonstration. For him it was in effect a neutralizing and dispersal strategy.

So they ascended by fours and were released one by one. For the most part, none had friends in the courtroom. A few, however, would emerge from behind the low balustrades to be greeted by someone. They would shake hands, embrace, clasp arms, run their fingers through someone's hair. A few times a teacher would put his arm around a boy and pull the boy's head down to his shoul-

der. The students were in fact like soldiers back from some inexplicable and foreign war, and the people waiting behind, at home,
equally brave, were saying, as best they could, be proud of your
tears and your efforts.

The reports from students of the events were varied save for
one detail, the violent horror of the bust and the total unfairness
of the act. "There was so much hatred in that building," a freshman boy had said. "You could see it in their eyes. They hated us.
They hated." Another commented on the size of the state troopers.
"They were so large. So damned large. So enormous. We locked
arms and were willing to go peacefully, really, you know, but they
were swinging everywhere, breaking anything." Still another young
man told of the noise, the shouting and screaming, the mace, the
wet cloths in case of tear gas, and the thumping and clubbing,
the people falling, dragging each other down, being yanked by the
hair, and being shoved viciously into a dean's office, a desk or
cabinet slamming against someone's spine. And always the noise.

One by one they came out of the courtroom, a slow process,
seemingly unending. One hundred eighty-four people seems so
many, so few. Every once in a while one saw fresh head wounds
and the swollen welts of purple and red flesh and jagged stitch
marks and the blood on the back of their necks and on their shirts
or dresses. There were rumors of someone having sustained a
broken back after falling through or being pushed out of a window. The students wondered about this. Some offered help. But
the faces of these people seemed so active, so pure, even as the sullen fatigue and fury of the night flushed all color deeper, deeper
inside. Within the courtroom, in the rear, some older people, the
audience, looked on, some laughing, totally amused at the sight
of frizzy-haired boys and girls in an array of grotesque costumes.
Two postmen came in to watch, rested awhile, then returned to
their East Cambridge routes.

Outside the courtroom at the edge of the circular lobby a young
man and woman sat facing each other, their legs pulled up under
their chins, their heads buried together in and among their en-
tangled arms and legs and hair. They were weeping. They explained to me that they had not been in the bust, but they

refused my offer of help. Now they simply couldn't take it anymore and so in their love and friendship together they cried.

When finally some of us could make arrangements to bring in
food on the pretext that we had brothers and sisters inside, the
jail scene was disclosed to us. All of the girls were penned together.
Some sat on the cold floor along the walls, their legs either
stretched out, touching the girl on the opposite wall, or tucked
under them. Many asked for cigarettes. Then a chant erupted:
"We want food. We want food. We want food." Their energy
spent, they soon were quiet again. The boys were located in three
or four cells, all very crowded. One cell was nothing more than
the receiving garage where presumably all the students were
dumped on their arrival. The back of this area had a metal door
which kept these prisoners from the outside. A flat light stretched
along the bottom of the door permitting two boys to read a newspaper. There was no place for them to sit except the floor. I spoke
with a friend here. His tired face lit up. "They want cigarettes.
Can you get some cigarettes?"

"Have you got any food on you? You know, like a candy bar?"

"What's happening on campus? I'm all right."

"Hey, where's Bill?"

"I heard you had been hospitalized?"

"He ran away before the cops came."

"No," he laughed.

The girls, behind criss-cross metal grating, watched us. The
jailors walked around behind, peering into the cells. Clutching
slips of paper they lined up the next foursome at the door where
the stairs leading up to the courtroom began.

"Are all the kids from the hospital back?"

"Yeah. Everyone's fine. I think, though, one girl broke her
back."

They were leaning in, our faces now inches apart, all of our
hands wrapped around the base of the window opening between
the anteroom and this garage-type chamber.

In another cell I spoke to some SDS leaders. One was almost
completely hoarse, an ugly bump appeared high on his nose.
"We're all right. What's happening on campus?"

"Who is that? Is he on the faculty or a dean?"

"They're meeting. The students are meeting in the church. They're angry and something's happening."

"What the hell are you doing here?"

"Good."

Around the edges of this cell other boys sat, utterly exhausted. I knew many of them as indefatigable workers and talkers. Now, however, without strength they looked thin, hideously weary but not yet beaten. It was nothing short of bizarre to see students from Lowell and Adams Houses, Sever, Emerson and William James Halls in jail. But their sentencing this morning was just the beginning. This was but the first strategy. They had to get out now, to meet again. To organize.

"The students aren't going to help. They're going to be seduced by the bust and not be aware of the issues. We've got to get back and speak in all the houses. Is Alex here?"

"No, he wasn't busted."

"Any food yet?"

"Oh, wow. What's Afro doing?"

"Tell that guy you'll bring in the food. He's O.K. He'll let you."

"I don't know."

"Are there deans and teachers upstairs?"

"Hey, officer. Sir. This guy says he'll get us some food. O.K.?"

"A couple."

"Yeah, I'll bet. Do we have enough bail money? You know what they did? They hid drugs on someone and got him on a narcotics rap."

"I'd give my arm for a peanut butter sandwich."

"No, that's not exactly right. I heard someone had tranquilizers and when the cops came in he threw the bottle away and someone picked it up. Why the hell is it taking so long?"

"Are we next? Where are they now?"

"They're up to the L's."

Upstairs in the business office opposite the courtroom a young blond woman stood hour after hour arranging for bail money. The students required to post bail came in, gave the information asked of them and lifted their right hands as they recited some words. A few were so exhausted they could barely repeat the oaths. Their right hands raised just above their hips, they dragged at cigarettes or shoved chocolate bars into their mouths with their left hands. Everyone about looked at their hair or clothes or partook of some bizarre prattle. It all was as if it wasn't happening. "Well, honey, if I had to be locked up, I'd like to be locked up with you." And she would smile and drag out some more bail money.

Early in the afternoon the women started coming out. The bail money was holding up and a transportation service back to campus had formed. Over and over again the procedure of bail was explained and the many rumors were clarified. Still stunned, one girl could speak only of how handsome the police had seemed. "They were tall, with slim aquiline noses. I remember their freshly pressed uniforms, baby blue. They looked like movie star extras." Another girl, relieved to get out, told of her impatience for many of her colleagues who had worried only about themselves. Frightened, they had lost the sense of company and the spirit of locked arms. But now, even as they signed release papers, everyone's intentions clearly were to return to resume and fight for their demands. "We've got to get organized. People have got to regroup." Before half of them had departed a meeting was scheduled for that night.

I, too, returned to the yard for a meeting, in Sever Hall, where the very next morning SDS pickets would circle the entrance arch, urging students to boycott classes. The meeting in Sever had been in session for some time when I arrived and I entered the room as, quite literally, a "point of grammar" was being raised. For an instant, a group of faculty members were stuck on the proper wording of a statement, and though they laughed their tension and concern were evident. Indeed, it was all evident now: the occupation of the building, the bust, the demands by these certain students that Harvard stop its expansion into Cambridge and abolish ROTC, that amnesty be granted to the sitters-in, that the faculty stay united, and that everyone respond to the ignominious fact that campus unrest, turmoil, violence, or whatever it's called had like thunder pounded down upon Harvard.

Not so very many years ago, I drove my father down Memorial Drive; that's the drive on the "Harvard side" of the river. He wanted to be shown the boundaries of Harvard and the Massachusetts Institute of Technology. I recall the power I felt showing him the long riverbank expanse of our campus and bragging of Harvard's capacity to purchase, to eat up, really, the property it needed so that it could huff and puff its way toward MIT. Almost as great, MIT, presumably, was doing the same thing, so that soon, I reasoned, Cambridge for all intents and purposes would be one incredible university. Nowadays they are called multiversities. The two schools seemed like marvelous giant machines, chewing up houses and people and spitting them out over their shoulders, and I and my whispering generation were all a hungry part of it, watching the destruction and construction, loving every new inch of Harvard and its gorgeous expanding brain, and hoping that someday Harvard might own it all. It was like playing Monopoly and having those unfortunate losers land right smack on your hotels on Boardwalk and Park Place.

God, it was great! All those little shacks and houses falling down would all be shoved aside for the monster brain eating its way to Boston, Somerville and Watertown. If only MIT wouldn't beat us to it. But they couldn't; how could they match our money and power and brains? Soon it would all be ours, and in those drives I would just about believe that it would be mine as well. My father used to ask questions about relocation or dislocation, but those terms, I used to think, had to do with higher economic strategies and no freshman or sophomore could be expected to deal with that. These were issues for my father's friends. It was adult talk.

But there are new representatives in this generation. The whisperers, dreamers and entrepreneurs remain, of course, but of the many voices within one single human being, some now are screaming. The prideful Monopoly game we used to observe, its tin markers trespassing on our own and others' real estate, have been thrown in our faces by a growing few, a noisy, knowing few. Then, when these voices are momentarily stilled, more voices are heard until a chorus of almost ten thousand persons fills a stadium to vote for demands and for the legitimacy of making demands so that they might whack their own blow at society's skull with the force of thousands shooting a right arm obliquely upward and outward toward some great marvelous plan, and screaming one word, STRIKE! STRIKE! STRIKE! STRIKE! STRIKE!

Somewhere in childhood each of us learns what essentially is the concept of simultaneity. We learn that many things happen in the world at precisely the same instant, so that while we eat or read or study, others are sleeping or fighting or dying. We learn that while young persons sweat out the hours before an arraignment, grocers whose valuable goods will refurbish these persons haven't yet read about a bust or maybe don't care that much about the whole thing. We learn that while a totally unprecedented political convention meets in a football stadium, lacrosse-playing colleagues of the conventioneers run through their warmup drills, and that while a faculty's liberal caucus meets on the second floor of a building, it barely hears itself above the unrecognizable score of a college musical comedy in dress rehearsal on the floor below.

To comprehend simultaneity means also to comprehend ambivalence. For apart from any choir or chorus or convention to which we have committed our voice for even a week, we alone possess innumerable voices: defiance along with doubt, concentrated anger along with exquisite fright, movement toward radical reform along with a prayer to keep things exactly as they are forever. It means fabrics of death wishes trimmed in hopes for immortality, and discrete strikes yielding diffuse guilts and a fluid shame. It means certainty and uncertainty, cogency and ambiguity, pleasure and pain. To one boy it meant occupying Harvard's University Hall, then moving out and walking about Cambridge, occupying the hall again, moving out again, this time so that he might telephone his parents. When they could not be reached, it meant returning. Then, wrapped with three others in the warmth of a blanket, a moist cloth in hand should tear gas be used, it meant bedding down to wait out a sordid and ugly night.

How often during those days did students speak of their phone conversations with parents. "Three thousand dollars a year and you're striking." "Go to it, son. Get yourself involved. I never did. And congratulations" "How could it happen at Harvard?" These were the phone calls, but the letters of alumni to their modern representatives and scion in the yard which the *Harvard Crimson* and *Alumni Bulletin* reprinted came to much the same thing.

Not surprisingly, messages of this sort made the sense and burden of the ambivalence even more exasperating: "I would have felt better if my father had opposed me right out. His siding with me only confused me more. Maybe someday I'll be free of them (my parents). I kept hoping that the strike wasn't going to be the thing that would drive us apart. They made me decide between studying, going back to work, or striking. No, that's not right. They made me decide between them and politics. I've never been involved this way. I can't go to the library when SDS is meeting. There's too much going on, and, you know, there's more here than books and lectures. They don't understand this . . . maybe they do . . . I don't know."

Much has been written about student revolutionaries, their seemingly inevitable upper middle class permissive parents, their superior intelligence, etcetera. But the often conflicting data from these studies only underscore the themes of ambivalence and simultaneity. For no human law prevents young people from manifesting the special warmth toward fathers Kenneth Keniston found in his study *The Young Radicals,* or the especially intense hostility toward fathers which a college senior recently reported in a thesis about his own political colleagues. If students in fact are preserving the politics forsaken by their parents, there may well be feelings of resentment, first, for having been psychologically coopted into this "profession," and, second, because their parents failed in it and chose instead business as usual. (All the same, the time seems right to "study" administrators and faculties, who by their actions or inactivities, that is by their own ambivalence almost make strikes and busts required courses of action.)

Faculty members, too, during these special "Harvard months," knew the ambivalence. The more they dug into the politics and meetings the more they sought ways of climbing out. "If the university's changing, what the students don't know is that the faculty may want out and have already found better places, different places to live and work." More than ever, there was mumbling of being around physically but pulling out spiritually.

But most poignant of all, perhaps, is the need to understand, to have the "whole mess figured out," analyzed — analyzed in the language of law, history, sociology or psychology, but somehow analyzed and thereby settled. A few days after the bust, with the buildings of Harvard veritably cracking under the force of meetings, caucuses, planning sessions, leaflet writing, multilithing and all the rest, a letter had been printed in the *Crimson* offering, ever so succinctly, the Oedipal interpretation of building take-overs and letter box pilfering. This represented, presumably, the reasonable and assiduous action for some. For others, the events seemed absolutely incomprehensible except for two issues: first, there was a pernicious evil in the world, actualized by the imperialistic invasion of Southeast Asia and maybe of Cambridge as well; and, second, Harvard was implicated. Whether it was through the corporation's investment of money, ROTC, the administration's irresponsibility, the faculty's posture of business as usual, Afro-American studies, or expansionism, Harvard itself seemed to be reeling from its own crude but effective arraignment and brutalizing day and night in court. Just who exactly, they asked, trespassed on whom or on what?

Does it not seem like trespassing when one heaps his values and philosophies of education upon us as if they were heavy burlap sacks of onions? And isn't it only natural, only human that we should reach back blindly for some feel or, better yet, handful of precedent upon which to lean? Isn't this after all where religion starts and where the very concept of history derives its life force? But why can't the young take our precedent, our history, our time, as immoral as they may be, as their own, and be thankful and done with it? Have they rejected our precedents and time? Do they now see in history only the efficacy of events like those occurring at Columbia, Nanterre, Berkeley and Chicago? Perhaps their sense of time implies the setting of new precedent rather than the acceptance of it, or the wish to prestructure the future rather than worship the stillness of a literary past. Theirs, after all, is the time of the now and the "us," not the inauthenticity of all the rest of "them" and last night, most especially last night and early this morning.

Well, apart from these magnificent schemes of time and space, it seemed as though the yard would be rippled by the contradictory tugs of the students toward a disjunctive relevance and, if necessary, disengagement, and of the faculty toward reasonableness, unity and, above all, continuity and grace.

Nonetheless, from the moment University Hall was "liberated," each of us not only sought an understanding and workable strategy for settlement, we also resorted to a new and strange vocabulary. Perhaps it is "back-room" political talk left over from high school government days, or "Parliamentese," perhaps "intellectualese." Whatever it is, as it comes to be employed replete with marvelous but overused terms like "negotiable," "legitimacy of demands," and "friendly amendment" and its rules of a special and sacred social grammar, one feels the chill of an exhilarating, fresh, maybe omnipotent involvement only to discover that so much and so many have been dehumanized. Is this the purpose of such a language? Even the students, as direct and honest as they have been, as clever or injudicious as they may seem, have a way of lapsing into dehumanizing language which makes it seem that from time to time they, too, forget that at the root of any violent or nonviolent political demonstration are people: administrators, deans, teachers, students, peasants, workers, policemen, people.

Two of these people, policemen in fact, who several nights before had liberated University Hall in their own way, spoke of the sitters-in as good people, "doing their job as we do ours, I suppose." Neither had been inside Harvard before. One couldn't remember ever before being in Cambridge for that long a time. Quite easily they recalled their anger and sense of a part pride in, part embarrassment over their action. They were put off by the girls, and as they spoke I tried to put together in that inevitable hunt for analysis their feelings of the erotic nature of the arrests with the not quite carnival, but ocean-liner-about-to-depart eroticism some of us had felt in the building that night. Touching bodies even in the course of sitting-in or making arrests is a not so simple part of anyone's job. Funny, the police, even in their street clothes, were handsome men, movie star extras maybe. They hated anarchists, resented rich kids, but not as much as violence. They hoped that "a small minority wouldn't ruin one of the really

good places left in the commonwealth." In but a few moments
with them, I thought they seemed confused, somewhat washed out
by the arrests, and thoroughly ingenuous. I was uncomfortable
speaking with them. They knew it and helped as best they could
to put me at ease.

Like many others, I am always impressed by how gentle these
"central figures of violence" seem, both the "cops" and the "kids."
Surely many of the students are. Almost despite their layers of
battle plans and divisions of the world into us and them, a forth-
rightness and sweet gentleness slips through. On the evening following the faculty's decision to defer debate on the Afro-American
studies program, I saw and spoke with angry, bitter and hurt students. Single file they stalked out of a closed meeting like a professional football team returning to the field, while the rest of us
stood around seeing how many we knew by name or would even
speak with us. Having pledged themselves to the sacredness of
their program and of their very destiny, these people were out to
do battle. They had spoken a bit, in private, naturally, of a little
history they too thought worthwhile preserving.

Yet with all the battle readiness of this handsome cadre, I
couldn't help but think of the young women who that afternoon,
hours before, had stood watching their tall, white faculty emerge
from the Loeb Drama Center. Patiently the women had waited
through discussions about a Committee of Fifteen, ROTC and
university expansion only to learn that fatigue and mysterious
pressures would win out over the urgency of their demands for a
Black Studies department and with it, as they say, a new day. The
women had just stood there on that Brattle Street curb crying.
And how many centuries of ritualized order and precedent kept
us from touching and comforting them? Couldn't someone just
have arisen to proclaim, finally, what was at stake and what after
all has worth? Were all the genuine heroes gone forever?

Even without them, a change in the conception of the Harvard
family had occurred. What had worked in the maintenance of an
elite and rather awesome kinship group seemed as if it wasn't
going to work any longer. Children who once seemed "illegitimate"
now were climbing into rather central roles, while distant elderly

relatives, the ones who visit once a year at graduation, had come under a most unbecoming attack. They had been advised to stay around all the time or cease visiting. The outside was inside and the inside had everted itself. "We're right at the center of everything," a student mused. "You remember when you're a child and your older brother is the big star, or your big sister is doing all the things? Now it's us, we're right in the center reading about ourselves in the newspaper. It's youth. Everything is youth and us."

How ironic it seems that the occupation, such as it was, took place in the very center of Harvard, and that the bust meant an invasion by foreign police and other guardians of the law like deans. There was, furthermore, all the talk by parents like If Harvard doesn't throw you out, we'll reach in and pull you out. But expulsion meant leaving, whereas sitting in meant staying. With this, not so incidentally, came the justifiable fear that expulsion decrees might be leveled when students were out for the summer. There was also talk of the incoming freshmen and how future admissions policies would be altered. Tomorrow's Harvard, someone quipped, will be comprised of Atlanta Jews, Scarsdale blacks and various, assorted but ever innocuous gentiles.

The outside was inside, the inside had everted itself, and the elite family structure of Harvard just shook. One corporation member, anyway, sat right up alongside SDS "rebels" under the hot lights of educational television. This spontaneous debate, which went on for hours, by its very form symbolized the sloshy fluctuations and realignments within the Harvard family, as every so often new people would come, and new facts, new issues, new political perspectives and new interactions doused in the juices of antipathy would be born. Then there would be a time out for an explication by members of the press.

One faculty member had said that in his early years at Harvard he saw the institution somewhat like a hotel, the faculty as resident hosts and the students as honorable guests, but guests nevertheless. Now he saw that it was really one large family.

But if it was that to him, it was more an expansive block party or budding commune to many of the students. For in their attempt to rap their elders they very explicitly registered votes for keeping the university open to the entire community, to the family of (elite) man, if you will. Their unanimous stadium vote to repudiate the corporation's right to close their university testified to this, as well as to many other things.

It hardly need be said that the occupation, the bust, the strike and the meetings of various sorts and duration didn't all go smoothly. In fact it's a little difficult to determine where exactly they were supposed to go. So many people were and remain bewildered. Decisions and ensuing political positions, predicated on carefully selected and measured bodies of data, collapsed like houses of cards or block towers erected by little boys when a better or brighter, louder or older person came along. Wednesday's dogma dissolved into the weekend's immaturity. Yesterday's satisfaction with reading *Crimson* and New York *Times* editorials was burned out in the conflagration of SDS, stadium and student residence house meetings. Boys living in the luxury of riverside towers sang evenly structured chorales about rent control, subsidy rates and negative income taxes. And a larger group than ever before spoke of the war. Over and over again, not just out of fear of the draft, they spoke of the war.

Saddest of all is not that while the strike went on athletes ran and played and Radcliffe honor students lay sunning half naked on the roofs of their dormitories; saddest of all, perhaps, is the fear among gifted people, among all people, that their dread of war, anger at the poverty in Appalachia, or the starvation in America, Biafra and India, or their disbelief of the expansion in Cambridge may be clichés. Saddest of all is that because Cronkite or Huntley-Brinkley portray so many scenes of a real war and real deaths and real misery that to "reiterate" these facts is "corny," "unoriginal," or "trivial." Suddenly, without cognitive warning, these events belong to the category "Well, I mean, you know." "It's just a cliché," one Harvard senior said in referring to his generation having grown up in the shadow of an atomic war. Despite the essays of Arendt and Keniston and the speeches by Wald, Spock and Chomsky, it's just a cliché.

But the A-bomb drills in third, fourth and fifth grades, the recollection of giggling children burrowing together under desks in the basement of the school and tittering about missing class minutes and what they would do if a war, whatever that meant, broke out on the hockey field or in the front hall or gymnasium has stayed with a certain group of students exactly like their shadows. And the gloom and inexplicable horror of it all, the fuzziness of the future and the commotion of the present have grown, just as the cliché says, like their very own shadows. Waiting for the cops to come as one crowds under a desk or rests his head on the angular frame of a file cabinet may, after all, symbolize a more contemporary form of A-bomb drill.

So, by God, the war broke out right in the middle of the yard, and before the Harvard faculty could even meet, the self-consciousness born of the various media's slogans and clichés choked off some people's feelings to the point where literally they could not budge, they could not take a step, they could not work. Or maybe the feelings simply overwhelmed them and they cried, as they had cried some six years before when their President had been slain.

As the clichés reinforced the depersonalization of events like revolution and war, the impression of having seen unadulterated fear on the faces of policemen over six feet tall, on the faces of grown men masked in clear and shiny white plastic, made it all seem very human and frightening again, especially to those who waited through the night on the outside. Even weeks after the bust at least one form of the fright remained. It is terribly difficult to describe, much less explain, but it has to do, somehow, with feelings of the university being "brought down" or being no more, and a sense, I suppose, of the dissolution of the entire world and all human groups. It has to do with attacking authority, seen and unseen, then being repulsed and not being sure anymore what in fact constitutes honorable, decent authority or how it feels when one is manipulating someone or being manipulated.

It is not uncommon for persons in the throes of such actual battles to reaffirm their belief in an ultimate power which is intended mechanistically to control all behavior and action everywhere. It's a power almost in the guise of a fabulous secret or colossal master plan, hidden somewhere, who knows, maybe locked

in a dungeon or in a University Hall file. It is spoken of often
when violent transitions like beginnings or endings are about to
take place or when the movement of the clouds suggests that a
storm is moving in upon us. It's a manipulating power of sorts
upon which one works out his feelings of dependence and independence, trust and mistrust. Usually it comes into play precisely
when one publicly seeks personal autonomy or challenges for a
right to control his fate. It takes the form of presidents, faculties,
corporations, boards of trustees, and perhaps even God. But one
thing is clear: there remains at Harvard College, and presumably
elsewhere, a population which, although it may not be large, has
not yet made either peace or war with this power and even today,
years later, confesses to feelings of naughtiness if not guilt about
its political urges as well as confusion if not despair.

Some students actually clapped at the news that soon after the
bust a Harvard dean was stricken and lay ill in a Boston hospital.
Others, horrified and nauseated by the announcement, discovered
that a certain strength they had employed and counted on for political action had died away. This just wasn't supposed to happen.
This wasn't part of the bargain. But then again, neither were those
forty cracked heads with the jagged stitches supposed to happen.
So they were right back where they started, and nothing yet had
been resolved.

Still, even with the naughtiness and confusion, a sense of prideful commitment to something has taken root in the lives of many
students and faculty members. Although they may never have been
revolutionaries, and although they probably have stopped attending SDS meetings, where they used to sit around the edges and in
the balconies, they have changed. They have become "radicalized,"
as the saying goes; they have changed in a big way, and it has not
been due simply to the fact that they saw their brothers abandoned
by authority and clobbered in the middle of the Harvard Yard.
More likely it is due to the fact that for all kinds of reasons, even
with all of the ambivalence, they have become politicized. And
when young bright minds imbibe facts and strategies while learning of the hypocrisy and immorality extant on their campuses, in
their communities, and in their country, there's going to be trouble

and there's going to be change. Only the tempo of this change seems incalculable.

One change, not of great proportion but of interest nevertheless, is the frequent description nowadays of "good people's" politics as radical. Only a few years ago among the middle class we used to hear (and say), "You'll like them. They're really bright, sensitive, liberal people." Now the same sentiment for the same people goes, "You'll really like them. They're involved, active, radical, good people." Or "They're just not the same now. They've been radicalized."

Of greater significance is the change in fighting back against unjust, insensitive authority. It is not, I feel, mere games or "acting out" of power that students display. Their strikes, boycotts, demonstrations of all sorts inevitably point to something horrible in their world, and in our world too. Their tactics and language may seem violent, unreasoned, unreasonable, impetuous, angry, or whatever, but even their own ambivalence and our depersonalizing language cannot hide these horrible things. In their very actions, the students inform all powers how to stop campus revolts. Every day of their lives students point, however clumsily, to the problems and the exact geographical regions where these problems reside. And they just may be telling us, with their many voices, with their rage as well as their love, their intrusiveness as well as their reticence, their anarchy as well as their supreme rationalism, what we may have to do in order to survive. Although they so often are at the political scene before us, we both face embarrassment, severe costs and quite a unique danger.

[2]

So now, having made it through the months following the Harvard bust, and witnessing a Harvard and much of the world, for that matter, struggling to awaken itself from what Kant called the dogmatic slumber, I have been especially troubled by my inability to sort out my own present and past, my own conventionalities and resentments. Am I wrong in thinking that the suggestions of many people really are founded on a notion that we must all return to a time gone by, and hence to a logic built upon the piles of an anachronistic structure? Is the university truly collapsing? Is it just the concept of higher education that is fading, or are there actually campuses going under? Will I be better off if they do or if they don't go under? And what about the millions of others who know universities far better than I, or far less, who because of their varying intimacies with this one serene institution might suffer more or less than I will? And whose rhetoric do I trust when my own private history, especially the sections on education, trembles and compels me to reconstruct and rearrange my past as well as "merely" recall it or call it into play? Too frequently it seems as though I have been there both before and after the others and now must support the costs of these adventures and accidents.

Perhaps the Harvard of ten years ago was in fact a delicious place "developing our capacities for intellectual excitement," as a classmate has written. But some of us weren't as ready for it all, apparently, as some others. Or maybe the intellectualism drowned out, or failed to wake up, a whole slew of qualities and activities that I thought went with college but never quite got. I wasn't ready for the whole thing; that is undeniable. But neither, in its way, was Harvard, and this is the point that stays with me.

Even as I think of the 1950's, I'm not quite able to get a fix on the context into which college experiences should be observed or judged. I know we all prided ourselves in knowing the few Negroes on campus. I know they weren't called blacks in those days. I know too that many of the Jewish boys would speak silently together about the one or two of their kind who were actively trying to get into what Harvard calls a final club. They used to speak of a mystic rotation for some clubs that would determine when a Jew might be permitted entrance. Certainly the Negroes then had no problems. In fact there was no Negro problem in those days. Indeed, the clubs offered no problems either. It all seemed fair enough. After all, the "prep" school boys came from the families who founded the country, hence they deserved, no, through birth they had earned special rights to be in their own clubs. That's the way it was even if that's not quite the way it might ideally have been.

On Mondays, I recall, we used to walk to class and look at some of our comrades in their army and navy suits, all dressed up like little soldiers and sailors, disappearing inside secret buildings behind the biological laboratories that no one ever could locate or even bothered to speak about. They had it good, those guys, it was said. They had their whole way paid; ROTC didn't really take that much time, and actually their summer outfits in particular looked rather good on them. One night a week they would become handsome and look not at all like the rest of us. You wouldn't dare call them "wonks" because they were in the army and navy and they were just as gentle on Monday in their khakis or blues as they were on Tuesday in their dungarees and sport coats and ties. But then again, who, after all, would join if he didn't have to? Who really wanted to march and get all caught up in that authoritarian style of life where they make you get a crew cut, even if the courses were "guts"? Probably only the poorer kids went out for ROTC, we used to think. And we would reminisce about the initials. Rotten Old Tin Cans is what they stood for someone in Chicago had told me. I knew he was kidding.

As incongruous as they seemed, the little soldiers could almost be excused their necessities next to the student council boys. Now here were really the power-hungry guys, so it seemed, anxious to better their extracurricular records for business and law school admissions officers. How often in those shady days of the 'Fifties did we darling products of high school student governments strut about the Harvard Yard snarling over the rather aggressive and abrasive sorts who would run for class marshal or president or representative to some supreme committee. Just whose prestige and well-being were they pursuing with their well-groomed Cambridge uniforms and regular two-week interval haircuts? I ask you that, we'd say. Just who are they trying to kid? Not us, certainly.

Then there were the days — each of us knew them — when our parents would come to visit. Everyone would welcome his parents to whom he would give that casual but conceited tour of the yard and the libraries, buildings and sports facilities. That's when we would take them for that ride down Memorial Drive. And we would tell them about the greatest collection of books in the world second only to the Library of Congress and France's Bibliothèque.

Or was it the third-largest in the United States? No, Harvard's scale was the world. It had to be. We would walk them past the Union and Lamont Library and point out how no girl, Radcliffe or otherwise, could get into Lamont, except of course in the summer, because it was one of the few air-conditioned places on campus and anyway the summer didn't count because Harvard Summer School had this policy of opening its doors to just about anyone. I mean, you know, it wasn't really Harvard because all those other kids could come and buy their little Harvard notebooks and green book bags and for eight weeks make believe they were in the big time. It was just so obvious then that every boy and girl in America wanted to go to Harvard and probably could have afforded it too. And if they couldn't, Harvard would have gladly given them a scholarship.

I think that what made school great in those years was that nothing happened in the world to disturb our work and efforts in Cambridge. There were no wars that mattered, no problems in cities, not even an overuse of the word "urban," no school difficulties, no pollution, no population fears. Castro was among the great ones. He came to speak once. There was Hungary, of course, but Harvard, we all knew, would open its doors to those sad refugees. And Adlai Stevenson, but the country wasn't smart enough to accept him as we had. The country with all its unequivocal anti-intellectual feelings and its blatant envy of Harvard. Stevenson's losses were proof of something good and special. It was important that he didn't win. It made us all the more elite and privileged, but still not like Yale where they had those indecent secret societies or, worse, Princeton where Jews still could not be admitted and where "colored boys" waited on tables in the eating clubs. We saw all of that. It wasn't rumor.

School of course was often a bit boring, but that's the way school was supposed to be. Relevant materials could be discussed at the dinner tables, but the real intellectual stuff came in class. Anyway, it was all preparation for some later events and experiences, and boredom and aloneness were the price you paid for being the best, or at least being in the best place.

Oh God, how pitifully out of it so many of us were. Just to

recall that whispering generation of ours, those hordes who actually believed that most anyone had a chance to "make Harvard" or at least was born to parents who could afford to take those immodest tours we doled out. Can we for a moment taste again that male chauvinism, those feelings we had for women and the ideologies in which our feelings of love and sexuality were cradled. And the Jews and the blacks and the poor? Did we not ignore their worlds and fail to question the condescending, hypocritical and just ghastly way we treated them all? And what about them, not yet able to scream loudly enough to be heard over the melodies of courses or of the band or glee club or just the sounds our cordovans made on the cobblestones? Is our memory of all that as accurate as it now seems? Is our memory of these other people correct? Not the ones who came; the other ones. The ones in Roxbury where some of us would go occasionally to tutor a little black-faced child during the day, and where we might return on a Saturday night, frightened to death in this strange and eerie world of taverns and storefronts, looking for black meat! It is not too difficult to remember all of these stories and adventures. When I think, for example, of the treatment given to students merely because they came from those vacuous Midwest states like Nebraska and Indiana, and the equally absurd honor paid to sons of great men who lived in great houses and used words like dowry and legacy. My impressions may be horribly inaccurate, of course, but it just seems that we were far removed from everything that mattered yet felt ourselves to be right in the middle of the nation's most significant action.

It is difficult, however, to recall what we felt about America then, what with all that talk about Communism. Did many of us really understand the shudder from the faculty which came from Senator Joseph McCarthy and was surely in the winds when we entered the yard for the first time on those deliciously beautiful September days? Did we understand the meaning of or even know of HUAC or liberty? Those were the days, after all, before identity crises, and that was the era when eyebrows rose in fury and confusion when a comrade spoke of "dropping out" for a year with no set plan or life purpose. We seemed to spend quite a bit of time then collecting lists of famous men of Harvard. Wasn't this really a favorite pastime for many of us? Eliot, Bernstein, Roosevelt, both Roosevelts for that matter, Emerson, Agee. No, we didn't know Agee yet. Then, as on a scavenger hunt, we sought as well the famous names on the faculty. I recall that there was somehow a magical belief that to be with these men (as there were so few women) for but the minutes it takes to walk through the yard and out beyond the Cambridge Common on an icy February morning would bring us success, accomplishment and dare I say fame? Perhaps their honors might, like dandruff, fall on our shoulders. We followed after people, believing always America to be so fine — not perfect of course, but fine. And we believed too that Harvard was just as fine, just as deserving of that casual and I-couldn't-care-less infatuation that we felt, and that many of us maybe still feel. We loved it even through the crises when small problems arose somewhere. But probably they were partly our own faults anyway.

One could go on and on, describing the utter differences between now and ten years ago or, if they aren't true differences but only differences of the imagination, then the intense variations in historical continuity that make this present generation stand so uniquely apart from the one that ruled but half a generation ago. This must be one of the most incomprehensible aspects of youth: that such remarkable change has come about so quickly, or fast enough that we, their bare elders, are rattled and flushed with excitement and perplexity while they just ingest everything and march on, hoping that a bit more change may be initiated with each new step and that the sounds of a new America may awaken them each morning.

On the social level, the changes we all speak about so openly now probably were not *that* sudden, for had we paid the slightest active attention to our society we would have seen much of them coming. We might even have pushed them along a bit and expressed greater care for the society about to be transformed, however little. Yet in the main, there just seemed fewer conflicts then between public political events and private career aspirations. But we were the workers and whisperers, the products of a psychological age and the students who too often let the pleasures and privileges of college spray over us, often to the exclusion of most everything else. A constrained hedonism existed then, and self-indulgence seemed sublime.

It's nothing short of ironic to look at the two Harvards, ours and theirs, and realize that our four years were truly what today's students with all "their" drugs and "turn-ons," would call an "ego trip." We were so self-satisfied and isolated, protected and removed as very gradually we worked our way to degrees and honors with but the slightest concern for that other world, except the parts where we would belong, until we got there. How many of us really took that outside as seriously as the inside? Was it not almost as if the shock and blessed sheen of a Harvard acceptance refused to wear off in time to permit us to enter all the worlds which in fact Harvard would gladly have helped us enter?

But it's not this way any longer. The days of self-interest have not passed, of course, but there are rumblings and explosions now which make it evident that some students not only have discovered and rediscovered a structure and a society, but want change. Not all of them want change, but certain ones want it even if it means great personal cost. This quality of concern is one of the major differences between this generation and ours. Their notion of care implies being hurt and living without, if not making a sacrifice altogether. They are more than a bit ambivalent, naturally, about forfeiting many things, but they are honestly presenting themselves and their goals and asking us to respond if we can transcend our authoritative impulses to evaluate and analyze. Many no longer play that best behavior for admissions officers and teachers game, as demeanor and decorum no longer are sacred. They're yanking and pulling the university into the world like never before. Some would mount whole campuses on dollies if they could and wheel them into Roxbury, Watts, Oceanhill-Brownsville, Washington and Hanoi.

Their strategies and tactics have been abhorred, vilified, re-pressed, encouraged, copied; but the small group I have in mind is a socially conscious, politicized band of students who whatever the results will not abide by an anachronistic university or tolerate

the sense of privilege so many of us felt and presumably worshiped. If it stands as a privilege, they say, then let all have a
chance, let all have a go at it, and then call it by some other name.
Above all, they feel their plans and efforts have worth, and it
seems that their sense of worth is identical to the sense I felt in
the 1950's when I contemplated my own life-style, career, and
most elaborate destiny.

The inevitable dilemma of the alumnus is that his very soul is
trapped between two times and between two histories. Only naturally does he hope that his donation or presence at a reunion or
athletic event will either reunite these two times or blot one out
so completely that only his own special time survives to be witnessed. To recapture those four extraordinary years, or even just
those clear September afternoons before the autumn registration
and the commencement of the first classes, or to know again emerging adolescence and the muscles and hormones that carried the
weight of all those hours would indeed be a lovely and bittersweet
reward. But it is not to be. For when we turn about, we do not
retrace steps, we merely head our futures into a misplaced geography. Our imaginations, moreover, have withered. So the magic of
donation and reunion gains its strength from the engagement it
augurs for the present, as clumsy and irksome as it seems.

We cannot be temporal imperialists suffocating today's children
with the time of our childhoods. We need not forfeit our adolescence nor our "college days," as smirkingly we used to call them,
but we're going to have to let them sit there, proudly but permanently immobile between high school and young adulthood.
And we're then going to have to support and teach, argue with
and respond to today's young people and, even more important,
react sensibly to today. "They" have the advantage, not because
everything is founded in their time but because, shockingly, so
much of the battle is fought on their turf.

I have been harsh; too extreme, perhaps, as much with myself
as with the others with whom I walked. Naturally, I too would
want a last peek at a privileged time. Still, I feel it essential that
when we visit our old schools — and each of us now, despite our
dedications and activities, are in many respects but visitors, our

claims having lessened with time — we must speak with the students who live where we lived, study where we studied, and find as hideaways our very own secret haunts. Perhaps too we must make special efforts to speak with those students who by their very appearance trouble us and cause us to resent the fact that the world is such that they are free to trespass on hallowed ground which we had worked so hard to touch. How sad it is, really, that so many of us had but four swift years to make a kind of mark or impact we cannot make again. Sadder still is the fact that millions of us in this country cannot make any such mark at all and know it. This is at least one paradox we overlooked and that students now have discovered.

Toward the end of the Harvard spring of 1969, as Harvard tried to get itself and its people and followers together, I received a letter from a Radcliffe College senior named Deborah Komaiko. The year before she had written me of her plan to do community work rather than honors academic work during her senior year. She felt simply that the former offered greater worth. Then, soon after the strike and the bust and the days of rain and brilliant sunshine, she wrote to me again:

"First, I abhor both sides for using the police as a universal punching bag in what amounts to an intra-class struggle. I did not approve of the tactics of taking the building. But I approved less of calling the police. Still, the frustration with this society has reached a point of no return for many. (It strikes me at this level: we can find ample justification for spending ten billion dollars a year to murder the Vietnamese, but we can't dig up two billion extra dollars to feed our own malnourished people!) This is my inheritance. This is the 'justice,' 'love,' and 'brotherhood' which I can claim a full adult right to! . . .

"How is a twenty-one year old woman supposed to be decent, humane, loving, committed, intelligent while still absorbing the myths of 'justice,' 'love,' and 'brotherhood' (not to mention 'academic freedom') . . . . Is poetry to be the solace, the escape, or the elitist corruption in my adulthood? Not that I expect you or anyone else to answer these questions. It will be agonizing enough looking for your own answers."

chapter 12

The Spring of Death

Ecstasy affords the occasion and expediency determines the form.
Marianne Moore, "The Past Is the Present." [1]

One doesn't walk up to construction workers in the same way one approaches the faculty in their offices or the "kids" in "the grill" or on "the meadow." One stands a bit more erect, not proud, exactly, but manly and strong, displaying the toughness from high school days.

"Excuse me, I wonder what you men thought of all the action on the campus recently."

"I don't have any thoughts about it. None of my business. Maybe they do." He gestures to his colleagues.

"No. I see. But you must have some thoughts."

"We don't work here, fella. When they picket on Sheridan Road I get my equipment and gang outa here. We don't work for Northwestern. They got problems, we go somewhere else. We don't work, we don't eat. It's just that simple."

"What about the antiwar demonstrations?" Now the hands smack toughly on the hips and the weight slams over to the other leg. Far more tough than the three men who watch the girls from behind sunglasses.

"Everything comes down, right? It all goes downhill, right? Shit runs downhill. It's all bullshit, right? It's none of my goddamn business."

Strange. Many at Northwestern that week thought for the first time they might have been running uphill, against the grain and the eternal incline. Some of the faculty had been catapulted out of their self-confessed ivory tower complacency for the first time ever.

In a few cases, the jolt had been so devastating that those few who prior to the strike had announced their resignations so that they might take sweeter jobs elsewhere were now beginning to feel a parental guilt of abandonment. For them, the strike had integrated the community, or enough of the community (is it an experiential community?) to such an extent that for one to leave meant an unraveling of "the plan," a shredding of a political force growing now practically out into the lake beyond the land that Northwestern had invented, brought from nowhere to blanket their bit of Lake Michigan.

The strike had come. With Kent State and Jackson State, large groups of people were manning bellows to keep it all alive — the issues, the spirit, the festival — to keep the force of it alive for today, through one week, through the summer and into the new academic year which would mean permanence in the future. In his office, a gentle professor spoke about his new political life and his hopes, his admiration for a young black woman now leading her student colleagues, one hoped, into that new day, that new dawn "they" speak so much of during the fervor of religious ceremonies and political upheavals. He cupped his left hand, fingers up, and gracefully lowered his right hand, also cupped, fingers down over his left. It was a magician preparing for some sleight of hand trick, or a marshmallow cloud falling on a five-legged bug caught on his back but eager nonetheless to be shielded from the heat. Then, leaning forward in his chair, his face above a yellow tablet on which incomprehensible formulae were written and both of us beneath the sign that admonished IF YOU CAN'T DIG IT, DON'T KNOCK IT, he told how a new university will grow in the midst of an old one, and how nothing will be destroyed. A combined academic and political institution will form from the molds of traditional, classical scholarship and what everyone is calling social relevance. The university, he said, will become a force of persuasion with an effect on public opinion.

"You know, it's the darndest thing. I come out here every day and watch these girls. And millions of 'em go by. But just today I figured out I'm probably seeing the same ones seven, eight times a day. Oh brother, get a load of this crossing the street. . . ."

But where to start in such an enormous university; where to go
to collect truth, for surely once the story is born everyone will
agree on it and everything will fit together. They'll all know the
same things and care about them equally. But why those guys
playing catch on this important morning, and why those people
floating lawn darts into the circle on the grass? The figures moving
from class to class and the sunbathers on the lawn speak of other
things this morning.

". . . I told him if he continues to act like that I'll give him
back the ring and we'll just call it . . ."

A group of Northwestern faculty and students, essentially to
keep the strike vital, hurriedly and spiritedly had attempted to
construct a New University. For some it was an antiwar college,
where traditional courses would be investigated for their possible
"connection" with the war but where "relevant" courses also would
be taught. With little time to prepare, certain faculty members
had dropped their regular curriculum routines and had begun to
teach under the syllabus of the New University. Faculty who had
not even been teaching during the year undertook to salvage the
semester's political activity, and so they lent their heads and hands
to New University programs.

Everything under the sun, a new sun it seemed, was being
offered: Role of the Computer in Society; The War at a Feeling
Level; Northwestern, Whither Goest Thou?; Draft Resistance
Seminar; Sociology of Math; The Press and the Strike; The Mis-
represented Middle: A Positive Position; Reflections of a Diluted I;
Socialization of Sex Roles and Aggression; Pacifism: Christian
Ethics and Tradition as a Basis for Alternative Social Action
within the Militant Society; Food Buying Co-ops; Persuasion (of-
fered by the School of Speech); and Towards a Psychology of
Conscious Values.

Approximately thirty-five new courses had been developed for
the New University and fifty or so "old" ones, that is, courses that
had been underway during the semester were being moderately or
more drastically adjusted to meet the challenge of the new syllabus.
Working out of their new Goodrich Hall office, a temporary New
University steering committee with an equitable faculty-student

representation was about to meet to establish a more permanent standing body. Everyone, it seemed, was getting in on it, hoping that an enormous effort might carry the package, the enterprise on a wave of political magic and exhilaration into the following autumn. Those in the administration who said it would all blow over in a day would eat their words.

". . . You ought to meet my daughter, Chuck," the construction worker was saying. "She don't wear these miniskirts. She keeps a law. Two inches above the knee. Quite a young lady."

To help students excuse themselves from business as usual, Northwestern's faculty voted to introduce a new grade, the T. Essentially the T gave the student credit for any course in which he enrolled at Northwestern, even if he chose to forsake it and enroll in up to four New University courses. The option, then, was work for the traditional grades or do politics, talk to the crucial issues and take T's. However, the choice produced a self-conscious tension among many students. What would a law school, graduate program, or medical admission committee that waited in an unclear future say about a T? Was it a bad mark? T for troublemaker. T for trial and temptation. Contemporary students seem so disquieted by the conflict of politics and the remains of a Protestant ethic that teaches them to work their slim and nagging work and take the chance that one is rewarded by unknown forces making their presence known in concrete, irrefutable forms. Like an A— or a B+. Someone said that T's reminded him of the brands worn by SS officers. Not the victims this time. The servants of the rulers.

And the sign above them in the grill read: YOU GET WHAT YOU NEED.

It all seemed impossible. No destructive faculty polarization occurred, as some had feared. Students were teaching in the New University, although the credit would be of the B level variety in contrast to the D and E levels accorded graduate and "super-graduate" courses.

The festival of the strike, its glamour and anguish, confusion and spiraling engagement had broken the inertia. The question, for one man, anyway, became "how to transform effervescence into an organizational infrastructure." The department of sociology grew weighty about me as I visited various offices, and with it I sank deep into society's ground. But this one man truly knew the sense of it all. Since there's not going to be a revolution, he said, you preserve your revolutionary credentials. Then you put aside the notion that it all might die away and get to work. And, while little has remained from the past, this just might be the time to really do something radical. It's like trying to fill an inside straight.

It was indeed a time for rash playing. And the sign read: BE REALISTIC. DEMAND THE IMPOSSIBLE!

Maybe it happened at Northwestern because the faculty, as he said, couldn't put on airs. As they weren't setting national standards, they couldn't say to their students, "How do you get off telling *me* what to teach!" Maybe it happened because young faculty had a genuine voice in the destiny of the handsome school that sits astride a lake where some still swim. But it may be risky to indulge so fully in the periodic politics that sweep a campus, once usually in the fall, once again usually in the spring, but bigger this time, biggest of all. But it has to be risky if academic reform, if any sort of reform is to kick the old or recalcitrant upstairs and then out for good. The New University in Evanston was predicated on bringing about this reform. It provided, as they will explain to anyone, possibility for the most pressing exigencies. It would preserve history and do action. It would stop routines, slash at inertia and put us all off balance. And after all, he said, the whole business of a university is to deal with uncomfortable things. That's why there are walls around universities.

13 May, 1970

It must be emphasized that this "course" has no bearing on the immediate purposes of the strike or on the attempt to stop the war. Those who wish to argue that it should, are invited to attend. Those who wish to engage in directly political activities — activities we consider entirely appropriate at this time — should contact the agencies on campus that have been set up for that purpose. [course announcement]

At Northwestern the decision to enroll in a New University course was the student's. Hundreds of students had pledged to carry through on the political events they would soon meet in their new courses. Some faculty spoke of a college without grades, without degrees or diplomas, and without the slightest hint of job preparation. Let's bring back the myth and nostalgia of learning, of education, he said. But the strike had to be maintained. It was as if a human spirit were being fed by an iron lung. The factionalism and hot-shot takeover politics where garrulous men grab for open microphones at mass rallies and organizations overreach for power as though their very self-esteem and pride were on the line had to be squelched, and a new learning brought into the brilliant daylight. And quickly!

Two young men hurried along Sheridan Road.

". . . Harry had two for four and missed a homer by this much on his last trip . . ."

Many on the freshly politically seeded acres of the campus were doing their best to heed his words, something about how attempting the impossible should liberate you rather than hang you up. Some were trying to shed the politics of guilt and the opprobrium that drenches prospective careers and, worse, the success that dances all about the globe like a chorus line introducing the star attraction, seductive fame. The atmosphere was humid, fluid; the old forms melted, the molds of a new form remained soft, pliable. But time was eroding the moisture. While one audience watched, doubted, walked away, then back again to wait, another audience studied it all from a distance. Little was said about leaders. Perhaps the students did not want any this time. "If they wanted one, they'd find one. Right?" Or maybe the ones they found had been killed, or chose to commit a political brand of suicide. So the story wasn't fitting together. It wasn't fitting together at all.

IT'S NOT EVERY MAN WHO CAN BLOW HIS OWN THING IN HIS OWN TIME. That's what the sign said, and it had sex and a social politics emblazoned all over it.

The New University at Northwestern seemed capable of absorbing wide variations in political styles. For some it was educational reform, for others a home where students would learn antiwar politics. It may be the proving ground for gradeless courses, since grades oppress and crush the freedom that learning knows to be

its parent. So say some. A value-free university? Even the myth of
it was laughable. Anyway, that is what that one special teacher
had implied as he staged the structure of freedom and the chance
for everyone everywhere to come to Northwestern to study and
to learn, to dance, and to find a sacred music. In the past, or so it
seemed to him, universities had been dry and hollow, an adolescent bore and, naturally, utterly bourgeois.

A Communication to Members of the Evanston Community

The students of Northwestern University want dialogue with the
Evanston community. We need to work with you at this crucial time. We
want to know your ideas and we want you to know what we think. Now
the time has come for us to reorder our priorities and work together for
humanitarian goals. Now, isn't it possible for us to work in harmony for a
better nation and world? For these reasons, we are trying to reach out to
members of the Evanston community. Enclosed are the facts about the
Northwestern University strike. Please take the time to read them carefully. We implore you to think open-mindedly about these facts and to
act in accordance with your conscience.

For Immediate Release — May, 1970

As Mayor of Evanston, I want to keep the lines of communication open
between the city of Evanston and the students, and I stand ready to help
maintain our longstanding cooperative relations.

Everyone would be able to "do his thing" here except ROTC.
That had to go! No one sought to throw out the traditional elements, although costume party graduating ceremonies that never
speak of peace or war, or education for that matter, but merely of
passing on into adult careers, which turns out to be collegese for
"business as usual," might have their leases revoked. You wait, you
administrators who feel next year will be a fresh start. We'll never
be the same here. We'll strip you of all certificates and you'll be
naked, humiliated by a new, sane, and for once sensible politics.
We're going to learn about the war, repression at home and university complicity.

. . . But the New University cannot and should not be an alternative
to continuing the strike. The New University must continue the demands, because in the New University people will be free of outside constraint, and free to determine their own lives and actions. In the New

University people will be free to learn because they want to. They will be free to unite thought and action. And they will be free to incorporate their personal values in all they do. . . .

This New University will destroy the myth that education is value-free; it will be an institution that recognizes the values implicit in its activities. Its politics will be up front . . .

JACK SAWYER
Daily Northwestern, May 14, 1970.

Two girls were speaking near a phone booth. "And two weeks after I use it, the black begins to show through at the roots again. I'm going to quit . . ."

Well, I don't know. The professor was scratching his head, he who is knowledgeable, preoccupied, famous and kind. And I, timorous, envious, hoping that the patterns of all universities would appear suddenly in brilliant color and thick black outline right there in front of us amidst the mound of success and business heaped upon his artless desk. "The New University," he mused. Then terms like "thoughtless," "gimmick," "local demands" were there in the room with us. Presumably more courses with political content and totally new types of courses would step forward, he suggested, but they would bring problems, too, like the fragmentation of knowledge, an overemphasis on the instrumental conceptions of information, and a new, sleeker model of the objective-subjective dichotomy. So far none of these movements had left a mark and the growing void seemed an omen. Didn't I think so? The classic scenario had played itself out at Northwestern, he said. The radicals were frustrated; the system had been brutally exposed so all could see it as from an amphitheater one watches weary surgeons rip open the bodies of the strongest soldiers and sew them up again.

The antiwar stuff had been dead for two years. Now it was back without the anti-imperialist rhetoric and, surprise of all surprises, advertising within-the-system political altercations. Draft resistance booths stood alongside tables with leaflets for the Hatfield-McGovern Amendment. Conventional politics flirted with what the sophisticated like me once thought to be radical action. And even if the war was just a symptom, you had to do something with symptoms, like doctor them or cure them. The radical effort of the last years had left a presence, he observed, a mist; not a political party, but a purpose, a goal, a temperature. The world outside would no doubt wonder about universities while the students would recompute grade averages, throw out the T's, and assess their chances for the future. Some would opt for that future and go to it, now as alone as one might ever be. Others would begin to believe there is no future until they act or reach out for it. So hearing the voices of their elders, who like parents on the sidelines urged them to hold that line, they contemplated going for their own inside straights and spending the summer campaigning for antiwar candidates in Duluth or Urbana and then waiting to see just how destiny would decide to put their lives together after that.

On the blackboard outside an office someone had written, *I wish I could convey information, create art and shut up otherwise.*

On the door outside a building a sign announced: THE HISTORY DEPARTMENT OPPOSES WAR; URGES THAT THE UNIVERSITY STAY OPEN; SUPPORTS THE T, AND PLEDGES TO REDIRECT ITS ACTIVITIES.

Many agreed that the strike had not been against the university. Indeed, the object was to keep the university open so that a new harvest might flourish inside. The original name Alternate University soon had been changed to New University, a fact which pleased many liberal faculty but made some radicals squirm from their fears of co-optation. It also brought a discriminating temper forward. Not everyone was about to gobble up the new doctrine and shuck old tricks and principles.

12 May, 1970

"The New University," voted into existence by faculty representatives Monday night, May 11, is an absurdity from both the academic and political point of view. The types of courses proposed by the department representatives for the New University seem likely to have neither educational value nor political effect. Instead of being designed to examine questions about the ends of education, the political and social significance of the various fields of study, and the values and aims now dominant in American society, these courses take for granted that the answers to such questions concern themselves mainly with techniques of organizing and expressing opposition to the war. In this respect, the New University is a parody of the Old University, in which it was often assumed that questions tended to concentrate on technique.

The courses proposed have almost no intellectual content and they are not interesting. Moreover, since they are designed to be little more than workshops of political action, they can have little effect in altering the perspectives of those many students who do not already take a critical view of American society and policy. And as short-term political instruments they promise to be feeble. Numerous action groups sponsored by ASG [Associated Student Government] are already hard at work on plans to take protest directly into the community outside the University. Why should anyone interested in *direct* political action bother to attend a seminar in its techniques when he can participate in such action out in the community itself? Students interested in direct action will likely take "T" grades in their courses and will join one of the groups working on programs in Evanston, Wilmette, etc.

Finally the New University fails to provide a model for the sort of completely restructured University which many of us wish to try to develop in the coming years. Since the courses are almost wholly devoted to short-term political goals, they represent no basis for the long-term transformation of Northwestern into an institution which promotes critical values.

Staff Member
Department of English

While classes would meet only once or perhaps twice a week for the remainder of the semester, the alternate educational pursuit born as the New University had brought an exuberance to a waning spirit, and a sculptured form, a tangible whole, a building, a place, a fresh school, almost, to people badly needing a victory. There was a glow about these people. Nothing had been destroyed; no one was being stomped on. And if their information about a similar program at the University of Illinois Circle Campus in Chicago was absolutely wrong, well, it could be attributed to the pride that comes from accomplishing something special and for the moment while knowing how supreme is the political value of collective solidarity, wishing openly that maybe yours is the only successful project of its kind in all the world.

[2]

The alternate university at the University of Illinois hardly fizzled the way some of the Northwestern crowd had suggested it would. Here on the Circle Campus on Chicago's Near West Side, under a hot sun coming through a polluted sky, the commuting students had gathered informally in an open theater in the round to listen to a rock band and intermittent political announcements and speeches. In the darkened, damp passageway near the main lecture centers and out beneath the ramps supported by modern columns leading to the theater, new friends spoke together of the cops, Southern Illinois University, the board of trustees and the collective courses of Strike University.

The rhetoric, the new handshake, Brother, Sister, the Frisbees flying practically through the musicians, much of the audience sunbathing, we stood together right on the spot where, I was sure, a marvelous Greek restaurant used to be and where pretending intellectuals and the real people would drink retsina and hear the few words that might tie them closer to a culture whose history no one then could possibly foresee.

"So if the trustees fuck us over, we gotta do something about it. We're not going to let 'em fuck us over this time. We got a lotta people on our side. Hey now. The Cultural Explosion Collective is going to be meeting at . . ."

Collectives, "courses" of a most modern nature, were being arranged under the guidance of a deliberately leaderless coordinating collective of thirteen people, twelve undergraduates and one graduate student. Whereas for the months of the school's infancy barely two hundred to three hundred students ever joined in anything political, now even the university public relations staff had estimated that thirty-five hundred students were committed to the spirit of the strike and all that might be born from its fire and fury. The plan was simple as could be: working-class students to build a People's University upon the pilings and girders of a modern, workable socialism.

"So Northwestern thinks we fizzled, eh? Goddamn lefty libs!"

At the time, thirty collectives, essentially designed and "led" by students, were underway, with some faculty involved. For the most part, collectives would meet once or twice before the year ended, but the hope was that some of them might be listed on the official fall academic calendar. According to the students, two thousand of the sixteen thousand of them on campus had signed up to attend one or more collectives. It was also their impression that about one-half of the faculty supported the notion of collectives. No grade changes like the Northwestern T had been instituted, but on the Circle Campus students were allowed to withdraw from any course as late as the end of the quarter. It remained up to instructors and students, therefore, to work out the administrative details of dropped courses and added collectives.

From the *Report of the Organizational Collective:*

3. Strike University alternative to the present structure, comprised of collective action projects through which people, undistinguished as to student, faculty, or non-student, assemble to take action on a particular issue. While action must develop out of information and understanding, these collectives will direct themselves beyond theory and rap and will build education out of participation in action.

The collectives themselves resembled Northwestern's New University courses, but there were some significant differences, notably the Latin Community Collective, in which students would work with the local community and so-called "gang boys" to coordinate the strike and bring to the community the very university that contributed to much of its destruction. There was also a GI Action Collective, which had recently leafleted the Great Lakes Naval Training Station; a High School Collective, designed to "bring the message" to young people; and a Labor Action Committee, formed to assist teamsters and post office workers in their own picketing activities.

Importantly, the strike, Jackson State, Nixon, Agnew, Cambodia, Kent State, the heat and the despair had melded what but a few months before would have seemed an outlandish amalgam of political positions. Almost like booths with their respective leaders hawking the new line, a Black Community Collective accepting whites, a Women's Liberation Collective, and a Cultural Explosion

Collective opened up for business with their own special dignity alongside a Vote Action Collective in which students labored to obtain signatures for support of the Hatfield-McGovern Amendment. During the summer days, if the energy would last, some students would do "legitimate" campaign work. In the evenings they would rap with their colleagues doing what we continue to call "community organizing" with the Vice Lords. If universities are not Indian reservations guarding distinct tribes on sacred and always sequestered land, then they may just be political melting pots boiling a pungent fare right where the restaurants of Greek Town and the great Italian neighborhoods once stood, perhaps shabby and poor but always constant and tough.

"Don't let 'em fuck you over this time," he yelled at them. "And something else. We're going to liberate the johns. No more of this men's room, women's room distinction. You know, man, when you gotta go and the nearest door says 'women,' I mean, like wow, that's a drag!"

The students in the outdoor amphitheater were applauding, laughing and stamping their feet; the Frisbees sailing overhead, red, white, now two red; men with their shirts off, women with their skirts pulled up catching the sun but leaving a line; checking out the politics, dreaming of co-ed johns, a world without constraints, the conflicts of career and politics; being more or less than or maybe the same as their parents, the one hour each way commute; the morale of the school, and then what the trustees who would meet in elegant Chicago hotel suites might decide. They could pound the collectives pretty hard and make the administration end it all. Maybe they would issue decisions over the summer when most of the students were away. Maybe, too, "The faculty will fight 'em by giving us all A's."

"We already got people working on this campus to cool the strike. That's what they're paid to do."

The students waited around, the band played, girls returned from gym class, sunglasses sparkled and the political ones huddled, isolated, in the passageways under the sun, on the grass in animated discussion. So much to be done that day. In the background, in what would be the foreground any other day, the mobs attended class. Straight, unpolitical, credential-career-success-mobility-fame-progress rendering class. Did these particular students think it a "cop-out" to return to regular classes? Are the concepts resumption and continuation themselves a "cop-out?"

But how do we know when we never do get to speak with most of the kids? Perhaps we must speak more with them and less about them.

"I've got four papers to write in ten days. All I need now's my NoDoz." A sunbather.

"Hey. Get in touch with me if you need some hippie color for your article." The political yeller.

"Naw. Most of 'em are good kids. It's just every once in a while you gotta stop 'em before they break something or hurt themselves." A campus policeman.

"Off the pig." They said that a lot, especially when they would speak of "co-optable liberals," the seriousness of their political machinations, the hope for a socialist revolution and their concern that faculty members fail to understand revolutionary action. But they're up against a pudgy, indolent society, not only in Daley's quarters and in Washington but in the offices of their advisors and teachers. Everyone has other ideas about SDS, militancy, and the shallow paroxysmic politics of the "kids." It's all child's play, they say, almost as if they might fear that he who speaks with students, sides, votes or fights with students abandons adult responsibility and sophistication, professional training and "the proper perspective."

"The only way now," the professor said later that afternoon, "is to campaign. We'll send thousands of kids into political campaigns around the state. They'll make a difference. Maybe we get the school to close for two weeks before the November elections."

"And the majority goes to Florida?"

"Then the minority will make the difference," he responded. "I'll take anything I can get. Nixon's asked for it. We're going with the system this time."

A people's university. No longer would "they" let a campus expand over the homes, alleys, markets and taverns that once were simply places or streets but now are called a community, a term implying that real lives together comprise it. Still, very few of us know exactly what a community is. A people's university that would far transcend any black studies program or "working-class" commuter college of low prestige, questionable and fluctuating morale and rather peculiar location in the middle of cities like Chicago, New York, Detroit, Boston and L.A. A people's university. It would mean that even the architecture would have to be transformed: the elitist ambience of an intellectual bastion would have to be wrung out of the concrete and brick palaces and wild collapsible buildings, as they looked from blocks away driving west on Congress Street. At times the entire campus, especially when seen as a single circumscribed community so apart from the city to which it belonged, appeared as a monstrous stage set, low-ered each morning before the first commuter arrived, raised again up beyond the dusty clouds each evening when the last of the staff had completed his cleaning and inspection. Someday they would have to replace that Greek restaurant, make it reappear, and that Italian place too, where everyone bragged how you could dine with the "in" people of Chicago and maybe even sit alongside a Mafia agent putting out his contract as he offered to share a hunk of freshly baked bread. A people's university.

[3]

"You wanna go to Jew Town, Mack?" the taxi driver had asked. "No, the University of Chicago."

Well, there would be no people's university in Hyde Park. Trouble was, the young woman had said several times that morn-ing, the University of Chicago faculty still prided itself on being leftist. But that's nothing more than a holdover from the 'Thirties when they all liked to refer to themselves as the hotbed of com-munism. The Chicago *Tribune* had practically manufactured the isolated and impregnable mystery that many required to be able to do their work. Now "everyone knows the faculty is plenty con-servative." I wasn't sure everyone knew that.

The slogans, leaflets, and waiting to be signed petitions comprised still another political gallery, theater, base of operations. Two handsome Danish graduate students spoke softly and eloquently of the spontaneous generation of the University of Chicago's contribution to a new politics. From a New University Conference project formalized but two weeks before, the notion of an organization in which people could be free to do political work had emerged. The purpose was to train organizers and then initiate — but here it was again — a people's university. Although not original, its name would be Right On Training Center.

"But that's R-O-T . . . You're putting me on."

"Hell no, baby," the girl on the phone had said, and I, so foolish, forgot the ironies and the antipathies toward so much of what we stand for, which brilliant students sneak into their crystalline humor. There were the special handshakes again, the view of the austere faculty club, the look of students in this famous university, their insistence, efforts, earnestness, and their knowledge of the harassment that their purposes would provoke forever and for always.

"They take down our signs."

"Don't let 'em fuck us over," the kid had screamed. "If the trustees give us trouble, we'll make noise and more noise."

At the University of Chicago, the small growing list of ROTC courses were focused around that phrase "bringing the community into the university." The walls separating the comfortable from the uncomfortable were to be razed, and the bricks that made them strong would either be used to trash some merchant or, more likely, be the material for constructing totally new theories of education and a totally new political stance. And it may just work.

Liberation classes were neatly blocked in on a schedule just like the ones we used to carry around in high school. Monday morning 10:30, Postermaking and Publicity. Art students were involved here as well. Monday and Wednesday 11:00, Self-defense. "Self-explanatory, right?"

"You mean like women's lib?"

"Right on."

Monday 12:00, Anti-riot Clauses of Federal Student Aid. Monday 1:00, Panther Defense. Bail money is always needed and June 8 of that year marked the opening of Bobby Seale's trial in Chicago. New Haven set a tone; they had sent a message. Chicago had RSVP'ed. Panthers would get help from the whites who ran ROTC in Mandel Hall. Everyone knew they must play it perfectly, for the blacks invariably receive most of the hostility and the retribution even when they're innocent or totally ignorant of situations in which they are made heroes or, more likely, villains.

"Man. You can't believe how the pigs hassle the spades. They stop to light a cigarette and whamo, they put 'em in chains."

"This university doesn't even like the blacks it has urban renewed."

There were other courses: American Antiwar Movements; Radical Critique of the Uses of Psychology in Community Relations; Fascism; working with Hyde Park youth in a coffeehouse named the Blue Gargoyle; Legislative Records of Peace Candidates; Why Invade Cambodia?; Radical Education and High School Organizing; and Guerrilla Theater.

The guerrilla theater had just reenacted the shooting of Bobby Hutton. The students pinned police badges on their workshirts and carried cap pistols. They had run around, made noises, called out in agony and shot their pistols. One body had fallen. All over again, Bobby Hutton was dead, but closer to a fantasied home this time. It had been effective, they reported. It had even changed the stilled mood of those who sprawled in the quad preparing for the Brandenburg Concerti concert by the small University Orchestra. Even the handsome woman who danced alone had stopped. So had the young men who joked about her and later on would try to peer beneath her skirt as she choreographed an expression of freedom. But later on that afternoon in a liberation class a young faculty member leading the discussion of socialism would discover that some University of Chicago students were so hampered by the "irreality" of television and a cognitive inability, so it seemed, to separate televised from untelevised reality that they would call the demonstrations at the Democratic Convention guerrilla theater.

"Hey. Have you signed the petition to open Ida Noyes to the community?"

There used to be, well, there still is a big building on Chicago's

Midway where many student activities find a home. The *Maroon,* the student newspaper, still works and sleeps there. There are basketball courts and is there not a swimming pool where the "students' violent nonaction" group held their weekly nude swim parties? I think that's right. In my day, we could dance at Ida Noyes one night a week if the townies didn't barge in on us and if we flashed our student ID cards. It seemed reasonable enough then. Now the building was liberated. That certain group of students called it the Fred Hampton Memorial Community Center.

"Hey. It's a petition to open Ida Noyes to the public." The black man looks. Fred Hampton. Anger appears on his face, but quickly it is soft again, and he smiles. Then a bit of triumph and he signs his name. And so do I, a resident of another state touched by the decency of it all and horrified by the report of Chicago's grand jury on the Hampton, or is it the Hanrahan case. It gets so confusing. So many petitions, so many causes, impressions and all that "data."

"Some graduate student really oughta do a study of the whole thing . . ."

TO UNIVERSITY OF CHICAGO

We, the undersigned, people of this community, demand that Ida Noyes Hall be opened to the people in our area as a recreational facility. The University of Chicago has taken many things from our community and has yet to give anything in return.

1. It has taken valuable land from the people, and has not used it for the benefit of the community.
   A. The university has torn down buildings and fenced in the property in order to keep the people out. And, when the university has rebuild (sic) on cleared land, the buildings are too expensive for the people to live in.
   B. Specifically, it has done nothing about building needed recreational facilities.
2. The university police tell people to get off street corners, even though there is no place for the people to go.

Therefore, the University of Chicago owes us, at least, the use of Ida Noyes Hall.

Tuesday 2:00, Third World Rip-off. Several days before our meeting, five UC students had worked their way into a board meeting of Standard Oil of New Jersey. Stemming from an idea New University Conference calls its anticorporate campaign, the students had preached anti-imperialism and demonstrated in front of the stockholders who, for that moment, also had to make the grainy resolutions of a televised and nontelevised society. There they were, the students, as big as life. As big as the biggest company, gloating, laughing, politicking, wondering perhaps for that unpredictable instant about their own parents' investments. They must have seemed bigger than ever, bigger even than in living anti-imperialist color.

Tuesday 2:00, Third World Rip-off in Fred Hampton Memorial Community Center where, with a little help from their friends, high school boys had just about liberated a gym so that it might stay open during the summer. Quite a fight was going on in America that day just to let a new generation, the newest, know a summer of mindless play.

High school students generally were enjoying an important role in the strike. They dug it. They were knowing, cunning, ironic, savvy. College entrance be damned this month; they wanted into everything: Women's Liberation, Gay Liberation, and the radical caucus even now populated by more than two hundred fifty people. Like a political carnival, the booths were everywhere. The whole campus spectrum screamed aloud and floated atop the Brandenburg Concerti. There was real world work to be done. The Vice Lords, too, were part of it. Trying somewhat to emulate the Panthers, they would be a liaison between the university and the community. But in the meantime someone had to be found to teach them Marxism. Someone was found. As for the students willing to go on the political firing lines, someone had to be found to tell them how not to rap with community groups. Someone was found.

Strike Central at the University of Chicago, a barefooted young woman manning the desk worked that hot day on ROTC courses and on Ida Noyes. The community desired to have facilities available to them but the university, so she said, claimed the community should care for itself; it had the bread to do it. The energy for the summer, therefore, would be directed essentially to this one project. Liberation classes presumably might slow up or even fall away, but this one issue might radicalize more students in the next months and bring some campus factions together.

ROTC was lily white; the students knew it. It was started by "the same old political types." Students knew that, too. There was resistance from the faculty and from students but, even more, indifference and lack of concern hung like a thick, ragged velvet curtain across their stage. "They confuse me with all these local issues. I know Cambodia and Kent. I don't know about Ida Noyes and I don't want to." A water fight in the quad had drenched a group of students and two wonderful hooligans galloped away. We all couldn't help but giggle as we fled from their childlike excitement and self-appointed battleground.

IDA NOYES SERVES THE PEOPLE

Today at four o'clock a group of local high school students liberated Ida Noyes Hall. The plan is to open Ida Noyes to all community people. This includes all the facilities.

The decision to move on Ida Noyes Hall was suggested and implemented by the high school students. Those University students who supported the action see it as part of the demand to "shut the university down in order to open it up."

To the students who kept one ROTC alive while wishing death for the other, course credit was unimportant. If the faculty failed to support them, they'd go it alone, but this time with the community in tow. They would have to be able to resist the harassment of Buildings and Grounds who, they alleged, tore down their posters, petitions and announcements.

"The students do whatever they want. I just clean up, do my job. Ask him, he's with me all the time. I mind my business and keep my nose clean. They want to burn the building down, well, that's one less place I got to clean. You know what I mean?"

But it's the many men and few women who soil the buildings, not those who empty the baskets and sweep up late in the darkest hours, who annoyed this one group of what they call radical students. More than anyone, it was the president who closed his university for a day or so after the Kent State tragedy, closed it again in memory of still more deaths in the South, and "then has the audacity to claim the place is politically neutral." A group of "gang boys" were asked to cancel a dance in honor of the Jackson deaths. The administration, according to some students, could not see that their dance in a university building *was* in honor of their dead brothers and sisters. Cultures sit astride those sagging university walls, laughing their heads off during the day, but moaning with the police sirens at night.

The university's president, they claimed, undercut strikes started by computer and library workers. The students had joined them, but when the school was closed the strikes within the strike dissolved right before their eyes. A construction worker picket line of the "informational" variety was also strangulated when workers were told they could either resume work or be fired. So the students quit the line and the workers thanked them for their support and their sensible decision to back off. No one was being used, and on that one day the grains of elitism sank deep within the earth, out of sight, and the scent of a people's university was just barely recognized on the ground where an effete democracy had been trampled.

"I wonder, do you have any reactions to that thing in New York with the construction workers and the students? You know when the police . . ."

"Look. You start something, everyone's got an equal chance. I mean, you know. I got the same chance you got. Everybody's got the same chance. You know the name Saipan? I was on Saipan during the war. Five out of two hundred men in my battalion lived through it. We all had the same chance. I used to think, I got just as good a chance as anyone out here. You know what I'm talking about?"

"Yessir."

In between urging people to sign the petition and grabbing a sandwich on the run, her soft light hair resting lightly against the faded blue denim shirt, a young woman explained New University Conference's attempt to build toward a viable socialist party. Long-term revolutionaries is what they were. No big explosions were to come from these people, anyway, that summer or during the following months. But soon socialism would stand tall on the shoulders of a supporting education. Right On Training Center was part of that support. So was the Ida Noyes Project. And so was the young woman who manned Strike Central during the long morning hours and right through lunchtime when it seemed that all America had halted and no one moved anywhere except in the gray, cool college corridors.

IDA NOYES IS DEAD

As of Saturday night the facilities of the Fred Hampton Community Center (formerly Ida Noyes) are open to the community. This building is being used as a center for the implementation of the three national strike demands:

1. U.S. troops out of Southeast Asia
2. End political repression — free all political prisoners. Free Bobby Seale
3. End university complicity with the war machine.

This building is open. Students: don't pull rank. Leave your ID's at home!

FRED HAMPTON LIVES

A basis for a people's university was being constructed and no one was demanding any special political talent from anyone else. They sought a model of education, an education to precede action. People had to breathe the sense of excitement and take away from it the credentials of something permanent. Maybe the radical caucus would be that permanence, that bridge spanning the summer and linking Cambodia, Kent, Jackson, linking America to such a different fate that all the traffic of the past would be rerouted or led right to the very edge.

And if there's violence, if some of them are pushed over the cliff? "Well, violence is a tactic." The girl with whom I was speaking moved slightly on the hard bench. I leaned in response. The Brandenburg Concerto was delicious. Another girl held her sandwich between her teeth, steadied the petition with one hand and wrote with gorgeous script her simple name, then left. "Concrete blows must be leveled against imperialism," she went on. "We have to make it harder and harder for them to wage war. You gauge what you can get. We didn't have a militant picket line here 'cause we didn't want to get people killed."

"And if they call you a fascist, a young German, a teutonic mad-
man? I mean, you appreciate what I'm asking. I'm not suggesting,
naturally, that you are, but there are some people who . . ."

"Yes. Yes. Yes. I know. Look. I'm no fascist. I'm not waging war
in Vietnam. It was the German people who acquiesced to fascism."

It was the first Brandenburg. No, the second. One should know
them. Maybe they were playing a Bach suite. I saw her for the last
time near 58th Street. Behind us some young children, younger
than us certainly, played in a small lot now renamed Kent State
Memorial Park. It was just a lot. My hand fumbled awkwardly
in hers as again I forgot the handshake. Then we parted.

[4]

ROTC was not the only educational development to pop fully
grown from the strike at the University of Chicago. It also happened that a group of seven or eight political scientists formed
study groups. Other professors also shifted their courses, while
still others needed to make no changes at all: their academic purposes were already political; even before the sudden concatenation
of political events, the most punctilious of students would have
called their courses "relevant." The study groups, however, in-
augurated by the political scientists seemed to have gained the
most attention, an attention that grew when some sociologists
joined them.

If the students at Strike Central believed their faculty to be
reactionary, well, moderate ("No that's right, you can say I said
reactionary when you write your article") the faculty, or some of
them, felt they had been rather remarkable. Some were working
with students on political projects. Like the men at the Circle
Campus and Northwestern, professors were in touch everywhere
with students getting caught up in local campaigns. The faculty
had also voted to change the 1970–1971 calendar year. Summer
vacation would be shortened to make possible a ten-day recess
prior to the November elections. And for the first time the faculty
took a political stand as a corporate body. They "came out" against
the war.

"I'm not so sure that's so good."

"And if they decide to vote someday for, shall we say, aid to the Arab nations, what do I do then?"

"Big deal. So they voted against the war. Big fucking deal."

No major grading changes were instituted at the time, but UC students at least were allowed to take P's (passes) with greater frequency than before.

"I have my doubts about all this," he said. "My responsibility as a teacher is to teach even if only one student wants to continue with the regular material. Educationally and politically it is absolutely essential that the university stay open. If one kid wants to do business as usual, we must do it with him. It isn't my responsibility to tell students what to do politically."

TO THE FACULTY OF THE COLLEGE. May 8, 1970

I trust it will be understood that in extending ourselves now we should not detract from the academic accomplishments of our students by abandoning our standards.

Although it may not be possible or desirable always to observe customary schedules, I expect each of you to make whatever effort is required to discharge your responsibilities as teachers.

"You gotta do the same work, but you can get a P. That's supposed to be accommodation? That's supposed to be liberal?"

At times the pieces fit together, at times it seems as though what's happening on these campuses are bits of myriad puzzles, their content and texture having nothing to do with one another. One says the least they should do is let us off before the elections to do campaigning. Another says he'll support that if he can figure out a way that the lower income students who must earn money during the summer will not be penalized by an abbreviated vacation. Another says the university need not worry about that since it never admits poor students anyway. And another says, "We aren't asking for vacation to campaign. We're digging socialism, education and big action to follow. You mark my words."

Many faculty, apparently, had gone as far underground intellectually as the Weathermen had politically. Some were stopping work they adored to lobby in Washington. It would be hot there, and maybe foolish or wasteful, but they were going to do it for themselves, for the children, adolescents and adults who watch them walk to work or watch them drink and smoke and luxuriate in the uncomfortable mysteries and vague notions that make academic life so drab to the outside, but so splendid within. They would be going to Washington with the planes and the cabs and the suitcases and the air conditioning to deal with the real political machines and the men who grease them and get filthy and filthy rich and powerful in the process. They would be going to Washington to speak with men whose ideas infuriated them and whose exuding life-styles depressed and maybe offended them. The stratified arrangement of the academy would stand, however, for it reflected the country, the politics, the times. They would all fly together, maybe even in tourist class, but while the young ones would lobby with senators, the big shots would seek out Laird and Agnew. The grains of elitism come back to pollute these isolated palaces, these Indian reservations.

The faculty had other ideas, too, like research projects on Vietnam body counts, the workings of the Justice Department and the Illinois National Guard, the legitimacy of bureaucracy and a careful study of the relationship between social scientists and the government, especially that portion of the government that makes war and not love, that portion not finding war unhealthy for children and other living things. Classified research, if it still existed on the campus, would have to be exposed. It might prove embarrassing. To a group of young political scientists, moreover, the events of that spring, the Spring of Death, might mean instituting the dream of a Federation of Social Scientists proposed by Chicago's David Easton. More and more political statements would have to come from intellectuals, but reshaping the profession would not be a part of it. It would mean, simply, politicization, and now was the time.

It is said that the strikes called at these three Chicago campuses had been tolerable to administrations and faculties essentially because they were not leveled against the universities. As one professor remarked, the strike offered him an occasion to speak to students about his job and watch amazement gleam on their faces as they learned of the honest freedom he earns and cherishes by token of his employment. But while the strike meant that some would feel a sense of community (again that word), for others, it was a diffuse attack, a swaying hierarchy of sentiments, and once more a time to exhort political expediencies and probably some less socialized passions as well.

[5]

No one anywhere can fully explain these phenomena nor describe the events on a campus he loves so dearly and that he thereby assumes he understands as well. It cannot be done. A man or a woman is a fool to believe that the data he collects in his head, with his hands or his tools, through his imagination and vision, or by dint of allowing his philosophy to brush up against those presumably innocent ones who stand aside to view the demonstrations tell much more than a bare truth. The scene and the very connotation of the word "scene" shift so drastically as one goes to describe it for himself that entire new language forms and rituals must be learned with every new trip, with every new blink, with every new stride. Counting bodies in the Ellipse, in the picket line, floating face down in a Cambodian river, lying every which way on battle carts is only part of that bare truth, only part of that shifting scene.

For some, the object, in psychological terms, is to prolong the latencies. If only attitudes might hold firm a bit longer; if only positions, tactics, slogans, handshakes would mean in May what they meant in November. In settling the air with but one truth each of us seems to come so soon to what we feel to be a lie or a betrayal, and all the world, in our country anyway, feels intimidated, out of it, royally screwed by a group they believe they can pinpoint and then characterize right out of existence. The students and faculty, administrators, presidents and alumni all feel stymied, stricken, gypped and forgotten. No one looks out for anyone anymore, and no one's word is trusted or honored. No one seems willing to make a house call.

The scene dissolves, and the latencies, the periods of response and reaction, dissolve with it. Entire personalities or their public sectors are radically altered. Like floating bodies in space we hurtle about, moving back perhaps from a place on the left we thought we would never desert. Inevitably, some of us collide only to oblige others to follow us or to turn away to find their own direction and purpose. Suddenly it is the period when history, even in its diminutive forms, returns to us those who departed so quickly and resolutely but a year or two ago. Men return from the war, fathers from work, students from politics and settled positions, professors from sad ideas, administrators from inane meetings. In a furious traffic of self-righteousness and narcissism, bolts of extraordinary governmental energy disrupt an already chaotic world and make it impossible for anyone to rest or daydream in the midst of this strange kinetic overflow.

Always we feel ourselves to be out of touch with the "real" power of the country and the "real" anger that ultimately puts Kent State and Jackson State on our cognitive maps for good and for always. Television, press conferences, editorials and second-hand reports, a rumor, a fantasy — something always stands between those of us in universities and the wars, the board meetings, the privileged accounts and the center. Surely grades oppress people and make learning a horrifying experience. But have not thousands and thousands of people salvaged joy and marshaled careers from all that oppression, or is that not the issue? And if the professor argues that all students seek is for us to listen, is it also not the case that his own profession might worry about its inability to gain a hearing with the community outside the gates? Do "they" listen to professors anymore? Should they? For those who care to hear it, not only are the strains of McCarthyism creeping back through the stone archways, they have been heard, as recently as any yesterday in full orchestration, in all their explosive might on the shores where "they" always fear the "Commies" themselves will land. Is there not an orchestration of politics and society that one need know about?

Patriotic Political Action
OF THE
DEMOCRATIC NATIONALIST PARTY

This year *must* be the year of political counter-attack against the insidious forces of diversion and subversion within our midst.

THE SAM ADAMS COMMITTEE OF PUBLIC SAFETY has been founded to re-
assert the political functioning of the White folk majority within our
United States of America.

Since the turn of the century, our American political scene has been
dominated by various factions and self-interested minority pressure
groups whose goals have generally *not* included the promotion of the
general welfare and the survival of the Nation.

There is only ONE SOLUTION . . . rebuild the political organization of
the ineffective White folk majority, and concentrate its united will upon
the political questions of the day.

THE SAM ADAMS COMMITTEE OF PUBLIC SAFETY will attack the local Trot-
sky-type politicians of both the Democratic and Republican Parties.

It will conduct a campaign of propaganda and physical terror against
the guilty individuals and their associates.

It will drive these traitors from public office, and reduce them to a position where suicide will be the only salvation for their crimes against
their own society, their own people, and their own Civilization.

The Sam Adams Committee of Public Safety

The educational reformations that bury themselves within the
smokey vaults of the campus strikes seek to explode universities so
that they may never again stimulate only the rich and the privileged with their swanky libraries, handsome gymnasiums and
sexful swimming pools. Some students want to push these facilities
through the gates and smash down the walls so that the whole
world like children in a wonderland may scurry through the
buildings and make love on the land. At the same time a large
group of equally noble people studies the vulnerabilities of its
fortresses and prays that by its own new presence in the community outside the walls the space within may be preserved for that
much longer. Who really is the good guy, one professor had asked;
the one who closes the university in response to the strike or the
one who works to keep "the place" open?

Strangely, universities bring upon themselves the mirror images
of national and international dilemmas and tragedies. If young
men refuse to go to war, they arrange to bring soldiers to their
campuses; and if real ammunition is employed and real orders to
kill are obeyed, then the scene has shifted still one more time and
all of us learn that war games are replications of the real thing,
not rehearsals for it. Is it only a matter of time before the highest
administration will alter its policies and report that troops have

been sent to invade America's intellectual sanctuaries, or at least those within twenty miles of huge American cities? Will it be, then, that bodies and politics like rough cement blocks will slide by one another and the hard friction will etch scars of irreparable damage on an entire society, and not merely on the face of higher education? But that's exactly what some want; so we'll have to wait for history to make its decisions and discriminate between the ineffable and the desecrating.

The targets of the so-called antiwar colleges are not as distinct when one visits a campus as they are when one reads the reports of others who care just as much and who see just as keenly. The movement of ideas, generations and personnel makes it impossible to know what one is supposed to store away. Strike University, New University and ROTC may not survive one summer. And Ida Noyes may shut down before the kids with the basketballs squirm their way in. But there are a lot of soldiers, policemen, Israelis and Arabs, a lot of Indochinese and now, evidently, a lot of students who also may not make it through the summer. For in the middle of our always intriguing, sometimes obscene way of abstracting everything, especially politics, we forget that human lives are at the center of it all, and that nothing short of life and death issues are what make us weep and love, forget and kill. Yet, while I can write this now and believe it with all my strength, I know full well I cannot live by these words for even the remainder of this glorious afternoon, much less through tomorrow, which, as the song says, marks "the first day of the remainder of my life."

But when I tell the professor, my friend, that Reggie Brown of SIU had his leg amputated, so I heard, because of a bomb explosion and no one seems to know the details, and he says "it's just another case of fumble fingers; don't be so paranoid," I know that the humanity of politics continues to lag far behind its power and excitement. But I know, too, that sensitive, decent people now trying so hard to find a niche in a system that might yield one stinking gleam of possibility and triumph are beaten in their souls and literally battle-weary even in their safe offices that now stand where a marvelous Italian restaurant used to be.

part 4: Conclusion

chapter 13

Time's Children

On my last birthday I was ninety-three years old. That is
not young of course. In fact it is older than ninety! But age is
a relative matter. If you continue to work and to absorb the
beauty in the world about you, you find that age does not
necessarily mean getting older.

                    Pablo Casals, *Joys and Sorrows*

I have nothing to do, but watch the days draw out,
Now that I sit in the house from October to June,
And the swallow comes too soon and the spring will be over
And the cuckoo will be gone before I am out again.
A sun, that was once warm, O light that was taken for granted
When I was young and strong, and sun and light unsought for
And the night unfeared and the day expected
And clocks could be trusted, tomorrow assured
And time would not stop in the dark!

                    T. S. Eliot, *The Family Reunion*

To speak or write about youth means, I think, confronting the time of one's past, that is, one's prior self. Perhaps,
too, it means examining one's priorities. Anyone who lives or
works with young people knows that to look out across at them
must be to look back at them, in a way, though not down at them.
It is to look back at them across the grain and purpose of time.
Often it seems so right being with people much younger; it
"works," as the artist might say, since our times and life-styles
seem to move together, cautiously but successfully. At other hours,
however, as for example during the first few days of school each
autumn, when we see the new crop and feel them to be so unjustly
young, our respective times seem disjointed and the space between
us seems unbridgeable. The feeling is like what parents feel when,
in a moment of endless duration, they turn swiftly about only to

discover that their children are no longer children, that they are no longer young and no longer wholly together as part of a family. The parents turn about and realize that their children have vanished, leaving as an after image a swirling glow in a suddenly sorrowful room. Parents and some of us who teach discover, too, that the children who depart take a chunk of time with them, an irretrievable chunk which makes us feel that we may never again get close to young people or, even worse, to the remnants of our own childhoods.

Sadly perhaps, gratefully perhaps we find that the motion of young people everywhere is in a sense the motion of ourselves. It is a reminder of the passing of our own private and unshared years as well as a conclusion to the public and social years we spend with children or as children. The motion of youth and the passage of years imprint time upon all of us, or at least upon those of us belonging to that generation now feeling its age. Children, certainly the very youngest people, it often seems to me, are time itself; not its embodiment, really, but its flame and reality. The future seems to them, or ought to seem, so open and endless, complicated, to be sure, but ultimately possible. And their past, I imagine, is unusually pure, even with all the errors and impertinences it contains. The hours of their past become friends with the present, and the present remains each second changed, barely altered by a culture and civilization which crash into the environments of the famous and the disenfranchised, the young and the old.

Time in these years of youth moved, as I recall, at its appropriate and appointed tempo, a tempo marked somewhere at the head of a logically computed but still artistic score. The moments of speeding advance and trudging retreat were all part of a plan for youth, all part of a temporal mechanics for living. The moments constituted a tempo that gave direction and motion to us even though our actions and sentiments must have seemed and maybe still seem like random notes and random rests to those who observed us and cared for us. These were the people, of course, who taught us constraint and promulgated the values that ultimately held us and our culture barely together. And so we keep in our memory those special and particular experiences and those particular people who in their way tie us to a tradition, a convention, a family and a name. And later on we reason that it must have been the constraints on psychic and social action which preserved the tonalities not just of ourselves but of entire generations.

Time and youth were once somehow together, the one being the other, both enduring for themselves, both enduring for the other and presenting to us spans of splashing aliveness and testimonies of achievement, excitement and critical pain; presenting to us as well the fibers of expectation and inference and every taste that can be had of death. We grew up to learn that a measured flow of time had been bequeathed to us for as long as, well, for as long as our spidery tenure might last. A peculiar word, "last." It gives promise of endurance and pronouncement of finality. So do the words "youth and time."

We matured, changed, displayed before ourselves some bit of what was being transacted behind our own eyes. And we all believed, even truthfully reported that a mutual understanding, a truce made in and of time had been completed, and that we had resolved all that life and death and being young and old might mean. But of course no truce existed, for in our aging we were soon enough obliged to look again, not upward this time but backward to where we had been. Like time itself, youth was again appearing to engulf us.

Then, in maybe the single discovery we made apart from the younger ones, apart from our own youth that is, they became us and we them. Or so it seemed. The young surround us so naturally, their bodies and chants pushing, urging, punishing us; they lead and follow us. As though in battalions, they order us to march in the footsteps of their pride and diffidence or gallop amidst their sexuality and adventure. How is it possible that they arrive before us and after us, smaller and larger, more amusing and urbane, more naïve and unexposed?

To examine youth, therefore, means either to walk in their tempo for those instants when the tempi of the generations may be contiguous, or to settle in among the years which accumulate for us, confront head-on the clashing of the present and the past,

and hear the explosion of regrets and life plans made so long ago
they hardly seem to carry our name anymore. But so much time
has accumulated that our examination seems false and uncertain.
We have passed into what we all call adolescence and early adulthood only to find that photographs of our childhood have become
crusty through our own disbelief. They seem foreign and un-
friendly. The space of the photograph is reminiscent of something: the high school room, the smell of lockers or hideaways, the
feel of streets, beaches and stony concrete. But the faces must be
identified through an act of inference normally reserved for dealing with the future; hence it is hard to believe that we are recalling
and not prophesying. Isn't this the case? We look at the picture
and say, yes, I remember that schoolroom. I used to sit next to
Bobby and Henry. And that teacher, Miss Marshall, and . . . and
. . . is that what I looked like then? I guess so. It must be. That
must be the past.

It seems ironic, though, that these self-conceptions linger this
way in the past and that they must be guessed at or reasoned out.
It seems impossible, even a trifle unjust. How can there be such
displacements and discontinuities in time when at most all we can
admit to feeling are the slight but delectable interruptions of sleep
and dreams? If the days follow along in line, we argue, like children well behaved on their way to a fresh, green park, why is last
year or five years ago, why is our youth so separated from us now,
and at times so incongruous? Why is it that the children at the
head of the line have already disappeared? Very small children
have similar reactions when they in turn undertake their examinations of youth. We see the sentiment in a three-year-old's expression as he sees a photograph of himself of two years before: "Baby.
See the baby! What's the baby's name? Who is that?"

[2]

Everyone, presumably, protects his own notions and treasures
of the past and of youth, extending or limiting their boundaries
and seasons. And everyone of a certain age, an age which institu-

tions and cultures help to compute, eventually decides he is no longer young. When one becomes that age, whole measures of time seem to be dismissed, dropped from the repertoire of habits, and the years and months, the congeries of time undergo a preparation and are put into storage. But they are stored, these years of the past, in peculiar fashion, for often we feel that we have continued on in the identical modes and styles of our youth, in the ways, that is, of our parents, so that the past doesn't seem dead at all.

Yet often, too, we find ourselves performing actions which bespeak what seem to us a historic urgency and dazzling spontaneity. Suddenly nothing has to do with yesterday's styles or childhood or our parents. Everything is new and totally recast as if our lives were made of clay hardening in society's molds and emerging finally in the forms of single days. These particular actions do not necessarily appear genuine or reasonable to us, but they come about, so we imagine, without preparation or rehearsal. Somehow we just do them. They just happen. We may even wonder where such actions and responses came from. Where was the action waiting? Was it pausing, perhaps, in some interior anteroom? Some of us wonder too where actions or reactions live after they have been sent from us, presumably to return to time. Are they retrievable or but bolts of quicksilver showing us their face a mere once and no more?

Youth has this uncertain way about it, for in one sense we as young people did not contemplate time the same way we did only moments after our departure from the buildings and persons we associate with being young and hence come to define as our younger years. The flow of time is gradual, as the buildup of a conception of the past grows in proper and tolerable duration. But then miraculously, often violently, we recognize that while most assuredly we are with people our own age we are no longer with young people, no longer with people young as young meant before. We begin to think about age in a new way, especially on our birthdays, and in the beginning of this series of recognitions and required reconciliations it is first the past which closes itself off to us. Exhibiting an antipathy and haughtiness, the past turns a heavy shoulder toward us and bids us in unbending fashion to move ahead, although there remains a voice somewhere daring us to seek impossible replications of prior years.

Do we not know an uneasy feeling when we think of how the play and freedom of childhood (and for some of us college as well) have been altered by the constraints and opportunities of adulthood? The constraints are like iron edges pricking our personalities and somehow destroying the smooth and linear flow of sweet time. Time, too, so it seems, possesses these edges, angularity amidst its unequivocal forms. For we learn that no one returns to the past, no matter what.

Before we truly understood this, however, time seemed to have played a casual game with us, offering freedom and caprice. One might even say that time played jokes on us and on itself. For the long and magical moments of childhood the years meant so little, and maturation for the most part went unfelt. Life was adventure and defeat, trial and setback, but it was encased in a resiliency sanctioned by a usually stern but frequently mischievous sense of history. One could come back and try something again, repeat a day of fun or a whole year in school perhaps. One could pass as a young man or young woman, and a culture fragmented into chips from the cracking of social reordering on its surface let it all happen. At least some of the culture's chips, the richer ones probably, permitted these youthful gambles and lines of failures. Let them have their fun now, we used to hear, for soon they won't be able to get away with this kind of light foolishness and aimless leisure. Soon their interminable dance will be stilled.

Yet in other parts of our culture it seemed as though water had seeped in between the cracks of the years and had frozen to a thick, crusty shell. It seemed as though water had trapped those persons whose simple measured destinies precluded free and capricious movement and some final hopeful liberation. Large groups of young people and old people stayed right where they were, frozen in the houses where their parents and grandparents lived what some have felt to be lives deprived of a substance and a joy that come from sleight of hand tricks with time, like rearranging the flow of preordained histories or shocking everyone

with absolutely audacious expectations. We don't always think of
it this way, but not becoming what your father was, living better
than he did, more enlightened and more dramatically, is, after all,
reordering history and, hence, performing rather nifty sleight of
hand magic with time's sense of direction.

We have names, however, for those unable to perform such
magic, just as we have names for the cultures, states and forgotten,
monochromatic towns where their children march to school and
then, cerebrally, march among their day-by-day lessons, abiding by
the social and educational currents, honoring the brittle habits of
teachers and bosses, and then march home. We say about these
towns, or about the poor parts of our own cities where the people
stamped for avoidance were dumped and remain penned, that
only the day matters, that only the single beat matters, presenting
its force and slim royalty once every turn of the world. One by
one, one by one. We say this and much more about the places we
see from the trains entering or leaving the smokey, smelly stations
of enormous cities where concrete platforms hold the very world
upright and stand bracing the black iron beams, old and tired,
sweating their rust and decay. The beams are themselves like the
men who brought them there and lifted them into a position and
posture so that others might be kept safe before their own depar-
tures for better times and better places.

We say about these rotting places that some of us study from
time to time that they offer a special glory in their day-by-day,
beat-by-beat theater. But we also say the children there lack a
drive to become all that they might, that the years have frozen
them solid, and that they actually prefer the meager tonalities of
their own compositions, their own flamboyant street styles and
the lugubrious architecture of their own craftsmen and fathers.
We say these children do not speak aloud to themselves or dream
too much or even wish. And we say that because of an evil accumulation of years discolored by the blackness of the mines, or the
frazzled whiteness of cotton fields owned by the good but still the
very richest, or by the coldness of the brown earth surrounding the
falling fences, or the forests that literally upped and moved just to
stay out of sight of their churches, stores, latrines and grave sites,

the genes which no man has yet begun to comprehend have been
disabled or discredited and made malignant.

There is, then, something called our time, the time we inherit
from our own and bequeath to our own, and something called
their time, the time of *them,* and the time of their youth. The two
times coexist, of course, which is to say little more than that they
hack their rhythms, their periodicities all they like, just as long
as nobody gets hurt. But does this mean that a truly universal
youth exists, a youthfulness that everyone shares? Or is there
instead a segregated youth, a time divided so that now youth has
reassessed itself and chosen to open its time only to those of the
same color or of the same demanded style? Does youth now stand
begging to hold together its isolated strength and greatness, or are
the disparities of culture so great that we continue to think first
of our own youth and then of the youth belonging to all the others?

An anger has arisen in this land, a momentous rage with a force
almost as great as life itself. Its smell is sweet, its heat is delicious,
its voices are assuredly young. One result of this anger is that time
has been made groggy by this youth force and has found itself
scarred so that it may just contemplate throwing off the capes of
its own original laws and begin anew, as "they" do when buildings
are razed on dusty lots where moments before people lived. Time
has been urged by youth to contemplate starting fresh, from
scratch, or pay a cataclysmic consequence. Thus we live in a time
where there will be more and more thorny discontinuities and
entire redefinitions of what it means to be young; what it means
precisely to be twelve or eighteen.

[3]

It is a well-known fact that recent years have brought young
people to a dominant position in our country. They have been
stretched "upwards" by capitalism, by wars and universities, and
by their firmness if not sophistication in debate and protest. Perhaps also by their overeagerness and nerve. The styles and language which they advertise but which to a great extent we manu-

facture have reverberated in our own placid "adult culture" such that they now shock the persons who designed them in the first place. Many have written that young people, as another of America's minority groups, have received some of the treatment accorded their minority group siblings. Sexual potency and wild eating habits, irresponsibility, street dirtying, animalism, ignorance and positively incomprehensible language and music patterns supposedly characterize them as much as any other group that has come under the glowering eye of America's "middle" ways and "middle" people, the people, that is, who guard the "middle years."

There is, however, a curious turn about the young, or of any group which because of its peculiar nature the rest of us tend to sequester or grant a semi-citizenship. It has to do with the fact that at some point in our relationships with other groups we project onto these groups the traits, drives, and maybe too the ambitions and animus we despise or at least find uncomfortable in ourselves and in our groups. The denigration of those who appear to us beneath our eyes, for example, helps us to stand a bit taller. We look down at some people and, intentionally or not we appear like a man bending to crush a cigarette under his foot and then straightening out again to his full height. Our attack on someone of another category is most likely an attack on all of that category, and because it is it serves to integrate our own groups a bit more and enhance our own delineated categories. The attacks or disapproval imply that along with our publicly announced proposals for equality there lives a fear that inevitably all categories might actually come together, blurring our distinct personal edges as they do and thereby destroying our precarious sense of uniqueness.

The machinery behind these attitudes, however, is not so recently learned. The infant's early confusion with names and classification generally, mommy as baby, baby as daddy or nonsense syllables serving for all three, reminds us that at some level in our actual or fantasy engagements we sometimes steer so closely to others that we not only fuse with them, we believe that we superimpose our tissue one on another. At times the child feels he has become a parent, then both of his parents. At times the parents fantasize totally incorporating the child unto themselves so that the family may truly be one organism. The parents wrap their arms and their coats and blankets so tightly around the child's tiny frame that in one instant he has disappeared and in the next he has been suffused among the mysterious creases and folds of adult bodies. Then there is only one again. Ring around the rosie, pocket full of posie, all join hands and become one again.

Some of us call this suffusion, identification. It resembles the "group grope," where we are instructed to hunt in the dark or, even better, in the most dazzling daylight with our eyes closed for the other people in that temporary family, the group. Using only our hands, we begin to build a filmy identity but a definite foundation nevertheless among their bodies, hair, and barely remembered first names. The suffusion of persons resembles too the ideas of communes, communality and community. No longer do two people alone share a baby and take responsibility for introducing him to the earth. Now there are places where worlds upon worlds of a constantly changing mini-nation claim birthrights to all of these most fragrant arrivals. "Come on people now, smile on your brother. Everybody get together, try to love one another right now."

This in part is what sits at the bottom of our involvements with other people. May we call it identification? In a way, we find ourselves becoming the other as well as becoming the image of the other. Not just during insanity but always, or from time to time, or once in a while. Or once. We force ourselves to wrench at the instruments guiding our perceptions so that husbands and wives whom we know and whom we care for might actually look alike. We make them look so much alike that they too become one, a fusion or confusion of each other. Then, when we have rendered them one, they come to share the same soul or speech as well as the same name and much of the same time, but certainly the same portion of the nation. But really it is incredible, as we think of it, that over time, as the crooked line of lived societies has made its way to the present, we have devised means for assimilating the most disparate times: not the times of generations, but the times of young men and young women. From women men learn periodicity and that special sense of ineluctable continuity. And from men women apprehend and tolerate the military game males play with destiny and what we call "lady luck." Nonetheless, it happens that despite the anger, the denigration and the proverbial gap that might remain between the generations the sexes find ways of moving together and concocting the ceremonies we know to be marriage.

When a baby is born, the instruments of our perceptions are again coerced, at the moment of birth even, to see the likeness between it and its parents. At the very instant of birth, at which instant we as children wrongly believed all babies look exactly alike, we as parents or the friends of parents not only detect an unequivocal difference among babies, we imperiously proclaim that the newly awakened spirit resembles its mother. "Is that unbelievable! It's the same face! Don't you see it?" We experience the same thing in families where the children are not the biological inheritors. "Uncanny," we say, the "real" parents having never been seen. "Look, look there how that baby is the image of its father. Uncanny. The spitting image. Unbelievable."

But the image of this new family which drapes our perceptual scheme is in large measure the primordial image of family, of unit, of the many made into the not at all artificial one. This is what we mean by categories coming together. At first, each family member, each role is resurrected and preserved, and then with superhuman power the pieces of all families from the beginning of time, just about, are transformed into the mold of a single monument, a single unblemished family portrait. For in that perceptual likeness that we impose, in that similarity, even identity of form that we insist on seeing, the generations collide, age disappears, identification becomes identity, and the young and the old move together. And here begins our study of youth, or at least our interest in such a "subject."

In not dissimilar fashion, we experience the essence of simultaneity. For example, we know the experience of all events and all human beings flowing at once together. As we do with individual family members, we first make the separate and the isolated ones come together as in a marriage of convenience. The bringing of these many objects together simultaneously reminds us of images seen through a camera which in focussing all come together. The hazy becomes the defined, multiplicity turns into single aloneness, and the many images are reduced to one image mechanically captured and made permanent. We become composers in a flight of extraordinary purpose, slinging our notes upon the page in patterns only saints might decipher but returning at last to an order, to a molecular symmetry we call a chord or resolution. Indeed, the very concept of a tonality rests upon this need to bring the many and the disparate together into a structure that no one in his wildest dreams would have thought could be arranged from such a frizzy string of ideas and experiments. Yet the wholeness evolves, all becomes simultaneous, and then everyone is compressed into a fitting shelter and given his single name and single remembrance: the family, the one, the all of them uniquely separate yet all servants to a single household. The young and the old, the men and the women are together. "Come on people now, smile on your brother. . . ."

[4]

Youth, in this same rhetoric, becomes both the mirror on which is recorded the images of our lives past and present and the field on which the residues of our own triumphs and incompletions lie weakly asleep. The return of ebullient neighbor children each school afternoon triggers underground explosions of our own private attempts to return in time. Through youth's rhythms and tireless strength it feels as though we have surrounded the past and made a glorious reunion with the most personal of history. We edge back slightly toward the past, and the past, once again the generous partner it once was, moves quickly out of its own lane, racing ahead of itself, so it seems, and best of all reaching its years out to us all over again.

When in the morning the children leave, we wonder, all of us in the clean, dry fabrics of our familiar protections, what world it is that they might learn of that day. Are school and play our world

scaled to their size and their units of comprehension? Do their
schools constitute our world plus one something that makes them
in this way genuine possessions of children? Do we in our regulations and conventions liberate or choke young people? Do we ever
offer to young people an even exchange? Is even exchange a possibility? Can the young and the old really be together?

Just whose time is it that we consider in fabricating styles and
courses for the young? Is it our time sealed and finalized? Is it
some temporary time, some makeshift pier extending outward
between the generations, an isthmus giving earth and gentle foundation to their half-serious, half-solemn experiences? Is the time
of youth a real time, one that spreads its covering over the nation?
Or is the time of youth subdivided among its tenants such that
some are granted privacy and special rights while others are left
like the remains of a Christmas pie for certain ones among us to
devour? Do we grant the young a space, a moment, anything at all
that is really theirs; or like the poor do they receive our own tired
residues and hand-me-downs?

Are the young sent away each morning to our schools, their
schools, non-schools, or are some of them hovering about that half-
eaten pie from which most but not all of us get to steal delectable
tastes whenever we want? And when we look at youth, really check
them out behind the ears and under the nails, whose vision do we
trust? Our own, or the image the young reflect or transmit to us
through our age and activity? In that exhilarating consciousness-
of-consciousness happening that surely overtakes us in our examination of youth, are we not caught in the years of someone else,
someone older, someone wiser maybe? Are we not perpetuating
prior rituals and reawakening the temperaments of those persons
who once — it seems so long ago — made their own inspections of
us, then bundled us up, and sent us out to school and to play and,
well, to life?

One probably cannot view the children scrambling on that scaf-
fold forming the generation beneath ours without contemplating
the mirrors of petulance and energy they unwittingly hold up to
us. At times, the young seek to shatter our histories and our very
sense of emotion. In one instant of unconscionable gall they at-

tempt to forbid us our pasts, but then they reflect for us our own insides, perhaps, by skipping between their obsessions with monotonous compliance and audacious adventures. Where we have finally straightened the seams of previous trials and settled our anxious flurries with knowledge, sexuality, law, religion and politics, they come along ripping open these seams and delighting uproariously in their attacks on the fragile institutional and human surfaces which hold back our secrets and keep our morality together. Where we have decided on natural silence, they create explosions that sweep away the ground upon which we stand together and wreck the treasures we have worked lifetimes to procure.

Oh, that supreme of all supreme narcissism the young invariably sculpt and about which we invariably feel so ambivalent. That way they have of throwing their bodies at us like wanton spirits of mythological origin. And that unembarrassed irreverence and supposed openness of their plans, regrets, and their interminable bargains and resolutions. Every day for them seems to stand as the last day of the last year. Every night evokes celebrations and innovations that crowd their rooms much as the radios and televisions crowd their brains with a language and a music not even the most patient would undertake to review. But in these sounds nestle a few of the treasures which youth too, has worked to procure.

[5]

The sounds and language of their friends whom they surely love and surely despise with a single and collective strength bring young people "in touch" with all their scattered armies, with their international allies, as it were. The sounds recall as well their own private histories of momentous fear and diffidence. The radio sounds pouring into the dutiful listeners who march across the streets and fields replay the voices of parents. How easily we remember ourselves lying quietly, nervously in bed, frightened by the darkness and by the suddenly invisible status of objects we, like blind persons, had depended upon for our bearings. We remember, too, being frightened by the aloneness, the natural end-product of a black stillness, the newborn of the night. Radio and television serve to draw us away from that darkness and that aloneness.

Earlier it had been myriad friendships and yet a persistent drive toward individuality and autonomy that sparked much of our childhood. Late into the night the midnight sign-off would be heard, marking in those blackest hours the cessation of the noise that had just before guaranteed company and companionship, the very things preventing individuality and autonomy. We pulled the sheets up over our heads, and the radio was shoved down into the bed along with a dog or cat, or books or toys. Or maybe we recall lying nearer the radiance of heat, the brother or sister who shared the room and the bed, and hence the dreams they magically produced. Night continues to possess the hours of silent awareness which for some have meant the best time for doing homework but which for others have aroused a terror neither conquered nor comprehended.

Now radios and records endlessly blare reminders of the voices of a mother or father in the next room, or even of the old television or radio set which sat with them when they were babies and brought movement to a stale emptiness. They remain the identifying sounds, the call letters of infancy, childhood and adolescence. Sounds like these mean being in touch, tuned in, as well as the assurance that desertion and rejection by the young and old alike exist only as fantasies, never as perceivable events. Sounds like these drive the presence of parents, family, neighbors, probably of all society, deeper and deeper inside the heads of young people, and yet, apparently, farther away from where the young might be able to build something special and significant from these sounds. With noises from the outside cramming their interiors, the few sounds generated by youth that might escape have been temporarily silenced, hence some of the demons of creativity alive within these young psychologies have been neutralized, such that many young persons have been rendered mere consumers.

There are also the sounds of time, sounds that do more than merely symbolize associations with external reality and those who inhabit it. Sounds become the corridors of receptivity and extrusion. Perception, after all, has more than a perfunctory social context. When we recognize our mother's voice or father's footstep, for example, we recognize not merely the distinct characteristics of those who live close, we begin to recognize our own interior processes capable of discerning between voices and footsteps. When we hear the unqualified outside, furthermore, we hear the vague inside as well. We hear, as it were, the apparatus of our interior or of our psychology, or, if that's not it, we hear the image of the interior. Then, through this introduction to the images of senses and perceptions, we commence imagining the shape of our "innerness," our cognitive talents and most especially our values and feelings. Eventually we learn that located within ourselves is an interior where memories doze and personal hurts line cracking walls, and where sorrow, anger, pride and a peculiar sense of loss safeguard a troubled darkness. And this, some believe, is what youth is all about and what we older ones keep of our own youth.

One thing school is all about, or maybe should be somewhat about, is putting us in touch with this interior and the experiences sunk in its depths. But well before school, each of us discovers wondrous people who possess an influence over us, leaving their mark as a handwritten language on these interior walls. Voices that practically speak to us from the inside come to be recognized as the voices of those who work or sleep alongside us, share our dinner table, or at least provide for us in all sorts of ways.

Amidst our private instincts and collected cultural residues (should they turn out to really "exist in our science" as they obviously do in our humanism) float the sounds of intelligible voices waiting to be labeled. On the diamond surfaces of our consciousness, their messages remain indelible, their directives decisive. Like charms on a bracelet, the voices and moods and the language and manner they softly imply continue to appear, untarnished even in our oldest age, purely cut as the day they were linked to the chain. In this way, our youth and their youth stay with us. Then, at some incalculable hour, the ways of the generations before us, the tricks of the ones on the scaffolding above us find their way into the architecture of our own privacy and into our hidden resources.

Now we become genuinely linked to history, and yet somehow more separated than ever before from the generation immediately behind us. And this is only part of what many of us call the process of socialization.

Another part of socialization is the onset of the battle of battles, that war against oppression and imperialism fought out first in the hideaway tree houses and alleys of childhood. It is the battle against those by whose loins our existence owes its permanence. It is the battle that first dominates our drive toward the denial of our origins and sustenance and then urges us to believe that we may be immortal, the products of a virgin birth. Evidence of pure autonomy, after all, would be selfish independence or, better, discourteous abandonment and flight. This would be man totally in control of the stars! The proof of autonomy would be the demonstration of a parentless status, a familyless society. Part of socialization is found in the noises of the young which drive their families, their origins, the kingpins of the past neatly away. Part of it, too, is the rancor of their own interiors that soon produces its own sounds as well as visions and illusions enough to stimulate entire battalions of young frenzied soldiers.

The young have come loudly alive, redefining dependency and autonomy as they grow older. Family names may be dropped, personal names erased, and while some assume the names of peoples of different lands and different times (although many have been named for these in the first place) , thereby extending connecting hands to a more comprehensive history, others take on names as apparel, as they see fit, according to some social size or political style. And by this many young persons would believe that a personal strength has been assured and that a steady independence has been made eternally real and genuinely worthwhile.

It is all so humanly complicated. When the child is small and his language appears to be "little more" than the effusion of sounds he has by some miracle internalized as the sounds of adults together, he holds his possessions so tightly to himself and to his land that no one could take them from him. Surely no one his size would dare bargain with him for the right even to share. So we urge him to let the others play with his toys and books, to take turns, give and receive. Here is a friend, we suggest, your first real friend.

But the child doesn't give an inch. For at the core of his refusal to share and what consequently we see as his lacking a sense of a social self, a sense, that is, that would permit our sense of self to coincide with his, are the objects of an extraordinary new world which offer to him the companionship of living sources and resources. The toys he now protects will soon be part of his cognitive processes; his animals and dolls the confederates, real and imagined, with whom he'll work; the corners and cupboards of his room will be the boundaries, regulations and mysterious but thankful rituals of a comprehensive social life; and his books the cornerstones of intellectual and fantasy adventures. To lend out his toys and his books is to part with the seeds of his imagination and the images of what will evolve into the notion of microcosm that someday he will incorporate as the father of sensation and reality. He cannot, therefore, relinquish even one possession without suffering a loss not merely to an inchoate pride or ill-defined contract of ownership but to the buds of a yet undetermined assertiveness and maturation.

And yet we as elders discover that parting with possessions and people is precisely what is often required for the liberation of a well-formed conception of self and the restoration of and access to youthful energies. Where once the attachments to certain toys and certain sounds kept us young and "in touch," later on they were found to be abutments to the next, unpredictable but invigorating stage of life, the middle years. We found, in other words, that the possessions often constituted an anchor in the present and a curtain on the future.

[6]

This, then, is a part of the battle for autonomy and freedom and the quest for an end to an expanding social psychological oppression. Endlessly, youth wishes to secure an agreement that the direction and placement of each step will be its own. One goes, the young invariably decide, exactly where one has to, even though so many of their (our) freely chosen steps are in fact made in obeyance of those wondrously powerful ones. But, just as an irreconcilable tension exists between the boundaries of the single purposeful self and a scorning, controlling society, so is there a pressure to determine which steps one takes on one's own and which steps one takes as acts of loyalty and obsessive learning. How, youth asks, do I know when I'm doing something for myself alone because I elect to do it? It is not just of symbolic value, therefore, that we find schools offering, apart from the "required" courses, what are called "electives," bits of the pie in a well-baked pan from which the young may choose a preoccupation, even a destiny. An elective is one of those self-created steps.

But even electives are nowhere near enough. For there needs to be among these steps, along with the required and the electives, personally initiated steps like a decision to quit school, steps coming from out of the blue, or, more accurately, from the interior's darkness. Here in personally initiated action and effort change is strapped to energy awaiting a discipline, and all are held together, presumably, by work. Here is creativity in a peculiarly intimate and loving form, yet here too is the potential for unordered and unpredictable propaganda and politics. Here is the basis, sometimes resolute, sometimes precarious, of an individual moving freely and cleverly, sometimes within, sometimes without the usual structure designed by and composed of everyone else in the world. Here is what they call an extracurricular activity in the raw. Most importantly, here is the origin of a new adulthood of genuine autonomy: "I don't want to be like everyone else," they say. "I mean, you know, like anyone else. I want to be me. Is that so hard to understand?"

It is not so hard to understand knowing even a bit of the genetic tracks that govern and offer human individuality. But at the same time it is impossible to understand or grant that individuality or autonomy knowing even a bit of human experience and knowing that unfathomable push in each of us to render homogeneous any groups of people we see as being different from us, even as we stumble among the roots of our own identity in which the goals of uniqueness, specialness and personal worth loom so enormous. We saw before how, in making an environment sufficiently constant so that we may more easily trace our steps across it, we tend to collapse everyone and everything else in order that we may stand out, so to speak, in greater relief. We do this cognitively as well as with our social psychological snares in which older or younger people, teachers, the "establishment," men or women get slung together in a heap then crushed under our heel to the bottom of a bushel basket and disposed of. We do this with our families, this action of hording people then lumping them together for our selfish conveniences and esteem.

In school, the habit of hording and clumping people together is somewhat altered. We have our best friend whom we love the most, naturally, but from whom we also sustain antagonisms which if enlarged to adult proportions would with one stroke destroy whole empires and continents. But we stay with this one friend, learning more about what might be called the extended family of trust and fidelity. And in these hours with our best friend, how ghastly and earth-shaking is the threat of an intervention by a third person, who could so easily cause us to dissolve the friendship. The mathematics and natural logic of cultures, we think, should take measures to forbid any sort of dissension and personal separation.

All of this has to do with the emergence of personal autonomy, self-regulation, and the resolution of that slim tension between the person existing solely by himself and having to be with the others on whom he mightily depends.

"I don't like Billy, do you? He always wants to hang around with us."

"Line up by two's," the teachers used to order, sanctifying the bonds which, without our teachers' insistence, we as little people had already erected. Then we would walk as partners, as junior parents, as single selves together. We were learning how to share as well as how to be alone and (by) ourselves. Gradually the architecture of these unions relaxed, and additions, carefully designed of course, were constructed. Soon we had four friends, then eight friends, then pals, gangs, clubs, fraternities. Then we spoke of our race and religion, our sex and our age group, our parts of a whole society enjoined. Brothers and sisters. Members of the family. Members of the tribe.

But in taking each of these significant evolutionary steps of social and psychological consequence, we have at one time or another combined all the others, the "residual people," clumped them into categories of convenience and homogenized them almost as a mound over which our own ascent into society's positions commences. We speak of climbing inclines where success and fame are involved along with many, many people. In what appears as the physics regulating our social psychology, we push off from these people in an effort to gain secure and success-oriented footing as well as proper momentum. Sometimes the others provide a resistance, sometimes a solidity meant to support our travels, our daring, even our biological growth and misdemeanors.

In the end, however, we come to recognize the well-delineated stress points of independence and dependence. For, despite our protestations, it *is* essential that we believe that our place of origin, our home base, will not budge one millimeter under the impact of our energies, our shoving off, or our first steps and later stampeding in space. It *is* essential, in other words, that we maintain our ability to balance independence and dependence on one scale and perfect autonomy and trusted reliance on another.

Independence and dependence, slipping away and returning again, the slender animal moving each day a bit farther from its mother and from its group. Each day a bit farther until one day we felt ourselves to be far enough away. Then we were gone. We were the astronauts on the moon, our one small step preceded by touches and leaps on our own ladders. Down and up, down and up again. Then down for good, our commitments finally congealed. During all the school years we had waited our turn to be detached from the world of childhood and ushered into an entirely new world hung in an incomprehensible adult space, presumably out there somewhere. But for some of us, the two worlds continue to be as separated and foreign from one another as was, well, the eighth grade from the sixth, the senior high from the junior high.

"I'll never make it. God, they have all that homework. I don't want to go back to school in September. I don't want to grow up."

"But I thought you wanted to go. After all, you'll still be with Robert and Jeff and John and Ernest and Homer. You'll still be together. And someday you'll be as big and strong as Daddy."

[7]

To speak or write about youth, as is so fashionable today, is to wonder aloud whether or not siding with the young promises acceptance by them and therefore grants reentrance into a time we have forever lost. Such a notion would seem reasonable enough if its simplicity did not make it somehow weak and sterile. For one reason or another, writing about youth seems to have become the means by which some of us kick off from the young into an occult or transcendent life space all of our own. Then again, writing, with its sane aggressiveness, may just be a kicking at youth with such unequivocal force that the demons inside us, who prompt us to seek a return to childhood to see again our parents when they were young and so beautiful that we would fight with people bigger than ourselves just to preserve their image, might turn to stone and hence be silent forever.

Some of the statements recently made about youth, for example, at first glance seem naked of all truth. One author says that the political knowledge of any person twenty-five years old or younger is by definition superior to and more sophisticated than the political knowledge of any person over twenty-five. By definition, no less! Twenty-five, this writer has marked as the point in a real chronology as *the* time barrier, and here am I, barely reconciled to yesterday's announcement that the magic number, surely dripping death on its stems, was thirty. Barely as I age, the market of my youthfulness and adult illusions drops, and my stocks continue to sink.

Another writer has asserted that the anger mustered by "youth" and then directed toward the inequities of schools and societies not only is destructive from a political perspective, but represents little more than the "acting out" (that ungodly phrase) of infantile neuroses or adolescent antipathies. To this person, everything

seems to be displacement or overidentification. And someone else
said the other day: "All those political protests you see? They are
little more than psychodramas. Psychodrama pure and simple."

What's so frightfully complicating about this youth business is
that at the same split second all of these statements seem absolutely
false and absolutely true. True, that is, as the existence of youth
itself. To be sure, the sophistication of some young people is right
out in front; it cannot be denied. But like the motives or capabilities that fill each human being and challenge him to action, the
sophistication is a complex one, for it reflects all humanity in a
single pot, its contents far from melted but far, too, from their
original state. For some young people, sophistication has come
easily, for they have captured and contained the language of their
mother, which was poetic and rare. For others, the sophistication
has come easily from what at first appears to be a contradiction of
progress and passivity. Without invitation and, even worse, without exertion, television has plopped a new language world in the
laps of a generation. Its coming most certainly has raised the awareness of younger persons but, as John Aldrich has suggested in *In
the Country of the Young*,[1] lowered, maybe permanently, their
sense of quality. Now, almost laughably, and partly because of
television, teachers face the problem of making human biology or
literature interesting, while television personnel themselves, as
Daniel Boorstin has noted in *The Decline of Radicalism*,[2] must
market oppression, starvation and war in a new and dramatically
salable fashion. Whatever the consequences, and television exposure of inequities has many, technology seems to have conspired
against the older generation to sculpt this "sophistication of ease"
among the young. For now the young not only publicly dismiss the
pasts of the old, as they always have (their private conversations
often turn to these pasts), they have become the most acute per-
ceivers and rightful inheritors, so some say, of a most expanded
sense of the present.

"The times they are a-changing." In some ways, many young
people have become sophisticated, knowledgeable too, well beyond
the real and imaginary levels set by those like myself who obsess
over and compare the generations and argue by theory and obser-

vation that in most "battles" the young must triumph. But twenty-five, by definition! It is also the case that many of the young mirror in their intelligence much of the faulty sophistication of a world of utter escape and fantasy that technology has also offered to them. (We must not forget the almost immaculate and endless unreality that television heaps on us before and after its documentaries.) Their knowledge, in fact, is not comparable either in breadth or variety to the harder-earned knowledge of many of their compatriots and many of the adults with whom they study and work. Sadly enough, there are people under twenty-five whose interest in a world so enormous and problematic has, in some instances, become dulled. They have, these young people, restricted their engagements, ignored the realities that have literally undercut the lives of other children and turned to watching the classroom clock that ticks them and their families through schooldays, holidays and ritualized ceremonies reifying a bland chronology and a vacuous calendar.

For these people, time itself drapes long expansions of drudgery and sleep between the prongs of celebrations which honor repetition and predictability. For so many, life remains little more than weekends, Christmases, Fourth of July's and summer vacations. And nothing, or very little, appears to arouse their sense of either indignation or joy. The threat of a holocaust, the existence of hunger, the presence of oppression seemingly cause barely a tremor in their linear routines and responsibilities. They do exist, these people, and more than once in their lives they exasperate teachers whose task it is to make poetry or drama, psychology or politics, history, science, printing, drawing or just plain reading palatable. Probably, too, they exasperate television bosses who are obliged to adjust films of war and poverty to these persons' fluctuations of taste and interest. Let's be fair about all this and recognize that many of us gracefully avoid our suspicion that much of society houses utterly boring, insensitive and recalcitrant people.

Some of us might choose to assume that the majority of America's children have been murdered by schools or by those portions of society demanding compliance and conventionality. Maybe so. But a more pertinent issue than whether a spirit of humanity is so

quickly extinguished by schools is that every year of growth provides its own magic and its own rational and irrational check-
points. Eight-year-olds cry because they are not twelve; twelve-
year-olds wish a taste of the free pleasures of eighteen, and many
of us seem to be frightened and thrown backward by the notching
of decades: nineteen to twenty, twenty-nine to thirty, 1969 to 1970,
1999 to 2000. So it isn't that any real integer like twenty-five marks
the beginning or end to anything magical or profound. Certainly
sophistication, with its valuable as well as ludicrous qualities,
knows no birth or death date of twenty-five.

Now about youth's anger, an anger, one would think to listen to
some observers, that every day brings youth closer to philosophies
of hatred and nihilism. Were we perhaps misled by a certain group
of intellectuals who taught us that aggression was the most prominent activity of children and hence the cornerstone of life and
death? To read some authors, we would think that youth bleeds
and sweats its anger in a climate so hot that no negotiation or
"radical confrontation" could ever soothe it. Dammit, we cry, why
do they stomp so, their bitterness and pomposity sewn into their
clothes and combed into their hair? Why do they scream obscenities, disloyalty and malcontent without respite, without considera-
tion or apparent purpose? Why all of that stoked-up aggressiveness and crystalline anger? To touch angered youth, we fear, is to
be wounded and, even worse, to have our blood mix with theirs.
If we meet up with hostile, politicized youth on a rampage, we're
liable to be contaminated by the scent of their culture, bowled
over by their collective strength, or perhaps won over to what we
perceive as their free-swinging, fault-finding parade.

But if we count the seconds of anger, rudeness or aggression in a
child's life, or tally up the moments of unadulterated hate and
antipathy either exhibited or implied, if we count the instants of
militant action and open attack, we will miss nothing less than the
form and stuffing of everyday life. Anger just is not as dominant
a life-force as we might wish to believe. There is just too much to
existence. So how can we destroy for good and always the image
that a "delinquent" is delinquent every waking second and that
even in his dreams he plots the desecration of societies that bounce

him and his blood-brother "gangs" into the seedy corners and wrinkles of cities embarrassed by their own inadequacies and injustices? How can we destroy the image of a college student as a fulltime political warrior, draft card burner, trasher or whatever?

As in all acts of unmitigated anger and frustration, as in all confrontations with bitter denial, most delinquent acts and most student protests are but matches suddenly lit and as suddenly extinguished and thrown away. There are no flames burning down all that is good, no gutting of buildings yet; there is just the firing of nerves for good and understandable reason, probably explainable by some metabolic force and social science. No flames yet and no indication, either, that a young person's love and fear, mischievousness, fright and style of testing the world are not parts of that aroused state. Only the body's witches know the concoction for anger, spite, and revenge. But it would seem, even now in our own slowly receding ignorance, that human anger erupts in the presence of many, many ingredients.

In truth, when the description and diagnosis of anger become a fixation, as for some they have, then to a certain extent the data recorded by these people are an admission of their own anger, in part stimulated by those they study but perpetrated too by social factors as well as real people, whom we long ago or just today believed we had successfully by-passed or psychologically transcended. When we diagnose or analyze we sometimes liberate an energy from those we examine, but too often diagnosis and analysis also mean a neutralization of badly needed political dissent and a doubtful invasion into the hearts of real human beings. But this is the chance we take in scientific inquiries involving human beings. If we only psychologize youth's anger, therefore, we may successfully avoid those very real situations that contribute to their anger and make ourselves believe that anger is the mold from which pure youth takes its shape.

Still, the anger is there, and it cannot be ignored. Its facets are complicated, for just as there are times when situations make certain young people incensed, so is there inevitably a group of people on the earth who by the anger they carry about within themselves seem to ignite situations, institutions and customs which previously seemed so "neutral," innocent and calm.

The anger cannot be ignored, regardless of where it may appear. It is strange, for example, that during youth's sieges on the "establishment" or on their chosen objects of adult social order we rarely comment on the excruciating loss of purpose resulting from the inability of certain young people to temper the hostility they maintain towards one another. This is anger apart from well-recognized political disagreements and violent factionalism. But let no one call this anger "typical infantile self-indulgence," for the young own no monopoly here, and infantile self-indulgence knows no age barrier of twenty-five. The cruelty and hurt that the young can generate in a flash seems staggering to us, probably because we might like to believe that a period of years can be sustained, between childhood tantrums and the time when the children must go to war, in which the young actually live according to an ethic of uncorrupted love and gentle kindness. What happened to that sweet-smelling bundle I used to call my baby, we ask again and again.

When, but a few years ago, we saw the hate of adults, the lust for power, as they say, and the obsequious planning that launched human spaceships to unattainable heights of isolated strength and dominance, we said hurrah for those men, but heaven keep my children, now so clean and young, away from that power and that fire of self-aggrandizement and ambition. But as our wisdom grew, the truth emerged: if we are willing to forfeit our sensibilities of proportion, then adult power and hate and child power and hate look almost identical. The competitions, the thumping of others' heads, the smashing of others' dreams and desecration of their simple place on the land are all there, as big as a child's life, as big as an adult's life, if not bigger.

Like assassins, the young and the old plot to undermine the routes of youthful as well as adult travel and poison the wells of seemingly anyone's sustenance and luxury. At times these plots seem justifiable, vengeful but vindicable in some primitive legal sense. But at other times they seem, even to understanding observers, as being nothing short of bizarre and heinous. There are actions that seem so utterly bizarre they make one think that only demons could choreograph such horrible movement and render such sickening pain.

How can it be, for example, that children with barely the strength or control to climb to the back of a happy stone whale built by someone who remembered the ways in which children give birth to make-believe, unembarrassed, in the midst of adult traffic would mercilessly fling a smaller child with practically no strength or control to a pavement of iron-hard cement? How can it be that so much damage of superhuman scale is meted out by children with brains incapable of fathoming the mysteries of addition and multiplication? How can it be explained? Sibling rivalry is not a sufficient explanation. And instincts? Well, possibly so, if we knew exactly what instincts were.

[8]

In writing about radical students, many authors speak of the vilification of members of one political group by members of another. But the anger they observe is more than even vilification. For there is a burden in a particular brand of student defiance, a burden reeking of nothing short of death, the wish for it and the fear of it, a burden causing an exorbitant expenditure of energies merely to keep dreams of death back and out of sight. Anger has given birth to these dreams and has revitalized, as macabre as it seems, an interest in and fascination with death. Yet in observing this anger, we outsiders tend to see little beyond waste and self-demise.

In another sense, a more precious sense, moreover, "youth" complicates our own visions and impressions of death. Sometimes we feel that their age alone should prevent their comprehension or preoccupation with death; they are too young, not yet prepared for such thoughts. I wonder. Do they come from a land where death rarely travels and where a true belief in immortality and infinitude linger? The young seem to us to act as we imagine their bodies to be, either unaware of natural eventualities or preferring to laugh aloud with youth's cunning, speed and impulsiveness. We think the young enjoy life; we think it is their wish that all people should know freedom and not worry about death for a long, long time.

When young people inquire about death, their words almost convey a charm, not a gaiety, of course, but hardly the lugubrious grays and blues of the words directed to death whispered and written by those who recognize that their life lines have begun to trail out behind them. In a crazy way, youth protects or ought to protect our own stockpile of hope and of life. "Our only hope is with them," we say, meaning in part that they must inherit our place and our errors; but meaning as well that time's uncanny flexibility allows us to transplant the rightful property and spirit of youth's future onto our past, which means that occasionally we flourish through their aspirations and their notions of what is possible. In fact, we sometimes feel high and giddy, as though on drugs, from the excitement and freedom we imagine will soon come to our young people and then, somehow, to us. Our hope, we proclaim, is that the young might be spared a repeated trampling down of their intentions and robust eagerness; but no one yet has spared anyone this.

In their early years, the very young reveal a confusion of death and sexuality, a confusion about how life starts and stops and about the fact that family members young and old may die, walk out or vanish. These can be costly confusions and they can persist. For a long, long time it seems that despite our efforts to restrain it, something in our psychology urges us to try to comprehend absences and losses which at one level are at the root of anger, defiance and the concept of death. Absences and losses as well as those mysterious additions through birth, marriage and remarriage are also part of youth's experience. The young have become the grand accountants and census takers of a family and of a society that shift in population even as they tally up the members. People go and new people come to take their place or establish a special place on their own. The young will find that their concern with missing persons and the dead will remain with them forever. But the concern starts even as language itself forms.

"Daddy go to work now," the child tells his mother, defining for himself the departure of his father but, more essentially, hoping to assure himself of his father's reappearance and therefore continuing existence. Like a flag announcing the start of the race, the child's announcement begins the count of the workday hours, the count of hours of separation which contain for him the initial exposure first to desertion and aloneness and soon to the notion of simultaneity as well. For the child temporarily will lay his anxieties to rest with the recognition that death does not occur just because I am here while Daddy is there.

"Want to speak to Daddy on the phone?"

"Hello, Lucas, how are you?"

"Daddy at work?"

"Yes, I'm at work, Luke."

"Daddy come home soon!"

"Yes, very soon now. Can I speak to Mommy now? . . . Give Mommy the phone now, Lucas. Lucas!"

But there is confusion. Child here, parent there, people coming and going, people leaving, people left. It all has something to do with life and death, or moving in and out of life and death, not in a playful way, but as a means of touching the walls and railings of reality outside, and the layers of consciousness inside. Life and death, the outside and inside, the possible and impossible, past and future, self and other, actual and ideal, all heaped together, all pulling and falling over one another. The young become our children. With fingers locked and stretched they grip at our hands, dragging us to their ends, to safety and to danger. Now, perhaps because of their rising power, we feel ourselves to be in the last movement approaching an end to something, a decade, a century, an era. The sense of the present expands and then collapses. With each breath the lungs suck in heavy molecules of time then pump them out again, tired and used up.

[9]

To move about the dungeons and palaces where youth is kept and where the images of youth become institutionalized as schools, clubs or political fraternities is to recognize that the anger of youth accompanies the compassion of youth just as the hate accompanies love and the impulse to care for someone accompanies the impulse to hurt him. It is not merely, then, that some schools or teachers or administrators, that some of us, are good and some bad, or that some educational philosophies seem genuinely custodial or murderous whereas others seem more imaginative or, as they still say, "progressive." Dichotomies of this sort are usually cognitive conveniences, rarely gauges of the truth.

It is rather the antinomies and ambivalence, the intense feelings of such extraordinarily discrepant meaning and emotion and conflictual push to action and then away from action that cause us to wonder about ourselves and our institutions and then turn us into immobilized fools, distraught and humiliated right in the middle of personal and political revolutions. It is the ambivalence and confusion that attracts us to youth's expressions like "identity crisis," "copping out," and "getting it together." And if we are immobilized, struck down by two competing drives or wants, then most probably there are four, eight, sixteen drives pinning us to the tracks where moments ago we glided so easily into healthy life, that is into love and work. In these times we just cannot "get it together" no matter how intense our rage, for we have been stilled by the antinomies and the ambivalence.

What a profound conceptual contribution Freud made in the notion of the Oedipal configuration, not only because of the social psychological relationships it describes, but because of its inherent insistence that portions of a man's imagination simultaneously hold secret packages of feeling sometimes so discrepant, so foreign from one another it would seem that he would burst into hundreds of swollen pieces. It is the reverence for the parent and the impulse to kill him, not separated, not one in each hand, but both in one reality, both clutched in one fist, both stored in one mind. Assuming an almost religious magnitude, the respect and adoration become united with a hate and brutality supposedly known only to prehistoric monsters. Behind the ambivalence are masked demons dancing a curious and chaotic commotion in our souls.

Parents, teachers and the companions of the young breathe that life and death and dance that demonic dance. The young and the small at times wish that the old and tall might flop over dead. The old and powerful wish that the young and insignificant might recede or wander away or maybe find another country. Love it or leave it. The number of these kinds of murders committed each day must be fantastic! But at the same time, adulation and un-questioned obedience to much authority also stand high. Pride is swallowed one second, hate the next, the wish for love and the wish for death the next. So it is that we almost can see the signs of life and death flickering on and off the surfaces of authorities appointed to oversee youth's daily and nightly routines.

What complicates these matters even more is that our customs and rituals often cannot keep up with or comprehend the conse-quences of our changing sensations and private trials. Society seems to have no place for ambivalence and the indecision it yields. Often it is as if the social casings, the social roles into which we are obliged to fit our personal intrusiveness, our "real" selves, perhaps, cannot accommodate the presence of all of our feelings, especially the anger. And how unfair this is, not just for youth, since all these other feelings have as much right to be seen and heard as the ones for which the social customs and rituals were originally conceived.

More generally, societies and psyches have developed ingenious procedures for honing conscious and unconscious materials, pat-terns and processes that change and rearrange themselves as much in sleep as in action, as much in death as in life. Dangerous experi-ments with drugs are undertaken, flirtations with lunacy are re-peated, and undeniable self-destruction is sustained partly as a reaction to the realities of our societies, partly as a reaction to anger and loss, but partly as well to find and demonstrate that these marvelous and frightening experiences exist not as bizarre extensions of our world, not as cantilevered perches, but as hunks of the same substantial structure that houses language, rudimentary perception and pedestrian reasoning. What frightens us, I think, is that at times reality itself seems to overhang a valley entirely unsupported in a way that would make the most daring architects gasp. The young help to erect this new reality of political actions, ideologies, and life-styles. They build it, behold it, then, just as we believed we were adapting to it, they tear it all down and start in again constructing still a newer reality and a fresher definition of social order and peace.

By their hopes for the young and in their prayers that the young may liberate the world if only because they are young, the old seek a liberation of their own lives of increasing constraint and incapacities. On these prayers and the efforts they initiate glistens the love being transferred between the generations. But often, too, the old wish for the obliteration of the young, and in this curse they covet a paradoxical liberation, a liberation turned on its head with time running backward, for we just cannot be young again like the young. We must instead be young like the middle-aged, or young like the old. When care for and trust in the young are entertained, succeeding futures, also paradoxically, are preserved and the histories of prior generations finally safeguarded. But when enduring antipathies toward the young dominate the transactions between generations, a false freedom is born, a freedom conceived in the belief that if one liquidates another's future, one's own past is cured and one's own future is rendered limitless. Among so many inherited rights, aging confers the power of potential rejector on all who survive. Soon the son will become the father who leaves. Still, rejection is no new business, as the young practice it among their peers, often reaching a precision and dexterity with its weapons that make us think they have been advised of its lifelong utility. Quite possibly, they have been. It's funny and sad to think what we teach children in the name of "preparing" them for adulthood and for the time when we are no longer here.

It's also funny and sad to think of the number of false liberation movements attempted each day as parents and children wrestle with and among themselves in the hopes of "getting together" and moving apart all at the same time. In these moments, which seem to make up so much of our present society, the faces of the rejectors and the rejected are so frequently seen close together. But this is part of what "they" call maturation and ambivalence, love and hate.

It is also part of what "they" call "rapid social change." The place, resting and moving, of each person who lives or has lived has become so fragile today, so evanescent. Once we were taught to believe in the permanent sanctity of the dead. Surely *their* reputations were finalized, sealed and delivered and their skeletons left untouched to rot deeper and deeper into the ground. But no more. Dead men have been lifted and carted away as the bare scent of their posthumous spirits have come into disfavor and their corpses made the recipients of national animus. More recently, the racially segregated status of cemeteries has been violated in ways that make churchgoers tremble in their appeals to paradisic courts. For when a black man is allowed to lie alongside a white man, the time has finally come to alter the most grotesque of written histories and to rearrange the substance of individual memory. The time has come to mature, resolve or at least recognize ambivalence and find a place for it in society. The time has come, in other words, for social change.

To some extent, these are but a few of the demands that youth outlines, some of the supposed crimes that youth allegedly commits: the tearing down of saints, the ripping open of tradition, the denial and desecration of memory and custom; and the obliteration of authority. Our impression is that youth's many and often capricious philosophies teach that no man knows such worth that he cannot be expended and that no man maintains such control over his energies that he can be expected to embrace all of fidelity's covenants. Through their boisterous sexuality, for example, the young are said to every day chew away at the fibers not "merely" of society but of the realities it labors so hard to contain. It is said that the young rip the fibers of realities and throw them in the faces of generations they know planted them and nourished them.

But it isn't so. It just isn't so that they alone are the guilty ones.

We know this by the intensity of our own urges to run to the books and movies, drawings, music, poetry and life-styles which in their gaudy and flavorful way reenact the same fantasies we now project onto youth, rightly or wrongly, the true owners of these particular products. We know it, too, by the actions we somehow cannot help ourselves from taking that fortunately remain private and unsuspected. Yet even with our most impeccable constraints, the products of the young, or of what Philip Slater has called the "counter culture," kindle reminiscences of our own timorous advances and almost comical regrets: "When I was young and used to listen to the sixteen-year-old boys in the high school locker room," the young man recalled, "I used to dream about growing up, so that one day I too could do what these older boys did. Lie!"

[10]

To write about youth means confronting one's prior and future selves and generations and, even more, one's single self properly bound, trapped and free, in the single glowing point of now. It means confronting not just one child, one day, one dream, or one event, but all days, all dreams, all events, all the best friends, the few lovers and the ancestors too, and all according to the sequences and antisequences these people and these events dictate and underwrite. It means a confrontation in which no one is left out as well as an understanding that the physics governing our psychologies recognizes that an expenditure of energy is required in the movement we make toward generations and objects identical to that required in the movement made away from them. The physics, therefore, describes a logic in the sometimes violent separations from parents that occur at precisely the same instant as the sometimes violent couplings with new friends and in the same way, probably, with a new sex, the other sex. Strange how that special unit of time circumscribing psychic transactions can seem so small and yet retain so much. It seems less strange if we recall that enclosed in this unit of time are all the remains, all that so far has been constructed of a unique identity. All eternity, perhaps, as some philosophers have taught, recurs in that one unit.

The escape from home, for example, and the sniping at family values and peculiar social structures are not exactly the precursors of attachments to people and institutions outside the family. In the beginning, they are part of one single action disguised as fragments by a seemingly long extension in time. It is not, therefore, that the engine of sexuality runs only when the engine of generational obedience is turned off. More precisely, the engine of obedience runs its energy into the engine of sexuality. When everything in that first engine is seemingly flat and impotent, the other engine appears to catch. But while it may seem as though the engine of sexuality proceeds under its own power, it remains attached to its parent engine in a single system for quite a while. (Only later on does the child dare examine the possibility that these engines may be separated and thereby gain the health and wisdom that this separation yields.) In the beginning, however, the major source of attraction and attachment to people and the fundamental linkage between people and the autonomy provided by their friendships is still the family, or at least relationships defined by kinship networks and authority.

Although it is true that with each decade aspects of maturity bloom earlier and earlier, the concept of adolescence has not yet lost all its validity. Gradations of psychological and social growth persist which, ironically, seem more and more in evidence as the young increase in what we call sophistication and awareness. So like a child running away from home to claim a vital independence and a chance to choose and own, the child running into love and sexuality, protest and freedom, the child running, really, toward the border between adulthood and childhood (a border that *does* in fact exist in our minds and in our societies) must pack together and stuff into his pockets the coins, food and mementos of his entire life. For they represent his first social psychological and economic arrangement with the family. With little preparation and even less warning, everything in this all-or-nothing transaction is packed, as if by the act of physically moving the child might lure away the memories of those places and people with such a devastating impact and finality that he might alter the content and rationality of his future and, most especially, of the reveries that future will hold.

The child takes the currency and foodstuff and runs to those he loves, and like a despotic general burns the villages behind him, the bridges, the outposts and the supply depots. Through this militant outburst the past presumably is pillaged and a sparkling new present and future are made to wait for him, his goals, and his greatness. And who's going to stand up and say it isn't so or it doesn't happen this way!

To write about youth and youth's lives of attachments to things and people and work implies a presence of myriad feelings, all the feelings and emotions that human beings can generate, and all at once; feelings generated in varying formulas, in varying proportions and saliences. Perhaps the metaphor of emotional debits and credits has worth, for it does seem that we run some emotional accounts into the red when we absolutely require clean and crisp capital in other accounts. Possibly, too, when we come to know emotions and feelings well, there will emerge a principle of balancing payments and monies received. But the systems of feelings now are so incomprehensible that to call any behavior, or political revolt for that matter, actions of love or hate, actions of guided or misguided purpose, actions of children or adults can be only partially correct. Too few actions will be so clear-cut that they might be assigned merely to one account or another. For there *will* be anger in love; there *will* be bitter regret in vast hope. And, regardless of what the words mean to us, there *will* be adult maturity in childlike expressions and childlike imagination in adult impressions.

To label or diagnose, observe or record, which after all constitute the process of writing about youth, is to select images and language from realities only thinly "in touch" with the magic of one's own conscious and unconscious worlds. In some ways and in some glorious times, we are one with or feel ourselves to be united with this "other reality," this counter culture, joined, that is, with these people and their generation. But, mainly, the source of our impressions, the grist, as it's still called, is our own interiors, interiors that do more than pay homage to materials that once lived outside of us or before us. It is *our* love and hate, *our* feelings of despair and courage, plasticity and conservatism, and *our* ambivalences that haunt the pages on which we print and draw a transient, flickering youth. It is unspoken talent and shameless temerity as much as it is insight and sensitivity.

Now, in the "real" sciences we could not exonerate such blasphemously personal thrusts at the truth. But somehow, in the outlandish physics systematizing and ordering social and psychological action, whatever it is that accepts our invitation to be written on a particular morning when the night before we had all but convinced ourselves that we were, finally, written out becomes part of the reality we have chosen to study. It becomes a part here just as much as it explicates a part there, and for a moment we are young like the young. The parts must appertain, moreover, for we have chosen youth, of all things, as this reality. But the parts must also be connected to the currency, food and souvenirs we, too, once stuffed together, hurriedly and without forewarning as we made our plans to pillage a past and thereby create a dazzling present and bountiful future.

But now, writing about youth seems impossible, since everything happens so quickly, pouring forth so rapidly that too little time is left over to catch much of anything anymore. Perhaps it wasn't this way once, in our youth, when resiliency was assured and our bodies were proud and indestructible and maybe our souls immortal. But it all happens so quickly now that no one seems to treasure even the impressions that emerge, unrefined, still dripping with the fluids of unconscious and conscious substance. Everyone demands finished products, all perfectly intelligible. Yet even worse, it all happens so quickly that we have begun to lose people from our land. What really is happening to the poor and the sick, and those who once were strong but whom failure has made frail and scared? Because of the rushing lives of so many people it is essential that we stop absolutely still, that we stop writing and stop talking and through our simple impressions, thoughtful and impure, regain those whom we have before turned away and restore the rare collection of time they have broken and hidden from us.

There is no life that can stand our taking away its fragile estimations of worth, just as there is no life that can come away unharmed from the tensions and deprivations endemic in our contemporary patterns of training, growth, education, bureaucracy, socialization, and career. All of us suffer in our way, the rich and the poor, and no one waits out the time of the temporary well. No one manages perfectly or completely a splintered life of demands heaped on demands. No one knows youth; no one knows aging; no one can adequately speak for another, even in a democracy. But each of us guards impressions of a life space colored and swept by time, and a sense of what it means to have morsels of the world we're able to see change, and what it means to have things resist even our most forceful efforts, singular and collective, to alter them. When the bewilderment of change, of time, really, and the reconciliation of the unchangeable properties of reality come to be internalized, then everything everywhere seems to have "gotten together," and identity arises as a part of that everything. Life now is fat, and death, even to the very young, a bit less terrifying.

The arc of time diminishes; youth waits its turn, then takes its sometimes foolish gambles with predestination and immortality. The rest of us work our narrow work, hoping that the markers separating the generations might move again and that when sophistication, knowledge and anger, style and unbecoming pride are for an instant laid away, each day and each person in that day might repossess a fundamental dignity.

Notes

Chapter 4

1. Erik H. Erikson, *Young Man Luther* (New York: W. W. Norton, 1958, p. 112.

Chapter 5

1. James Agee and Walker Evans, *Let Us Now Praise Famous Men* (Boston: Houghton Mifflin, 1969), pp. 289–291.
2. See Jerome Bruner, "The Conditions of Creativity," in *On Knowing: Essays for the Left Hand* (Cambridge: Belknap Press, 1962), pp. 17–30; Abraham Maslow, "Creativity in Self-Actualizing People," in *Toward a Psychology of Being* (Princeton, Van Nostrand, 1968), pp. 127–137; Robert Coles, "The Words and Music of Social Change," *Daedalus*, 98 (1969), 184–198; Paul Goodman, "Youth Subculture" and "An Unteachable Generation," in *Compulsory Mis-education and the Community of Scholars* (New York: Random House, 1962), pp. 271–294 and 113–121; Michael A. Wallach and Cliff W. Wing, Jr., *The Talented Student: A Validation of the Creativity-Intelligence Distinction* (New York: Holt, Rinehart and Winston, 1969).
3. Andrey Voznesensky, *Selected Poems*, trans. Herbert Marshall (New York: Hill and Wang, 1966).
4. Stéphane Mallarmé, *Selected Prose, Poems, Essays and Letters*, trans. Bradford Cook (Baltimore: The Johns Hopkins Press, 1956).
5. Jean-Paul Sartre, *The Words*, trans. Bernard Frechtman (New York: George Braziller, 1964), pp. 230–231.
6. Arthur Rimbaud, letter to G. Izambard, in *Illuminations*, trans. Louise Varese (New York: New Directions, 1946).
7. George Orwell, *Such, Such Were the Joys* (New York: Harcourt, Brace and World, 1953).
8. Sartre, *op. cit.*, pp. 220–221.
9. Bertolt Brecht, *Selected Poems*, trans. H. R. Hays (New York: Harcourt, Brace and World, 1947).
10. Martin Buber, *Ten Rungs: Hasidic Sayings* (New York: Schocken Books, 1947).
11. Albert Einstein, *The World as I See It* (New York: Philosophical Library, 1949).

12. F. Scott Fitzgerald, *The Letters of F. Scott Fitzgerald,* ed. Andrew Turnbull (New York: Charles Scribner's Sons, 1963), pp. 32–34.

Chapter 6

1. *Bristol Township School District Program,* p. 26.

Chapter 7

1. Yvonne Criswell, "Mixed Emotions: My Year at Wellesley," in *The Searcher,* Wellesley High School. Reprinted in *How Old Will You Be in 1984?,* ed. Diane Divoky (New York: Avon Books, 1969), p. 185.
2. See his *White Racism: A Psychohistory* (New York: Pantheon, 1970).
3. For a more detailed account of these events, see Peter Schrag, *Village School Downtown* (Boston: Beacon Press, 1967).

Chapter 8

1. See Kenneth Haskins, "The Case for Local Control," *Saturday Review* (January 11, 1969), 52 ff.
2. See Theodore R. Sizer, "The Case for a Free Market," *Saturday Review* (January 11, 1969), 34.
3. See Peter Schrag, "Little Brother Is Watching," *Change,* 2 (January–February 1970), 5–6.
4. See Talcott Parsons and Gerald M. Platt, "Considerations on the American Academic System," *Minerva,* 6 (Summer 1968), 503.
5. See Joseph Featherstone, "School Managers," *The New Republic,* 160 (February 8, 1969), 13–14.
6. Cited in Murray Friedman, "Is White Racism the Problem?" *Commentary,* 47 (January, 1969), 61–65.
7. See Harvey Pressman, "Schools to Beat the System," *Psychology Today,* 2 (March, 1969), 62.

Chapter 9

1. These groups do not necessarily represent all university voluntary tutorial programs. They may be unique in terms of their individual approaches.
2. Quotation from Ann Cook, at the time a student at Sarah Lawrence College, Bronxville, New York, in the *New York Times,* Sunday, July 14, 1963.
3. No systematic attempt was made to investigate fully the backgrounds of these so-called generations. Historical descriptions of revolutionary leaders, however, may be found in Crane Brinton, *The Anatomy of Revolution* (New York: W. W. Norton, 1938), pp. 113–148, and Pitirim Sorokin, *Sociology of Revolution* (Philadelphia: J. B. Lippincott, 1925), part III.
4. See Hans Toch, *The Social Psychology of Social Movements* (New York: Bobbs-Merrill, 1965), pp. 130–157. In this context see also Henry W. Riecken and George C. Homans, "Psychological Aspects of Social Structure," in *The Handbook of Social Psychology,* ed. Gardner Lindzey (Reading, Mass.: Addison-Wesley, 1954), pp. 786–832.

5. It may be interesting to compare Reform and Uplifter organizations in terms of the differentiations noted by Neil Smelser in his discussions of Norm- and Value-oriented movements. See his *Theory of Collective Behavior* (New York: The Free Press of Glencoe, 1963), pp. 270–382.

6. These notions of bureaucracy are taken from Max Weber, *The Theory of Economic and Social Organization* (Glencoe, Ill.: The Free Press, 1947).

7. See David Riesman, "The Search for Challenge," *Merrill-Palmer Quarterly of Behavior and Development,* 6 (1940) 218–234, and "The College Student in an Age of Organization," *Chicago Review,* 12 (Autumn, 1958), 50–68. See also Ernest Schachtel, "On Alienated Concepts of Identity," in *Man Alone,* eds. Eric and Mary Josephson (New York: Dell Company, 1962).

8. See Toch, *op. cit.*

9. For relevant theoretical discussions see Ross Stagner, "Personality Dynamics and Social Conflict," *Journal of Social Issues,* 17 (1961), 28–44, and "Studies in Aggressive Social Attitudes," *Journal of Social Psychology,* 20 (1944), 129–140.

10. See Toch, *op. cit.,* pp. 185–203.

11. For theoretical and empirical examinations of the effect of sexual identity on behavior, see Guy Swanson and Daniel Miller, *Inner Conflicts and the Mechanisms of Defense* (New York: Holt, 1960), and Paul D. Lipsitt, "Defensiveness in Decision Making as a Function of Sex Role Identification," Diss. University of Chicago 1965.

12. Eric Hoffer, *The True Believer* (New York: Harper and Row, 1951), p. 88.

13. See Toch, *op. cit.,* pp. 136–137.

14. This discussion is somewhat reminiscent of Lewis Coser's *The Functions of Social Conflict* (Glencoe, Ill.: The Free Press, 1956). For a somewhat different theoretical perspective see Raymond W. Mack, "Components of Social Conflict," *Social Problems,* 12 (Spring 1965), 388–397.

15. Weber, *op. cit.* See also Ernst Troeltsch, *The Social Teaching of the Christian Churches* (New York: Macmillan, 1931), vol. I.

16. "Organizational Change: A Study of the Women's Christian Temperance Union," Diss. University of Chicago 1954.

17. The previous phrase is taken directly from the title and substance of Erving Goffman, *The Presentation of Self in Everyday Life* (New York: Doubleday, 1959).

18. Interestingly, the developmental process of trust, autonomy, initiative, and industry, strongly reflects the stages of psychosocial crises advanced by Erik Erikson in *Childhood and Society,* 2nd ed. (New York: W. W. Norton, 1963), pp. 247–274. In this light, it may be fruitful to explore the phases of social movements, generally, in an epigenetic framework.

19. See his "Alienation and Labor" in the *Economic and Philosophical Manuscripts,* in Marx, *Early Writings,* trans. T. B. Bottomore (New York: McGraw-Hill, 1964).

20. Saul D. Alinsky, *Reveille for Radicals* (New York: Random House, 1969), p. 157.

21. Hoffer, *op. cit.*, p. 108.

22. *Ibid.*, p. 109.

23. This notion was indirectly suggested by Morris Rosenberg in his *Society and the Adolescent Self Image* (Princeton, New Jersey: Princeton University Press, 1965).

24. See for example Talcott Parsons and Robert F. Bales, *Family, Socialization and Interaction Process* (Glencoe, Ill.: The Free Press, 1955); Morris Zelditch, "Role Differentiation in the Nuclear Family," in *The Family*, eds. Norman Bell and Ezra Vogel (Glencoe, Ill.: The Free Press, 1965); and Fred L. Strodtbeck, "Husband-Wife Interactions over Revealed Differences" and "The Family as a Three-Person Group" in *Small Groups*, eds. Paul Hare, Edgar F. Borgatta and Robert F. Bales (New York: Knopf, 1962).

25. For some relevant perspectives on these notions, see Carl N. Degler, "Revolution Without Ideology: The Changing Place of Women in America," and Edna G. Rostow, "Conflict and Accommodation," in *Daedalus*, 93 (Spring 1964), pp. 653–670 and 736–760.

Chapter 10

1. See his essay in *Religion in America*, eds. Robert N. Bellah and William G. McLoughlin (Boston: Beacon Press, 1968). See also his "Religious Evolution," *American Sociological Review*, 29 (1964), pp. 358–374.

2. See Kenneth Keniston, *Young Radicals: Notes on Committed Youth* (New York: Harcourt, Brace and World, Inc., 1968).

3. R. D. Laing, *The Politics of Experience* (New York: Pantheon Books, 1967).

4. See, for example, Philip E. Slater, *The Pursuit of Loneliness* (Boston: Beacon Press, 1970).

5. Susan Sontag, *What's Happening in America* (New York: Farrar, Straus and Giroux, Inc., 1967), cited in *Natural Enemies? Youth and the Clash of Generations*, ed. Alexander Klein (New York: J. B. Lippincott Company, 1969), pp. 222–223.

Chapter 11

1. Cited in Fred Weinstein and Gerald M. Platt, *The Wish to Be Free: Society, Psyche and Value Change* (Berkeley: University of California Press, 1969).

Chapter 12

1. From *The Complete Poems of Marianne Moore* (New York: Viking Press, 1967).

Chapter 13

1. John Aldrich, *In the Country of the Young.* (New York: Harper and Row, 1970).

2. Daniel J. Boorstin, *The Decline of Radicalism: Reflections on America Today* (New York: Random House, 1969).

Bibliography

Bales, Robert F. *Personality and Interpersonal Behavior*. New York: Holt, Rinehart and Winston, 1970.

Beels, C. Christian, and Ferber, Andrew. "Family Therapy: A View." *Family Process*, 8 (1969), 280–332.

Bion, Wilfred R. *Experiences in Groups and Other Papers*. New York: Basic Books, 1959.

Dunphy, Dexter. "Social Change in Self Analytic Groups." Diss. Harvard University 1964.

Erikson, Erik H. *Childhood and Society*. New York: Norton, 1950.

Ferber, A. S., and Beels, C. C. "Changing Family Behavior Programs," mimeo. 1969.

Freud, Sigmund. *Group Psychology and the Analysis of the Ego*. New York: Bantam Books, 1960.

Gibb, Jack R. "Climate for Trust Formation," in *T-Group Theory and Laboratory Method*, eds. Bradford, Leland P., Gibb, Jack R., and Benne, Kenneth D. New York: John Wiley and Sons, 1964.

Higgen, Gurth W., and Bridger, Harold. "The Psychodynamics of an Intergroup Experience." *Human Relations*, 17 (1964), 391–446.

Lacan, Jacques. "The Mirror-phase as Formative of the Function of the I." *New Left Review*, 51 (1968), 71–77.

Laing, Ronald D. *The Politics of Experience*. New York: Pantheon Books, 1957.

Mann, Richard D. with Gibbard, Graham S., and Hartman, John J., *Interpersonal Styles and Group Development*. New York: John Wiley & Sons, 1967.

Mills, Theodore M. *Group Transformation: An Analysis of a Learning Group*. Englewood Cliffs, New Jersey: Prentice-Hall, 1964.

Redl, Fritz. "Group Emotion and Leadership." *Psychiatry*, 5 (1942), 573–596.

Slater, Philip E. *Microcosm: Structural, Psychological and Religious Evolution in Groups*. New York: John Wiley & Sons, 1966.

Stock, Dorothy, and Thelen, Herbert A. *Emotional Dynamics and Group Culture*. New York: N.Y.U. Press, 1958.